HOLT *Traditions*

Fifth Course

M000239490

Language and Sentence Skills Practice
Support for *Warriner's Handbook*

▶ **Lesson Worksheets**
▶ **Chapter Reviews**
▶ **"Choices" Activities**
▶ **Literary Models**
▶ **Proofreading Applications**

FOR
■ **Grammar**
■ **Usage**
■ **Mechanics**
■ **Sentences**

HOLT, RINEHART AND WINSTON

ISBN 978-0-03-099706-8
ISBN 0-03-099706-2

2 3 4 5 6 073 12 11 10 09 08

Contents

Contents

Chapter 4

THE CLAUSE:
INDEPENDENT AND SUBORDINATE CLAUSES

Chapter 5

AGREEMENT:
SUBJECT AND VERB, PRONOUN AND ANTECEDENT

Contents

Contents

Contents

Chapter 13

PUNCTUATION:
END MARKS AND COMMAS

Chapter 14

PUNCTUATION:
OTHER MARKS OF PUNCTUATION

Contents

Contents

Using This Workbook

The worksheets in this workbook provide practice, reinforcement, and extension for *Warriner's Handbook*.

Most of the worksheets you will find in this workbook are **traditional worksheets** providing practice and reinforcement activities on every rule and on all major instructional topics in *Warriner's Handbook*.

You will also find in the workbook several kinds of **Language in Context worksheets,** which have been developed to expand the exploration and study of grammar, usage, and mechanics. The Language in Context worksheets include Choices worksheets, Proofreading Applications, Literary Model worksheets, and Writing Applications.

- **Choices** worksheets offer up to ten activities that provide new ways of approaching grammar, usage, and mechanics. Students can choose and complete one independent or group activity per worksheet. Choices activities stimulate learning through research, creative writing, nonfiction writing, discussion, drama, art, games, interviews, music, cross-curricular activities, technology, and other kinds of projects, including some designed entirely by students.

- **Proofreading Application** worksheets help students apply what they learn in class to contexts in the real world. Students use proofreading symbols to correct errors in grammar, usage, and mechanics in practical documents such as letters, applications, brochures, and reports.

- **Literary Model** worksheets provide literary models that demonstrate how published authors use various grammatical forms to create style or meaning. Students identify and analyze each author's linguistic choices and then use grammatical forms to create style or meaning in their own literary creations. Students are asked to reflect on their own linguistic choices and to draw connections between the choices they make and the style or meaning of their work.

- **Writing Application** worksheets are similar to the Writing Application activities in *Warriner's Handbook*. Following the writing process, students use specific grammatical forms as they create a publishable document such as a letter, report, script, or pamphlet.

The Teaching Resources include the **Answer Key** in a separate booklet titled *Language and Sentence Skills Practice Answer Key*.

Symbols for Revising and Proofreading

Symbol	Example	Meaning of Symbol
≡	Fifty-first street	Capitalize a lowercase letter.
/	Jerry's Aunt	Lowercase a capital letter.
∧	differant	Change a letter.
∧	The capital Ohio	Insert a missing word, letter, or punctuation mark.
⌐	beside the river	Replace a word.
⌐	Where's the the key?	Leave out a word, letter, or punctuation mark.
⌐	an invisibile guest	Leave out and close up.
⌒	a close friend ship	Close up space.
∩	thier	Change the order of letters.
(tr)	Avoid having too many corrections (of your paper) in the final version.	Transfer the circled words. (Write *tr* in nearby margin.)
¶	¶"Hi," he smiled.	Begin a new paragraph.
⊙	Stay well	Add a period.
∧	Of course you may be wrong.	Add a comma.
#	icehockey	Add a space.
⊙	one of the following	Add a colon.
∧	Maria Simmons, M.D. Jim Fiorello, Ph.D.	Add a semicolon.
=	a great=grandmother	Add a hyphen.
∨	Pauls car	Add an apostrophe.
(stet)	On the fifteenth of July	Keep the crossed-out material. (Write *stet* in nearby margin.)

Choices: Investigating Parts of Speech

The following activities challenge you to find a connection between the parts of speech and the world around you. Do the activity below that suits your personality best, and then share your discoveries with your class.

INVENTION

What's a Neologism, Anyway?

Every day, your world is changing, and new groups are forming. What are some of these new groups? Make up names—collective nouns—for these new groups. For instance, what would you call a pile of old electronic devices that no longer work? What would be a good name for a group of people who visit the same chat room? Brainstorm a list; then, create a collective noun naming each group.

COMPUTER SCIENCE

Bits and Bytes

Nowadays, you can talk to computers, and they will understand! How did computer programmers accomplish this feat? Investigate speech-recognition software. Find out what parts of speech these programs use. Also, try to find out what the limitations of such programs are. When you've answered these questions, let your classmates in on how this new technology works.

REPRESENTING

Separating Sheep from Goats

Are you a pro at telling an adjective from an adverb? Do your classmates a favor by showing them how you do it. Compose a flowchart detailing the steps you follow when you identify one of these modifiers. Be sure to include a step for identifying the word modified (figuring out which word is modified is what confounds some people). Copy your chart onto poster board and post it in the classroom so that everyone can refer to it.

BUILDING DEXTERITY

Chameleon Conjunctions

Have a contest. Who can find a word that can function as the most parts of speech? The winner must have written complete sentences appropriately using his or her word as each part of speech. Winners must present and defend each entry.

ART

Cut and Dried

Make a collage of words that have been derived from people's names, such as *watt* and *pasteurize*. You could cut these words from newspapers and magazines, draw them, or print them out in different fonts. Be sure to capitalize them if necessary! Add illustrations wherever possible. Post your work where the class can see it.

VOCABULARY/PERFORMANCE

Talk On

Have you ever heard the words *gab* and *yak*? They are both synonyms for *talk*. Use a thesaurus to look up the word *talk*. Make a list of all the synonyms. If you don't know the exact meaning of some of the entries, look them up in a dictionary. Then, show your classmates that adverbs aren't the only words that show "how"; verbs can, too! Demonstrate how to "talk" in a number of these different ways. Be ready for applause.

RESEARCH

Deep Roots

Get together with a group of friends, and divide up this project. Look up the etymologies of the parts of speech—*noun, pronoun, adjective, adverb, verb, preposition, conjunction,* and *interjection.* Where and when did these words originate? Check out a good dictionary, such as *The Oxford English Dictionary.* Why were these names chosen? Present your research to your classmates, and post each etymology (including the first use of each word) in the appropriate place on a time line.

Common, Proper, Concrete, and Abstract Nouns

| **1a.** | A *noun* names a person, a place, a thing, or an idea. |

A *common noun* names any one of a group of persons, places, things, or ideas. A *proper noun* names a particular person, place, thing, or idea.

COMMON NOUNS   actor, language, attorney general
PROPER NOUNS   Audrey Hepburn, English, Janet Reno

A *concrete noun* names an object that can be perceived by one or more of the senses. An *abstract noun* names an idea, a feeling, a quality, or a characteristic.

CONCRETE NOUNS   petunia, computer, artichoke, cloud, Joe Schilling
ABSTRACT NOUNS   enthusiasm, health, spirituality, tolerance

EXERCISE A   In the sentences below, underline the common nouns once and the proper nouns twice.

Example 1. The new course he is taking will be taught by Juanita Martinez.

1. Have you ever read *The Crucible* or any other plays by Arthur Miller?

2. Call Miss Sacks if you are on her committee.

3. The Louvre, a famous museum in Paris, was once a palace.

4. Dr. Athelstein will visit Civics I tomorrow to discuss the history behind Memorial Day.

5. The beach was littered with driftwood that had been blown there by Hurricane Hugo.

6. Al's Garage and Towing Service employs the best team of mechanics in town.

7. Address all suggestions to the Human Resources Department in Building Two.

8. How much of these vitamins does a person need every day?

9. We enjoyed our vacation at the coast but want to see the Smoky Mountains this year.

10. Are you going to the classes at Glenwood Hospital?

EXERCISE B   In the sentences below, classify the underlined noun as concrete or abstract. Above the noun, write *C* for *concrete* or *A* for *abstract*.

Example 1. August Wilson won a Pulitzer Prize for the play *The Piano Lesson*.

11. In this play, a brother and sister engage in a conflict over a piano.

12. The piano becomes a symbol for ambivalence toward African American history.

13. Wilson's discouragement with the treatment of African Americans has spurred him to use theater to raise consciousness.

14. Wilson has written a series of plays, each set in a different decade.

15. One of Wilson's influences was the blues, especially the blues singer Bessie Smith.

2

Collective Nouns and Compound Nouns

The singular form of a *collective noun* names a group.

  EXAMPLES herd   squad   fleet

A *compound noun* consists of two or more words that together name a person, a place, a thing, or an idea. A compound noun may be written as one word, as separate words, or as a hyphenated word.

  EXAMPLES courthouse   Vietnam Memorial   sister-in-law

EXERCISE A In the following sentences, classify each underlined noun as collective or compound. Above each, write *COLL* for *collective* or *COMP* for *compound*.

                        COMP

Example 1. What does a chief executive of a professional sports team do?

1. In 1988, Susan O'Malley became one of the few women in North America who ran a major sports team.

2. The National Basketball Association (NBA) is a major professional sports league.

3. O'Malley was hired as the president of the Washington Bullets, an NBA franchise, now known as the Washington Wizards.

4. The owner of the team, Abe Pollin, said that he offered O'Malley the job because of her outstanding work and her brainpower.

5. As a college student, O'Malley ran a group that delivered balloons.

EXERCISE B In the following sentences, underline the collective nouns once and the compound nouns twice.

Example 1. My father-in-law helped the brigade fight the fire at the feed mill.

6. The vice-president introduced her family to the committee.

7. Edith, who is my partner on the debate team, uses push buttons to control her wheelchair.

8. A gaggle of Canada geese landed in the courtyard in front of city hall.

9. Congress is considering a bill to lower income taxes.

10. That crowd of people has lined up to buy season tickets.

11. My stepbrother is a systems engineer.

12. Mom asked how much the bushel of corn cost.

13. The reporter announced that the secretary of state had just arrived at the press conference.

14. The pack of wolves descended from the rocky hill.

15. Jim and Peter have just built a barn in the backyard.

Pronouns and Antecedents

1b.   A *pronoun* is a word used in place of one or more nouns or pronouns.

The noun or pronoun that a pronoun stands for is called the *antecedent* of the pronoun. Sometimes the antecedent is understood or unknown.

EXAMPLES   Have **you** seen the art of Carla Markwart and Betsy Youngquist? **Each** has **her** own style, **which I** like, but **one** is quite different from the **other.** [The pronoun *you* is understood to refer to the reader. *Each* and *her* replace the nouns *Carla Markwart* and *Betsy Youngquist. I* is understood to refer to the writer. *Which, one,* and *other* refer to the noun *style.*]

EXERCISE A   Underline the pronouns in the sentences below.

Example   1.   Leona herself has been to Hong Kong, but most of us never have.

1. On July 1, 1997, Great Britain relinquished its control of Hong Kong to China.

2. The people of Hong Kong probably found themselves wondering about their future.

3. I. M. Pei, who himself is an Asian American, designed the Bank of China building there.

4. Which of the Boston Museum of Fine Arts wings did he design?

5. Often, many who shop in Hong Kong have found the prices of certain items to be much lower than those of identical items at home.

6. I can't imagine that!

7. This is the postcard that I got from my friend Leona when she was in Hong Kong.

8. "We were astounded by the smells, sounds, and colors of Hong Kong," she wrote.

9. Leona and her parents treated themselves to dim sum, a meal that anyone might enjoy.

10. What would you choose to eat from a Chinese menu?

EXERCISE B   In the following sentences, underline the pronouns once and their antecedents twice.

Example   1.   Marco and Alex, who are aspiring musicians, enjoyed the concert immensely.

11. Mrs. Carter decided to take her children to see the holiday decorations downtown.

12. Did Sonia know she was going to receive the award?

13. After she caught the flu, María took good care of herself and recovered quickly.

14. Tim bought the oranges at the market because they were very sweet.

15. Katerina finally found the perfect outfit for the dance and exclaimed, "That's the dress!"

Personal, Reflexive, and Intensive Pronouns

1b.   A **pronoun** is a word used in place of one or more nouns or pronouns.

A *personal pronoun* refers to the one speaking *(first person)*, the one spoken to *(second person)*, or the one spoken about *(third person)*. A *reflexive pronoun* refers to the subject of a sentence and functions as a complement or as an object of a preposition. An *intensive pronoun* emphasizes its antecedent.

    PERSONAL   I will let **you** see **my** notes. Did **you** give **him yours**?

    REFLEXIVE   My little sister can get dressed by **herself.**

    INTENSIVE   Dr. Minton **himself** will perform the operation.

EXERCISE   In the sentences below, identify each underlined pronoun by writing above the pronoun *P* for *personal, R* for *reflexive,* or *I* for *intensive.*

    Example **1.** The Service Dogs Charity Walk was a success for the dog-training center; a side

                                                    P   *R*

             benefit was how much we enjoyed ourselves.

  1. Have you ever participated in one of these benefits yourself?

  2. This year our club helped the trainers raise money for their work.

  3. Some city officials and business owners donated their time to help us with publicity.

  4. The dogs and owners representing the center are themselves the stars at any of its events.

  5. One trainer told me that the dogs in her program are often strays from a local shelter—they

      may even have been recommended by its staff.

  6. Her dogs learn to open doors by themselves and to respond to sounds.

  7. In addition, she makes sure that they learn to retrieve objects as part of their skills training.

  8. She and her staff try to teach the dogs basic skills within the first year, and later they teach

      specific jobs when dogs are matched with owners.

  9. The training itself is expensive, so fund-raisers like ours are important.

 10. My friends and I will continue to commit ourselves to helping this organization.

Demonstrative, Interrogative, and Relative Pronouns

1b.	A *pronoun* is a word used in place of one or more nouns or pronouns.

A *demonstrative pronoun* points out a specific person, place, thing, or idea. An *interrogative pronoun* introduces a question. A *relative pronoun* introduces a subordinate clause.

DEMONSTRATIVE   **That** is my sister's notebook.

INTERROGATIVE   **Who** is coming to the party?

RELATIVE   The girl **whom** they nominated for class president is Gloria.

EXERCISE A   In the sentences below, identify each underlined pronoun by writing above the pronoun *D* for *demonstrative*, *I* for *interrogative*, or *R* for *relative*.

                   I   *R*

Example   1. <u>What</u> did Maria learn <u>that</u> helped her to solve the equation?

1. Of those colleagues, <u>whom</u> will you take to the session <u>that</u> begins at noon?

2. <u>This</u> is an outline <u>that</u> explains how to study properly.

3. Of the cat's newborn kittens, <u>these</u> are the two <u>that</u> I will adopt.

4. Aunt Phyllis saw my book and asked, "<u>Whose</u> is <u>this</u>?"

5. Inez is among <u>those</u> <u>who</u> are trying out for roles in the spring musical.

6. <u>Which</u> of <u>those</u> does Angelo think is the better design for the new student center?

7. <u>These</u> are the problems for both teams: the weather, <u>which</u> doesn't seem to be improving, and transportation to the stadium.

8. Jackson said, "Many people have told me <u>that</u>. Why should I not believe the story <u>that</u> I have heard?"

9. He read aloud Browning's sonnet, <u>which</u> was the most touching poem <u>that</u> I had ever heard.

10. Lomasi told Henry, <u>whom</u> she trusted, something <u>that</u> she wanted him to keep secret.

EXERCISE B   In each of the sentences below, underline the type of pronoun given in parentheses at the end of the sentence.

Example   1. <u>Who</u> is coordinating the planning for this year's event? (*interrogative*)

11. Those involved with music are preparing for the annual music festival. (*demonstrative*)

12. The crowd, which was very large last year, is expected to double. (*relative*)

13. The bands that will draw the largest crowds should begin at noon. (*relative*)

14. Several of these, whose music many have heard, have won competitions. (*demonstrative*)

15. Who could ask them whether they will play rock or blues or both? (*interrogative*)

Indefinite Pronouns

1b.   A *pronoun* is a word used in place of one or more nouns or pronouns.

An *indefinite pronoun* refers to a person, a place, a thing, or an idea that may or may not be specifically named.

> EXAMPLES   They spent **most** of the weekend planning their trip.
>
>   Did **someone** call my name?

EXERCISE   Underline all the indefinite pronouns in the following paragraphs.

Example [1] Are any of the native insects, plants, and animals losing their habitat, and thus their

lives, to ones arriving from other countries?

[1] Around the globe, species alien to a given area are changing the environment and the

economy for anyone or anything already established in that area. [2] Some of these unwelcome

guests have traveled to their new homes via humans, animals, or insects; others have arrived in

ships, suitcases, clothing, and even old tires.

[3] The intrusion of a few of these creatures and the changes that many of them have brought

have not always been accidental. [4] Much of the fish habitat in U.S. inland waters has been

changed forever because too many of the nonnative species were knowingly mixed in with the

native ones. [5] Nutria, animals that were previously one of the popular substitutes for mink, have

been released into swamps and marshes; by consuming root systems, each has contributed to

habitat and species loss and to erosion.

[6] However, the case has usually been that someone or something unknowingly introduced the

pests that annoy and destroy. [7] Zebra mussels and plants such as leafy spurge, hydrilla, and

floating fern clog many of our U.S. waterways and irrigation systems. [8] In the Black Sea area of

Europe, several of the fisheries already in trouble because of polluted waters closed when a good

many were infiltrated by the Atlantic jellyfish.

[9] Present in the U.S. since the 1980s, both of the mites that infect honeybees have destroyed

much of keepers' colonies and ninety percent of all of the nation's wild honeybees. [10] Finally,

nobody wants to contract one of the seventeen diseases carried by the Asian tiger mosquito or to

experience the painful sting of the imported red fire ant.

GRAMMAR

Adjectives and the Words They Modify

1c.   An *adjective* modifies a noun or a pronoun.

Adjectives modify nouns or pronouns by telling *what kind, which one, how many,* or *how much.* The most frequently used adjectives—*a, an,* and *the*—are called *articles.*

     EXAMPLES   **A bright orange** zinnia danced in **the** wind.

                  We will be **happy** to buy tickets to your **new** play.

EXERCISE   In the sentences below, underline each adjective. Then, draw an arrow to the word it modifies. Do not include articles.

Example 1. Miss Oseola McCarty will be remembered for her scholarship fund set up for

               deserving students at the University of Southern Mississippi.

1. This gracious African American woman, whose ninety-one years were filled with hard work

    and many dreams, was Miss Ola to family and friends.

2. Lucy, her hardworking mother, inspired her money-saving habits.

3. Once Oseola began attending elementary school in Hattiesburg, Mississippi, her lifelong

    home, she would come home each day and help with laundry bundles to earn even the least

    bit of money, saving these small amounts until she had enough to open a savings account.

4. Even then, her every thought was to provide whatever care she could for her grandmother

    and other members of her family who had no one.

5. The life of this young girl changed forever when she left sixth grade to care for a sick aunt and

    never returned to follow her own dream of becoming a nurse.

6. In the following years, Miss Ola continued to keep long hours in her laundry business and to

    deposit her savings in various local bank accounts.

7. Because her formal education was incomplete, she wanted to set up a scholarship to give other

    black students the education she had missed.

8. Two bank employees, longtime friends, had been helping her make conservative investments

    so her savings would grow.

9. Those two women, the trust officer of the bank and an attorney, helped her establish a scholar-

    ship for African American students at the University of Southern Mississippi.

10. The amazing story behind a scholarship fund of such significance as hers has been told often

     in print and on national television.

Adjective or Pronoun?

| **1b.** | A *pronoun* is a word used in place of one or more nouns or pronouns. |

| **1c.** | An *adjective* modifies a noun or a pronoun. |

Some words may be used either as adjectives or as pronouns. A word may be used as one part of speech in one context and as a different part of speech in another context. Remember that an adjective *modifies* a noun and that a pronoun *takes the place of* a noun or pronoun.

ADJECTIVE   I have **another** shoe just like **this** one somewhere in my room. [*Another* modifies the noun *shoe*. *This* modifies the pronoun *one*.]

PRONOUN   I have **another** just like **this** somewhere in my room. [The pronoun *another* takes the place of *shoe*. *This* takes the place of the pronoun *one*.]

EXERCISE A Identify each underlined word by writing above it *ADJ* for *adjective* or *PRON* for *pronoun*.

Example 1. Will these ballots be distributed to all of us?

(these = ADJ, all = PRON)

1. Several of those subjects are easy for me: Algebra II, Spanish III, and American history.

2. Hakim, please explain why both of these formulas are correct.

3. I didn't know whether one topic would be more fun to research than the other.

4. Whose were those gym clothes left lying in a heap on the bench?

5. For much of our vacation, Dad had found another route for us to follow.

6. May we have a little more time to finish both parts of the application for admissions?

7. Neither of us knows which is the more difficult job, gardening or baby-sitting.

8. Each runner may pick up a sweatband and a water bottle in either color.

9. What did Salma do with each item?

10. The nature of this chemical is such that neither combination will be successful.

EXERCISE B In the sentences below, identify the italicized words by underlining the adjectives and circling the pronouns. Then, draw an arrow from each underlined adjective to the word it modifies.

Example 1. Was *that* the largest pumpkin entered in the fair *this* year?

11. *Few* people appreciated how long it took *most* of us to get into costume.

12. Renee hoped *some* guests would arrive early, so she could enjoy visiting with each *one*.

13. The bricklayers finished *most* of the new wall before *many* businesses were open.

14. Once you have decided *which* era you will explore, *whose* is the story you will tell?

15. *Both* golfers played an outstanding round, *each* scoring in the low 70s.

Adjective or Noun?

1a. | A **noun** names a person, a place, a thing, or an idea.

1c. | An **adjective** modifies a noun or a pronoun.

Some words can be used as nouns or adjectives.

NOUNS	ADJECTIVES
spaghetti	**spaghetti** sauce
high school	**high school** teacher
American Indian	**American Indian** business

EXERCISE A   Identify each underlined word by writing *ADJ* for *adjective* or *N* for *noun* above the word.

               ADJ   N
Example 1. The <u>Blackfeet</u> Indians consisted of three tribes living on the <u>Great Plains</u> of the

               United States and Canada.

1. The <u>Blackfeet</u> hunted buffalo on foot until they acquired horses from <u>European American</u> settlers.

2. These <u>Plains</u> people lived in tepees made of <u>buffalo</u> hide.

3. In the early part of the <u>nineteenth</u> century, <u>beaver</u> trappers entered the <u>Blackfoot</u> hunting ground.

4. After an initial conflict, the <u>European Americans</u> began to trade goods such as tools, metal

   knives, and <u>glass</u> beads with the Blackfeet in exchange for beavers.

5. Some Blackfeet refused to trade because they considered the <u>beaver</u> a sacred animal.

EXERCISE B   In the sentences below, identify the italicized words by underlining the adjectives and circling the nouns. Then, draw an arrow from each underlined adjective to the word it modifies.

Example 1. Have you ever seen the ⟨*wool*⟩ used for *Angora* sweaters?

6. This year, Mother has cooked our *holiday* turkey in her *earthenware* oven.

7. Conrad did not stir the contents of his *chemistry* beaker enough to complete his *test*.

8. Doesn't the *green* in this shirt clash with that *purple* jacket?

9. Melina, please explain how much *electricity* this *light* bulb will use.

10. Plain *cheese* sandwiches were my favorite until I tried one with broiled *tomato*.

11. What happens when you put *Iowa* corn into an iron pot, put on the lid, and apply *heat*?

12. Ms. Ramirez calls the *pop* quizzes that she gives each week *practice* tests.

13. Every *fall*, we helped to collect sap from the *maple* trees.

14. Kitchi asked the *mail* carrier to slide the *mail* under the door.

15. That is the kind of *service* every *tow truck* driver should provide a motorist in trouble!

Proper Adjectives

1c.   An **adjective** modifies a noun or a pronoun.

An adjective that is formed from a proper noun is called a *proper adjective*.

NOUNS	ADJECTIVES
China	**Chinese** tea
Easter	**Easter** Sunday
America	**American** car
Buddhist	**Buddhist** shrine
Hong Kong	**Hong Kong** harbor

EXERCISE A   On the lines provided, write the proper adjectives for the proper nouns given. You may consult a dictionary.

Example 1. California _____Californian_____

1. Sweden _____

2. Egypt _____

3. Socrates _____

4. Homer _____

5. Italy _____

6. San Francisco _____

7. Labor Day _____

8. Iraq _____

9. Java _____

10. Mars _____

EXERCISE B   In the following sentences, underline all common adjectives once. Do not include articles. Underline all proper adjectives twice.

Example 1. Examples of Etruscan art, greatly influenced by the Greeks, can still be found in ancient tombs.

11. The Bensons just installed Mexican tiles throughout their new home.

12. Explain five differences between the Turkish and Ottoman empires.

13. Do you think the Japanese culture encourages a stoic attitude toward difficult situations?

14. Next Thursday will mark the last annual meeting of Spanish-American War veterans.

15. After twenty laps, Jacy threw himself with a Herculean effort into the finish-line tape.

GRAMMAR

Action Verbs

1d. A *verb* expresses action or a state of being.

An *action verb* expresses either physical or mental activity.

PHYSICAL ACTIVITY	paint	jog	write
MENTAL ACTIVITY	think	anticipate	hope

> **EXAMPLES**   The carpenter's team **finished** the repairs before noon. [physical]
> They **did** not **forget** about the rain gutters. [mental]

EXERCISE A For each sentence below, identify the type of action that the underlined verb shows by writing above the verb *P* for *physical* or *M* for *mental*.

Example 1. Since last year, my sister Nadie has wanted a bicycle to ride to school. *[M]*

1. With his excellent school record, Hiromi was accepted to the medical school.

2. Pilar wondered why the air often smelled smoky during autumn.

3. Simon feels more energetic when he exercises in the morning.

4. Maggie quickly thought of the correct answer after Mr. Howard called on her.

5. In the winter, trees that lose their leaves look bare and lifeless.

6. I cradled the puppy, which was asleep in my arms.

7. Teddy stopped by here earlier, before he left for the train station.

8. Lee believed that his bicycle was working well, but Jay did not agree.

9. While Emilio will eat cold cereal all year, Della dreams of oatmeal on cold mornings.

10. The ship's captain sounded the alarm, and the crew scrambled on deck.

EXERCISE B Underline each action verb in the sentences below.

Example 1. Kristi Yamaguchi, the figure-skating champion, helps others who dream of success.

11. Her Always Dream Foundation (ADF) works with groups in California, Nevada, and Hawaii.

12. These groups encourage and support economically and socially disadvantaged children.

13. Yamaguchi hopes ADF will expand into a nationwide network of groups.

14. Many of the children never thought they would have enough clothing or school supplies.

15. Others learn new skills when they work on computers that ADF provides.

Linking Verbs

1d.   A *verb* expresses action or a state of being.

A *linking verb* connects the subject to a word or word group that is in the predicate and that identifies or describes the subject. Such a word or word group is called a *subject complement*. All linking verbs are intransitive, since they do not have objects.

The most commonly used linking verbs are forms of the verb *be* and other verbs such as *appear, become, feel, grow, look, remain, seem, smell, sound, stay, taste,* and *turn.*

EXAMPLES   DeAnn **became** a famous artist and sculptor. [The compound subject complement *artist* and *sculptor* identifies the subject *DeAnn*.]

Don't the new chimes in the bell tower **sound** wonderful! [The adjective *wonderful* describes the subject *chimes*.]

Some verbs may be used as linking verbs or as action verbs.

EXAMPLES   The skirt **turned** scarlet from the dye Mina added to the water. [linking]

Dwayne **turned** the car around in the driveway. [action]

EXERCISE A   In the sentences below, underline linking verbs once and subject complements twice.

Example 1. These grapes taste sweeter than those.

1. When Roberto received the compliment, he turned red with embarrassment.

2. Did the bananas at the grocery store look good this morning?

3. Paula felt much calmer after talking to her grandmother.

4. The tree seemed taller today than it did yesterday.

5. The travelers grew tired after the long journey.

EXERCISE B   In the space above each underlined verb below, identify the verb by writing *L* for *linking* or *A* for *action.*

Example   April 4, 1974, **[1]** *L* was a day that **[2]** *A* will always be remembered in baseball history.

At 2:40 P.M. in Cincinnati, Hank (Henry) Aaron of the Atlanta Braves **[6]** tied what **[7]** had been Babe Ruth's unbroken record—714 home runs during a major league baseball career. He **[8]** turned a 3 ball, 1 strike pitch into a home run that **[9]** sailed over the wall.

Four days later, on April 8, Aaron **[10]** made history again. The stadium **[11]** looked packed, and millions **[12]** were watching the game in their homes. The weather **[13]** was cool and cloudy. The Dodgers **[14]** were leading 3 to 1, and the Braves **[15]** had one player on first base. The pitcher **[16]** threw a fastball, and Aaron **[17]** knocked it over the left field fence. The crowd **[18]** must have been wild with excitement! Aaron **[19]** had hit number 715 and **[20]** had broken Ruth's record.

Main Verbs and Helping Verbs

1d.   A *verb* expresses action or a state of being.

A *verb phrase* consists of at least one *main verb* and one or more *helping verbs* (also called *auxiliary verbs*).

> **EXAMPLES**   John **must be feeding** the cats now. [*Must* and *be* are helping verbs. *Feeding* is the main verb.]
>
> **Do** you **have** a favorite artist? [*Do* is the helping verb. *Have* is the main verb.]

EXERCISE A   In the sentences below, underline the main verbs once and the helping verbs twice.

Example 1. Have you ever seen any paintings by Mexican artist Rufino Tamayo?

1. Rufino Tamayo was born in 1899.

2. During Tamayo's childhood, his aunt would sell fruit in a market in Mexico City.

3. His eye for color was probably influenced by this experience; red, green, and yellow are

   included in the dominant colors in his paintings.

4. Some of his work was inspired by the paintings of Spanish artist Pablo Picasso.

5. Our art teacher has shown us slides of Rufino Tamayo's paintings.

6. Tamayo's art has been exhibited in museums throughout the United States and Mexico.

7. In 1936, Tamayo was living in New York City, where he could pursue his goals as an artist.

8. Tamayo's painting *Children Playing with Fire* may have been created in reaction to the Mexican

   Revolution.

9. Tamayo may have worried that people would destroy themselves and the earth through war.

10. Didn't several other artists of the 1930s and 1940s have that same concern?

EXERCISE B   In the paragraph below, underline the verbs and verb phrases. Then, circle the main verbs.

Example [1] Have you ever seen the actor Mario Moreno?

   [11] By the 1940s, this popular Mexican movie personality had become an international success.

[12] He was more commonly known as Cantinflas. [13] Mexicans had fallen in love with his

charming but clumsy character who was always dressed in baggy pants, a white T-shirt, and a hat.

[14] You may have seen the 1956 movie *Around the World in 80 Days*, in which Cantinflas appeared

as the character Passepartout. [15] Rufino Tamayo must have also appreciated the work of

Cantinflas because he painted a portrait of the Mexican star in 1948.

Transitive Verbs and Intransitive Verbs

1d.   A **verb** expresses action or a state of being.

A *transitive verb* has an object—a noun or a pronoun that tells *who* or *what* receives the action. An *intransitive verb* does not have an object.

TRANSITIVE   Arliss **will ask** a **question**. [The object *question* receives the action of *will ask*.]

INTRANSITIVE   Mrs. Gelburg **had** quietly **walked** into the classroom. [No object receives the action of *had walked*.]

INTRANSITIVE   Many of us **were** happy to see her. [No object receives the action of *were*. The adjective *happy* describes the subject *Many*.]

A verb can be transitive in one sentence and intransitive in another.

EXAMPLES   Colleen **washed** her hands. [transitive]

We also **washed** before dinner. [intransitive]

EXERCISE A   In the sentences below, underline transitive verbs and circle intransitive verbs.

Example   1.   The president had spoken for ten minutes before he answered questions.

1. Next year, Belinda will help us with the homecoming plans.

2. Tama showed us her sketches of the scenery for the drama club's next play.

3. Lightning flashed across the dark sky as the storm quickly approached.

4. What will Sergio do for his part of our report on life in Plymouth Colony?

5. The tire was flat, and the spare had barely enough air in it.

6. We walked the entire distance in the 10K benefit for cancer research.

7. Dimitri was eager for his grandparents' arrival so that they could see his new calf.

8. Yesterday, Reggie worked until the garage was clean and the trash was in bags.

9. Have Etta and Robbie arrived yet with the napkins and plastic plates, cups, and silverware?

10. Pour the batter into a greased and floured baking pan.

EXERCISE B   In the paragraph below, underline transitive verbs and circle intransitive verbs.

Example   [1] I have heard of Senator John Chafee of Rhode Island.

[11] As a Marine, he faced the many challenges of Guadalcanal in the Pacific during World War II. **[12]** When the military recalled him to active duty during the Korean War, he served his country once again. **[13]** Later, he spent six years in the Rhode Island House of Representatives. **[14]** He became governor in 1962 and was reelected in 1964 and 1966. **[15]** He began his Senate career in 1976 and later led efforts toward the reduction of the federal budget deficit.

Adverbs and the Words They Modify

1e.   An *adverb* modifies a verb, an adjective, or another adverb.

An adverb tells *how, when, where,* or *to what extent* (*how long* or *how much*).

EXAMPLES   The professor arrived **early** for the debate. [*Early* modifies the verb *arrived,* telling *when.*]

Did that person seem **too** busy to help us? [*Too* modifies the adjective *busy,* telling *how much.*]

EXERCISE A   In the sentences below, underline each adverb once and the word or words it modifies twice. Then, draw an arrow from each adverb to the word or words it modifies.

Example   1.   I could have danced forever, but I was very tired.

1. Small children certainly do need careful supervision.

2. Hector proudly showed his parents his excellent report card.

3. Josh worked on the project enthusiastically.

4. Surely we are meeting at my house?

5. I will not eat at that outrageously expensive restaurant.

6. Kuni carefully felt his way through the totally dark hall.

7. The neighbors suddenly seemed too ready to leave for their summer vacation.

8. The defendant responded quite sarcastically to the prosecuting attorney.

9. You can eat inexpensively in this restaurant.

10. Odessa ran rather quickly to get her purse and jacket.

EXERCISE B   In the space above each of the following sentences, add at least one adverb. Use a caret (⌄) to mark where each adverb should be inserted.

Example   1.   Would you *someday* like to follow the route of one of Marco Polo's trips?

11. She called me from Houston with an urgent message.

12. Tina was lucky to find her gold ring.

13. The dog waited for its owner's return.

14. Construction crews will begin work at 6:00 A.M.

15. Would you mow the grass and wash the car for me?

Noun or Adverb?

1e.   An *adverb* modifies a verb, an adjective, or another adverb.

Some words may be used as nouns or as adverbs.

EXAMPLES   Raz and Donna are studying **tonight** with Shari and Jim. [adverb telling *when*]

   Tonight is their last chance to review their notes. [noun, subject of sentence]

   Yuri gave Rosita a ride **home** from the party. [adverb telling *where*]

   He found her street and her **home** with no problem. [noun, object of verb]

EXERCISE A   In the sentences below, determine whether the underlined words are used as nouns or adverbs. Above each, write *N* if it is a noun and *A* if it is an adverb.

Example 1. Fran decided that she would go to the library <u>today</u>.   *A*

1. <u>Yesterday</u>, I chose my books carefully for my reports about events between 1890 and 1920.

2. <u>Yesterday</u> was the first time I had ever seen book reviews on the school's Intranet.

3. Will we ever be able to access books entirely with computers at <u>home</u>?

4. Trudy chose her book quickly so she could go <u>home</u> to begin her book report.

5. He liked only one of the reviews he read <u>tonight</u>.

6. <u>Tonight</u> is the night I will read those book reviews.

7. <u>Tomorrow</u>, Cecile will read the review that rates a book three stars.

8. <u>Tomorrow</u> will be the day they update the Intranet book reviews.

9. The <u>forward</u> on the team scored twice.

10. Please run <u>forward</u> until I say "stop."

EXERCISE B   In the space above each sentence below, add at least one adverb. Use a caret (∧) to mark where the adverbs are inserted.

                   certainly   *ever*
Example 1. I would ∧ like to know why a cat would ∧ chase a squirrel.

11. The caravan arrived at the oasis, and everyone helped to set up camp.

12. Sailboats filled the harbor as people crowded into the town for the celebration.

13. Is this the best day for the soccer playoffs, or will another day be better?

14. When the dog needs to have a bath or to have its nails clipped, I take it to a groomer.

15. "Mechanics Want You to Know . . ." was the name of the seminar that Mom attended.

The Preposition

| **1f.** | A *preposition* shows the relationship of a noun or pronoun, called the *object of the preposition,* to another word. |

A preposition, its object, and any modifiers of the object form a *prepositional phrase*.

EXAMPLES   The spider is walking **across its web.** [*Across* is the preposition; *web* is the object of the preposition.]

According to the weather report, the snow should begin falling soon. [*According to* is the preposition; *weather report* is the object of the preposition.]

EXERCISE A   In the following sentences, underline each preposition once and each object of the preposition twice. Some sentences have more than one prepositional phrase.

Example 1. In spite of the rough terrain, the Incas built an empire among the Andes Mountains.

1. The Incas of South America offered gifts to their gods.

2. The Incas worshiped the mountain gods along with the sun.

3. If the gods viewed the Incas favorably, crops would be abundant during harvest.

4. Beneath the rocky mountain soil, archaeologists discovered small silver statues.

5. The figures were made of seashells and dressed in clothing like that worn by Inca women.

6. Machu Picchu, a fortress city surrounded by terraced gardens, was not discovered until 1911.

7. Cuzco, which is near Machu Picchu, was the capital of the ancient Incan civilization.

8. On the slopes of Mount Ampato in 1995, anthropologist Johan Reinhard and his friend Miguel Zarate found the frozen mummy of a teenage girl.

9. According to a textile expert, she wore a shawl that was the best-preserved example of Incan clothing ever found.

10. Andean people today maintain a reverent attitude toward the Andes Mountains.

EXERCISE B   In the space above each of the following sentences, add at least one prepositional phrase. Use a caret (ʌ) to mark where the phrases are inserted.

Example 1. ʌI would like a new coat. [*In addition to new gloves, for winter*]

11. Someone sneezed loudly.

12. I will read three books.

13. Bring me the wrench and a hammer.

14. Who will answer this question?

15. We have fed and watered the livestock.

The Conjunction

1g. A *conjunction* joins words or word groups.

COORDINATING CONJUNCTION	It has not yet begun to rain, **so** I will go to the game.
CORRELATIVE CONJUNCTION	**Either** Alice **or** Yoshiro will drive to the field.
SUBORDINATING CONJUNCTION	**Because** it was beginning to rain, we left early.

EXERCISE A In the following sentences, underline the coordinating conjunctions once and the correlative conjunctions twice. Circle the subordinating conjunctions.

Example 1. Why does this acreage have fewer trees and shrubs than that one does?

1. Not only did I feel foolish, but I also looked ridiculous.

2. You may not believe me, yet I'm telling the truth!

3. We plan to travel through Europe by train, for there is much we want to see.

4. Would you like to join the computer club since you enjoy creating computer programs?

5. I can't find my other shoe, and my bus is here!

6. The coach had tried to guide the team so that they could succeed.

7. Both Jules and Tess have passed the preliminary college entrance exams.

8. Though the sky is filled with many constellations, my favorite is still the Big Dipper.

9. Neither Ken nor Uni had seen the movie.

10. I hopped on one foot while I pulled off the wet sock.

EXERCISE B In the paragraph below, fill in the blanks with appropriate conjunctions.

Example [1] Akira and I had planned to play soccer on Saturday; it was raining, though,

_____*so*_____ we decided to try something new.

[11] _____ Akira _____ I had been to the new museum, _____

we had heard many good things about it. [12] _____ the Museum of Modern Art was

crowded, we still saw many amazing paintings and sculptures. [13] We looked at some of the

museum's permanent collection, _____ a traveling exhibit was what most people had

come to see. [14] _____ we both like photography, our favorite part of that exhibit was

a group of scenes by a local photographer. [15] Our first trip to the museum was an enriching

experience, _____ we will definitely return.

The Interjection

1h. An *interjection* expresses emotion and has no grammatical relation to the rest of the sentence.

An interjection is often set off from the rest of the sentence by an exclamation point or a comma. An exclamation point indicates strong emotion. A comma indicates mild emotion.

EXAMPLES   **Wow!** We won!

Oh my, I'm sorry that I'm late.

EXERCISE   Underline the interjections in the following sentences.

Example 1. Why, I'm amazed to see so many fans here today!

1. Hooray! Daria saw Halley's comet on the wrap-around screen at the science theater.

2. Hey, have you visited the memorial to the Japanese Americans of World War II?

3. Tomorrow we have an algebra test, and—yikes!—I still need to study!

4. Grace thinks that we will be, oh, only fifteen or twenty minutes late.

5. Yay! Construction has begun for the National Museum of the American Indian.

6. Wow! October 1, 1999, was the fiftieth anniversary of the People's Republic of China.

7. "After trimming trees and planting shrubs all day, am I tired! Whew!" Onita said.

8. Ouch! I stubbed my toe on the curb!

9. Say, I enjoyed visiting the birthplace of Margaret Mitchell, who wrote *Gone With the Wind.*

10. Ah! That swim in the pool was quite refreshing.

11. Oops! I didn't mean to type an *l* instead of an *I*.

12. Yikes! The lid on that antique ceramic jar is very delicate.

13. Sh. The baby is sleeping in the other room, and I don't want to wake her.

14. My, what a beautiful apartment you have!

15. Now, where do you think they keep the soup bowls?

16. Where in the world could my wallet be? Aha! I found it!

17. Psst. When do you think this movie will end?

18. Oh, what a wonderful way to spend a holiday!

19. Well, I believe I'll call Monica tonight.

20. Ahem. Can I have your attention, please?

Determining Parts of Speech

1i. The way a word is used in a sentence determines what part of speech the word is.

> **EXAMPLES** Will you please find another station on your **radio**? [noun]
> The newest **radio** station in town plays country music. [adjective]
> We gave a party for **those** of our friends who were leaving. [pronoun]
> **Those** friends of ours recently moved to the East Coast. [adjective]
> **Before** the pop quiz, we hardly knew what questions to expect. [preposition]
> I sharpened the only pencil I had **before** the class began. [conjunction]

EXERCISE A In the following paragraphs, identify the part of speech of each underlined word by writing above it *N* for *noun, ADJ* for *adjective, PREP* for *preposition, PRON* for *pronoun, ADV* for *adverb, CONJ* for *conjunction, V* for *verb,* or *INTJ* for *interjection.*

Example June **[1]** has written an essay **[2]** about the rise of cities.

[1] From the sixteenth century on, the Industrial Revolution **[2]** caused many cities around the world to experience **[3]** tremendous growth and **[4]** change. Particularly in Europe **[5]** and North America, these cities **[6]** quickly became centers of **[7]** large-scale manufacturing. As a result, **[8]** many social problems developed in **[9]** them.

Early on, **[10]** skilled craftspeople had **[11]** difficulty finding work **[12]** because machines did their jobs **[13]** more quickly and inexpensively. Many **[14]** city people began working **[15]** in factories where conditions were poor. Improved **[16]** agricultural methods **[17]** reduced the need for farmworkers. Cities grew **[18]** as factories attracted more and more workers. **[19]** Unfortunately for many, living **[20]** conditions were unhealthy and **[21]** unsuitable. Many lived in crudely built houses, **[22]** apartment buildings, and even cellars. In early industrial cities, **[23]** alas, widespread disease and pollution caused the death **[24]** rate to rise dramatically. Over time, the quality of life in most industrial cities got **[25]** better.

EXERCISE B In each sentence below, underline all the words that function as the italicized part of speech given before the sentence.

Example 1. *conjunction* We lacked neither pen nor paper.

26. *pronoun* These are your books, and those are mine.

27. *verb* By the time the bus arrives, Nadine will have been waiting for an hour.

28. *adjective* When I was little, four hours seemed long.

29. *adverb* Always remember to accept gifts graciously and to send a thank-you note.

30. *preposition* In spite of the dry weather, the garden yielded ten bushels of snap beans.

Review A: **Parts of Speech**

EXERCISE A In the following paragraphs, identify the part of speech of each underlined word by writing above it N for *noun*, ADJ for *adjective*, PREP for *preposition*, PRON for *pronoun*, ADV for *adverb*, CONJ for *conjunction*, V for *verb*, or INTJ for *interjection*.

                                  V   ADJ
Example [1] Follow the instructions for [2] this grammar exercise.

In [1] America today, grammarians are [2] rarely heroes to students. Nevertheless, the opposite [3] should be true. Just ask any student [4] who has trouble with [5] high school English.

Probably the most famous American [6] grammarian is Noah Webster, who [7] died over a century ago. However, Webster is not usually remembered for his work [8] as a grammarian. [9] Because of the dictionaries [10] that have been named after him, he has become famous; however, he had nothing at all to do with most of them!

One of the [11] most interesting grammarians of the [12] twentieth century is the Harvard scholar George Lyman Kittredge. Working with a colleague, in 1913 he [13] published a book called *An Advanced English Grammar.* His book treats grammar with a [14] well-known firmness. [15] Oh, Kittredge's overpowering [16] personality inspired many legends [17] and stories [18] about his imperious and dramatic manner.

That Kittredge's book [19] happens to be available for the [20] rest of us is fortunate. [21] Well, what other grammarian today would write what Kittredge did on the very first page of his [22] grammar book? One sample sentence on that page [23] states categorically, "A man who respects [24] himself should never condescend to use [25] slovenly language."

EXERCISE B In each sentence below, underline all the words that function as the italicized part of speech given before the sentence.

Example 1. *noun* We drove past many fields of cotton.

26. *pronoun*   Of all the fabrics used, cotton cloth is one of the oldest in the world.

27. *verb*   Five thousand years ago the inhabitants of India grew and spun cotton.

28. *adverb*   Cotton was also used frequently in ancient Egypt, China, and Pakistan.

29. *preposition* It was not until A.D. 700 that Europeans began to grow cotton in their fields.

30. *adjective* The weaving of cotton fabrics was one important factor in the English Industrial Revolution.

Review B: Parts of Speech

EXERCISE A Each of the following sentences contains a word that is used twice. Above each underlined word, identify its part of speech by writing one of the abbreviations below.

N for *noun*	ADJ for *adjective*	ADV for *adverb*	CONJ for *conjunction*
PRON for *pronoun*	V for *verb*	PREP for *preposition*	INTJ for *interjection*

                                                    N   V
Example 1. In an obstacle race the contestants race over hurdles and climb walls.

1. Two workers were trapped in the mine when the tunnel caved in.

2. Carol's mother, a busy person herself, sometimes asked Carol, "Couldn't you please busy yourself with some work?"

3. The Red Cross workers help in any emergency where their help is needed.

4. The girl with the black hair was dressed entirely in black.

5. That delivery truck has driven past our house several times in the past hour.

EXERCISE B In the following paragraphs, identify the part of speech of each underlined word by writing above it one of the abbreviations below.

N for *noun*	ADJ for *adjective*	ADV for *adverb*	CONJ for *conjunction*
PRON for *pronoun*	V for *verb*	PREP for *preposition*	INTJ for *interjection*

                            ADJ   PREP
Example Nearly **[1]** every person knows **[2]** about gold rushes.

   The famous **[6]** ones occurred in California and in the **[7]** Klondike **[8]** during the 1800s. Stories

have been told and **[9]** retold about fortunes made and lost in the **[10]** gold fields, especially near

[11] San Francisco and Dawson. However, on **[12]** all of the North American continent **[13]** these

were not the first sites of gold fever. Several years **[14]** earlier, the discovery and lure of the gold

drew a **[15]** swarm of prospectors **[16]** to Auraria in northern Georgia.

   Auraria (Latin for "City of Gold") is in Cherokee County. Formerly **[17]** an unexplored region

[18] between two obscure rivers, **[19]** this small town became **[20]** both a name on the map and a

word on people's lips. **[21]** When they heard tales of **[22]** enormous gold nuggets in the late 1820s

and early 1830s, people **[23]** flocked to the nearby hills of Auraria. **[24]** Its stores and law offices

soon **[25]** were serving more than a thousand people.

   [26] Well! The boom was exciting **[27]** while it lasted. However, by the 1850s Auraria, once so

[28] full of promise, was merely a small town with a glittering **[29]** past. Today, all that

[30] remains is a ghost town.

Review C: **Parts of Speech**

EXERCISE A   In each sentence below, underline all the words that function as the italicized part of speech given before the sentence.

Example 1. *verb*   Just a short time ago the most popular definition of *hardware* was "articles that are made of metal."

1. *noun*   I am astonished by the incredible operating speed of modern computers.

2. *preposition*   Data fed into a computer can be stored for future use and retrieved quickly.

3. *adjective*   American companies increasingly depend on electronic parts.

4. *adverb*   Companies might often use databanks to manage information efficiently.

5. *pronoun*   Many people who once feared electronics are now ordering personal computers for themselves.

EXERCISE B   Each of the following sentences contains a word that is used twice. Identify the part of speech of each underlined word by writing above it one of the abbreviations below.

N for *noun*	*ADJ* for *adjective*	*ADV* for *adverb*	*CONJ* for *conjunction*
PRON for *pronoun*	*V* for *verb*	*PREP* for *preposition*	*INTJ* for *interjection*

Example 1. She ground the eggshells into the ground with her shoe.

6. The bright light shone through the light material.

7. When the tennis ball went over the fence, Carmen's partner wanted to start the game over.

8. Color the letters on the poster with a color that is highly visible.

9. Southside's quarterback sped down the sideline to make the crucial first down.

10. These socks belong to Diego, and these are Juanita's, so those must be mine.

11. Before you play computer games, you should sit before your desk and finish your homework.

12. Gene cast about, searching for a helpful manual about car repair.

13. We receive three daily newspapers, but we do not always have time to read all of them daily.

14. At his uncle's farm, Theo milks cows and processes the milk to make butter and cheese.

15. Tomorrow, and especially our dress rehearsal tomorrow, will be here before we know it.

for **CHAPTER 1: PARTS OF SPEECH OVERVIEW**   pages 17–18

Literary Model: Descriptive Narrative

The radiance was that of the full, setting, and blood-red moon, which now shone vividly through that once barely discernible fissure, of which I have before spoken as extending from the roof of the building, in zigzag direction, to the base. While I gazed, this fissure rapidly widened—there came a fierce breath of the whirlwind—the entire orb of the satellite burst at once upon my sight—my brain reeled as I saw the mighty walls rushing asunder—there was a long tumultuous shouting sound like the voice of a thousand waters—and the deep and dark tarn at my feet closed sullenly and silently over the fragments of the *"House of Usher."*

—from "The Fall of the House of Usher," Edgar Allan Poe

EXERCISE A

1. In the passage above, most of Poe's adverbs modify verbs. List the adverbs that modify verbs. (Hint: "Rushing" is not a verb; it is a participle modified by the adverb "asunder.")

   _____   _____

   _____   _____

   _____   _____

2. What adverbs are used to modify the same adjective? _____   _____

3. What part of speech other than verbs and adjectives can an adverb modify? _____

EXERCISE B   Read the passage aloud, leaving out the adverbs. Then, read it aloud with the adverbs. Without the adverbs, would the story's ending be as exciting? How do the adverbs contribute to the passage?

_____

_____

_____

_____

_____

_____

_____

_____

_____

GRAMMAR | Language in Context: Literary Model

Literary Model (continued)

EXERCISE C   Drawing on the mood and tone of Poe's conclusion to "The Fall of the House of Usher," write your own brief, suspenseful ending to a story yet to be written. The action you describe could be as familiar as enduring the last few seconds before the beginning of a final exam or achievement test, as simple as losing a helium balloon on a windy day, or as unsettling as losing your balance on rain-slick steps. As you write, use adverbs wherever possible to add details to your story and to establish and maintain the intended mood.

_____

_____

_____

_____

_____

_____

_____

_____

_____

_____

_____

_____

_____

_____

_____

_____

_____

EXERCISE D

1. Look over your paragraph, and underline the adverbs that you used.

2. Re-read your paragraph, leaving out the adverbs. How does leaving out the adverbs affect your paragraph's style or meaning?

_____

_____

_____

_____

Writing Application: Newspaper Article

The *5W-How?* questions (*Who? What? Where? Why? When? How?*) can generate descriptive modifiers for your writing. Let them prompt you to include sensory details.

LESS DESCRIPTIVE   The tourists greeted their tour guide.

MORE DESCRIPTIVE   The travel-weary tourists greeted their confident, smiling tour guide gratefully.

WRITING ACTIVITY

Good reporters take readers to the scene of the event, letting them experience it vividly through carefully chosen modifiers. Write a brief article of about two hundred words for your school newspaper. In the article, describe a school event that you enjoyed greatly. Include at least three adverbs and at least three adjectives that convey to readers a sense of "being there." Avoid overused modifiers like *very* and *really*.

PREWRITING   Using the *5W-How?* questions listed above, recall the event in as much detail as possible. Generate more details than you need; then, choose the most interesting and significant from among them.

WRITING   Journalists usually write very short, concise introductory and concluding paragraphs, and they usually order events chronologically. Move quickly from a one- or two-sentence introduction into your description of the event.

REVISING   Let a friend read your article; then, ask the friend what details he or she remembers. Details that are forgotten probably need more vivid description. Brainstorm for sensory details, since these bits of information often stay in readers' minds.

PUBLISHING   Check your article for errors in grammar, usage, spelling, and punctuation. Be sure that you have included six modifiers. If you have used any proper adjectives, be sure to capitalize them. Submit your article to the paper's editor, following any submission requirements carefully.

EXTENDING YOUR WRITING

You may wish to develop this exercise into a longer essay. You could develop your account of the event more thoroughly, turning it into a personal-experience essay in which you explore why the event matters to you. Did it affect you strongly, change you, or challenge you to think about your ideas?

GRAMMAR | Language in Context: Writing Application

Choices: Investigating Parts of a Sentence

The following activities challenge you to find a connection between the parts of a sentence and the world around you. Do the activity below that suits your personality best, and then share your discoveries with your class.

ANALYTICAL WRITING

The Chicken or the Egg

Grammar has been studied for centuries. However, the question remains: Is grammar something that has been imposed on language, or is it something inherent in language? If grammar is inherent in language, what does this fact say about the human brain or about language itself? Is grammar something that exists in the human brain? Write an essay exploring these questions.

DESCRIPTIVE WRITING

Dream House

A dream house—everybody's got one. What is in yours? Think about it. Make a list of everything you want in your house. Use your list to write a few paragraphs detailing your dream house. Of course, those paragraphs will be full of complements that identify or describe aspects of the house. After you have written your paragraphs, highlight all the complements and consider how they help to flesh out your descriptions.

LINGUISTICS

The Defining Moment

Don't like the definition of *sentence*? Make up another one! Working with a team, compose several alternative definitions of what a sentence is. Then, put your ideas to the test. Present your definitions to your classmates for discussion, and choose the best one.

VISUAL REPRESENTATION

Know Thyself

Have you ever analyzed the structure of your own writing? Doing so can help you become a better writer. Take a look at a paragraph you wrote recently, and count the number of words in each sentence. Then, label each sentence as declarative, interrogative, imperative, or exclamatory. Record your findings in a bar graph.

LINGUISTICS

Curator of the Minipolitan

Prepare a mini-museum of fabulous or interesting sentences. First, let your classmates know that you will be accepting entries for your museum. Next, do some searching of your own. Dictionaries of quotations could be a treasure trove for this project. Choose a number of selections. Then, prepare museum cards for each one. On each card, note the author, the date, and the title of the work from which the sentence comes. Identify the sentence's purpose and any unusual elements. If you use any of your classmates' submissions, be sure to give them credit. Finally, with your teacher's permission, set up your museum in the hall.

VISUAL REPRESENTATION

I Did It My Way

Do you have trouble with sentence diagramming? No problem. Design a new way of visually representing sentence structure. Use color, shape, position, or even texture if you like. Then, try out your innovations on your classmates.

REAL LIFE

What Goes Around

Here's a topic you might enjoy—common exaggerations that people say. You know common lines—ones like *That's the best dog in the world*. Brainstorm a list of familiar statements. Then, divide them into four categories—declarative, imperative, interrogative, and exclamatory. Also, divide each of these categories into things you like to hear and things you'd rather not hear again. Share your list with your classmates.

Sentences and Sentence Fragments

2a. A *sentence* is a word group that contains a subject and a verb and that expresses a complete thought.

SENTENCE FRAGMENT   The window in the kitchen.

        SENTENCE   The window in the kitchen could not be opened.

EXERCISE A Decide whether the following groups of words are sentence fragments or complete sentences. On the lines provided, write *F* for *fragment* or *S* for *sentence*.

Example   __*F*__ **1.** Looking for a pen so I can finish writing my report.

_____ **1.** Hercules defeated the monster Hydra.

_____ **2.** A plant thought by some to have great healing powers.

_____ **3.** How many pages of the article in the magazine?

_____ **4.** Kiyo, wearing her soccer uniform, posed for her team picture.

_____ **5.** As my grandmother observes the weather.

EXERCISE B On the line provided, write *S* if all of the sentences in the item are complete or *F* if the item contains any fragments. For each fragment, insert a caret (∧) and add words above the line to make the fragment a complete sentence.

Example   __*F*__ **1.** Kenya's Joseph Chebet won the men's division of the 1999 New York City

                      Marathon. Mexico's Adriana Fernandez ∧*won* the women's division.

_____ **6.** For Chebet, this win broke a string of second-place finishes in previous marathons in

        New York City and Boston. In April 1999, also won first place in the Boston Marathon.

_____ **7.** Chebet's victories put him in the record book with Alberto Salazar and Bill Rodgers.

        Salazar won in 1982, while Rodgers won in both 1978 and 1979.

_____ **8.** Like Chebet, Adriana Fernandez had also finished in second place in the 1998 New

        York City Marathon. In 1999, the first Mexican woman ever to win an international

        marathon.

_____ **9.** In addition, nearly $2\frac{1}{2}$ minutes ahead of her nearest competitor. Her time was only 26

        seconds short of the record that Australia's Lisa Ondieki set in 1992.

_____ **10.** Chebet and Fernandez each felt they had run a strong race. At 4 minutes 43 seconds,

        the time for one of the miles that Chebet ran the fastest in the race.

GRAMMAR

Subjects and Predicates

2b. | Sentences consist of two basic parts: *subjects* and *predicates*. The **subject** tells *whom* or *what* the sentence is about. The **predicate** tells something about the subject.

SUBJECT	PREDICATE
We	laughed.

SUBJECT	PREDICATE
Each of the books	must be logged in.

PREDICATE	SUBJECT	PREDICATE
How much has	your peach crop	produced this year?

EXERCISE A   In each of the following sentences, identify the underlined word group as the subject or the predicate of the sentence by writing above the word group *S* for *subject* or *P* for *predicate*.

Example 1. <u>Some of the worst disasters in history</u> have been caused by volcanic eruptions.

1. <u>Volcanoes and volcanic eruptions</u> have long been a source of fascination and terror.

2. They <u>have even played a role in the religions of many cultures.</u>

3. <u>Have</u> scientists <u>given</u> the world any explanations of volcanic activity?

4. On November 14, 1963, <u>a volcano</u> created a new island off the coast of Iceland.

5. Have <u>articles about volcanoes or geothermal energy</u> appeared in any magazines lately?

6. From the internal heat of the earth comes geothermal energy.

7. In Iceland <u>geothermal energy</u> is released by the internal heat of the earth.

8. In 1980, the volcanic eruption of Mount St. Helens <u>shocked the world.</u>

9. Because of geologists' efforts to predict the eruption, <u>loss of life</u> was minimal.

10. Eyewitnesses of the event <u>will not soon forget the sight.</u>

EXERCISE B   In each of the following sentences, underline the subject once and the predicate twice.

Example 1. <u>Pliny the Younger, a Roman writer and statesman,</u> <u>wrote descriptions of volcanoes.</u>

11. Have you read this article on central Italy and Mount Vesuvius?

12. Pliny the Younger was the first to describe the various stages of an eruption.

13. In addition, Pliny described the height of the cloud of ash above Vesuvius as well as the effects of the eruption on people.

14. Mount Vesuvius is situated a little over five kilometers northwest of Pompeii.

15. Part of the caldera around Vesuvius, known as the Somma Rim, was formed approximately 17,000 years ago.

Simple and Complete Subjects

2c. The *simple subject* is the main word or word group that tells *whom* or *what* the sentence is about. The *complete subject* consists of the simple subject and any words or word groups used to modify the simple subject.

SIMPLE SUBJECT   Waiting to be rescued, **people** sat on rooftops or climbed into trees.

COMPLETE SUBJECT   **Waiting to be rescued, people** sat on rooftops or climbed into trees.

SIMPLE SUBJECT   How could the **tap water** at the shelter be made safe to drink?

COMPLETE SUBJECT   How could **the tap water at the shelter** be made safe to drink?

EXERCISE A   Identify the underlined words or word groups in the following sentences by writing above them *SS* for *simple subject, CS* for *complete subject,* or *SS/CS* for *simple subject and complete subject.*

                                   CS

Example 1. The research for his term paper led Robert to this Web site.

1. The home page had links to Native American businesses and services.

2. Included were a variety of organizations from North, Central, and South America.

3. Several of the Web sites provided more links to education and employment services.

4. Robert found the links to cultural research centers and newspapers helpful.

5. Also useful was the American Indian Science and Engineering Society site.

6. Did he tell you about the resources at the Seventh Generation Fund site?

7. His favorite Web site was that of the Wordcraft Circle of Native Writers and Storytellers.

8. The American Indian Center of Chicago will be a great site for his family history search.

9. Did he view the links under "Native Businesses"?

10. The Native American home page is now bookmarked in his computer's Internet program.

EXERCISE B   In each of the following sentences, underline the complete subject once and the simple subject twice.

Example 1. These days, American Indian businesses are becoming more diversified.

11. Many American Indian groups have expanded income sources well beyond tourism and art.

12. Some groups expanded by opening businesses on reservations.

13. American Indians have also begun providing support services as government contractors.

14. Some have taken advantage of scenery and location to add hotel and recreation facilities.

15. To work with non-Indian companies, a number of tribes incorporated and set up separate business offices.

Simple and Complete Predicates

2d. The *simple predicate*, or *verb*, is the main word or word group that tells something about the subject. The *complete predicate* consists of the verb and all the words used to modify the verb and complete its meaning.

SIMPLE PREDICATE   I **have read** about the hundreds of active volcanoes on earth.

COMPLETE PREDICATE   I **have read about the hundreds of active volcanoes on earth.**

SIMPLE PREDICATE   **Did**n't you ever **see** that movie before?

COMPLETE PREDICATE   **Did**n't you **ever see that movie before**?

EXERCISE A   Identify the underlined words or word groups in the following sentences by writing above them *SP* for *simple predicate* or *CP* for *complete predicate*.

Example 1. Vicki had bought a new CD organizer. *[CP]*

1. Our band fund-raiser will be selling popcorn in cans trimmed in the school colors.

2. By this time tomorrow our train will have arrived at the next stop on our tour.

3. Gayle's alarm clock has awakened her an hour early each day.

4. For how many seasons did Yogi Berra play baseball in Yankee Stadium?

5. Mom and Dad have always kept a road-emergency kit in the car.

EXERCISE B   In each of the following sentences, underline the complete predicate once and the simple predicate twice.

Example 1. Mavis and David were certainly happy about the prize.

6. Wes had been searching for his carburetor.

7. Did you paint with tempera or watercolors in art class today?

8. Slowly, the fog was rolling around the hills and down into the valley.

9. Feeling a little awkward, Sharon offered her help.

10. Grandfather teased me playfully.

11. Tomorrow, bring pens, pencils, papers, and erasers with you for the final exam.

12. How far from NASA headquarters does the flight-crew coordinator live?

13. Canada geese slowly made their way to the pond.

14. Grandmother used a washboard for the laundry on washday.

15. Do you know any tricks with a yo-yo?

Complete and Simple Subjects and Predicates

2c. The *simple subject* is the main word or word group that tells *whom* or *what* the sentence is about. The *complete subject* consists of the simple subject and any words or word groups used to modify the simple subject.

2d. The *simple predicate,* or *verb,* is the main word or word group that tells something about the subject. The *complete predicate* consists of the verb and all the words used to modify the verb and complete its meaning.

EXERCISE A In each of the following sentences, underline the complete subject once and the simple subject twice.

Example 1. The widespread use of computer technology has changed work.

1. Computer programs frequently replace pencil and paper, slide rules, and small calculators.

2. They can provide rapid analysis and impact reports on changing data.

3. With easy-to-use Internet resources and communications, data can be shared more quickly.

4. The result of using computers for many tasks is usually a savings in time and money.

5. All of this technology produces much more efficient and productive work environments.

EXERCISE B In each of the following sentences, underline the complete predicate once and the simple predicate twice.

Example 1. With industry moving toward high technology, not only businesses but also their

clients have been affected.

6. Ivette Carcas, an architect from Florida, has seen a number of changes in her field.

7. Pencil sketches were previously the norm.

8. Now, she constantly uses computer-aided design (CAD) programs.

9. These programs give her more flexibility.

10. Because of this new resource, clients sometimes pressure the professional for a quick answer.

11. Without thorough discussion, the result could be unrealistic expectations or incorrect plans.

12. Another Florida architect, Miguel Rodríguez, would agree with Ms. Carcas's assessment of computer technology in their industry.

13. According to Mr. Rodríguez, thought processes for problem solving cannot be rushed.

14. The client's desires must be balanced with the schedule.

15. Local regulations and building codes also must be considered in any design.

Compound Subjects

2e. A *compound subject* consists of two or more subjects that are joined by a conjunction and that have the same verb.

EXAMPLES   **You** and **Cody** ought to be proud of your grades this term.

Is **news, weather,** or **sports** covered first each night in the newscast?

Last night, neither the **car** nor the **motorcycle** would start.

EXERCISE   In each of the following sentences, underline the parts of the compound subject.

Example **1.** Did either a <u>mountain lion</u> or a <u>bear</u> make that sound?

1. Increased wages and additional benefits were the results of the negotiations.

2. Will Mark or Sara pick you up at the bus stop?

3. There are many charts and graphs in our new economics book.

4. Trains, buses, and the subway make up the mass-transit system here.

5. Neither swimming nor boating is possible yet at the site of the artificial lake.

6. The radius of this circle and the height of that rectangle should be equal.

7. Is soy, corn, or wheat more important in the U.S. economy?

8. Wire cages or netting can keep young plants safe from hungry birds and animals.

9. One coat, two caps, and four sweaters were on Nettie's shopping list.

10. Neither Kevin nor Sean had seen this kind of caterpillar before.

11. Has either the deer or her fawn been eating at the trough with the cattle?

12. Tomorrow, the coach or the team captains will speak at the pep rally.

13. Alfalfa or soybeans will grow in those fields next year.

14. Newsstands and newspaper vending machines are located throughout the airport.

15. Snips and snails and puppy dogs' tails are not really the ingredients of little boys.

16. Are plant nutrients and dirt really derivative products of rocks?

17. Electricity and computers certainly caused changes in industry in the last century.

18. Mathematicians and astronomers agreed on the location and size of the new planet.

19. This weekend, four or five of us will walk in the benefit for cancer research.

20. Either next weekend or the one after might be better for our class picnic.

Compound Verbs

2f. | A **compound verb** consists of two or more verbs that are joined by a conjunction and that have the same subject.

EXAMPLES   Ian **collected** his thoughts and **began** to write.
              Have you ever **seen** a movie or **read** a book about the Sasquatch?
              You can either **take** the subway or **ride** a bus to the state fair.

EXERCISE In each of the following sentences, underline the parts of the compound verb.

Example 1. We will either <u>wash</u> dishes after dinner or <u>clean</u> the den.

1. Survey crews may either finish the job now or wait until after the thunderstorm.

2. My father usually sleeps during the day and eats his breakfast at 7:00 P.M.

3. Evan would have walked, run, or bicycled to the first game of the season.

4. The driver turned off the road, parked on a side street, and waited.

5. Mom did an excellent job, was awarded a paid day off, and earned a raise.

6. Our supermarket manager looked but could not find the product either.

7. Juan dropped his duffel bag on the sand, doffed his sandals, and raced into the ocean.

8. Do mail carriers work in bad weather or wait for better conditions?

9. You should finish all the problems but still have enough time for a quick review.

10. The poet Paul Valéry rose at dawn each morning and wrote for hours.

11. For orange paint, add equal parts of red and yellow and blend thoroughly.

12. Court stenographers hear all the testimony but should not discuss any of it with anyone.

13. Harold, Mel, and I compared our notes and reviewed the chapter before the civics test.

14. Shall I call some of my friends and invite them to the show?

15. In the morning, the aircraft mechanics will either repair or replace the part.

16. Firefighters needed more water and chemicals but couldn't get them fast enough.

17. Biologists could neither recognize nor categorize the new strain of bacteria.

18. Helen liked stories by Robert Louis Stevenson but could never remember any of the titles.

19. My cat always recognizes the sound of my father's car and meets my father at the door.

20. Will Ruby and James bring fruit for a salad or buy some at the grocery?

Compound Subjects and Verbs

2e. A *compound subject* consists of two or more subjects that are joined by a conjunction and that have the same verb.

2f. A *compound verb* consists of two or more verbs that are joined by a conjunction and that have the same subject.

    COMPOUND SUBJECT **Nancy, Tim,** and **I** want to sign up for the track team.

    COMPOUND VERB The baseball game **ran** late and **delayed** a cricket demonstration.

EXERCISE A Underline the compound subjects and compound verbs in the following sentences. Then, on the lines provided, write *CS* for *compound subject* or *CV* for *compound verb*.

Example ___CV___ **1.** In the 1970s, Thomas Bewick developed a method of carving wood and popularized it for printmaking.

_____ **1.** Bewick would cut away pieces of a block of wood and leave a raised, printable image.

_____ **2.** Grace Albee (1890–1985) began her engraving career by creating linocuts but later, in Paris, learned Bewick's technique.

_____ **3.** Either her artistic skill or her eye for detail would have made her work successful.

_____ **4.** She inked, screened, and laid the prints on the dining room table.

_____ **5.** Her works and those of artists such as Rockwell Kent have been called regionalist art.

EXERCISE B Combine each of the following sets of sentences to create one sentence with a compound subject or a compound verb. Write each new sentence on the line provided.

Example 1. Grace Albee grew up in Rhode Island. She studied art there.

    Grace Albee grew up in Rhode Island and studied art there.

6. In 1927, she entered work in a Providence Art Club print exhibition. Her husband did also.

_____

7. The couple moved to Paris in 1928. They began working and taking classes there.

_____

8. Painter Norman Rockwell was among their friends. So was printmaker John Taylor Arms.

_____

9. Albee's prints of plants contrasted soft against sharp. They also played light against shadow.

_____

10. A museum displays some of her prints. The Boston Public Library displays some, too.

_____

How to Find the Subject in a Sentence

A simple way to find the subject of a sentence is to ask *Who?* or *What?* before the verb. Remembering the following guidelines will also help you find the subject of a sentence.

(1) The subject of a sentence expressing a command or request is always understood to be *you*.

　REQUEST　[**You**] Bring me that book of poems, please.

　COMMAND　[**You**] Turn out your light and go to sleep, Mariana.

(2) The subject of the sentence is never in a prepositional phrase.

　EXAMPLE　**Some** of these poems are difficult to understand. [*Some* is the subject of the sentence. *Poems* is the object of the preposition *of*.]

(3) The subject of a sentence expressing a question generally follows the verb or a part of the verb phrase.

　EXAMPLE　Do **you** like this poem best? [*You* do like this poem best.]

(4) The word *there* or *here* is almost never the subject of a sentence.

　EXAMPLES　Here are the **pliers** and **hammer**! [What are here? *Pliers* and *hammer* are here.]

　　　　　There were several **books** of poetry on the shelf. [What were? *Books* were.]

EXERCISE A　In each of the following sentences, underline the subject once and the verb twice. If the subject is understood to be *you*, write *You* after the sentence.

Example 1.　Please begin now, class, with your small group discussions. *You*

1. Here is a poem by Alice Walker, an African American writer and a Pulitzer Prize winner.

2. Was Alice Walker dismissed once from college because of her participation in a civil rights demonstration?

3. Didn't she later win a scholarship to Sarah Lawrence College?

4. There are several novels by Alice Walker in our library.

5. Claudia, please pick up a collection of Walker's short stories at the bookstore.

EXERCISE B　In each of the following sentences, decide whether the underlined word is the subject. If it is, write *S* above it. If it is not, find the subject and circle it. If the subject is understood to be *you*, write *You* after the sentence.

Example 1.　How often is the (poetry) of Langston Hughes read?

6. Gregory, listen to the rhythm in the poem "Harlem," by Langston Hughes.

7. There is a line in that poem about "a raisin in the sun."

8. The writer of the play *A Raisin in the Sun* took the play's title from that line of poetry.

9. Wasn't there a movie produced under that title also?

10. Was Langston Hughes one of the most influential African American poets of his day?

Language and Sentence Skills Practice

GRAMMAR

Complements

2g. A *complement* is a word or word group that completes the meaning of a verb.

A complement may be a noun, a pronoun, or an adjective and may consist of one word or a group of words.

DIRECT OBJECT	Did Shana lend you her **notes**?
INDIRECT OBJECT	Did Shana lend **you** her notes?
OBJECTIVE COMPLEMENT	Did you find the notes **helpful**?
PREDICATE NOMINATIVE	This test will not be the semester **exam**.
PREDICATE ADJECTIVE	The test is rather **long**, though.

EXERCISE Underline all the complements in the following sentences.

Example 1. Last summer a guide showed <u>us</u> the <u>Frederik Meijer Gardens</u>.

1. The garden also includes a top-ranked sculpture park.

2. How many landscape awards has the garden won?

3. We enjoyed the botanical garden because the weather was perfect.

4. Even if the weather had been bad, the guide would have shown us the indoor sculptures.

5. Our group did not attempt a tour of the entire 118 acres.

6. Leonardo da Vinci's *Horse* was the main attraction for us.

7. Da Vinci had named his massive bronze creature *Il Cavallo*.

8. People rediscovered the horse as early as 1966.

9. The notebook in which the designs were found is called the Madrid Codex II.

10. Da Vinci designed the horse but never constructed it.

11. One person who read about the notebook and design was Charles Dent.

12. He considered the sculpture a dream project of major importance to the U.S.A. and to Italy.

13. However, when he died in 1994, the da Vinci horse was not yet complete.

14. The prearranged sale of some of Dent's art collection proved lucrative.

15. The sale gave Dent support for the project.

16. At the same time, Fred Meijer negotiated both the garden's support and funding for the project.

17. Sculptors at the foundry poured, assembled, and shaped two of the huge bronze horses.

18. Each sculpture had a stainless-steel frame and weighed nearly thirteen tons.

19. Milan, Italy, witnessed the unveiling of its *Leonardo da Vinci Horse* in September 1999.

20. How welcome the 24-foot *American Horse* was.

Direct Objects

2h. A *direct object* is a noun, pronoun, or word group that tells who or what receives the action of the verb or that shows the result of the action.

A direct object answers the question *Whom?* or *What?* after a transitive verb. A direct object may be compound and, for emphasis, may precede the subject and verb.

EXAMPLES   Liana had read that **book** before she met the **author.**

Should we elect the **secretary** or the **treasurer** next?

Do bacteria cause **whooping cough**?

What muscle **tone** and **stamina** that exercise program creates!

EXERCISE   In the following sentences, underline the verbs once and the direct objects twice.

Example 1. You should have goals for your job.

1. Did our neighbor stake her new plants?

2. Have you read those chapters yet?

3. Had the enormous whirlpool trapped the schooner?

4. Dad and Mom planted decorative native grasses along the back fence.

5. Letitia, Ira, and Colin helped the pep squad and me with the goal post decorations.

6. After you remove all liquid from this solution, determine the amount of sodium remaining.

7. Once a week, Pearl added a fictional adventure to her journal.

8. Travel agents usually can answer questions about your destination.

9. During today's practice, Coach wants cooperation.

10. Where does Mr. Jepson keep the markers, poster board, and gluesticks for this project?

11. Everyone cheered the football team wildly because it had reached the state finals.

12. At the farmer's market we will buy spring onions, black-eyed peas, and peaches.

13. What great coordination Odelle, Jillian, and you bring to our defense!

14. For the awards banquet next month, invite someone as your guest.

15. Six of Eliot's great-grandchildren attended his ninetieth birthday party yesterday.

16. Graph the tallest mountains in the fifty states.

17. DeNiequa should be taking both of you with her when she buys groceries.

18. Mei-Ling watched the toolmaker as he finished the point on the shovel.

19. How much oil do sunflower seeds yield per pound?

20. What a wonderful fabric you have selected for the upholstery on the sofa and chairs!

GRAMMAR

Indirect Objects

2i. An *indirect object* is a noun, pronoun, or word group that often appears in sentences containing direct objects. An indirect object tells *to whom* or *to what* (or *for whom* or *for what*) the action of the verb is done.

> **EXAMPLES**   The librarian handed **me** the pile of books to reshelve.
> Has the senator given the **League of Women Voters** his answers?
> Furnish the **jurors** a copy of this map for use in their deliberations.

EXERCISE A   In each of the following sentences, underline each indirect object.

Example 1. Amy Tan shows <u>readers</u> her world.

1. In her books, Amy Tan provides her fans a glimpse into her own Chinese heritage.

2. Tan gives her audience stories that are based on her family history.

3. Many stories that she heard while growing up furnish the author material for her books.

4. In her book *The Joy Luck Club*, Tan shows readers the relationship between Chinese American mothers and their daughters.

5. Relationships among her own family members gave her the inspiration for the book.

6. In the dedication of *The Joy Luck Club*, Tan gives her mother the assurance that she has not forgotten her Chinese heritage.

7. The author also offers her editor, her agent, and her family thanks for their encouragement.

8. Book reviewers afford Tan much critical acclaim for her first efforts as a novelist.

9. Throughout her books, she presents the public a new and refreshing point of view.

10. Her second novel, *The Kitchen God's Wife*, also has won Tan critical praise.

EXERCISE B   In the following sentences, underline indirect objects once and direct objects twice.

Example 1. Who gave <u>N. Scott Momaday</u> another <u>name</u>?

11. Tsoai-talee, a mountain sacred to the Kiowa, provides Momaday that name.

12. Anglo-Americans have given this Wyoming mountain the name Devil's Tower.

13. My teacher told us the story of Momaday's name and of its meaning, which is "Rock-Tree Boy."

14. Before Momaday was a year old, one of his father's relatives gave him this name.

15. The Pulitzer Prize Committee awarded the writer the 1969 fiction prize for his book *House Made of Dawn*.

Objective Complements

2j.   An *objective complement* is a word or word group that helps complete the meaning of a transitive verb by identifying or modifying the direct object.

An objective complement may be a noun, a pronoun, or an adjective. Only a few verbs can take an objective complement: *consider, make,* and verbs that can be replaced by *consider* or *make,* such as *appoint, call, choose, elect, keep, name, cut, paint,* and *sweep.*

EXAMPLES   The judges called Jeremy the most promising **pianist** at the recital.
We wanted Caroline as our representative, but they elected her **theirs.**
Sweep the kitchen floor **clean** and keep it **shiny** with a light coat of wax.
What beautiful **shades** of blue the students painted those posters!

EXERCISE A   In each of the following sentences, decide whether each underlined word is an objective complement. If it is, write *OC* above the word. If it is not, find the objective complement and circle it.

Example 1. Ayita named her <u>brother</u> the (sales manager.)

1. The manufacturers called their product the greatest <u>invention</u> since the toaster.

2. My parents consider my <u>sister</u> and <u>me</u> dependable.

3. The student council reelected <u>Carlos</u> president this year.

4. After lunch, Deandra wiped the table and the countertops <u>clean</u>.

5. The athletic committee named Kimama <u>"Outstanding Athlete of the Year."</u>

6. How useless the electrical storm rendered our <u>computers</u>!

7. Mr. Peterson considers <u>Italian, French, or Latin</u> excellent preparation for college.

8. My brother appointed me official <u>guardian</u> and <u>protector</u> of his baseball card collection.

9. The managing director appointed <u>Ms. Latham</u> assistant director.

10. What a successful <u>student</u> her determination made her!

EXERCISE B   Underline the objective complements in the sentences below.

Example 1. Would your grandfather declare this dish <u>first-rate</u> or <u>top-notch</u>?

11. My grandfather called Julia's lasagna delicious.

12. Granddad finds eating both necessary and pleasurable.

13. His friends dubbed him "The Connoisseur" because he always makes some remark about his food.

14. Granddad appointed my sister Julia tester and taster of his new recipes.

15. How fulfilling and "filling" she considers the experience!

GRAMMAR

Direct and Indirect Objects and Objective Complements

2h.	A *direct object* is a noun, pronoun, or word group that tells who or what receives the action of the verb or that shows the result of the action.
2i.	An *indirect object* is a noun, pronoun, or word group that tells *to whom* or *to what* (or *for whom* or *for what*) the action of the verb is done.
2j.	An *objective complement* is a word or word group that helps complete the meaning of a transitive verb by identifying or modifying the direct object.

EXERCISE A In each of the following sentences, decide what type of complement the underlined word is. Above the word, write *DO* for *direct object*, *IO* for *indirect object*, or *OC* for *objective complement*.

                                             DO

Example 1. Sara could not explain her <u>forgetfulness</u>.

1. By the turn of the century, how many apartments filled the <u>island</u> of Manhattan?

2. The photographer gave <u>us</u> one of the pictures she had taken of the school.

3. Sweep the chimney <u>clean</u> at least once a year and the firebox after each use.

4. Please do not send any <u>more</u> of these samples unless someone requests them.

5. Ms. Van Sterben deemed her faithful nurse <u>worthy</u> of a share of the fortune.

6. Had she allowed <u>herself</u> and her <u>staff</u> any spare time for emergencies?

7. What <u>folly</u> future historians may consider many twentieth-century "innovations"!

8. In addition, this housing provides the <u>immigrants</u> few extras.

9. The director and the cast discussed the first <u>act</u> but decided not to change it.

10. Who would award an <u>architect</u> a prize for an undesirable structure?

EXERCISE B Identify each complement in the following sentences. Underline once each direct object, underline twice each indirect object, and circle each objective complement.

Example 1. The energetic child pushed the <u>door</u> (open.)

11. Roberto took a huge bite out of the sandwich.

12. Everyone congratulated Nancy on her award.

13. Dad lent Wally his car for the evening.

14. Jane always likes her vegetables well cooked.

15. The mayor quickly issued the public a statement regarding his decision.

                                                     HOLT HANDBOOK | Fifth Course

for **CHAPTER 2: THE PARTS OF A SENTENCE**   pages 42–43

Predicate Nominatives

2k. A *predicate nominative* is a word or word group that is in the predicate and that identifies the subject or refers to it.

> EXAMPLES   Each building's exterior had previously been adobe **bricks** and **plaster**.
> This news report was the same **one** that we watched an hour ago.
> The new business in town is **Husani's Egyptian Restaurant**.
> Computers had become a **necessity**.

EXERCISE A   In the following sentences, underline linking verbs once and predicate nominatives twice. Be sure to include all parts of verb phrases.

Example 1. Computers will remain both work and play in tomorrow's world.

1. Shirley Chisholm became the first black woman to serve in the U.S. House of Representatives.

2. The antique table, which we found in the basement, must have been a valuable one.

3. When viewed from above, the design of the building seemed the shape of a figure eight.

4. Hasn't the ocean turned a beautiful color from the light reflecting off the clouds?

5. Frances Perkins, the first woman in the history of the United States to hold a Cabinet post, was secretary of labor during Franklin Roosevelt's administration.

6. The seeds you planted are becoming vines and fruits all over the garden.

7. Are your e-mails about Kimi's trip to Norway the ones with last month's dates?

8. The most innovative idea for an air shaft was yours.

9. Germany, Austria, and Hungary were the countries with the most representatives.

10. The helpful woman who called yesterday from the local insurance agency is she.

EXERCISE B   Underline the predicate nominatives in the following sentences.

Example 1. The hacksaw and two pipe wrenches are what I need next.

11. Next year's class representatives will be George Running Bear and Sylvia Flying Hawk.

12. How stirringly Sidney Poitier became Justice Thurgood Marshall in that teleplay!

13. The honor of meeting such an influential business leader was mine and theirs at last.

14. Dr. Martin Luther King, Jr., a nonviolent activist and civil rights leader, was a recipient of the Nobel Peace Prize.

15. The main difference between wasps and bees is that wasps have long, narrow bodies and slim waists.

Predicative Adjectives

2l.	A *predicate adjective* is an adjective that is in the predicate and that modifies the subject.
EXAMPLES	At this point, my plans for the future remain quite **indefinite.**
	Does the sky look **green** to you?

EXERCISE A In the following sentences, underline linking verbs once and predicate adjectives twice. Be sure to include all parts of verb phrases.

Example 1. After all, this Web site has been extremely informative.

1. When did doctors become aware of the importance of antiseptics?

2. Four tables for two will be available at about the same time.

3. Mom's apple-blueberry muffins are delicious.

4. To Edith and Sol, the circus's high-wire act appeared thrilling, dangerous, and glamorous.

5. My plan to listen to that CD through my headphones sounded good to Mom and Dad.

6. Bev's seat covers were navy and tan.

7. Your essay on pet food should be informative but entertaining.

8. Smoke billowing from the warehouse fire smelled pungent and oily.

9. Who has seemed happiest about your acceptance to that college?

10. Stretching your muscles during exercise can be helpful.

EXERCISE B Underline the predicate adjectives in the following sentences.

Example 1. How anyone can stay warm out here is amazing to me!

11. The rose garden smelled lovely.

12. With four holes still to play, the amateurs' golf tournament leaders were confident.

13. A person with a balanced diet, enough rest, and plenty of exercise should stay healthy.

14. Will the CDs sound clearer because of your new speaker system?

15. How fortunate you and Sheila are to get tickets to the concert!

16. Should dependability be essential in any car you might consider buying?

17. Do the floats in this year's holiday parade seem bigger and more colorful than last year's?

18. Explain for us why corn can grow so tall in this particular climate.

19. Most carpet layers with whom I have worked are experienced, efficient, and neat.

20. Ruben felt a little nervous as the time grew near for his driving test.

for **CHAPTER 2: THE PARTS OF A SENTENCE**   pages 42–43

Predicative Nominatives and Predicative Adjectives

2k. A *predicate nominative* is a word or word group that is in the predicate and that identifies the subject or refers to it.

    EXAMPLE   Kudzu is a fast-growing **vine.**

2l. A *predicate adjective* is an adjective that is in the predicate and that modifies the subject.

    EXAMPLE   The waves that crested soon grew **higher** and **rougher.**

EXERCISE A   In each of the following sentences, decide what type of subject complement each under-lined word is. Above the word, write *PN* for *predicate nominative* or *PA* for *predicate adjective.*

    Example 1. Drifting across the yard, the guitar music was <u>tantalizing</u>. *(PA)*

  1. You will remain <u>president</u> of this organization for the rest of the year.

  2. Is Raymond Dawson the <u>author</u> of *The Chinese Experience?*

  3. Tiffany had been typing for an hour, and she looked <u>discouraged</u> and <u>tired</u>.

  4. The food at the banquet was <u>tasteful</u> and <u>appealing</u> in its presentation.

  5. After three days of thunderstorms, Tranh felt <u>depressed</u> and <u>languid</u>.

  6. They became <u>heroes</u> and <u>celebrities</u> practically overnight.

  7. Should Arturo be the <u>leader</u> of the expedition?

  8. Seditious groups were a <u>threat</u> to the new regime.

  9. How <u>content</u> my uncle seemed in his remote cottage on the Outer Banks of North Carolina.

10. My grandmother seemed <u>happy</u> and <u>surprised</u> because we had come to visit her.

EXERCISE B   Add a subject complement to each of the following groups of words to make a complete sentence. You may include words modifying the subject complement.

    Example 1. To Rita, the Scotch pine seemed *the perfect landscape tree.*

11. Edna, at the age of eighty-four, was _____

12. After his retirement, Detective Forbes became _____

13. When he completed his project, Sergio felt _____

14. All of the gardens in the tiny Japanese village were _____

15. Todd thought that the job application looked _____

Parts of a Sentence

2b. Sentences consist of two basic parts: subjects and predicates. The **subject** tells *whom* or *what* the sentence is about. The **predicate** tells something about the subject.

SUBJECT	Did **William Faulkner** ever live in New Orleans?
PREDICATE	**Did** William Faulkner ever **live** in New Orleans?

2g. A **complement** is a word or word group that completes the meaning of a verb.

DIRECT OBJECT	Rafiq told Caroline a **story** in which he named a **lizard** Leo.
INDIRECT OBJECT	Rafiq told **Caroline** a story in which he named a lizard Leo.
OBJECTIVE COMPLEMENT	Rafiq told Caroline a story in which he named a lizard **Leo.**
PREDICATE NOMINATIVE	The story was a good **one,** but it was far-fetched.
PREDICATE ADJECTIVE	The story was a good one, but it was **far-fetched.**

EXERCISE A In each of the following sentences, underline the sentence part indicated in parentheses.

Example 1. (*objective complement*) The city dyed the river green for St. Patrick's Day.

1. (*complete subject*) Each person on the roster is eligible for a T-shirt and a cap.

2. (*simple predicate*) What had been happening to the wildlife in the forest and the lake?

3. (*predicate adjective*) Drivers must stay straight in the narrow lanes along this section.

4. (*simple subject*) Only Marvin could think of a solution like that for this problem.

5. (*direct object*) Bring all of your favorite recipes to contribute to our booklet!

6. (*simple predicate*) Shadows had slowly fallen across the dusty hills.

7. (*predicate nominative*) The audience became a wall of sound.

8. (*indirect object*) Could you furnish this court any evidence of your whereabouts?

9. (*complete predicate*) How long that mechanic must have worked to repair our car!

10. (*objective complement*) Did the minister say, "I now pronounce you husband and wife"?

EXERCISE B Underline the complements, and above each write *DO* for *direct object*, *IO* for *indirect object*, *OC* for *objective complement*, *PN* for *predicate nominative*, or *PA* for *predicate adjective*.

Example 1. My grandmother prefers her peaches very ripe.

11. Juanita offered Caroline a seat next to her in the theater.

12. The film's plot seemed overly complex and hard to follow.

13. The student council elected Aurelio treasurer for next year.

14. My part-time job at the law office is good experience for the future.

15. Our school's historical society keeps our heritage alive in its production of plays.

Classifying Sentences According to Purpose

2m. Sentences may be classified according to purpose.

(1) A *declarative sentence* makes a statement and ends with a period.

(2) An *interrogative sentence* asks a question and ends with a question mark.

(3) An *imperative sentence* makes a request or gives a command. Most imperative sentences end with a period. A strong command ends with an exclamation point.

(4) An *exclamatory sentence* shows excitement or expresses strong feeling and ends with an exclamation point.

DECLARATIVE	Fruit juice is good for you.
INTERROGATIVE	Will you support this recommendation?
IMPERATIVE	Please pass the prune juice.
	Watch out for the bus!
EXCLAMATORY	How terrible that tastes!

EXERCISE Identify the purpose of each of the following sentences. On the line provided, write the abbreviation that classifies the sentence's purpose. Then, add an appropriate end mark to the sentence.

DEC for *declarative* INT for *interrogative*

IMP for *imperative* EXCL for *exclamatory*

Example _INT_ **1.** When you need a little help, will you call me ?

_____ **1.** What a strange sight that was

_____ **2.** Elizabeth Blackwell, the first female physician in the United States, opened a hospital in 1853

_____ **3.** If you don't mind, could you stay after class to help clean up

_____ **4.** What a terrific day I've had

_____ **5.** Did the playwright Henrik Ibsen become cynical as he grew old

_____ **6.** Set the table for dinner, please

_____ **7.** He asked how you knew whom to contact

_____ **8.** Don't move from that spot

_____ **9.** How fabulous Denny's birthday party was

_____ **10.** Think before you speak, Rich

GRAMMAR

Review A: Complete Sentences and Sentence Fragments

EXERCISE Decide whether the following groups of words are sentence fragments or complete sentences. On the lines provided, write *F* for *fragment* or *S* for *sentence*.

Example __*F*__ **1.** Unlocked key to understanding hieroglyphics and Egyptian culture.

_____ **1.** Supported by a vast array of resources and new findings, Egyptology.

_____ **2.** Egyptologists arranged a tour of artifacts dating from about 2650–2150 B.C.

_____ **3.** Artifacts from the time of the first pyramids, the Sphinx, classic statues.

_____ **4.** Over 230 items from thirty museums and ten private collections were included.

_____ **5.** Exhibition of outstanding quality, most not ever viewed together before.

_____ **6.** Three of the world's best Egyptologists agreed to work on this project.

_____ **7.** Were senior, or head, curators of Egyptian art at their museums.

_____ **8.** Chose articles that would show this time period in a new way.

_____ **9.** As an example of how difficult the selection process was.

_____ **10.** Of the British Museum's 100,000 artifacts, only sixteen were included in the exhibit.

_____ **11.** Fifteen from the Louvre, thirty-five from the Metropolitan, and twenty-seven from the Cairo Museum.

_____ **12.** In all, the curators spent three years collecting objects for the exhibition.

_____ **13.** To show life during the Fourth Dynasty and the style of Egyptian art.

_____ **14.** Most important was the way in which the human form was used in this art.

_____ **15.** Copied for centuries to come, carvings and paintings showed human profiles.

_____ **16.** The eye and eyebrow looking straight out, now considered typically Egyptian.

_____ **17.** Experts and scholars disagreed on the dates to assign the various items.

_____ **18.** Visitors easily followed the time-line approach used to display items.

_____ **19.** Catalog of architecture, paintings, statues, the dynasties, and more.

_____ **20.** Much of the modern fascination with Egypt is rooted in this era.

Review B: **Parts of a Sentence**

EXERCISE A In each of the following sentences, underline the simple subject once and the verb twice.

Example 1. There are many varieties of spoken English.

1. Most of us recognize the differences in English pronunciations—for instance, the difference between American and British pronunciations.

2. We are also familiar with many varieties of American speech.

3. We oftentimes know Texans by their drawl and recognize Bostonians by their pronunciation of *a*'s and *r*'s.

4. Usually, however, an educated Texan and an educated Bostonian write a nearly identical kind of English.

5. In fact, the Texan and the Bostonian share this written brand of English with most other writers of English in all parts of the world.

EXERCISE B Underline the complements in the following sentences. Then, above each complement, write one of the following abbreviations to identify the type of complement.

    DO for *direct object*   PN for *predicate nominative*

    IO for *indirect object*   PA for *predicate adjective*

    OC for *objective complement*

Example 1. The pilot told the passengers the plan of the flight.

6. Helen Frankenthaler proclaimed her painting finished.

7. Nick gave us directions to the Ruben Blades concert.

8. Martina Arroyo was happy about her role in *Aïda*.

9. Stories by Eudora Welty were his favorite reading material.

10. Did you give Tawana her Emily Dickinson book?

11. Gwendolyn Brooks was the winner of a Pulitzer Prize in 1949.

12. Many Hawaiians welcomed the news of fair skies after the hurricane.

13. Her supporters judged her qualified to be elected to Congress.

14. The sky seemed bright and clear in the morning.

15. Enthusiastic applause greeted the conductor.

Review C: **Parts of a Sentence**

EXERCISE A In each of the following sentences, underline the complete subject once and the complete predicate twice.

Example 1. Marsupials exist primarily in Australia and on some adjacent islands.

1. Pouched mammals, such as the kangaroo, differ from other mammals in significant ways.

2. Most of these marsupials carry their young in pouches.

3. At birth, the young of all marsupials are astonishingly small in comparison with the full-grown adults of the species.

4. A newborn kangaroo or wombat, for instance, measures only about an inch long and remains utterly helpless for a long period of time.

5. There are a great many types of marsupials, including marsupial moles and marsupial mice.

EXERCISE B Underline the complements in the following sentences. Then, above each complement, write one of the following abbreviations to identify the type of complement.

DO for *direct object*   PN for *predicate nominative*
IO for *indirect object*   PA for *predicate adjective*
OC for *objective complement*

Example 1. Professor Martinez gave her students some excellent advice.

6. The stories of Mary Wilkins Freeman are often portraits of strong-willed women.

7. Baseball player José Canseco hit a double in the first inning of the game.

8. The author promised me a free copy of his book.

9. The poems of Langston Hughes are fluid and evocative.

10. Is the Citadel a military college in South Carolina?

11. Shannon Jones, a Philadelphia attorney, presented the case for the defense.

12. We considered the new baseball field perfect for our league.

13. Will you give Hernando the gift now or later?

14. The rain seemed heavier in the afternoon.

15. Rosa appointed Charla treasurer for the upcoming term.

Review D: Kinds of Sentences and Sentence Fragments

EXERCISE A Identify the purpose of each of the following sentences. On the lines provided, write the abbreviation that classifies the sentence's purpose. Then, add an appropriate end mark to each sentence.

DEC for *declarative*   INT for *interrogative*
IMP for *imperative*   EXCL for *exclamatory*

Example __IMP__ **1.** Be careful of that first step.

_____ **1.** How many birthdays have you celebrated in the United States, Mr. Nguyen

_____ **2.** Tomorrow is the beginning of the spring semester and also of basketball season

_____ **3.** What a clever idea you had

_____ **4.** Add the distance between points A and B to the distance between points C and D

_____ **5.** Please take home any food dishes or games you brought for the party

_____ **6.** Ranch hands rode for several miles before they found the first tracks of the cougar

_____ **7.** If we ask Ms. Okada, don't you think she will let us finish these last two algebra

problems

_____ **8.** Lucia's graph identified the ten senators who had served the longest in Congress

_____ **9.** Hurry, Noelle

_____ **10.** Had Thi and Willis planned on camping and hiking all weekend long

EXERCISE B Decide whether each of the following groups of words is a sentence fragment or a complete sentence. On the line provided, write *F* for *fragment* or *S* for *sentence*.

Example __F__ **1.** Waiting for Sam Maskewit to repair the computer speaker wires.

_____ **11.** Planting trees takes preparation, time, and patience.

_____ **12.** Visit the wildlife park.

_____ **13.** Covering outside pipes or wrapping them can prevent their freezing.

_____ **14.** Any animal and habitat loss you know of in these highlighted areas.

_____ **15.** Had prescribed something to ease her patient's allergic reaction to cats.

_____ **16.** Darryl checked on the first-aid methods and materials available in the clinic.

_____ **17.** Callie Begaye made the winning goal that sent our soccer team to regional finals.

_____ **18.** So that we can enjoy a walk on a sunny afternoon.

_____ **19.** New kitchen cabinets should arrive in two weeks and will be ready for painting.

_____ **20.** Examined the leaves under the microscope to determine chlorophyll levels.

GRAMMAR | Language in Context: Literary Model

Literary Model: Poetry

The surface of the earth is soft and impressible by the feet of men; and so with the paths which the mind travels. How worn and dusty then must be the highways of the world, how deep the ruts of tradition and conformity!

—Henry David Thoreau, from *Walden*

A poem should be palpable and mute
As a globed fruit,

Dumb
As old medallions to the thumb,

Silent as the sleeve-worn stone
Of casement ledges where the moss has grown—

A poem should be wordless
As the flight of birds.

—Archibald MacLeish, from "Ars Poetica"

EXERCISE A

1. Identify the following elements in the first sentence of the Thoreau excerpt.

Subject: _____   Verb: _____

Subject Complements: _____ _____

2. In the second Thoreau sentence, what is unusual about the arrangement of sentence parts before the comma? What predicate adjective describes "the ruts of tradition and conformity"?

_____

_____

3. List all of the predicate adjectives in the excerpt from the poem "Ars Poetica."

_____

EXERCISE B How do both writers use predicate adjectives to draw comparisons between two things?

_____

Literary Model (continued)

EXERCISE C Try using a series of subject complements poetically to express a changing view of time. Use a subject and a linking verb as an opener, or use one of the following to illustrate the way a child might regard time: *Saturday morning used to be . . . , A summer vacation appeared to be . . . , Crisp fall afternoons seemed to be. . . .* Close with a line or two expressing an adult's perspective.

_____

_____

_____

_____

_____

_____

_____

_____

_____

_____

EXERCISE D

1. Identify predicate adjectives and predicate nominatives in the lines you wrote.

_____

_____

_____

_____

2. Copy one of your lines containing a predicate adjective. Revise it to include a predicate nominative that acts as a metaphor. Which version has more impact? Explain.

_____

_____

_____

_____

_____

_____

Writing Application: Essay

Fragments can be effective in certain writing circumstances, such as in dialogue or ads.

FRAGMENT   "Because I said so!"

FRAGMENT   "All Merchandise 50% Off"

However, in formal writing, fragments are unacceptable. Remember that a complete sentence has a subject and a predicate and expresses a complete thought.

WRITING ACTIVITY

Select and cut out three advertisements that contain fragments. You can find ads in magazines and newspapers that you may have at home or that your teacher has brought to class. You can also find ads online and print them out. For each ad, write a brief paragraph in which you identify the sentence fragments and rewrite them as complete sentences. Then, consider which are more effective: the ads with sentence fragments, or the ads as you have rewritten them. Write a closing paragraph in which you relate your thoughts on why sentence fragments might be effective in ads.

PREWRITING   As you choose your ads, be sure that they have at least one fragment each. Examine each ad. How do the ad's graphics and copy (words) work together to get readers' attention? Did the ad succeed in making the product attractive to you? Why or why not? Jot down your thoughts on each ad.

WRITING   As you rewrite the copy in complete sentences, you may have to gather various pieces of information from different places in the ad. Rather than combining these pieces randomly, decide on an effective organization. Perhaps you will talk about the product first, its price second, and its availability third. Perhaps another strategy will work better. Avoid producing a list of vaguely related facts.

REVISING   Be sure that your complete sentences cover all of the information in the ad. Let a friend attempt to match your rewritten copy to the ads. If the friend mismatches them, rewrite your copy so that it more clearly describes the product.

PUBLISHING   Check your writing for errors in grammar, usage, spelling, and punctuation. Be sure that you have not written any sentence fragments. Post the ads and your rewrites on a piece of poster board, and present your products to your class.

EXTENDING YOUR WRITING

You may wish to develop this exercise into a longer essay. Today, readers are used to advertisements featuring very few words; in fact, some ads today use no words at all. Ads fifty years ago, by contrast, were heavy with text and took some time to read. Find and make copies of two or three ads from newspapers and magazines of the 1940s. For a history or sociology class, compare them to the ads you used in the exercise, and comment on why and how ads and their audiences have changed.

for **CHAPTER 3: THE PHRASE** | *pages 53–69*

Choices: Exploring Phrases

The following activities challenge you to find a connection between phrases and the world around you. Do the activity below that suits your personality best, and then share your discoveries with your class.

WORD PROCESSING

Now You See It, . . .

Adjective and adverb phrases lend detail to a description. Where would we be without them? Find a wonderfully descriptive passage—a couple of paragraphs or so from your own writing or that of a favorite author—and type it into a word-processing program. Proofread and print this copy. Make another copy, and highlight each of the adverb and adjective phrases. Make a list of the details that the phrases add. Then, delete all of the adjective and adverb phrases. Proofread and print this copy. Mount your list of details and your three copies of the passage on poster board. Use this poster as you explain to the class how important these phrases are to the author's description. Be sure to identify each of the details that the phrases add.

LINGUISTICS

From the Top!

Pick any preposition, and then make a list of every idiom or expression you can think of that uses that preposition. For *from*, you could start with the expression used by a music conductor: *from the top*. Begin by brainstorming; then check a dictionary of idioms, and ask your friends and family for ideas. When your list is ready, pass out copies to your classmates (and to everyone who helped you).

HISTORY

To Be or Not To Be

Many a famous quotation begins with or includes an infinitive. How many can you remember? Brainstorm as many as you can; then look through a dictionary of quotations. Pick at least ten famous or interesting quotations that use infinitives. Write each quotation on a card. Include the work in which the quotation appears and its author and date. Then, mount the cards on poster board, and with your teacher's permission, display them in your classroom.

COOKING

One Beaten Egg

Every good cook knows how to use verbals. Check out a few cookbooks, and find as many verbals (participles, gerunds, infinitives) as you can. Start with *shelled*, as in *shelled peas*. Then, make a list of twenty verbals found in cookbooks. Which recipe contains the most verbals? When you have found the ultimate verbal recipe, make copies of it and give them to your classmates.

BUILDING BACKGROUND KNOWLEDGE

Contemplating Careers

Have you been thinking about a career? Notice the number of careers whose names are gerunds. *Accounting* is one. Create a list of at least ten others, and pass out copies of your list to your classmates.

MATHEMATICS

One Multiplied by One Equals One

You know quite a lot about mathematics. How would you translate the above equation into the terms of English grammar? Where is the participle? What is the verb? What grammatical function does each use of *one* serve? Think of ten other mathematical sentences to translate into grammar terminology. Explain them to the class.

HISTORICAL RESEARCH

Attila the Hun

Throughout history, there have been people who were known by their names and an appositive. Attila the Hun is one. Gather up to ten of these names. Then, using appositives, write a very short biography for each person. Share your research with your classmates. Be sure to point out which names use commas with their appositives and which do not.

Language and Sentence Skills Practice

Phrases

3a. A *phrase* is a group of related words that is used as a single part of speech and that does not contain both a verb and its subject.

VERB PHRASE	will be attending [no subject]
PREPOSITIONAL PHRASE	under the sofa [no subject or verb]
INFINITIVE PHRASE	to attend the play [no subject or verb]

EXERCISE A Above each underlined word group in the following sentences, write *P* if the word group is a phrase or *NP* if the word group is not a phrase.

Example 1. <u>Rushing up the sidewalk</u>, Suki excitedly waved the concert tickets. *(P)*

1. The bird <u>with the bright red feathers</u> is a cardinal.

2. You'll need to discuss that with Ms. Conlan, <u>the director of the community center</u>.

3. <u>Even when the sun is shining</u>, this forest is dark and gloomy.

4. Keith has never tried <u>waterskiing on this lake</u>.

5. <u>Seventeen trees in the neighborhood had fallen</u> before the storm ended.

6. The cat, <u>sitting serenely on the top shelf of the bookcase</u>, watched us cleaning up the mess.

7. The highway <u>that goes around the city</u> is usually less crowded than the one that goes through the city.

8. Don't forget <u>to wear a hat</u> while you're out in the sun!

9. <u>After seeing the movie</u>, Ryan decided to read the book.

10. What was the last book <u>that Mark Twain wrote</u>?

EXERCISE B For each of the following items, write a phrase that correctly completes the sentence.

Example 1. Mr. Ferguson, _____ *the tennis coach* _____, is also a biology teacher.

11. _____, we said goodbye until the next school year.

12. The small gray kitten was hiding _____ .

13. Jeremy was asked _____.

14. Lightning flashed _____, and the sound of thunder rolled across the countryside.

15. Dusty, _____, is a very intelligent dog.

Prepositional Phrases

3b.   A *prepositional phrase* includes a preposition, the object of the preposition, and any modifiers of that object.

EXAMPLES   Stain both sides and the edges **of the front door** this color **instead of that one.** [*Door* is the object of the preposition *of; the* and *front* modify *door. One* is the object of the preposition *instead of; that* modifies *one.*]

Did you stain the door **on the front, back, and sides**? [*Front, back,* and *sides* are all objects of the preposition *on.*]

EXERCISE   In each of the following sentences, underline all prepositional phrases once. Then, in each phrase, underline each object of the preposition twice.

Example   1. The candidate withdrew from the race out of respect for her opponents' agendas.

1. With warm smiles they welcomed us to their school.

2. Rows of trees swayed gently in the breeze.

3. As soon as the cat comes in the house, it wants to go outside again.

4. The Space Shuttle *Discovery* carried the Hubble Space Telescope into orbit in 1990.

5. Have you asked your brother whether we can use his bike in the morning?

6. In the Roaring Twenties, the Teapot Dome scandal marred the presidency of Warren Harding.

7. If Kevin calls, please tell him that I've already gone to the game.

8. Soaring silently through the sky, the hawk watched carefully for its next meal.

9. Fifteen inches of snow fell in some parts of the state last night.

10. In addition to political cartoons, Thomas Nast also made drawings of Santa Claus.

11. For Suzanne's birthday, we gathered in the conference room for a party.

12. From the bridge, Julio saw the Manhattan skyline spread out before him.

13. Sally threw lettuce and tomatoes in a bowl and poured salad dressing on the mixture.

14. Pat scolded the dog, who had put its muddy paws on her dress.

15. The driver of the car said he was flying to Jerusalem to get married.

16. Acrobats did handsprings on the sidewalk in spite of the crowds rushing to work.

17. Due to bad weather, the plane did not arrive on schedule.

18. Joshua toddled around the house in his pajamas.

19. The kite dove into the trees, snagging on a branch before we could get it down.

20. By means of a crudely constructed wooden raft, he floated down the river.

Adjective Phrases

3c. A prepositional phrase that modifies a noun or a pronoun is called an *adjective phrase.*

An adjective phrase tells *what kind(s)* or *which one(s)* and generally follows the word it modifies.

EXAMPLES Some **of the carved wood figures in my aunt's collection** are **by Hopi artisans.** [*Of the carved wood figures* modifies *Some* and tells *which ones. In my aunt's collection* modifies *figures* and tells *which ones. By Hopi artisans* also modifies *Some* and tells *what kinds.*]

EXERCISE A Underline the adjective phrases in the following sentences.

Example 1. The furnace in your basement is nothing compared to the furnace that heats the earth from almost 93 million miles away.

1. The sun, which provides the light and heat required by life on earth, is nothing more than a huge ball of gas.

2. Almost all of this gas is hydrogen.

3. Hydrogen atoms collide in the core of the sun and combine to make helium.

4. These reactions produce energy, which eventually escapes the sun and makes its way to earth.

5. Tiny packets of energy called photons can spend over a million years escaping the sun.

6. However, after they reach the surface of the sun, they spend only eight minutes on their journey to earth.

7. From the ground, the sun appears yellow and the sky over our heads seems blue.

8. Sunlight is actually white, but when it passes through earth's atmosphere, the blue portion of the light gets scattered.

9. The sun cannot produce all this energy forever; it will eventually use up the hydrogen atoms in its core.

10. Fortunately, heat and light from the sun should last for another five billion years.

EXERCISE B In each sentence below, underline the adjective phrase once and the word it modifies twice.

Example 1. Five of the actors stayed late and helped the crew strike the set.

11. The top four teams from the conference will advance to the playoffs.

12. Next time you go to the store, get a carton of eggs.

13. A box of torn paper and ruined ribbons was all that remained.

14. Tanya was delighted with the book by Mark Twain you gave her.

15. Shadows in brown and gray dominated the painting.

Adverb Phrases

3d. A prepositional phrase that modifies a verb, an adjective, or an adverb is called an *adverb phrase.*

An adverb phrase tells *how, when, where, why,* or *to what extent* (*how long* or *how far*).

> **EXAMPLES** Unhappy **because of the delay,** we asked the clerk to refund our money. [*Because of the delay* modifies the adjective *Unhappy* and tells *why.*]
>
> **In the morning,** Deena caught the train to Philadelphia. [*In the morning* modifies the verb *caught* and tells *when.*]

EXERCISE Underline the adverb phrases in the sentences below. Then, draw an arrow from each phrase to the word or words it modifies.

Example 1. On Tuesday, two flocks of whooping cranes flew toward the nearby fields.

1. In five minutes we should leave for the airport.

2. Can Tina finish the report after lunch?

3. Upset about the mess, the supervisor fired the two painters.

4. Our shuttle flight between islands will land soon because of the short distance.

5. Jarod moved the desks out of their rows into small clusters of four or five.

6. For two hours the rains drifted slowly but steadily across the valley.

7. We watched the huge owl perched high in the pine tree.

8. After practice, we can finish changing the oil in your car.

9. Juanita is always punctual for choir rehearsal and softball practice.

10. The movie we saw last night was outstanding in terms of scenery and costumes.

11. How many books will still look new after this year's classes?

12. By midmorning Wanda had sorted the books for the auction by topic and author.

13. Should I mention that today the stores are open from 8:00 A.M. until 10:00 P.M.?

14. In just six years, Irene had earned degrees in marine geology and surveying.

15. Didn't Grandmother seem surprised by the large crowd at her birthday party?

16. Harriet finished the college entrance test within the two hours allowed.

17. Aaron seemed satisfied with the additional provisions of his employment contract.

18. None of the departments are receiving interoffice mail this afternoon after 2:00 P.M.

19. Later tonight during the meeting of our family band, we will play kazoos and spoons.

20. One section of Etta's job application was incomplete in regard to her education.

Adjective and Adverb Phrases

| **3c.** | An *adjective phrase* is a prepositional phrase that modifies a noun or a pronoun. |
| **3d.** | An *adverb phrase* is a prepositional phrase that modifies a verb, an adjective, or an adverb. |

EXAMPLES   Judo has been called the gentle art **of self-defense.** [The adjective phrase *of self-defense* modifies the noun *art.*]

Doesn't our instructor teach a class **for advanced students in the afternoon**? [The adjective phrase *for advanced students* modifies the noun *class.* The adverb phrase *in the afternoon* modifies the verb *Does teach.*]

EXERCISE A   In each sentence below, decide whether the underlined phrase is an adjective phrase or an adverb phrase. Above it, write *ADJ* for *adjective phrase* or *ADV* for *adverb phrase*.

                                                           ADV

Example 1. Will you show me your favorite Web site <u>after school</u>?

1. The illustrations <u>in this book</u> are certainly beautiful.

2. Ahanu's mouth slowly opened <u>in a huge yawn</u>.

3. LaNelle's collection <u>of antique dolls</u> has become quite valuable.

4. No one <u>at the council meeting</u> understood the question.

5. The birthday presents were wrapped <u>with care</u>.

EXERCISE B   In each sentence below, underline the prepositional phrase or phrases. Then, identify each as an adjective phrase (*ADJ*) or an adverb phrase (*ADV*). Finally, draw an arrow from each phrase to the word it modifies.

                              ADV   ADV   ADV   ADV

Example 1. Langston Hughes stayed <u>in college</u> <u>for a short time</u> before leaving <u>for Harlem</u>.

6. Some of Hughes's poems had appeared in his elementary school's magazine.

7. In high school Hughes enjoyed studying and writing poetry.

8. Hughes moved to Harlem in 1921 and later traveled in Africa and France.

9. Frequently, he would send poems to American magazines.

10. He once left some poems beside the plate of a well-known poet.

11. This poet spread the word about Hughes's abilities as a poet.

12. As a result, Hughes's poetry became better known after 1925.

13. Two books of his poetry were published before he got his college degree.

14. Hughes went around the country and spoke to many audiences.

15. He also wrote books about the careers of various African American heroes.

Participles

Verbals are formed from verbs but are used as nouns, adjectives, and adverbs. The three kinds of verbals are the *participle*, the *gerund*, and the *infinitive*.

3e.	A *participle* is a verb form that can be used as an adjective.

There are two kinds of participles. *Present participles* end in –*ing*. Most *past participles* end in –*d* or –*ed*. The perfect tense of a participle is formed with *having* or with *having been*.

EXAMPLES   **Growing** teenagers need nutritious diets. [*Growing*, a form of the verb *grow*, modifies the noun *teenagers*.]

Toby's shirts, **having been washed** and **pressed,** were hanging in the closet. [*Washed* and *pressed*, forms of the verbs *wash* and *press*, modify the noun *shirts*.]

EXERCISE   In each sentence below, underline the participle once and the word it modifies twice.

Example 1. The African dinosaur, having been found, now needed a name.

1. Searching, we found several baseball games on television.

2. Raul plays the part of a wandering minstrel in our skit.

3. Six birds huddled in the branches under the pouring rain.

4. Having won, the Panthers agreed that the co-captains should accept the trophy.

5. The spruce trees, having been planted and nurtured, were ready to harvest.

6. In what ways do the entwined DNA strands communicate information?

7. Exploring, the botanist collected a few seeds during his walk.

8. The farmer hoped that his hay, cut and baled, would bring a good price.

9. The growing children constantly needed larger shoes.

10. For our lemonade Mimi added frozen cubes of orange juice instead of regular ice cubes.

11. The leading candidate gratefully acknowledged people's support in the election.

12. The geese, having landed, seemed reluctant to take off again.

13. In an algebra problem, the derived value of *x* may not always equal *y*.

14. The setting sun cast a beautiful light over the meadow.

15. The judges handed the presenter the sealed envelope that contained the winner's name.

16. Having overslept, we caught the last commuter train on the morning schedule.

17. The chosen applicants must attend the orientation meeting Monday morning.

18. Final grades, having been recorded and posted, were also mailed to us.

19. Kate's vest was of a woven fabric that she had designed and made herself.

20. Soaping, rinsing, and drying, the dishwasher efficiently cleaned the pots and pans.

Language and Sentence Skills Practice

Participial Phrases

3f. A *participial phrase* consists of a participle and any modifiers or complements the participle has. The entire phrase is used as an adjective.

An *absolute phrase* consists of (1) a participle or participial phrase, (2) a noun or pronoun that the participle or participial phrase modifies, and (3) any other modifiers of that noun or pronoun. The entire word group is used as an adverb to modify an independent clause of a sentence by telling *how, when,* or *why.*

EXAMPLES **Carefully guarded for many years,** the secret codes in quilts that slaves made have been revealed. [The participial phrase *Carefully guarded for many years* modifies the noun *codes.*]

National interest in such codes having grown in recent years, Raymond Dobard and Jacqueline Tobin decided to write a book that explains the codes' meanings. [The absolute phrase *National interest in such codes having grown in recent years* modifies the independent clause.]

EXERCISE In each sentence below, underline the participial or absolute phrase once and the word or words it modifies twice.

Examples 1. The sun setting behind the mountain and clouds, the photographer captured the beautiful panorama on film.

2. Dribbling the basketball, Ryan moved up the court.

1. Spinning like a whirlwind, the gyroscope became a green-and-white blur.

2. A child having been lost in the woods, search parties were organized, and dogs and helicopters were requested.

3. Our basketball team, headed for the playoffs, focused on attitude and teamwork.

4. Receiving the award as Teacher of the Year, Ms. Wilkinson laughed, then cried.

5. Having sunk this putt, has Tiger Woods made the lowest score in today's round of play?

6. Yuri missed all the wildflowers among the grasses, mown just the day before.

7. The framing timbers prepared, the carpenter could begin the room addition.

8. Prop managers will need to arrange the scenery found in the storage area.

9. Alerted to expect a pop quiz, we were surprised not to have one.

10. This is the first letter, having been stamped and mailed today, to be sent on the new stationery.

Participles and Participial Phrases

3e. A *participle* is a verb form that can be used as an adjective.

3f. A *participial phrase* consists of a participle and any modifiers or complements the participle has. The entire phrase is used as an adjective.

An *absolute phrase* consists of (1) a participle or participial phrase, (2) a noun or pronoun that the participle or participial phrase modifies, and (3) any other modifiers of that noun or pronoun. The entire word group is used as an adverb to modify an independent clause of a sentence.

> **PARTICIPLE** The **darkening** skies made the campers hurry their preparations.
>
> **PARTICIPAL PHRASE** **Waiting for the bus,** we discussed the trick plays in today's game plan.
>
> **ABSOLUTE PHRASE** **The dog having waited inside all day,** we hurried to let him out.

EXERCISE A In each sentence below, circle the noun or pronoun that the underlined participial phrase modifies.

Example 1. Tapping his pencil on the desk, Mitch considered the last test question.

1. The baby, crying from hunger, awakened everyone in the house.

2. Cooked too long, the roast was dry and tasteless.

3. Spinning on our skates, we attracted the attention of all the other skaters.

4. The money collected by the students went toward their class trip.

5. Glancing at the calendar, Mika remembered her dentist appointment.

EXERCISE B In each of the following sentences, underline each participial or absolute phrase once and the word or words that it modifies twice.

Example 1. Ticking loudly, the grandfather clock in the hall struck midnight.

6. The music having finished, Jerry and Eileen walked slowly off the dance floor.

7. Jiro, engrossed in the chemistry experiment, completely forgot what time it was.

8. Jumping into the air, the collie caught the stick.

9. Gary and Felix, tossing a football back and forth, talked about the upcoming game.

10. Onto the stage walked the comedian, straightening her jacket.

11. Riding through the park, the friendly cyclists greeted everyone.

12. Having removed his shoes, Takao stepped into the living room.

13. Cara, checking her rearview mirror, noticed how closely the car was following her.

14. Tired from his long hike, Jorge flopped into the chair.

15. Highways named for famous people cross many sections of the country.

Gerunds

3g.   A *gerund* is a verb form ending in *–ing* that is used as a noun.

> EXAMPLES   **Bicycling** is the perfect exercise for me.
> Tommy prefers **jogging** to other forms of exercise.
> Give **stretching** a try before you begin an activity.

EXERCISE A   Underline all the gerunds in the sentences below.

Example 1. When a tropical dry forest is the focus, <u>studying</u> can be a pleasure.

1. Exploring enables botanist Mark Olson to find unusual or rare habitats.

2. In order to examine some plants, collecting has played an important part in his work.

3. The small amounts of rainfall are predictable and make forecasting a dependable science.

4. Under these climatic conditions, surviving is not what one would expect from such a wide variety of plant life.

5. Whether in Madagascar or Mexico, the thrill of discovering never fades.

EXERCISE B   Underline the gerunds in the following sentences. Then, above each gerund, identify its function in the sentence by writing *S* for *subject*, *PN* for *predicate nominative*, *DO* for *direct object*, *IO* for *indirect object*, or *OP* for *object of preposition*.

Example 1. For tomorrow's job market, are the important skills <u>researching</u> *PN* and <u>programming</u> *PN*?

6. Rosa quit dancing for six weeks after she sprained her ankle.

7. Carita had to decide between golfing and swimming.

8. Taxiing is the airplane's method to move between airport terminal and runway.

9. American artisans have kept alive the crafts of tatting and crocheting.

10. Darla gave sleeping a high priority after she finished her final exams.

11. Isaac did enjoy in-line skating when he had the time.

12. After an hour of searching, Bettie had enough information from the Internet for her report.

13. Would painting have held his attention longer if he had been able to sell his work?

14. The sawing and hammering made so much noise that the baby woke up.

15. Exercising is my favorite way to reduce stress.

Gerund Phrases

3h. A *gerund phrase* consists of a gerund and any modifiers or complements the gerund has. The entire phrase is used as a noun.

EXAMPLES **Working efficiently** is key to **finishing a job**.
I like **walking in the park** or **sitting in the porch swing**.

EXERCISE A Underline the gerund phrases in the following sentences.

Example 1. Connie kept <u>handing out toys</u> until every child at the shelter had received one.

1. Equipment for sledding and ice-skating around this pond may be rented over there.

2. On tonight's program, let's give engineering in this century a closer look.

3. Departing and arriving through customs is now easier for international passengers.

4. Tullie didn't mind licking the new, mint-flavored stamps.

5. Many students support local charities by volunteering time after school.

6. Voting for your favorite candidate is the best way to promote responsible government.

7. Without excavating further, the archaeologist could not estimate the age of the site.

8. Doesn't raising the flag on the mailbox tell the letter carrier we have mail for pickup?

9. Once the train left the station, it made up time and began running on schedule again.

10. Two important parts of Stan's business were greeting customers and managing time.

EXERCISE B Underline the gerund phrases in the following sentences. Then, above each gerund phrase, identify its function in the sentence by writing *S* for *subject*, *PN* for *predicate nominative*, *DO* for *direct object*, *IO* for *indirect object*, or *OP* for *object of preposition*.

Example 1. Give <u>visiting Australia</u> a second thought.   *IO*

11. Riding on the top level of a double-decker bus lets tourists see better.

12. All the actors gave singing in the melodrama their wholehearted effort.

13. Grandmother loves dropping in for a visit with us.

14. According to the committee's air quality report, carpooling for work would be an asset.

15. Is autographing books for their fans a task most authors enjoy?

16. First on Juan's checklist was verifying names, addresses, and phone numbers.

17. The electrician began removing the knockout circles on the box for the light switch.

18. Our cheering and yelling at the celebration party took the team by surprise.

19. Gary's job at the grocery store today was sorting and arranging items on the pasta aisle.

20. My running out of thank-you notes happened at a very bad time.

Language and Sentence Skills Practice

Gerunds and Gerund Phrases

| **3g.** | A *gerund* is a verb form ending in *–ing* that is used as a noun. |

| **3h.** | A *gerund phrase* consists of a gerund and any modifiers or complements the gerund has. The entire phrase is used as a noun. |

> **GERUNDS** Boris likes **hiking** and **camping.**
>
> **GERUND PHRASE** **Waiting on tables** is a good way to earn money in the summer.

EXERCISE A Underline the gerund in each of the following sentences.

Example 1. Traveling is more fun with family or friends.

1. When the day is over, reading is a pleasant way to relax.

2. The teacher discouraged whispering.

3. When the water temperature is right, diving can be an exhilarating experience.

4. Weeding is essential for a healthy garden.

5. After exams are over, dancing helps to get rid of tension.

EXERCISE B In the following sentences, underline the gerund phrases. Then, above each gerund phrase, identify its function by writing *S* for *subject, PN* for *predicate nominative, DO* for *direct object, IO* for *indirect object,* or *OP* for *object of preposition.*

Example 1. Swimming at the beach is our usual summer activity.

6. Understanding quantum physics is difficult for many people.

7. Gareth was soon bored with weeding the garden.

8. For Leo, acting in the school play was the greatest thrill.

9. Vivian exercises by jogging through the park.

10. Admitting his guilt was not easy but made Jerry feel better.

11. Howard enjoyed coaching the children's soccer team.

12. Volunteering with Big Sisters helped Mari decide to become a counselor.

13. Gordon gave designing skyscrapers as a career his best effort.

14. Cristina's mistake was signing the contract without legal advice.

15. Writing to a European pen pal can be a rewarding experience.

Participial Phrases and Gerund Phrases

3f. A *participial phrase* consists of a participle and any modifiers or complements the participle has. The entire phrase is used as an adjective.

3h. A *gerund phrase* consists of a gerund and any modifiers or complements the gerund has. The entire phrase is used as a noun.

PARTICIPIAL PHRASE   **Designing a chair,** he first made several rough sketches. [participial phrase used as an adjective to modify *he*]

GERUND PHRASES   Evan likes **designing the work** and **drawing the sketches.** [gerund phrases used as direct objects of *likes*]

EXERCISE   In the paragraph below, identify each underlined phrase by writing above it *PART* for *participial phrase* or *GER* for *gerund phrase*.

Example   GER
[1] <u>Winning the Iditarod Trail Sled Dog Race four times</u> has brought Susan Butcher a

certain amount of fame.

[1] <u>Determined and driven toward her goals,</u> Butcher raises her own dogs. [2] <u>Tucked away in the Alaskan wilderness not far from the Arctic Circle,</u> her kennel is a four-hour drive from the nearest grocery store. [3] Butcher believes that only when she remains this isolated from society can she concentrate on <u>creating a tight bond with her 150 dogs.</u> [4] <u>Having been a veterinary technician previously,</u> she has raised huskies in her own unique way for more than twenty years. [5] From the moment each puppy is born, <u>getting it used to her voice and her touch</u> requires plenty of time. [6] <u>Breathing on a newborn puppy so that it can also learn her scent,</u> she handles and talks to the puppy frequently. [7] <u>Growing closer and closer to Butcher,</u> the puppy is personally fed, trained, and even sung to and massaged by her. [8] When the puppy is four and one-half months old, Butcher begins <u>training it in harness.</u> [9] By <u>showing the dogs her love for them,</u> Butcher gains the devotion needed to create championship teams. [10] In the Iditarod, <u>crossing approximately 1,160 miles of mountains, frozen seas, and snowy wilderness between Anchorage and Nome</u> is the ultimate test of a dog team's devotion.

Infinitives

3i.	An *infinitive* is a verb form that can be used as a noun, an adjective, or an adverb. Most infinitives begin with *to*.

NOUN	**To write** has long been my dream.
ADJECTIVE	This is the coat **to buy.**
ADVERB	Arthur was unable **to sleep.**
OMITTING *TO*	Please let us [to] **talk** to Jan.

EXERCISE A   Underline the infinitives in the sentences below.

Example 1. Let's go.

1. With so many leaves and so little breeze, we should start to rake now.

2. Uncle Stan and I took the canoe out onto the lake to fish.

3. In *Any Given Day,* 98-year-old Jessie Foveaux had many entertaining memories to tell.

4. To succeed had always been Barbara's goal for her golf game.

5. Rhode Island's senator felt that in his position integrity was not too much to expect.

6. Is it true that to question is an indication of intelligence?

7. What made you laugh?

8. To live, you must dream.

9. Our team's first wish for the final game of the season is to win.

10. On this record, will we hear Hoyt Axton sing?

EXERCISE B   Underline the infinitives in the sentences below. Then, indicate how each infinitive in the sentence is used by writing above it *N* for *noun, ADJ* for *adjective,* or *ADV* for *adverb.*

Example 1. If Ellen could help me wash and dry, I could go home on time.

11. For you, what is the easiest number to remember?

12. To graduate has great significance in Judy's family.

13. Before 7:00 A.M., sixty students had already logged on to register.

14. Why did Jim decide to leave early?

15. Because we had come to the park to camp and hike, Ben started setting up tents.

Infinitive Phrases and Infinitive Clauses

| **3j.** | An *infinitive phrase* consists of an infinitive and any modifiers or complements the infinitive has. The entire phrase can be used as a noun, an adjective, or an adverb. |

NOUN	I want **to nap before dinner,** Joe.
ADJECTIVE	Mr. Melomo is not the first **to leave the factory.**
ADVERB	I was happy **to hear about your job.**

An *infinitive clause* consists of an infinitive with a subject and any modifiers and complements the infinitive has. The entire clause is used as a noun.

| **EXAMPLE** | The choir director wanted **them to sing louder.** [The clause is used as the direct object of *wanted*. The pronoun *them* is the subject of *to sing*, and the adverb *louder* modifies *to sing*.] |

EXERCISE Above each of the underlined word groups, write *IP* for *infinitive phrase* or *IC* for *infinitive clause*.

Example 1. Who would have expected <u>computers and programming to interest Lord Byron's</u> *IC* <u>daughter?</u>

1. Augusta Ada Byron King seemed born <u>to use words as effectively as her poet father had.</u>

2. Her mother, Lady Byron, did not want <u>to stress literary skills in Ada's education.</u>

3. Ada's studies seemed <u>to emphasize algebra, calculus, logic, and physics.</u>

4. It was unusual during the early 1800s for <u>a young woman to receive this type of education.</u>

5. After meeting Charles Babbage in 1833, Ada was eager <u>to learn more about his work.</u>

6. Babbage was already working on a machine <u>to replace his unfinished Difference Engine.</u>

7. Ada used Babbage's formulas in programming his new Analytical Engine <u>to add, subtract, multiply, and divide numbers in any requested sequence.</u>

8. <u>To show related branches being calculated within equations</u> was Ada's goal in using the Bernoulli numbers found in trigonometry.

9. Among all the women <u>to contribute to the computer industry</u>, only Ada has had a language named for her.

10. The military and the aerospace industry sometimes use the language Ada <u>to power their computer programs.</u>

Infinitives and Infinitive Phrases

| **3i.** | An *infinitive* is a verb form that can be used as a noun, an adjective, or an adverb. Most infinitives begin with *to*. |

| **3j.** | An *infinitive phrase* consists of an infinitive and any modifiers or complements the infinitive has. The entire phrase can be used as a noun, an adjective, or an adverb. |

INFINITIVE   The top shelf was too high for him **to reach.**

INFINITIVE PHRASE   **To achieve your goals,** you must work hard.

EXERCISE A   In each sentence below, indicate whether the word *to* is part of an infinitive or of a prepositional phrase by writing *I* for *infinitive* or *P* for *preposition* on the line provided.

Example ____*I*____ **1.** Their request to visit the new aquarium was granted.

_____ **1.** To appear at a royal court is an honor.

_____ **2.** When the boats were due back, we ran down to the pier.

_____ **3.** There was nothing left for us to do at the end of the day.

_____ **4.** Evan was trying to help me with chemistry.

_____ **5.** Mr. Taosie gave the manuscript to the new editor.

EXERCISE B   Underline the infinitive phrase in each sentence below.

Example 1. Have you gone <u>to see the exhibit of Hiroshige's work?</u>

6. My uncle wanted to show me his new picture by Hiroshige.

7. To see an original print by Hiroshige is a joy.

8. Most artists of his time liked to paint women or actors.

9. Hiroshige wanted to depict the natural world.

10. His first major job was to draw illustrations for a book.

11. Later, he went on to complete large sets of prints.

12. At some point he must have decided to concentrate on landscapes.

13. Hiroshige apparently loved to populate his pictures with human figures.

14. Many Western artists, including van Gogh, liked to imitate his scenes.

15. Hiroshige managed to produce over five thousand prints in his lifetime.

HOLT HANDBOOK | Fifth Course

Verbal Phrases

Verbals are formed from verbs but are used as nouns, adjectives, and adverbs. The three kinds of verbals are the *participle,* the *gerund,* and the *infinitive.* A *verbal phrase* consists of a verbal and its modifiers and complements. The three kinds of verbal phrases are the *participial phrase,* the *gerund phrase,* and the *infinitive phrase.*

PARTICIPIAL PHRASE	**Attending this seminar,** we were part of a video conference.
GERUND PHRASE	Next year, **attending the conference** will be much simpler.
INFINITIVE PHRASE	May we apply now at their Web site if we wish **to attend the next conference**?

EXERCISE A   In the sentences below, identify each underlined phrase by writing above the phrase *GER* for *gerund phrase, PART* for *participial phrase,* or *INF* for *infinitive phrase.*

Example 1. In dollars today, how much would Abraham Lincoln have spent <u>to be elected</u>
     INF
     <u>President of the United States?</u>

1. <u>Creating a united nation for all African peoples</u> was Julius Nyerere's goal in life.

2. Former Irish Prime Minister Jack Lynch did his best <u>to foster peace in Ireland.</u>

3. Name the record credited with <u>being this company's first million seller.</u>

4. How many hours does it take <u>to fly from New York City to the South Pole?</u>

5. <u>Hiding behind a boulder,</u> I watched the pronghorn run across the plain.

6. Laws have continued <u>banning the sale of lead-based paint.</u>

7. Is Wilt Chamberlain the only basketball player ever <u>to score 100 points in a single game?</u>

8. <u>Playing for the Minnesota Twins,</u> Rod Carew won seven American League batting titles.

9. Nathalie Sarraute will be remembered for her literary style, <u>called Roman Nouveau.</u>

10. The team <u>having been moved out of Washington, D.C.,</u> the mascot changed also.

EXERCISE B   In each sentence below, identify the use of the underlined phrase or clause by writing above it *N* for *noun, ADJ* for *adjective,* or *ADV* for *adverb.*

Example 1. In 1997 in the United States, what caused <u>the work hours per person to increase?</u>
     N

11. The methods used <u>to develop plutonium</u> have been applied to DNA and RNA research.

12. The novel <u>describing the struggles of a family</u> was my favorite.

13. Did <u>owning the oldest pencil in the world</u> make Count von Faber-Castell famous?

14. Langston Hughes helped <u>found the Harlem Suitcase Theater.</u>

15. We decided <u>to spend our vacation day touring the wildlife park</u> just a few miles away.

Appositives

| **3k.** | An *appositive* is a noun or a pronoun placed beside another noun or pronoun to identify or describe it. |

EXAMPLES The new algebra teacher, **Mr. Rawlings,** will also teach a calculus class. [The noun *Mr. Rawlings* identifies the noun *teacher*, the subject.]

Evergreens, pine trees and fir trees grow new leaves before shedding the old ones. [The noun *Evergreens* describes *pine trees* and *fir trees*.]

EXERCISE A Underline the appositives in the sentences below.

Example 1. The Latin name *Picea* is shared by the blue spruce and the Colorado blue spruce with pines, firs, and other spruces.

1. Sometimes, the needles of a spruce tree might not have their famous color, blue-green.

2. Spruce trees usually are found growing along water sources, streams or springs.

3. *Picea glauca,* the white spruce, may have blue-green needles.

4. Also called a Canadian spruce, this tree prefers a milder climate, the forest.

5. Mass plantings of this spruce in a landscape, windbreaks, continue to be popular.

EXERCISE B Underline the appositive in each sentence below. Then, draw an arrow to the word that the appositive identifies or describes.

Example 1. At the end of the novel, Chapter 17, the cowboy rode off into the sunset.

6. Walter paid less for ten high-density diskettes, a package, than he had a month ago.

7. Did you help our guest, Aunt Tovah, get settled in the guest room?

8. Traffic on the freeway was in its usual congested state, gridlock.

9. Celebrities, the young couple usually traveled in disguise.

10. Our debate is scheduled for tomorrow, Thursday, instead of Friday.

11. Han's new book, a novel, will be in bookstores by the middle of the month.

12. All of the new baseball team members, rookies, reported for practice a week early.

13. Sally made an appointment to discuss her schedule with her counselor, Ms. Whitson.

14. Follow these easy steps to make my favorite dessert, gingerbread.

15. The cartoon characters Tom and Jerry tickled my funny bone.

Appositive Phrases

| **3l.** | An *appositive phrase* consists of an appositive and any modifiers the appositive has. |

> **EXAMPLES** The charts, **each in a different format,** show the changes in income and expenses this year.
>
> Will you vote for her and him, **the best-qualified student council candidates**?

EXERCISE A Underline the appositive phrases in the sentences below.

Example 1. Artie, show these people, <u>our newly hired accountants</u>, the latest reports.

1. One of our salesclerks, a girl named Shauna, sets a good example.

2. Do we note the pattern, the number and width of their stripes, to tell the zebras apart?

3. Rosalie was sure she had seen a black hole, a cavernous dark spot in the night sky.

4. When it's time to leave for the airport, the new one near the east freeway, let me know.

5. Did the R.M.S. *Titanic,* that most luxurious of cruise ships, have only one gash in its hull?

6. Calculate the values of these variables, x and y, for this equation.

7. The duckbilled platypuses, odd-looking mammals, seemed to be playing chase in the river.

8. I enjoyed *The Last of the Mohicans*, both the television movie and the book.

9. Looking over his truck, Jett decided to add two things, a step and a grab bar by each door.

10. Our neighbors, the new family two houses away, are planting yuccas in their front yard.

EXERCISE B Underline the appositive phrase in each sentence below. Then, draw an arrow to the word that the phrase identifies or describes.

Example 1. Would that metal worker, <u>the one next to the forge</u>, teach me this trade?

11. Describe three achievements of Margaret Thatcher, the former British prime minister.

12. Dr. Martin Luther King, Jr., a leading advocate for the end of segregation, worked to get unfair laws changed.

13. As long ago as 1949, scientists were investigating the nutritional value of plankton, small ocean creatures.

14. Have you ever wondered what makes emeralds, such amazing gemstones, so beautiful?

15. Researchers compared tuberculosis strains, both the active and the nonactive, looking for what did and did not cause the disease.

Appositives and Appositive Phrases

| **3k.** | An *appositive* is a noun or a pronoun placed beside another noun or pronoun to identify or describe it. |

| **3l.** | An *appositive phrase* consists of an appositive and any modifiers the appositive has. |

> APPOSITIVE After you left, your friend **Ramala** called.
>
> APPOSITIVE PHRASE Jesse Sheng, **the vice-president of the bank,** sent me a card.

EXERCISE A Underline the appositive phrase in each of the following sentences.

Example 1. No one else, at least not a person in this class, wrote a paper on NASA.

1. I took my stereo to Otto Shultz, a local technician.

2. Sheriff Yvonne Hamilton, the first woman to hold that position, was cited for bravery.

3. Even Veronica, the best student in our class, barely passed this trigonometry test.

4. One of the most exciting cities in the world, Rio de Janeiro is filled with tourists.

5. Mr. Gonzales, the school newspaper's advisor, taught us how to lay out the front page.

6. An innovator in the shoemaking industry, Jan Matzeliger has been pictured on a stamp.

7. Bobby, their two-year-old toddler, did less damage than we expected to his birthday present.

8. My father transformed our backyard, a tangle of weeds, grass, and brambles, into a deck area.

9. That clock, a family heirloom, was my great-grandmother's wedding present to me.

10. Last Saturday we invited the Apontes, our new neighbors, to have dinner with us.

EXERCISE B Underline the appositives and appositive phrases in the following paragraph.

Example [1] General Ulysses S. Grant, a two-term President of the United States, had spent more than two years touring Europe and the Far East with his family.

[11] A viable candidate for a third term as president, Grant was relieved when James A. Garfield received the 1880 Republican Party nomination. [12] After losing this bid for another term in the White House, Grant settled into a quieter lifestyle with a considerable nest egg, savings that amounted to approximately $100,000. [13] He decided to put most of his savings into a business run by two people, his son and another man. [14] Still a poor judge of character, Grant was no more successful with this venture than he had been with some before the war. [15] Unfortunately, his son's partner, Ferdinand Ward, was as dishonest as some of Grant's Cabinet members had been.

Review A: **Prepositional Phrases and Verbal Phrases**

EXERCISE A In the sentences below, underline the prepositional phrases. Then, indicate how each phrase is used by writing above it *ADJ* for *adjective phrase* or *ADV* for *adverb phrase*.

              ADV

Example 1. <u>In colonial days</u> many Americans could not read or write.

1. At that time most schools were privately operated and charged fees.

2. Fees for schooling were usually not large; nonetheless, many families could not afford them.

3. While most of the towns and cities had schools, many rural districts did not.

4. Fairly wealthy rural families hired tutors or else sent their sons to boarding schools.

5. However, a member of the family was the only teacher that most daughters would have.

6. Anyone supervising apprentices was responsible for those children's education.

7. Following the American Revolution, textbooks, including Noah Webster's famous speller, began to appear.

8. Webster's text, and others, followed American pronunciation in teaching spelling.

9. During the 1800s, people started viewing free public education more favorably.

10. Advocates for these schools also wanted state education boards to establish goals for students.

EXERCISE B Underline the verbal phrases in each sentence below. Then, indicate the type of phrase by writing above it *PART* for *participial phrase, GER* for *gerund phrase,* or *INF* for *infinitive phrase.*

                                     GER

Example 1. Few people in those days thought of <u>going to college.</u>

11. There were few colleges in America; most of these had been established to educate ministers.

12. A boy applying for admission to a college would have studied Latin, Greek, and mathematics.

13. Preparing for college might also have included courses in history, rhetoric, and logic.

14. College preparatory schools, called academies, were the predecessors of high schools.

15. The problem for many was understanding the purpose of the curriculum in these schools.

16. Previously, some college preparation had been designed to give students strong trade skills.

17. Students at colonial colleges could expect to study science, literature, and modern languages.

18. Taking advanced classes in Latin, Greek, and mathematics was also common.

19. Instead of long assignments from textbooks, students had to learn by rote memorization.

20. Directed by a board of trustees, the president of the college managed its administration.

Review B: **Prepositional Phrases and Verbal Phrases**

EXERCISE A Underline the prepositional phrases in the sentences below. Then, indicate how each phrase is used by writing above it *ADJ* for *adjective phrase* or *ADV* for *adverb phrase*.

                  ADJ   *ADV*
Example 1. Events in the 1920s brought many changes to the United States.

1. So many men left their jobs to fight in World War I that women had to leave home and become a part of the paid workforce.

2. American women voted in their first national elections, leading to a large voter turnout.

3. The Red Scare adversely affected public opinion toward U.S. labor unions.

4. The Immigration Act of 1924 slowed the flood of newcomers from non-European countries.

5. A hero of the Twenties, Charles Lindbergh, flew a single-engine plane across the Atlantic.

6. The 1920s are sometimes called the Jazz Age because of the style of the decade's popular music.

7. A basketball team consisting entirely of African American players, the Harlem Globetrotters entertained delighted crowds across the country.

8. In spite of the Eighteenth Amendment, which legislated prohibition, many larger cities ignored this law as they grew through the decade.

9. President Wilson was successful in his efforts to establish the League of Nations.

10. People were delighted by electric lighting, airplanes, radios, and other inventions that improved their lives.

EXERCISE B Underline the verbal phrases in the sentences below. Then, indicate how each phrase is used by writing above it *PART* for *participial phrase*, *GER* for *gerund phrase*, or *INF* for *infinitive phrase*.

                                  PART
Example 1. Motion pictures featuring sound attracted large audiences in the late 1920s.

11. Going to the movies became fashionable.

12. No longer did moviegoers have to walk to the movie theater.

13. Riding in a Model T, the average American traveled with greater freedom than ever before.

14. For the first time ordinary people were able to own and operate automobiles.

15. Jamming the country's highways by 1929 were more than 22 million cars.

16. At first, the problem was finding enough restaurants or gas stations during a road trip.

17. Expanding rapidly during this period, American businesses looked toward a bright future.

18. In 1928, Herbert Hoover was elected to guide the nation's affairs.

19. Many people were involved in the tricky game of playing the stock market.

20. After the stock market crash of 1929, President Hoover failed to stop the recession.

Review C: Prepositional, Verbal, and Appositive Phrases

EXERCISE A   In the following sentences, identify each underlined phrase by writing one of the following abbreviations above the phrase: *PREP* for *prepositional*, *PART* for *participial*, *GER* for *gerund*, *INF* for *infinitive*, or *APP* for *appositive*.

Example 1. The curtains hanging in the study were dark. [PART]

1. The shaken driver crawled from the damaged car.

2. Shocked greatly, they stood silent and still.

3. An excellent form of exercise is walking vigorously.

4. Discouraged by his fruitless tracking, my photographer friend gave up.

5. To rest awhile seemed advisable.

6. The park's prize attraction, an obsolete tank, was my small brother's favorite "mountain."

7. Finishing an essay is sometimes hard.

8. Photographing migrant workers, Dorothea Lange's task, was often difficult.

9. After the heavy rain began, I no longer wanted to go outside.

10. A frog that did not jump would be a strange kind of frog.

EXERCISE B   In the following sentences, identify each underlined phrase by writing one of the following abbreviations above the phrase: *PREP* for *prepositional*, *PART* for *participial*, *GER* for *gerund*, *INF* for *infinitive*, or *APP* for *appositive*.

Example 1. Two girls from our class won awards. [PREP]

11. Taking pictures, one of Judy's favorite pastimes, keeps her busy on weekends.

12. Finding no one home, the salesperson left.

13. Owls are able to turn their heads almost all the way around.

14. We raised money by conducting a bake sale.

15. Margaret Coit, the Pulitzer Prize winner, wrote a book about John C. Calhoun.

16. The view across the river is magnificent.

17. Through the trees we saw smoke from a small cabin.

18. A signed form indicating your approval is required.

19. "Don't be afraid to ask questions," he told us.

20. Hedda Hopper's job was writing chatty columns about Hollywood.

Literary Model: Participles in a Poem

from I Hear America Singing
by *Walt Whitman*

I hear America singing, the varied carols I hear,

Those of mechanics, each one singing his as it should be blithe and strong,

The carpenter singing his as he measures his plank or beam,

The mason singing his as he makes ready for work, or leaves off work,

The boatman singing what belongs to him in his boat, the deckhand

   singing on the steamboat deck,

The shoemaker singing as he sits on his bench, the hatter singing as

   he stands. . . .

EXERCISE A   Circle the participles and participial phrases in the excerpt above. Hint: Clauses that act as modifiers or as objects of the participle should be treated as part of the participial phrases.

EXERCISE B

1. What is the effect of the repetition of the participle *singing*?

_____

_____

2. What does the poem emphasize—the action of singing, the singing itself, or the various people doing the singing? Explain.

_____

_____

3. How would the emphasis of the poem be different if Whitman had chosen to use *singing* as a verb rather than as an adjective (participle)? Explain.

_____

_____

Literary Model (continued)

4. How would the emphasis of the poem be different if *singing* were used as a noun (gerund)?
Explain.

_____

_____

EXERCISE C   Write a short poem in which you repeat a participle, such as *singing*.

_____

_____

_____

_____

_____

_____

_____

_____

_____

EXERCISE D

1. What is the effect of the repetition of participles in your poem?

_____

_____

_____

_____

2. Is this the effect you intended? Explain.

_____

_____

_____

_____

_____

Writing Application: Yearbook Entry

Writers and speakers often use gerunds and gerund phrases to talk about present or ongoing activity. Infinitives and infinitive phrases, on the other hand, often point readers to the future.

PRESENT ACTION   Coral-reef diving has long been a passion of mine.

FUTURE ACTION   Someday, I would like to dive at Australia's Great Barrier Reef.

WRITING ACTIVITY

You are being featured in your high school's yearbook, and the editors have asked you to write a few paragraphs about your favorite hobby or pastime. Your readers want to know what you are currently doing in your hobby. Use at least three gerunds or gerund phrases as you tell them. Tell them also what you would like to do someday. Use at least two infinitives or infinitive phrases to talk about your future plans.

PREWRITING   You may know right away what activity you will describe; otherwise, brainstorm several activities until you decide which is your favorite. Then, make a list to gather details. What talents does the activity require? What equipment do you use? How long have you participated in the activity? Write down a list of memorable events associated with the activity so that you can choose the one or two most interesting for your paragraphs.

WRITING   You may wish to arrange your paragraphs chronologically, beginning with your first attempts at the activity and working to the present and then to your future plans. However, the paragraphs may be more interesting if they focus on key events, which could be presented using order of importance. Remember also that your readers are not experts on the activity. You will need to explain any technical terms you use.

REVISING   You like the activity you have chosen to write about; now choose dynamic, specific verbs and verbals as well as bold modifiers to convey your appreciation of the activity to readers. Try to interest some readers in learning more about the activity and perhaps even experiencing it.

PUBLISHING   Check your paragraphs for errors in usage, spelling, and punctuation. Make sure that you have used gerund and infinitive phrases correctly. With your teacher's permission, you and your classmates may wish to collect your paragraphs and arrange them on a bulletin board, with pictures of each student engaged in his or her chosen activity.

EXTENDING YOUR WRITING

You may wish to develop this exercise into a longer essay. For a psychology class, you could explore why most people have hobbies and how hobbies enrich our lives. For a history class, you could research the origins and development of the activity in which you participate.

for **CHAPTER 4: THE CLAUSE** `pages 76–89`

Choices: Exploring Clauses

The following activities challenge you to find a connection between clauses and the world around you. Do the activity below that suits your personality best, and then share your discoveries with your class.

WRITING

In the Beginning

Think up twenty subordinate clauses with which to begin a story. Make some of them fantastic, such as "When strange flashing lights first appeared above the Franklins' house, . . ." Then again, make some of the clauses more ordinary, such as "Before Mr. Wiley and his dog moved in next door, . . ." Type or neatly write your clauses, and hand out copies to your classmates, who can use them as the beginnings of short stories.

BUILDING BACKGROUND KNOWLEDGE

For Which It Stands

Find some examples of famous quotations that include subordinate clauses. Your examples could come from historical documents, poetry, speeches, or other literary forms. You could compile a list from memory or consult a dictionary of quotations. Be sure to identify the clause's function in the quotation. Don't forget to give credit to the original speaker or writer of the quotation. Compile your clauses and the quotations in which they appear along with your classmates' contributions in a class dictionary of quotations.

REVISING

Pack a Wallop

Concentrated force is more powerful than force that is spread out in time or space. Clauses have their uses, but too many clauses can weaken an argument. Show your classmates how to reduce a clause to a phrase and a phrase to a word. Write five sets of three sentences. The first sentence should contain a clause that will become a phrase in the second sentence. The second sentence should contain a phrase that will become a word in the third sentence. When you're finished, use your examples as you explain how these revisions can create a more powerful argument.

ANALYSIS

Playing Favorites

Identify four of your favorite books and analyze the first and last paragraphs of each book. Count the number of sentences exhibiting each type of sentence structure. Illustrate your findings in a bar graph. Think about the trends you found. What do they say about you as a reader? Can they teach you anything about beginning and ending your own writing? Discuss your findings with a few classmates.

WRITING

Do the Demo

Now that you can identify the four basic sentence structures, take a look at them in action. Write five versions of the same paragraph. In the first paragraph, use only simple sentences; in the second, use only compound sentences; in the third, use only complex sentences; in the fourth, use only compound-complex sentences; and in the fifth, use each type of sentence structure at least once. Then, read the paragraphs aloud and lead the class as they compare and contrast them. Does each version contain the same information? Which paragraph is most interesting?

ANALYSIS

How About You?

Okay, you've studied the sentence structure of some of the world's great writers, but how about you? How do you use sentence structure? Look through your portfolio and pick out a few pieces of writing that are at least four paragraphs long. Then, analyze the sentence structures that you find. How many of each type of structure did you use? In what order did you use them? Can you identify any patterns? Write a paragraph analyzing your use of sentence structure and identifying any changes you would like to make. Save your analysis for future reference.

Language and Sentence Skills Practice

GRAMMAR

Identifying Clauses

| **4a.** | A *clause* is a word group that contains a verb and its subject and that is used as a sentence or as part of a sentence. |

Although every clause has a subject and a verb, not every clause expresses a complete thought. A clause that expresses a complete thought is called an *independent clause*. A clause that does not express a complete thought is called a *subordinate clause*.

SENTENCE   We had been watching the waves as they crashed against the cliffs.

INDEPENDENT CLAUSE   **We had been watching** the waves

SUBORDINATE CLAUSE   as **they crashed** against the cliffs

EXERCISE A In the independent and subordinate clauses in the following sentences, underline the subjects once and the verbs twice.

Example 1. Was this memorial the first that any state had created to honor an American Indian?

1. In 1909, funding was approved for this statue, which is located between Plymouth, Indiana, and the Yellow River.

2. It is a monument to Chief Menominee, who tried to save his people's land.

3. When he designed the statue, the sculptor depicted the chief in full Potawatomi dress.

4. Everyone will remember this peaceful chief as long as the monument stands.

5. The reservation where the Potawatomi lived had been set aside in an 1832 treaty.

6. Chief Menominee did not negotiate to sell the land, but three other chiefs did.

7. Because the treaty had given the land to all four chiefs, Menominee said the sale was illegal.

8. Chief Menominee and his supporters, who had committed no crimes, were simply ignored.

9. White settlers rushed onto the land, and the state militia moved the American Indians off.

10. The relocation trip to Kansas, which is now called "The Trail of Death," was a disaster.

EXERCISE B In each of the following sentences, underline the subordinate clause.

Example 1. Please give this message to whoever answers the telephone.

11. Then, I saw a side of her character that I had not seen before.

12. We finally found the key in the locker where I had left my luggage.

13. Luisa believed that she would not be recognized with a new hairstyle.

14. After 6:00 P.M., every door was locked so that it was impossible to leave or enter the building.

15. Chemistry is the subject with which he has the most difficulty.

The Independent Clause

4b. An *independent* (or *main*) *clause* expresses a complete thought and can stand by itself as a sentence.

An independent clause used by itself is generally called a *sentence*. The term *independent clause* is generally used when such a clause is joined with at least one other clause (either independent or subordinate) to make a sentence.

EXAMPLES   **He then gave the page to Edie,** and **she added hypertext for the links to other Web pages.** [two independent clauses joined by *and*]

These links are programmed with Hypertext Markup Language, or HTML, which is easier to say and to remember. [one independent clause combined with a subordinate clause]

EXERCISE In each of the following sentences, underline the independent clause or clauses.

Example 1. Before a computer can process data, <u>the machine must know</u> what and where the material is and how it relates to a Web page.

1. HTML can only describe to a computer the positions for information, graphics, and buttons on a display screen or Web page.

2. More efficient than HTML, XML (Extensible Markup Language) is a tool that tells computers how to find, relate, and share information.

3. XML tags information so that the computer knows the difference, for example, between the various numbers on a customer's order or credit memo.

4. Equally important, tags usually appear before and after any data that is being described.

5. Nesting is a convenient feature of tags because it allows grouping of related bits of data.

6. Anyone interested in XML should be able to follow the rules for using it.

7. Users can create tag labels in everyday language for their businesses.

8. Because tags can function as a tree, or outline, with any number of related groups, some labels will be more specific than others will.

9. Usually, a pair of tags is created for each bit of data; each tag is written inside angle brackets that look like arrow points, one facing left, the other facing right.

10. XML tags for movie listings, for example, might include the words *movies, title,* and *star.*

The Subordinate Clause

4c. A *subordinate* (or *dependent*) *clause* does not express a complete thought and cannot stand by itself as a sentence.

> **EXAMPLES**   to whom we sent the get-well card
>
> that Jim Flying Eagle knew about computers

The thought expressed by a subordinate clause becomes complete when the clause is combined with an independent clause. Like a word or a phrase, a subordinate clause can be used as an adjective, a noun, or an adverb in a sentence.

> **EXAMPLES**   Isn't my friend Angela, **to whom we sent the get-well card,** going home from the hospital today? [adjective clause]
>
> **That Jim Flying Eagle knew about computers** was obvious from his comparison of the new models. [noun clause]

EXERCISE   In each of the following sentences, underline the subordinate clause.

Example 1. Teddy knew <u>that someday soon he would have to finish his term paper.</u>

1. Louise Abbéma, who lived from 1858 to 1927, at first was most famous for painting portraits.

2. While she was an art student, the young girl continually amazed everyone with her ability.

3. An early influence was artist Rosa Bonheur, whose skill and renown Abbéma admired.

4. In Paris, where she had been studying with well-known artists and art teachers, her first portrait of Sarah Bernhardt gained her public recognition in 1876.

5. Because Bernhardt continued posing for Abbéma's portraits, they became good friends.

6. That Abbéma wore her hair short and often dressed as a French soldier added to her notoriety in Paris social circles.

7. She showed not only portraits but also still lifes as exhibits of her art continued.

8. Admirers wanted decorative panels, engravings, and illustrations that she had created.

9. Have you seen her *Portrait of a Young Girl with a Blue Ribbon*, which I happen to like?

10. She must have been proud when she received the Chevalier of the Legion of Honor for her artistic achievements.

HOLT HANDBOOK | Fifth Course

Identifying Independent and Subordinate Clauses

4b.　An *independent* (or *main*) *clause* expresses a complete thought and can stand by itself as a sentence.

4c.　A *subordinate* (or *dependent*) *clause* does not express a complete thought and cannot stand by itself as a sentence.

INDEPENDENT CLAUSE　**I play the guitar, and George sings.**

SUBORDINATE CLAUSE　**Where you go,** I will go.

EXERCISE A　Identify each of the following clauses by writing above it *I* for *independent clause* or *S* for *subordinate clause.*

Example　1.　whatever you expect to see on an island

1. Cuba is the largest island in the Greater Antilles

2. where more than six thousand species of plants grow

3. that the national flower is the mariposa

4. this flower is also called the butterfly jasmine

5. since the southern coast has mangrove swamps supporting birds and wildlife

EXERCISE B　To each of the following subordinate clauses, add an independent clause. Write your revised sentences on the lines provided.

Example　1.　If you buy that magazine, _If you buy that magazine,_
I'd like to read it.

6. Whenever you walk on the beach, _____

_____

7. Although summer is starting off hot, _____

_____

8. Because I live in this country, _____

_____

9. What I need now _____

_____

10. After I graduate, _____

_____

The Adjective Clause

| **4d.** | An *adjective clause* is a subordinate clause that modifies a noun or a pronoun. |

An adjective clause follows the word or words that it modifies and tells *what kind* or *which one*.

> **EXAMPLES**   I have always wondered about the people **who introduced new species of trees to America.** [The clause modifies the noun *people*.]
>
> The Chinese chestnut, **which arrived from China and Korea in 1853,** is resistant to the fungus affecting American chestnuts. [The clause modifies the noun *Chinese chestnut*.]

EXERCISE A   In each of the following sentences, underline the adjective clause.

Example 1. We laughed about the time that all of us dressed like clowns.

1. I looked for the book that Bahira recommended.

2. Red is a color that often signals danger.

3. The passengers suffered delays, which they thought were intolerable.

4. The lake where we camped last weekend is called Clear Lake.

5. Kaulana is the only one of you who is always punctual.

EXERCISE B   In each of the following sentences, underline the adjective clause. Then, draw an arrow from the clause to the noun that the clause modifies.

Example 1. Do you know anyone who might appreciate having these toys?

6. Sara went to the Bureau of Vital Statistics, where she hoped to find the answer.

7. The plants that we put outside last summer really thrived.

8. Robbie entered the library where they had first met.

9. South Carolina, which is one of the original thirteen states, has a rich and varied history.

10. Venus and Serena Williams are sisters who play professional tennis.

11. While visiting the pueblo, I saw jewelry that I loved.

12. Did the waterspout that swept inland destroy more than those two buildings?

13. The place where Luigi works is just half a mile from his home.

14. The sight that Darcy enjoyed most on her vacation was the sunrise.

15. Sometimes, customs that might seem to have vanished reappear.

Relative Pronouns

4d. An *adjective clause* is a subordinate clause that modifies a noun or a pronoun.

Usually, an adjective clause begins with a *relative pronoun*, a word that not only relates the clause to the word or words the clause modifies but also serves a function within the clause.

> EXAMPLES   My mother, **who has been called the Queen of Salsa,** began singing in the 1940s.
>
> This seems to be the ring [that] **my sister wants.**

An adjective clause may begin with *when* or *where*. When used to introduce adjective clauses, these words are called *relative adverbs*.

> EXAMPLE   Wayne Gretzky will probably never forget the day [when] **he was admitted to the Hockey Hall of Fame.**

EXERCISE A   In each of the following sentences, underline the adjective clause once and the relative pronoun or adverb twice. If the relative pronoun or adverb is understood, write it above the clause.

Example 1. Have you ever seen a comedy routine *that* Victor Borge has done?

1. My little sister has been inspired by the talent that Mom puts into a performance.

2. You should send a thank-you note to anyone from whom you received a gift.

3. Who are the people that most recently were awarded Kennedy Center Honors?

4. Name the writer who wrote that novel.

5. Mary Shelley, who was only nineteen at the time, wrote *Frankenstein.*

6. Have the tulip bulbs, which Mavis planted last fall, bloomed yet?

7. Watch this Harlem Globetrotters' basketball video, which was filmed by my uncle.

8. Gerald searched the classified ads, where he hoped to find a job.

9. The basic ingredients in the soup Mom makes in the winter are potatoes, beans, and carrots.

10. Please set aside a time when the admissions representative might meet with you.

EXERCISE B   Complete each of the following sentences by writing an appropriate adjective clause on the line provided.

Example 1. My aunt, *who has been visiting from Wisconsin* , will be returning home next week.

11. Tammy and I made plans to see the new movie _____.

12. The tree _____ has been there for over one hundred years.

13. The story is about a kitten _____.

14. Mr. Rubenstein, _____, will coach the football team next year.

15. Manny and Robin, _____, plan to attend the same college.

Essential and Nonessential Clauses

4d.   An *adjective clause* is a subordinate clause that modifies a noun or a pronoun.

Depending on how it is used, an adjective clause is either essential or nonessential. An *essential* (or *restrictive*) *clause* provides information that is necessary to the meaning of a sentence. A *nonessential* (or *nonrestrictive*) *clause* provides additional information that can be omitted without changing the basic meaning of a sentence.

    ESSENTIAL   We wanted to buy new candles **that were white.**

    NONESSENTIAL   We bought five candles, **which were white,** for the new candlesticks.

EXERCISE A   In each of the following sentences, underline the adjective clause once if it is essential and twice if it is nonessential.

Example 1. I liked the cat <u>that had the white paws.</u>

1. Meghan loved the turquoise and silver Navajo bracelet that we brought her.

2. Are more business leaders who can support nonprofit organizations doing so?

3. The first woman ever to lead the Lincoln Center for the Performing Arts was Beverly Sills, who is a well-known soprano.

4. We spoke to the mechanic, whose work on our car was excellent, about another repair job.

5. For a bedtime story, Hon Lu likes to hear the one that is about chickens.

6. Our friends to whom we sent a fruit basket last year have sent us a basket of oranges.

7. Dad likes to read Dave Barry's humor column, which appears in our paper every week.

8. Can you remember the name of the beach that we enjoyed so much last summer?

9. Hadji, who is my best friend, bowled his best today.

10. Charlie called the real-estate agent whose sales record seemed the best.

EXERCISE B   In each of the following sentences, underline the adjective clause once if it is essential and twice if it is nonessential. Then, draw an arrow from the clause to the word it modifies.

Example 1. The fence <u>that separates the two yards</u> is being repaired.

11. How do you locate someone who no longer lives in your town?

12. The horse, which had been grazing not far away, came trotting over to greet Tanya.

13. A dinner was planned to honor Mrs. Gibson, who was retiring at the end of the year.

14. The bake sale that has been scheduled for this weekend should be quite successful.

15. Can anyone tell me the species of cactus that grows tallest in the United States?

The Noun Clause

4e: A **noun clause** is a subordinate clause that is used as a noun.

A noun clause may be used as a *subject*, a *predicate nominative*, a *direct object*, an *indirect object*, or an *object of a preposition*.

EXAMPLES   **Whoever wants to come with us** is welcome. [subject]

Dinner time will be **whenever you arrive.** [predicate nominative]

I understand **how that works.** [direct object]

Ying Par will give **whoever asks** some help. [indirect object]

Sam told his story to **whoever would listen.** [object of a preposition]

EXERCISE A   In the following sentences, underline each noun clause. If the sentence contains no noun clause, write *none* at the end of the sentence.

Example 1. I saw a demonstration of how traffic signals work.

1. What Garrett Morgan invented in 1923 was the earliest traffic signal.

2. How he became an inventor after only six years of school is a mystery to me.

3. Less commonly known is that earlier he invented a breathing device.

4. Morgan had been trying to sell the gas masks that he invented to the Cleveland, Ohio, water company.

5. The company asked him to bring his devices to a tunnel that had caved in.

6. Twenty-four men were awaiting rescue by whoever had the necessary equipment.

7. Morgan, his brother, and two volunteers did whatever they could.

8. The city considered him to be a hero for saving most of the men who had been trapped.

9. Ultimately, Morgan sold his breathing device to whoever needed one.

10. Wouldn't people say that his invention is noteworthy?

EXERCISE B   In each of the following sentences, underline the noun clause. Then, above the clause, write one of the following abbreviations to indicate how the clause is used: *S* for *subject*, *IO* for *indirect object*, *PN* for *predicate nominative*, *OP* for *object of a preposition*, and *DO* for *direct object*.

Example 1. Mr. Harrison asked if anyone had read the *Gettysburg Address*. [*DO*]

11. Whether or not there is life on other planets is still a matter of speculation.

12. Mrs. Driscoe gave an orange to whoever wanted one.

13. Your success will be determined by how you plan your time.

14. Pilar's reason for being late was that she had overslept.

15. I finally understood what his real objection was.

The Adverb Clause

4f. An *adverb clause* is a subordinate clause that modifies a verb, an adjective, or an adverb.

An adverb clause tells *how, when, where, why, to what extent,* or *under what condition.*

EXAMPLES **Wherever you travel,** people will help you. [The clause modifies the verb *will help,* telling *where.*]

This speaker sounds much better **than that one does.** [The clause modifies the adjective *better,* telling *under what condition.*]

Our books should arrive tomorrow **since they were shipped on time.** [The clause modifies the verb *arrive,* telling *why.*]

EXERCISE A   In each of the following sentences, underline the adverb clause.

Example 1. Once Dad began to travel overseas, all of us wanted to go on a trip with him.

1. When we visited Kyoto, Japan, we stayed in a ryokan, a kind of lodging.

2. We always removed our shoes before we entered a room.

3. Dad reminded us if we forgot.

4. I vowed to try a new food every day provided that someone told me what it was.

5. After we finish eating dinner, couldn't we take a walk?

6. While we were at dinner, someone turned down our beds.

7. We have found this ryokan to be very nice since it provides robes and slippers.

8. If we have a bath tonight, will we sleep better?

9. The water in the bath was much hotter than I had expected!

10. My brother can sleep anywhere as long as he has a pillow and a blanket.

EXERCISE B   In each of the following sentences, underline the adverb clause once and underline twice the word or words it modifies.

Example 1. After my truck is repaired, I will drive to town.

11. Although it is very late, the birds are still chirping.

12. George was assigned to the Senegal office because he was a specialist in African affairs.

13. As soon as she was settled on the airplane, Hasna relaxed.

14. The singer worked whenever he could.

15. Alsatians are good police dogs because they are very intelligent.

Subordinating Conjunctions

4f.   An *adverb clause* is a subordinate clause that modifies a verb, an adjective, or an adverb.

An adverb clause is introduced by a *subordinating conjunction*, such as *after, although, before, if, since, so that, unless,* or *while*, that shows the relationship between the adverb clause and the word or words that the clause modifies.

EXAMPLE   Would you like traveling slowly **so that you could see the world of Marco Polo**? [The subordinating conjunction *so that* relates the clause to the adjective *slowly*.]

EXERCISE   In each of the following sentences, underline the adverb clause once and underline the subordinating conjunction a second time.

Example 1. As long as people read about Marco Polo's adventures, they will be inspired to

explore other countries and cultures.

1. Would the cities be larger or smaller than the present-day cities are?

2. Before I travel in China, I might try to learn a little about the language and customs.

3. Learning Chinese can be difficult unless you have a good teacher.

4. If we have time, we should walk along the top of the Great Wall.

5. Marco Polo described the market town of Kashgar, a crossroads now as it was then.

6. Wherever else I might go, I would definitely visit Kashgar's Sunday bazaar.

7. If the merchants allowed, I would sample the foods and teas.

8. Though the weather can be warm, Kazak men wear their traditional felt hats.

9. Older people in Yarkand get too little iodine from foods, as people did centuries ago.

10. Since its artisans produced fine fabrics, Khotan was an important stop along the Silk Road.

11. While Khotan was a center of commerce, it was also the gate through which Buddhism

traveled to Northern China.

12. You, too, could travel the Silk Road as if you were Marco Polo.

13. Until they reached China, the Polo family had traveled mostly through Muslim regions.

14. You can learn much from people of various cultures, as long as you keep an open mind.

15. While historians aren't sure of the date, the Polos arrived at the Mongol court sometime in 1275.

16. Because they had met the Mongol emperor, Kublai Khan, on an earlier trip, they were welcome.

17. The Polos stayed in the emperor's domain for sixteen or seventeen years once they arrived.

18. Although little is known about his life, many myths about Marco Polo have sprung up.

19. Wherever he went, Polo must have paid close attention to detail.

20. He subsequently wrote a famous account of his travels so that Europeans might learn of Asia.

Elliptical Clauses

4f. An *adverb clause* is a subordinate clause that modifies a verb, an adjective, or an adverb.

4g. Part of a clause may be left out when its meaning can be clearly understood from the context of the sentence. Such a clause is called an *elliptical clause.*

In the examples below, the bracketed words may be omitted because the meaning of the clause is clear without them.

> **EXAMPLES** **Although [she was] tired,** the soldier remained at her post.
>
> Luggage should be routinely transferred **once [it has been] tagged with a final destination sticker.**
>
> Can they bring supplies to you sooner **than I [can]**?
>
> Can they bring supplies to you sooner **than [they can bring supplies to] me**?

EXERCISE A In each of the following sentences, underline the elliptical clause.

Example 1. Since you understand this law better than even I, please explain it to the rest of our study group.

1. While taking trumpet lessons, Darla had learned several march tunes.

2. Please leave all other books and materials under your desks until finished with the test.

3. Should our express mail package arrive sooner than the one shipped first class?

4. Although in a hurry, Ahmed took time to stretch.

5. My mother has always baked a tastier blueberry muffin than I.

6. Though lost for a week, my algebra book finally turned up in our classroom.

7. For the final challenge, Cameron had to slice more onions than we.

8. How could their petition receive so many more signatures than ours?

9. Since using an irrigation system, Ruben has harvested ten percent more corn per acre.

10. Even though I play fewer video games than some teenagers, I still could follow Suki's strategy.

EXERCISE B In each of the following sentences, underline the elliptical clause. Then, insert a caret (∧) and write above it the words that are missing.

Example 1. Who knows as much as Gina ∧*knows* about making scenery?

11. At the restaurant, Chester and Erin ate more salad than I.

12. Once repaired, the tire held air pressure very well.

13. Can squirrels eat as much birdseed out of a feeder as raccoons?

14. The waves surprised me more than her.

15. Because of heavy evening traffic, air rescue arrived sooner than the ground team.

Identifying Adjective and Adverb Clauses

4d.	An *adjective clause* is a subordinate clause that modifies a noun or a pronoun.
4f.	An *adverb clause* is a subordinate clause that modifies a verb, an adjective, or an adverb.

EXAMPLES We sympathized with our friends **whose luggage was lost.** [adjective clause]

As long as we were there, we helped them look for their bags. [adverb clause]

EXERCISE A In each of the following sentences, identify the underlined subordinate clause by writing above it *ADJ* for *adjective clause* or *ADV* for *adverb clause*.

                                                                        ADJ
Example **1.** George Washington Carver, who was an African American scientist, was renowned

for his research on agricultural problems and products.

1. I clearly heard children shouting on the playground, as though the window were not closed.

2. Because she was holding the board carefully, Barbara was able to pound in the nail.

3. Rita attended band camp, and she met students who were interested in becoming musicians.

4. I managed the store alone while the owner was on vacation.

5. No one will read a newspaper that cannot report accurately the day's happenings.

EXERCISE B In each of the following sentences, underline the subordinate clause. Then, indicate what kind of clause it is by writing above it *ADJ* for *adjective clause* or *ADV* for *adverb clause*.

                            ADV
Example **1.** Will we see you when we get there?

6. If you are interested in driving to Macdonagh Lake, please telephone to let me know.

7. The lake, which is in the northwest corner of the state, has fishing and boating facilities.

8. I have looked at a map, and the drive, which is an easy one, will take a little under two hours.

9. I am looking for the park entrance where the boat launch is located.

10. If you wish to rent a boat, you can rent canoes, rowboats, and paddleboats at the boathouse.

11. On the boat ride, wear one of the orange life vests that are available in the boathouse.

12. Will someone alert me when the rest of you are ready to stop for lunch?

13. I plan to go for a swim in the lake, which is crystal clear.

14. There are always lifeguards on duty because it is a state park.

15. How long did I work on the plan that would let me make this trip to Macdonagh Lake?

Language and Sentence Skills Practice   **93**

Identifying and Classifying Subordinate Clauses A

4d.   An *adjective clause* is a subordinate clause that modifies a noun or a pronoun.

4e.   A *noun clause* is a subordinate clause that is used as a noun.

4f.   An *adverb clause* is a subordinate clause that modifies a verb, an adjective, or an adverb.

4g.   Part of a clause may be left out when its meaning can be clearly understood from the context of the sentence. Such a clause is called an *elliptical clause.*

EXAMPLES   This house, **which is near the park,** is a great deal! [adjective clause]

The front porch is **what I like about the house.** [noun clause]

Don't forget to bring the insurance papers **when we meet.** [adverb clause]

Their essay is not due any sooner **than ours [is].** [elliptical clause]

EXERCISE   In each of the following sentences, underline the subordinate clause. Then, identify the type of clause by writing one of the following abbreviations above it: *ADJ* for *adjective clause, ADV* for *adverb clause,* or *N* for *noun clause.* Then, also write *E* over each elliptical clause.

ADV—E

Example 1. As spoken, the words of that nonsense poem sounded hilarious.

1. Because mastering computer technology is one of the biggest challenges, schools must include computer training in the curriculum.

2. The referees assessed our opponents more minutes in the penalty box than us.

3. My grandmother, who is a former dancer, advised my sister and me in improvisational dance.

4. My politician grandfather often brags that he could "wheedle a vote out of an opponent."

5. Are you aware of the underlying political philosophy that this newspaper editor supports?

6. When the convention was held, feminists revolted against rigid gender roles.

7. My great-grandmother, who was one of the early suffragettes, lectured on the need for a federal law giving women the vote.

8. While complaining about vacuuming the living room rug, my kid brother tripped over the cord.

9. When organizing our foods-around-the-world party, please ask for paper plates and plastic silverware.

10. Whoever explains the riddle will win the prize.

Identifying and Classifying Subordinate Clauses B

4d.	An *adjective clause* is a subordinate clause that modifies a noun or a pronoun.
4e.	A *noun clause* is a subordinate clause that is used as a noun.
4f.	An *adverb clause* is a subordinate clause that modifies a verb, an adjective, or an adverb.
4g.	Part of a clause may be left out when its meaning can be clearly understood from the context of the sentence. Such a clause is called an *elliptical clause.*

EXAMPLES   This flower, **which was pink,** made me sneeze. [adjective clause]

What we need is a sense of humor. [noun clause]

After the leaves fell, we saw the nest. [adverb clause]

No one had misjudged him **any more than I.** [elliptical clause]

EXERCISE In each of the following sentences, underline the subordinate clause. Then, identify the type of clause by writing one of the following abbreviations above it: *ADJ* for *adjective clause, ADV* for *adverb clause,* or *N* for *noun clause.*

                                                              ADJ
Example 1. This novel, which is the latest best-seller, will be the perfect birthday gift for my

mother.

1. If there is an increase in the amount of carbon dioxide present in the atmosphere, plant growth

    also will increase.

2. Many Americans voted for the New Deal, which comprised the political policies of Franklin

    D. Roosevelt.

3. Researching the platforms of political candidates helped RaeAnn learn more than her friend.

4. Amy thought that "The Rockpile," by James Baldwin, was the most interesting short story in

    our literature book.

5. While he waited for the bus, Len read the latest novel by his favorite author.

6. The governor answered more questions about the proposed budget than they.

7. Please set that stereo where I can reach it.

8. In 1981, Sandra Day O'Connor, who had been an Arizona judge, became the first female

    Supreme Court justice.

9. Although carefully monitored, the toddler still managed to defoliate the plant.

10. That the Civil War pitted brother against brother is tragic.

Classifying Sentences According to Structure

4h. Depending on its structure, a sentence can be classified as simple, compound, complex, or compound-complex.

(1) A *simple sentence* contains one independent clause and no subordinate clauses. It may have a compound subject, a compound verb, and any number of phrases.
(2) A *compound sentence* contains two or more independent clauses and no subordinate clauses.
(3) A *complex sentence* contains one independent clause and at least one subordinate clause.
(4) A *compound-complex sentence* contains two or more independent clauses and at least one subordinate clause.

SIMPLE	Doyle and I practiced our speeches.
COMPOUND	Doyle evaluated my speech, and I evaluated his.
COMPLEX	As I practiced my speech, I grew calmer.
COMPOUND-COMPLEX	Before class started, I grew nervous, so I practiced my speech again.

EXERCISE Classify each of the following sentences according to its structure by writing one of the following abbreviations on the line before the sentence: *S* for *simple sentence, CX* for *complex sentence, CD* for *compound sentence,* and *CD-CX* for *compound-complex sentence.*

Example _CD-CX_ **1.** Of all the holidays, I like New Year's Day best; however, I seldom see all the

football games that I want to watch.

_____ **1.** Anyone who is a member may attend the FFA banquet.

_____ **2.** When the play was over, the cast returned to the stage, and we all applauded.

_____ **3.** After the storm, the river crested at fifteen feet above flood stage.

_____ **4.** Aren't people who are optimistic usually cheerful?

_____ **5.** Reserve your seats now, and then pay for the tickets tomorrow.

_____ **6.** The driver braked so suddenly that the car behind ours was forced to swerve.

_____ **7.** We campaigned as hard as we could; nevertheless, our candidate lost.

_____ **8.** From our dining room, we could enjoy a perfect view of the sunset.

_____ **9.** You must abide by the terms of the contract, or you will lose your job.

_____ **10.** Until you have the car's oil changed, you may not drive it.

Review A: Independent and Subordinate Clauses

EXERCISE A In each of the following sentences, identify the underlined clause by writing above it *I* for *independent clause* or *S* for *subordinate clause*.

Example 1. Although Spanish is the chief language of South America, dozens of other languages

are also spoken there.

1. The official language of Brazil, which is the largest of the South American countries, is

Portuguese.

2. The Inca language is still spoken by several million people in Colombia, Peru, and Bolivia.

3. In fact, many Bolivians speak Aymara or Quechua, and only a third of the people speak Spanish.

4. If you go to Guyana, you will find many Hindus and Muslims whose ancestors came from Asia

and who still speak Hindi and other Indian languages.

5. Dutch, of course, is the official language of Suriname (Dutch Guiana), and French is spoken

throughout French Guiana.

EXERCISE B In each of the following sentences, underline the subordinate clause. Then, identify the type of clause by writing one of the following abbreviations above it: *ADJ* for *adjective clause*, *ADV* for *adverb clause*, or *N* for *noun clause*.

Example 1. The educational systems of most South American countries are different from the

system that we are accustomed to in the United States.

6. The Spanish and Portuguese settlers who colonized South America brought with them the

educational traditions of their native countries.

7. Because the colonists established many schools and universities, they provided a general

education for many people.

8. What is considered the first Latin American university was founded in 1538 in Santo Domingo.

9. Because many students left school after three or four years, they did not benefit much.

10. The original philosophy was that only those in the professional classes should receive

advanced levels of education.

Review B: **Independent and Subordinate Clauses**

EXERCISE A In each of the following sentences, identify the underlined clause by writing above it *I* for *independent* or *S* for *subordinate*.

Example 1. Education in Latin American countries <u>that were settled by the Spanish and the Portuguese</u> usually followed the teaching systems of the colonists. [written above: *S*]

1. While almost all Latin American countries had state-supported secondary schools and universities, <u>relatively few students expected to attend these schools</u>.

2. Following the European tradition, the secondary schools usually offered an academic program <u>that emphasized classical studies and foreign languages</u>.

3. <u>The teaching in a secondary school consisted largely of scholarly lectures</u> on which the students were expected to take complete notes.

4. <u>Whoever graduated from a secondary school</u> had finished his or her general education.

5. Students could not go to universities <u>unless they wanted to prepare for specialized professions like law and medicine</u>.

EXERCISE B In each of the following sentences, underline the subordinate clause. Then, identify the type of clause by writing one of the following abbreviations above it: *ADJ* for *adjective clause,* ADV for *adverb clause,* or N for *noun clause.* Also write *ELL* above each elliptical clause. Then, identify each adjective clause as *essential (E)* or *nonessential (N)*.

Example 1. What do you, <u>who are so well traveled</u>, expect to see on a visit to one of our national parks? [written above: *ADJ, (N)*]

6. Parks such as the Grand Canyon, Mesa Verde, and Yellowstone are popular tourist attractions that are visited by millions of people.

7. Once established, these parks became important but today represent only part of the work of the National Park Service.

8. The bureau oversees more than 125,000 square miles of land of scenic, historic, or scientific interest, which is classified into more than a dozen major categories.

9. National rivers, which are among the categories, are overseen by the bureau.

10. The Appalachian Trail is what is known as a national scenic trail.

Review C: **Classifying Sentences According to Structure**

EXERCISE A Classify each of the following sentences according to its structure by writing one of the following abbreviations on the line before the sentence: S for *simple sentence,* CX for *complex sentence,* CD for *compound sentence,* and CD-CX for *compound-complex sentence.*

Example _CD-CX_ **1.** We enjoy seeing America, so we visit a different national park every time we take a vacation.

_____ **1.** Preserving national historic sites will help protect our country's heritage.

_____ **2.** In 1936, the Blue Ridge Parkway became the first national route of its kind; it provided the best access to the spectacular Blue Ridge scenery.

_____ **3.** Fort Laramie, which is called a national historic site, was first a fur-trading post; it later became an army post.

_____ **4.** The National Park Service will continue to grow; people of our nation wish to preserve places of scenic, historic, and scientific interest.

_____ **5.** From mansions to ranches and churches to wharves, the national historic sites use a variety of structures to showcase creative American craftsmanship.

EXERCISE B Classify each of the following sentences according to its structure by writing above it one of the following abbreviations: S for *simple sentence,* CX for *complex sentence,* CD for *compound sentence,* and CD-CX for *compound-complex sentence.*

Example 1. Would you like to read a novel that tells of a soldier's Civil War experiences?

6. Many soldiers who fought in the American Civil War wrote of their military experiences, and some of these writings have been published.

7. Most of these writers were amateurs, but one of them, John William De Forest, was a professional novelist.

8. The letters written to his wife during the war were later published under the title *A Volunteer's Adventures.*

9. The book also includes six of De Forest's magazine articles, which add to the lively anecdotes and descriptions in the letters.

10. In addition, editor James H. Croushore provided background information that helped to shape the chapters of the book.

Review D: **Classifying Clauses and Sentences**

EXERCISE A Classify each of the following sentences according to its structure by writing *S* for *simple sentence*, *CX* for *complex sentence*, *CD* for *compound sentence*, or *CD-CX* for *compound-complex sentence*.

Example *CD-CX* **1.** Divers now can explore underwater regions more safely and efficiently; equipment was developed in the last century that made possible more extensive underwater activity.

_____ **1.** Explorers who study the world beneath the sea have made important scientific discoveries.

_____ **2.** Undersea exploration requires sophisticated equipment to enable divers to breathe and to protect them from water pressure.

_____ **3.** For centuries breath-holding divers went thirty to forty feet (nine to twelve meters) beneath the surface without equipment; others used diving bells in shallow water.

_____ **4.** Today scuba divers have greater freedom and mobility because of the aqua-lung that Jacques-Yves Cousteau helped invent in 1943.

_____ **5.** Cousteau's inventions brought about many changes in undersea exploration; his observation vehicle, which he called a diving saucer, enabled divers to stay underwater for longer periods of time.

EXERCISE B In each of the following sentences, underline independent clauses once and subordinate clauses twice. Then, classify each sentence according to its structure by writing *S* for *simple sentence*, *CX* for *complex sentence*, *CD* for *compound sentence*, or *CD-CX* for *compound-complex sentence*.

Example *CX* **1.** Some proverbs, which often seem very simple, express important truths.

_____ **6.** A familiar proverb states that the longest journey begins with a single step; another tells us that little strokes fell great oaks.

_____ **7.** Many people have heard these wise sayings but haven't applied them to their own lives.

_____ **8.** For example, suppose you are required to read a 400-page novel before a test at the end of the school year.

_____ **9.** If you don't start reading the book until the last possible weekend, you will probably not read it well; furthermore, you may not have time to finish the book, and you will almost certainly not enjoy it!

_____ **10.** If you start now and read ten pages a day, you'll be finished within six weeks.

Literary Model: Short Story

> During the whole of a dull, dark, and soundless day in the autumn of the year, when the clouds hung oppressively low in the heavens, I had been passing alone, on horseback, through a singularly dreary tract of country, and at length found myself, as the shades of the evening drew on, within view of the melancholy House of Usher.
>
> —Edgar Allan Poe, "The Fall of the House of Usher"

EXERCISE A

1. Identify the following elements in the passage above.

Independent clause(s): _____

_____

_____

Subordinate clause(s): _____

_____

_____

2. Is the sentence simple, compound, complex, or compound-complex?

_____

EXERCISE B

1. What impression of the narrator's journey does the sentence create? For example, was it a fun journey, a scenic one, a short one? Explain.

_____

_____

2. Based on this opening sentence, what can you predict about the story that will follow? Explain.

_____

_____

3. How does the structure of the sentence contribute to this impression?

_____

_____

Literary Model (continued)

EXERCISE C   Using the opening sentence of Poe's short story as a model, write your own first sentence for a short story. First, decide on the overall impression you want readers to have. Then, write a sentence whose structure helps to create that impression.

_____
_____
_____

EXERCISE D   What is the structure of the sentence you wrote? How does this structure help to create the impression you intended?

_____
_____

If you wish, finish your story, keeping what you have learned about sentence structure in mind.

_____
_____
_____
_____
_____
_____
_____
_____
_____
_____

Writing Application: Narrative

Adverb clauses can provide readers with important information, since they often answer questions about how, why, when, where, and so on. If you leave these details out, readers may feel unsatisfied. Furthermore, the subordinating conjunctions that introduce adverb clauses communicate the logical relationship between ideas in the sentence.

LESS SATISFYING	The kids ran away.
MORE SATISFYING	When the door of the abandoned house swung open, the kids ran as if the ground beneath their feet had opened.

WRITING ACTIVITY

Write to an out-of-town friend whom you have not seen in a while. Explain to your friend that a recent event brought him or her to mind. Then, describe an event, positive or negative, that took you by surprise. Use at least five adverb clauses to tell the conditions under which the event occurred and to explain the event's impact on you.

PREWRITING   Choose a prewriting technique, such as listing or brainstorming, that will help you recall the details of the event. Relive the event in your mind, and write down your reactions. What about the event surprised you? How did you respond, both immediately and after reflection?

WRITING   Writers often organize personal narratives chronologically, but using a flashback might add suspense to your story and create a sense of surprise for readers. Outline several possible plots; then, choose the most effective. Remember, also, that readers love a good story well told. Tell your story with attention to sensory detail, and choose active verbs to keep the pace brisk.

REVISING   Every good story needs an audience. Have several friends read the narrative and give you feedback on which events interested them most. The events that they fail to mention may need embellishment, or they may not be important enough to include.

PUBLISHING   Check your narrative for errors in spelling and punctuation. Be sure you have used at least five adverb clauses to add details. If you use an adverb clause at the beginning of a sentence, follow it with a comma. Follow the standard format for letters as you write and print out the final version. Mail the letter to your friend, who will no doubt be surprised!

EXTENDING YOUR WRITING

For a psychology class, interview five or six people about what surprises them. Include a child, someone your own age, a young adult, and an older adult. Do a bit of research, either in the library or on the Internet, into what scientists say causes surprise. You may wish to develop this exercise into a full-length essay.

for **CHAPTER 5: AGREEMENT**   **pages 96–117**

Choices: Expanding Your Understanding of Agreement

The following activities challenge you to find a connection between agreement and the world around you. Do the activity below that suits your personality best, and then share your discoveries with your class.

ETYMOLOGY
Family Ties

What does each part of the word *antecedent* mean? Research this information in a good dictionary. Then, brainstorm and compile words that contain one or more of these word parts. Include a definition for each of these words. Then, use each word correctly in a sentence. Make copies and share your findings with your classmates.

BUILDING BACKGROUND KNOWLEDGE
Ducks and Geese and Chicks

Do you know what a group of several geese are called? There are dozens of specific names for different groups of animals. What are terms for these groups? Find out. Then, with your teacher's permission, lead the class in writing sentences that use pronouns to refer to each of these collective nouns.

RESEARCH
One Leg at a Time

Pants are one thing, but they take plural verbs and pronouns. What other words do likewise? Working with a friend or two, make a list. (You might want to consult a few reference sources for ideas.) When you've compiled a list of at least ten, find or create illustrations for each of these special nouns. Transfer your illustrations to poster board. Under each illustration, write a sentence in which you refer to the noun by using a plural pronoun.

LOGIC
All and *None*

These two indefinite pronouns play a big role in constructing a syllogism, a form of deductive reasoning. Find out more about syllogisms and their rules. Pay particular attention to the roles that the indefinite pronouns *all*, *none*, and *some* play in logical arguments. Then, prepare an illustration or two showing how these pronouns are used.

SURVEY
The Usual Suspects

Polish your listening skills. Listen for subject-verb agreement errors around school, at home, with friends, and out shopping. Which subjects and which verbs seem to cause the most problems? Compile a list of at least ten common problems. Then, ask your teacher for permission to let your classmates in on your findings.

WRITING
Every Dog Has Its Day

Many a proverb or saying uses the expression *many a* or *every*. Get together with a couple of friends, and make a list of at least ten of these sayings. Then, write each proverb on a poster, highlighting the verb and the expression *many a* or *every*. Have a couple of blank posters on hand when you present your list to the class. Challenge the class to add to your list, by either making up a proverb or quoting one. Write and highlight each new entry. When your project is complete, you could type up one big list and make copies for your classmates.

DISCUSSION
Culture and Language

Perhaps no other aspect of English is as bound to culture as usage. Just as a group can require certain clothes, it can also demand a certain language. Just as membership in a group can become part of who we are, so the language we use can become part of our identities. What are some of these requirements for some groups? Is language a part of our identities? On what bases should a person be judged? Aren't many of us bilingual or bi-dialectal, using one way of speaking at home and another in formal situations? How does agreement fit into the picture? With your teacher's approval, lead a discussion of these questions and others that arise.

USAGE

Number

Number is the form a word takes to indicate whether the word is singular or plural.

5a. A word that refers to one person, place, thing, or idea is singular in number. A word that refers to more than one is plural in number.

SINGULAR	gem	Web site	lily	alumna	politics	he	that
PLURAL	gems	Web sites	lilies	alumnae	politics	them	those

EXERCISE A On the line before each of the following words, write *S* for *singular* or *P* for *plural*.

Example __P__ **1.** wolves

_____ **1.** their   _____ **8.** myself   _____ **15.** mice

_____ **2.** monster   _____ **9.** Ferris wheel   _____ **16.** volcano

_____ **3.** crankshaft   _____ **10.** aspens   _____ **17.** youth

_____ **4.** thunderstorms   _____ **11.** deduction   _____ **18.** elves

_____ **5.** sisters-in-law   _____ **12.** monasteries   _____ **19.** we

_____ **6.** constitution   _____ **13.** it   _____ **20.** equations

_____ **7.** winches   _____ **14.** jeopardy

EXERCISE B On each of the following lines, write a singular or plural word to complete each word group correctly. Indicate the number of your word by writing after it *S* for *singular* or *P* for *plural*.

Example 1. three dozen ___peaches—P___

21. two main _____   **31.** each of the following _____

22. several _____   **32.** only the middle _____

23. a more alert _____   **33.** a long, hot _____

24. the other _____   **34.** these few good _____

25. all qualified _____   **35.** my favorite _____

26. every last _____   **36.** both exciting _____

27. too many _____   **37.** that sad _____

28. neither _____   **38.** any current _____

29. a classic _____   **39.** those amazing _____

30. no more than forty _____ **40.** not one _____

Language and Sentence Skills Practice

Subject-Verb Agreement A

USAGE

| **5b.** | A verb should agree in number with its subject. |

(1) Singular subjects take singular verbs.
(2) Plural subjects take plural verbs.

| **5c.** | The number of a subject usually is not determined by a word in a phrase or a clause following the subject. |

EXAMPLES   **Bart Bonnard plays** baseball for the Cougars. [singular subject and verb]
He and his **teammates have** won every game this year. [plural subject and verb]
To win the championship **was** their goal. [infinitive as subject]
The **introduction** written by the coeditors **appears** before the contents page.
The **musicians,** along with the conductor, **are** rehearsing.

EXERCISE A In each of the following sentences, circle the subject and write above it *S* for *singular* or *P* for *plural*. Then, underline the verb in parentheses that agrees in number with the subject.

Example 1. Job (opportunities) along with a variety of activities *(bring, brings)* people to cities.

1. Cities such as San Francisco *(attracts, attract)* many residents.

2. Residents of a large city often *(is, are)* faced with high taxes.

3. A major problem in many large cities *(involves, involve)* transportation.

4. Those residents who use public transportation *(helps, help)* the environment.

5. Pollution, as well as overcrowded highways, *(is, are)* reduced.

EXERCISE B Most of the sentences in the following paragraph contain an error in subject-verb agreement. Draw a line through each incorrect verb, and write above it the form that agrees with the subject. If a sentence is already correct, write *C* above the number.

Example [1] The Grupo de Teatro Popular Realista ~~were~~ *was* founded by Alfonso Sastre.

[6] Alfonso Sastre, who is one of Spain's leading playwrights, have been influenced by the works of Arthur Miller. [7] Some of his writing show the influence of Brecht and Beckett. [8] Sastre, along with these playwrights, usually place his plays in urban locations. [9] A major theme throughout his plays are criticism of society. [10] Despair caused by social injustices pervade Sastre's works. [11] The characters in almost every play face the problem of maintaining a sense of self. [12] Overcrowded living conditions, in addition to situations often demeaning, adds to the characters' misery. [13] However, he, as well as Miller, inject a sense of hope into the despair. [14] Perhaps the play that stands as the finest example of the theme of despair and hope are *Ana Kleiber.* [15] This playwright, who is considered one of Spain's most controversial dramatists, have also been called his country's most original.

Subject-Verb Agreement B

5b.   A verb should agree in number with its subject.

(1) Singular subjects take singular verbs.
(2) Plural subjects take plural verbs.

5c.   The number of a subject usually is not determined by a word in a phrase or a clause following the subject.

> EXAMPLES   **Aurelio arrives** by airplane at 7:00 P.M. tonight. [singular subject and verb]
>
> **Susan** and her **father plan** to attend a jazz concert this weekend. [plural subject and verb]
>
> **Playing** stringed instruments well **has** always **been** his passion.
>
> The **book** of poems **is** here.
>
> **W. H. Auden,** who wrote the poems, **remains** my favorite poet.

EXERCISE   In each of the following sentences, underline the subject. Then, underline the verb in parentheses that agrees in number with the subject.

Example 1. The school board, together with the Parent-Teacher Association, *(meet, meets)* on

Thursday evening to begin discussions.

1. The fabric for these skirts *(were, was)* so thick that I had to sharpen my scissors before I was

able to cut it.

2. *(Have, Has)* playing checkers always been a hobby of yours?

3. The newspaper, as well as Dad's morning coffee, *(are, is)* from the store down the street.

4. In that village, spending two days to polish one piece of black pottery *(are, is)* not unusual.

5. *(Are, Is)* four adults coming along on our trip to Washington, D.C.?

6. To help Suzanne and Anita find good seats at last night's annual band concert *(were, was)* my

main concern.

7. The quarterback of the Elmwood Eagles *(are, is)* Eduardo Valdez.

8. The students who are visiting our American history class later next week *(are, is)* from

Edinburgh, Scotland.

9. Calling ahead for reservations *(are, is)* the best way to ensure that we will get a table.

10. That book, which is a fantasy story about some tiny people, *(were, was)* my favorite when I was

ten years old.

Indefinite Pronouns A

USAGE

5d. Some indefinite pronouns are singular, some are plural, and some can be singular or plural, depending on how they are used.

> **EXAMPLES** **Everyone** who enjoys sports **likes** this program.
>
> **Many** who travel to France **visit** Paris.
>
> **More** of that book **was** interesting to me. [*More* refers to the singular noun *book.*]
>
> **More** of the students **are** here today. [*More* refers to the plural noun *students.*]

EXERCISE A In each of the following sentences, circle the subject and write above it *S* for *singular* or *P* for *plural*. Then, underline the verb in parentheses that agrees in number with the subject.

Example 1. (Someone) from one of the state offices *(are, is)* visiting our class tomorrow.

1. Few of the maple trees *(have, has)* changed color yet.

2. *(Do, Does)* any of the rules for debates apply in this case?

3. Many of the students *(are, is)* running for that student council position.

4. Nothing that we saw *(have, has)* changed our minds about going to the lake for a picnic.

5. *(Have, Has)* everybody interested in joining the two new quartets signed up for auditions?

EXERCISE B Most of the following sentences contain an error in subject-verb agreement. First, circle the subject of the verb that should be revised. Then, draw a line through each incorrect verb and write above it the correct form. If a sentence is already correct, write *C* above the number.

Example 1. (Some) of her friends who wanted to surprise Della ~~has~~ *have* filled her locker with birthday balloons.

6. Sadly, most of that nation's natural resources has been depleted.

7. Everybody on the two debating teams appear ready to begin.

8. Many who use these methods to restore pieces of art require extensive training.

9. All of the driveways on our block has been resurfaced with asphalt.

10. None of the actors was discussing the script changes with the director.

11. Each of the graduating classes are electing permanent class officers.

12. Only one of these suitcases slide under the seat on this plane.

13. Neither of the candidates state especially strong views about the issues.

14. Several among those watching the lunar eclipse was capturing its red phase on film.

15. Of the optional pizza toppings available, most on the list seems to be vegetables.

Indefinite Pronouns B

5d. Some indefinite pronouns are singular, some are plural, and some can be singular or plural, depending on how they are used.

> **EXAMPLES** **Nobody is** able to reach Martha by phone.
>
> **Several** of our neighbors **have** bird feeders in their yards.
>
> **All** of the tomatoes are ripe. [*All* refers to the plural noun *tomatoes*.]
>
> **All** of the food at this party **is** delicious. [*All* refers to the singular noun *food*.]

EXERCISE Most of the following sentences contain an error in subject-verb agreement. Draw a line through each incorrect verb, and write above it the correct form. If the sentence is already correct, write *C* above the number.

Example 1. None in this group of test answers ~~bear~~ *bears* any similarity to the following group.

1. No one among the visiting relatives tell as good a story as Aunt Vicki does.

2. Each of the actors have earned a curtain call for this afternoon's performance.

3. Some of the dancers moves with skill and grace.

4. Anyone who shows the carpentry skills necessary stand a good chance of being hired.

5. If all of these chemical elements is present in these quantities, name the substance.

6. Both of the statistical results seem out of balance when compared to practical experience.

7. In Miranda's opinion, more of the trees needs to be trimmed.

8. Under what circumstances does none of the laws of gravity apply?

9. For whatever reasons, no one in the various meetings have volunteered for this benefit.

10. Of those attorneys, several with fee-based cases was handling pro bono cases also.

11. Do anything besides golf and basketball relax you?

12. Please ask whether everybody already eating needs a refill on tea, juice, or ice water.

13. Because of the improved harvester, none of the wheat crop have gone to waste.

14. All of my tennis shoes that don't fit is handed down to my little brother.

15. Because of the fire, everything on these two floors were left in ashes.

16. While we watched, both of the cloud formations on the horizon was twisting into one.

17. Have somebody with a license offered to drive us?

18. This past Tuesday, some of the commencement practices was better than the rest.

19. Nobody in our town repair cars as well and as fast as Mr. Wilson and his mechanics do.

20. One of the fan letters to the band were sent from New Zealand.

USAGE

Compound Subjects A

A *compound subject* consists of two or more subjects that are joined by a conjunction and that have the same verb.

5e. Subjects joined by *and* usually take a plural verb.

Some compound subjects joined by *and* name only one person or thing and take singular verbs.

> **EXAMPLES**   **Gwendolyn Brooks** and **Judith Viorst are** poets.
> The **director** and **star** of the movie **is** Barbra Streisand.

5f. Singular subjects joined by *or* or *nor* take a singular verb.

> **EXAMPLES**   Neither **Marco** nor **Raymond has** ever **seen** an opera.
> **Has** the **project leader** or the **secretary arrived** yet?

5g. When a singular subject and a plural subject are joined by *or* or *nor*, the verb agrees with the subject nearer the verb.

> **EXAMPLES**   Neither the chorus **members** nor the lead **singer has come** to rehearsal.
> Neither the lead **singer** nor the chorus **members have come** to rehearsal.

EXERCISE In each of the following sentences, underline the simple subjects that are part of the compound subject. Then, underline the verb in parentheses that agrees in number with the compound subject.

Example 1. To pay for car repairs and to save for college *(take, takes)* all the money that

Sam makes.

1. Someone or something *(has, have)* dug a tremendous hole right in the middle of the front yard.

2. Chips and salsa *(is, are)* Kevin's favorite snack.

3. A month of hard work and years of experience *(have, has)* been poured into Han's new

sculpture.

4. Either the two-hour tape or the four-hour one *(plays, play)* smoothly and easily in this recorder.

5. *(Has, Have)* cleaning your room and washing the car been taking most of your weekend lately?

6. Red beans and rice *(happen, happens)* to be one of Dad's favorite foods.

7. Jonathan Winters, Robin Williams, and Dana Carvey *(are, is)* Yoshi's favorite comedians.

8. Neither tomatoes nor garlic *(were, was)* on the grocery list, but Diego remembered to buy

them anyway.

9. *(Is, Are)* Sonja or Gretchen leading at the halfway point of the mile run?

10. *(Is, Are)* a plumb bob or a trowel used in bricklaying?

USAGE

Compound Subjects B

A *compound subject* consists of two or more subjects that are joined by a conjunction and that have the same verb.

5e.	Subjects joined by *and* usually take a plural verb.

Some compound subjects joined by *and* name only one person or thing and take singular verbs.

EXAMPLES   **Jim** and **Doris were** the singers in the band.
The **singer** and **producer** of that CD **is** Enrique Ríos.

5f.	Singular subjects joined by *or* or *nor* take a singular verb.

EXAMPLES   Neither **Carl** nor **Amanda has** ever been to Carlsbad Caverns.
Either **Patrick** or **Jane was** at the meeting last night.

5g.	When a singular subject and a plural subject are joined by *or* or *nor*, the verb agrees with the subject nearer the verb.

EXAMPLES   Neither **the children** nor **the mother was** at home.
Neither **the mother** nor **the children were** at home.

EXERCISE   Each of the following sentences contains an error in subject-verb agreement. First, underline the simple subjects that are part of the compound subject. Then, draw a line through the incorrect verb and write above it the form that agrees with the subject.

Example 1. Many of Cora's friends and some of her neighbors ~~has~~ *have* arranged a surprise party for

tomorrow night.

1. A bake sale and a car wash is going to help us raise money for the charity.

2. Either the police officers or someone from the sheriff's office have to file a report about

   the incident.

3. Twenty-hour workweeks and a full load of schoolwork is not unusual for students.

4. How long is the welding crew and the carpenters scheduled to work on this job?

5. Our set director and costumes manager for the holiday skits were Joyce Proudfeather.

6. What has the student body and the faculty selected as the mascot for our new high school?

7. During every appointment, dental hygienists or the dentist advise me on tooth care.

8. Has the abstract paintings and the mixed-media works of Kathleen Holder been on exhibit for

   a long time?

9. Salt and pepper is the only seasonings that many people use on their food.

10. María Banks and Paul Stewart, who were well known in their community, was acquainted for

    seventeen years.

Language and Sentence Skills Practice   **111**

Finding the Subject

5h. When the subject follows the verb, find the subject and make sure that the verb agrees with it.

EXAMPLES Here **is** your **ticket**.

Where **are** the **tickets** that you had reserved for yourselves?

USAGE

EXERCISE A In the following sentences, underline every subject. Then, draw a line through any incorrect verb and write above it the form that agrees with the subject.

Where are
Example 1. ~~Where's~~ our tour guides taking us today?

1. By the way, here's the CDs that you ordered three weeks ago.

2. Does the water fountain and the ice machine still work okay?

3. There's the new vegetable gardens, plowed and ready to be sown.

4. Here's seven of the ten jackets for the new band members.

5. Is Marc and his brother really twins?

6. Where's the best places to eat our meals and to spend the night?

7. In addition to the greenery, was there any dried flowers in the bouquet?

8. As you requested, here's the plans for the next two weeks of my chemistry class.

9. Is there any more of those delicious cranberry muffins Shaniqua made?

10. Where's the candidates we are supposed to hear debate tonight?

EXERCISE B Most of the following sentences contain an error in subject-verb agreement. Draw a line through the incorrect verb, and write above it the correct form. If a sentence is already correct, write *C* above the number.

there are
Example 1. Today on television, ~~there's~~ several nature specials and a movie about whales.

11. Here's several newspaper articles about people donating money for children's schools.

12. Is my eyeglasses still where I left them on the table next to the couch?

13. There's not very many applicants for the firefighter jobs that are open now.

14. Do Jacob and Wanda intend to speak during the student congress meeting this afternoon?

15. Where's the shirts and pants for the dry cleaners?

16. Since there's more people coming to the reunion, we thought we'd bring extra salad.

17. Where's our soccer equipment and the uniforms going to be stored?

18. There's tomatoes and carrots in the refrigerator.

19. Here's the reference location and the description for the new Web site for our math class.

20. Have each of you decided yet on a place you would like to visit during our vacation?

Collective Nouns

5i. A collective noun may be either singular or plural, depending on its meaning in a sentence.

EXAMPLES   The **team plays** on Monday. [singular, a group as a unit]

The **team take** turns at bat. [plural, individual members of the group]

All **teams declare** themselves ready for the playoffs. [plural, more than one group]

USAGE

EXERCISE   In each of the following sentences, underline the collective noun that is used as a subject. Then, underline the verb in parentheses that agrees in number with the collective noun.

Example 1. The public still (*express, expresses*) their opinions in letters to newspaper editors.

1. The team (*like, likes*) to include their friends and relatives in activities.

2. This morning a number of the staff (*complete, completes*) training on waiting tables.

3. Next, the assembly at the United Nations (*vote, votes*) on the human rights issue.

4. How often (*have, has*) the choir worn robes for its performances?

5. She has asked whether the committee (*want, wants*) more time for their reports.

6. A small number of natural areas (*were, was*) named national monuments in 2000.

7. The audience of elementary students (*seem, seems*) to be enjoying the play.

8. By this time tomorrow, the battalion (*arrive, arrives*) at their assigned positions.

9. The herd (*turn, turns*) in unison toward this water hole each time we pass.

10. Which political party (*believe, believes*) that passing laws for lower taxes is within its ability?

11. A cloud of hornets (*were, was*) buzzing lazily about its nest.

12. The number of peaches in a bushel (*vary, varies*) with the size of the fruit.

13. During intermission, the orchestra (*check, checks*) their musical scores for the next act.

14. Ian's family (*meet, meets*) every year to renew friendships and exchange family news.

15. Can we assume that, when the time comes, the litter of kittens already (*have, has*) homes?

16. Wildlife (*search, searches*) for food longer and over a wider area during a drought.

17. Last night, a number of apple-tree buds (*were, was*) damaged by the frost.

18. The youth of today (*face, faces*) more competition for high-tech jobs than ever before.

19. The jury (*request, requests*) copies of the documents that were introduced as evidence.

20. (*Do, Does*) that couple spend a good bit of time volunteering at the blood bank?

USAGE

Expression of an Amount

5j. | An expression of an amount (a measurement, a percentage, or a fraction, for example) may be singular or plural, depending on how it is used.

> **EXAMPLES** We thought **six ounces** of grapefruit juice **was** enough for this punch mix. [The amount is thought of as a unit.]
>
> **Have** only **twelve percent** of the eligible voters cast absentee ballots? [The percentage refers to the plural noun *voters*.]
>
> **Two thirds** of our literature book **covers** authors who lived from 1600 to 2000. [The fraction refers to the singular noun *book*.]

EXERCISE In the following sentences, underline the correct verb in parentheses.

Example 1. Four miles (*was, were*) the distance we hiked.

1. Eight dollars (*is, are*) the price of a ticket.

2. (*Do, Does*) eight ounces of that sports drink really help you when you are exercising?

3. Recently, about five percent (*have, has*) been the interest rate for savings accounts.

4. If three cents (*are, is*) owed me, just put them in the basket for others who could use them.

5. Three eighths of a cup (*were, was*) the only difficult measurement in that recipe.

6. When you change a car's oil and filter, four quarts of oil usually (*replace, replaces*) the old oil.

7. Since I have been working here, seven percent of the employees (*have, has*) gotten raises.

8. Five dollars an hour (*seem, seems*) to be the current rate for baby sitters.

9. Approximately one third of my friends (*take, takes*) care of siblings after school.

10. Two yards from the end zone (*were, was*) the closest their team ever came to scoring.

11. Four days (*is, are*) all this business takes as state holidays.

12. If sixty percent of the students (*miss, misses*) class, the test will be postponed.

13. Five-liter bottles filled with spring water (*sit, sits*) chilling in a tub of ice.

14. Before you leave, please see that two hundred dollars (*are, is*) transferred to the account.

15. As many as sixty-five percent of our students (*commute, commutes*) ten miles or more.

16. One third of my classmates (*live, lives*) on the Ute reservation.

17. Six new thousand-dollar scholarships (*have, has*) been established this year.

18. According to the donor records, nearly five hundred pints of blood (*were, was*) donated.

19. Out of each dollar, three fifths (*pay, pays*) for school books and supplies.

20. (*Are, Is*) fifty hours of free computer-programming time a possibility these days?

Nouns Plural in Form

5k. Some nouns that are plural in form take singular verbs.

Nouns such as *civics* are plural in form but take singular verbs. Nouns suggesting "a pair of" always take plural verbs. Nouns such as *acoustics* may be singular or plural.

EXAMPLES   The **news comes** on at six o'clock.

Where **are** the **scissors**?

The **acoustics** in this auditorium **are** perfect for music and theater events.

Acoustics is an ever-changing field of study.

5l. Even when plural in form, the title of a creative work (such as a book, song, movie, or painting) or the name of a country, a city, or an organization generally takes a singular verb.

EXERCISE   In the following sentences, underline the correct verb in parentheses.

Example 1. (Aren't, *Isn't*) the book *Buildings That Changed the World* full of outstanding pictorials?

1. Last year, mathematics (were, was) my favorite course.

2. "The Hollow Men" (are, is) my favorite poem by T. S. Eliot.

3. (Are, Is) my eyeglasses on the table next to the couch?

4. According to the airline's president, statistics (show, shows) an increase in air travel.

5. Acme Chemicals (have, has) been a loyal supporter of the Special Olympics.

6. Molasses (are, is) the key ingredient in my favorite breakfast bread.

7. Your new binoculars (feel, feels) heavier than any of the others you have been using.

8. "Carburetors Today" (explain, explains) changes for future car-engine designs.

9. Don, please be sure that the shears (receive, receives) a good cleaning after each use.

10. We thought that measles (weren't, wasn't) contagious once we had had that variety.

11. (Isn't, Aren't) "Trees," the poem by Joyce Kilmer, often read?

12. The jury summons (require, requires) me to report to the courthouse next Monday.

13. Genetics (are, is) among the college classes Victoria may take.

14. The store ClaSupps (carry, carries) the basic supplies students might need for a class.

15. (Do, Does) the economics of the situation require further examination?

16. The United States usually (nominate, nominates) its senators in primary elections.

17. *Bemelmans: The Life & Art of Madeline's Creator* (are, is) Chi's favorite book.

18. Maroon pants (look, looks) just right with that white shirt and sweater, Margie.

19. 3D Plumbers (use, uses) the latest in miniature camera equipment to diagnose problems.

20. (Are, Is) the Aleutians a large group of individual islands or a long island chain?

Predicate Nominatives; *Every, Many a; Don't, Doesn't*

| **5m.** | A verb agrees with its subject, but not necessarily with a predicate nominative. |

| **5n.** | Subjects preceded by *every* or *many a* take singular verbs. |

| **5o.** | The contractions *don't* and *doesn't* should agree with their subjects. |

> **EXAMPLES** The leading **crop** is strawberries.
> **Strawberries are** the leading crop.
> **Every man** and **woman has spoken.**
> **Many a student works** after school.
> **He doesn't** go to the movies often.
> **Don't** we need to study today?

EXERCISE A In each of the following sentences, underline the subject. Then, underline the verb in parentheses that agrees in number with its subject.

Example 1. (*Haven't, Hasn't*) the pyramids of Egypt always been a popular tourist attraction?

1. Our idea for a great weekend (*is, are*) swimming and boating at the lake.

2. (*Don't, Doesn't*) Harriet and Gina live in that apartment house?

3. Many a citizen in our city (*have, has*) voiced concern over rising taxes.

4. Jugglers (*was, were*) the main attraction of the show.

5. Every cow and calf (*have, has*) been taken to the pasture.

6. Many an opening night (*find, finds*) more than one actor struggling with his or her lines.

7. Like all good fiction, (*don't, doesn't*) your story have an interesting ending?

8. I certainly (*don't, doesn't*) mind washing and drying the dishes after that excellent meal.

9. Not every basketball and program (*were, was*) autographed before the team left.

10. These days, many a car and truck (*come, comes*) equipped with front and side air bags.

EXERCISE B In each of the following sentences, underline the correct verb in parentheses.

Example 1. Many an alma mater (*don't, doesn't*) mind contacting the alumni.

11. This computer (*don't, doesn't*) come with a good software package.

12. About a year from now, many a student (*are, is*) planning to toss that graduation cap in the air.

13. Every CD and tape in the store (*have, has*) been marked down twenty-five percent.

14. Jim (*don't, doesn't*) like to brag, but his aunt Jewel makes the best blackberry cobbler.

15. Many a diver and swimmer (*share, shares*) an interest in the outcome of this swim meet.

Relative Pronouns

5p. When the relative pronoun *that, which,* or *who* is the subject of an adjective clause, the verb in the clause agrees with the word to which the relative pronoun refers.

   EXAMPLES   Gregory Hines, **who stars** in this movie, is also known as a dancer. [*Who* refers to the singular noun *Gregory Hines.*]
   I like films **that feature** tap-dancers. [*That* refers to the plural noun *films.*]
   Alligators are only one of the animals **that is** found in a swamp. [*That* refers to the singular indefinite pronoun *one.*]

EXERCISE In each of the following sentences, underline the relative pronoun and circle the word to which it refers. Then, underline the verb in parentheses that agrees in number with the word to which the relative pronoun refers.

Example 1. Installing lockers is one of the topics that *(have, has)* been hotly debated.

1. The manager needs workers who *(are, is)* fluent in Spanish.

2. I thought of two different answers that *(seem, seems)* correct.

3. Bobby is prepared to interview for that job, which *(are, is)* perfect for his skill level.

4. Lela is the only one of the students who *(have, has)* been to Peru.

5. Ask the manager who *(coordinate, coordinates)* the schedules about working overtime.

6. Perhaps my parents can lend you the novel that *(were, was)* assigned today.

7. We watched a program about the astronauts who *(has, have)* just returned from a mission.

8. Esther found the reference books that *(contain, contains)* the charts for our presentation.

9. The only one of the singers who *(knows, know)* this part is absent.

10. Unalakleet, which *(are, is)* a remote Alaskan village, was the first stop for Census 2000.

11. My best friend Aaron made an announcement that *(have, has)* startled everyone.

12. Larry and Beth are going to Twin Oaks Bikes, which also *(carry, carries)* parts.

13. The teacher who *(help, helps)* me understand calculus has accomplished a great deal.

14. We spent an hour making posters that *(attach, attaches)* to the float for the parade.

15. She is one of the poets who *(are, is)* busily creating new rhymes for us to enjoy.

16. The games, which *(is, are)* tightly scheduled today, need to start on time.

17. Robert's report is about one of the new planets that *(has, have)* not yet been named.

18. Since the only one of the pilots who *(fly, flies)* the route is ready, we should board now.

19. How do the puzzle pieces that *(are, is)* lost just suddenly reappear?

20. Gene used to have a calf that *(were, was)* named Burnsey.

USAGE

Number, Gender, and Person

5q.   A pronoun should agree in number, gender, and person with its antecedent.

> **EXAMPLES**   **Isaac Bashevis Singer** won many awards for **his** short stories. [singular, masculine, third person]
>
> **I** don't believe this physics book is **mine.** [singular, first person]
>
> **Students,** will **you** please sit down? [plural, second person]
>
> The **horse** rolled in the grass to scratch **its** back. [singular, neuter, third person]

EXERCISE   In each of the following sentences, underline the correct pronoun in parentheses. Then, circle the antecedent with which the pronoun agrees.

Example 1. Do the judges announce when ⟨she⟩ will actually receive (*her*, *their*) scholarship money?

1. Abdulrahman got the players' autographs and showed (*it*, *them*) to me.

2. Telma showed the class a photograph of (*her*, *their*) grandparents' farmhouse.

3. When you see Derek, would you please remind (*him*, *them*) to come to rehearsal?

4. My brother and sister and I prepared dinner so that (*we*, *they*) could surprise Mom.

5. The bread in both baskets was old and stale, so I fed (*it*, *them*) to the birds.

6. In a few minutes, our guest speaker will tell us about (*his*, *our*) search for dinosaurs.

7. That was the hardest marathon Eddie had ever run, but (*he*, *it*) still managed to win first place.

8. Frank doesn't like strawberries, so he asked for a small serving of (*it*, *them*).

9. Because of extra practice on her backstroke, Rhea has improved (*her*, *their*) lap time.

10. A sea turtle comes ashore to make a nest in which to lay (*her*, *its*) eggs.

11. May Connor borrow your map of Africa so (*he*, *it*) can finish our discussion?

12. We elected Marie and Joan cocaptains for (*her*, *their*) leadership of the golf team.

13. Kendra agreed to make (*her*, *our*) kraut salad for next month's potluck dinner.

14. We can return the yearbook proofs within the week if you leave (*it*, *them*) with us today.

15. Please ask Sondra to bring a computer tool kit to (*her*, *its*) class on repair techniques.

16. From (*his*, *its*) place at the head of the line, Brian will lead the class to the parking lot.

17. The gutters were overflowing from the hard, fast rain that filled (*it*, *them*) up.

18. Before you put your letters in the mail box, make sure to put postage on (*it*, *them*).

19. After (*our*, *its*) 4-H meeting, we put away the folding chairs and table.

20. Our dog Waldo always seems to know when it is time for (*his*, *its*) bath.

Indefinite Pronouns

5r. Some indefinite pronouns are singular, and some are plural. Other indefinite pronouns can be either singular or plural, depending on their meaning.

EXAMPLES   **Each** of the **women** on the team has improved **her** batting average.
Everyone in the **boys'** choir must learn **his** part during the next two weeks.
Some of that **program** is not working because **it** has not yet been debugged.
Some of the computer **viruses** do **their** damage slowly.

EXERCISE A   In each sentence in the following paragraph, underline the indefinite pronoun. Then, underline the pronoun or pronoun group in parentheses that agrees with it.

Example [1] Many of those whom Craig entertains recognize *(himself, themselves)* in his humor.

[1] Some of Craig's tales have the "rez" for *(its, their)* settings. [2] Anyone in the audience could imagine *(himself or herself, themselves)* as a mischievous child hiding behind Grandmother's skirts. [3] Each of his readers might recall *(his or her, their)* own butterflies in the stomach after hearing Craig's description of asking for a first date or of delivering that first oral book report. [4] Much of his humor shows *(itself, themselves)* in his "Muttonman" cartoon, which pokes fun at history and the pitfalls of living with two cultural standards. [5] In following the true-to-life misadventures of this unlikely hero, few fail to see that Craig's humor applies to *(his, their)* own lives as well.

EXERCISE B   In each of the following sentences, underline the pronoun or pronoun group in parentheses that agrees with the indefinite pronoun.

Example 1. Both of the trees are large enough to shade the ground around *(it, them)*.

6. Some of the best athletes will share *(his or her, their)* training tips with us.

7. Each of the members of the jury has voiced *(his or her, their)* opinion.

8. Neither of the girls has submitted *(her, their)* application.

9. Few in our town wanted to miss seeing *(his or her, their)* team in the regional playoffs.

10. Did all of the applicants leave *(his or her, their)* business cards with my secretary?

11. If some of your friends want to come with us, tell *(him or her, them)* to hurry.

12. One of the players left *(their, her)* basketball on the court.

13. Many of the spectators took *(his or her, their)* programs home as souvenirs.

14. Neither of my shirts is where I left *(it, them)*.

15. Anyone who wants to join the women's choir should schedule *(her, their)* audition.

Language and Sentence Skills Practice   **119**

USAGE

USAGE

Antecedents Joined by *And, Or,* or *Nor*

5s. Use a plural pronoun to refer to two or more antecedents joined by *and*.

5t. Use a singular pronoun to refer to two or more singular antecedents joined by *or* or *nor*.

EXAMPLES   While **Calinda** and **Yvette** were on vacation, I watered **their** plants.
Neither **Calinda** nor **Yvette** has finished **her** report.

EXERCISE On the line provided, complete each of the following sentences by adding a pronoun or pronoun group that agrees with its antecedent.

Example 1. The dogs and puppies have responded well to ___*their*___ trainers.

1. If the pipes burst, our basement and first story are sure to have _____ floors ruined.

2. Neither Gary nor Paul has completed _____ research project.

3. Yearlings and cows milled about, waiting for the rancher to feed _____.

4. Toby and Nell might share _____ picnic lunches with us if we ask nicely.

5. Meg, Will, and I hope to take _____ college entrance exams on Saturday.

6. Pull cords or light-adjustment wands for the blinds have _____ own part numbers.

7. Can you measure the success of rock-and-roll by _____ influence on musical styles?

8. Claire or Suzi promised to come by and lend me _____ notes for our civics test.

9. Room and board is included as long as you pay for _____ in advance.

10. Don't forget your shovel and pail; you'll find _____ essential for seashell hunting.

11. On Wednesday, will Jarod or Roger deliver mail for those of us on _____ route?

12. I can hardly wait to see whether Paula or LaShonda wears _____ new dress tonight.

13. Uncle Jake and Grandpa proved to us that _____ know how to play checkers.

14. We could elect José or Ray as student body president if _____ would run for office.

15. Neither Belle nor her sister could go to the movie _____ was wanting to see.

16. Every night after dinner, my brother and I clear the table before anyone asks _____ to do so.

17. Give Fred and Lainie a call since _____ have offered to bring us some wood for the fireplace.

18. The sleet and snow is going to be a mess when _____ melts.

19. Odds and ends of mementos sometimes show up where we least expect to find _____.

20. Which candidate included law and order in his platform because he felt _____ was missing in too many communities?

Number of Collective Nouns

5u.   A collective noun can be either singular or plural, depending on how it is used.

A collective noun takes a singular pronoun when the noun refers to the group as a unit. A collective noun takes a plural pronoun when the noun refers to the individual members or parts of the group.

   EXAMPLES   The **troupe** earned tonight's applause with **its** incredible performance. [singular]

   The **troupe** are slowly getting out of costume, as if **they** are quite tired. [plural]

EXERCISE A   In each of the following sentences, underline the collective noun. Then, underline the pronoun in parentheses that agrees in number with the collective noun.

Example 1. This group selects a new chief according to the laws of *(its, their)* elders.

1. During the debate, the faction for a tax cut were emphatic in *(its, their)* arguments.

2. The circle of friends and neighbors seem delighted that *(it, they)* are invited to the wedding.

3. Each morning, the staff check *(its, their)* mail and announcement bulletins.

4. Our marching band claim *(it, they)* are ready for today's competition.

5. This particular lot of wrenches has been selling quickly since we put *(it, them)* on display.

6. Has the committee selected *(its, their)* newest members yet?

7. An entire colony of ants invited *(itself, themselves)* to our picnic.

8. That new woodwind ensemble is practicing now, and I am eager to go and hear *(them, it)*.

9. The assembly have voted to close *(its, their)* session, today only, to all media coverage.

10. Without a leader, a herd of horses or cattle usually will wander about *(its, their)* range.

EXERCISE B   On the lines provided, complete the following sentences by adding a pronoun that agrees with the collective noun.

Example 1. The council want more public input before making ___*their*___ final decisions.

11. The minority has always known that _____ has a right to disagree with the majority.

12. A multitude of Internet service providers offer great value for the price _____ charge.

13. The crew have a responsibility to serve _____ captain and ship loyally.

14. Flying in with a heavy load of nectar, a swarm of bees approached _____ nest.

15. The mob rushed up to the doors, determined not to miss _____ favorite singer.

USAGE

USAGE

Nouns Plural in Form

5v. Some nouns that are plural in form take singular pronouns.

Nouns such as *civics, electronics, mathematics, news,* and *physics* are plural in form but take singular pronouns. Nouns suggesting "a pair of" always take plural pronouns.

> EXAMPLES   **Genetics** is **one** of those fields that seem to change and grow rapidly.
>
> Have you seen the **shears** since we used **them** to trim the hedges?

Many nouns, such as *athletics, ethics,* or *acoustics,* may be singular or plural.

> EXAMPLES   Is the **politics** of today's party really different from **that** of twenty years ago?
>
> His **politics** do not always make for smooth sailing, but **they** are never boring.

5w. Even when plural in form, the title of a creative work (such as a book, song, movie, or painting) or the name of a country or a city generally takes a singular pronoun.

The names of some organizations, though plural in form, may take singular or plural pronouns.

> EXAMPLES   ***Cats*** has a wonderful musical score; I could listen to **its** songs all day.
>
> The **Hebrides** are beautiful islands that welcome all **their** visitors.

EXERCISE In each of the following sentences, underline the noun with a plural form. Then, underline the pronoun in parentheses that agrees in number with the noun.

Example 1. <u>Mumps</u> can be a dangerous illness, especially when an adult has (*it*, *them*).

1. Gymnastics is such a great sport that we always try to watch (*it*, *them*) on television.

2. Which binoculars are being repaired, and when will (*it*, *they*) be ready?

3. Laces is a great roller-skating rink, and (*it*, *they*) has a cafe upstairs where we sit and watch people skate.

4. I washed my pajamas with something that was purple, and now (*it*, *they*) are purple, too.

5. My favorite class this term is economics because (*it*, *they*) helps me understand business and finance.

6. Alyson bought new shorts for summer camp but forgot to take (*it*, *them*) with her.

7. How do my sleeves turn (*itself*, *themselves*) inside out while going through the washer and dryer?

8. The news (*themselves*, *itself*) reports more information about technology than before.

9. *The Ways of My Grandmothers*, by Beverly Hungry Wolf, seems as though (*it*, *they*) might be a book I would enjoy reading.

10. If a summons is delivered to you, be sure to read (*it*, *them*) very carefully.

Gender and Number of Relative Pronouns

5x. The gender and number of a relative pronoun (such as *who, which,* or *that*) is determined by its antecedent.

> **EXAMPLES**   Each **boy who** needs **his** room assignment should not leave the registration area.
> The new **girl** at school, **who** drives **her** brother to junior high, seems friendly.
> The **birds that** flew just above our heads to **their** nests are purple martins.

EXERCISE In each of the following sentences, underline the pronoun in parentheses that agrees with its antecedent.

Example 1. What can you get for a brother who spends every cent on (*his, their*) stamp collection?

1. The oceanographers, who explained (*their, its*) work, had visited our diving club before.

2. A young mother who is proud of (*its, her*) new baby plans to have several pictures taken.

3. Have you seen my magazine, which somehow has lost (*its, her*) cover?

4. He sent me old jokes that had (*their, his*) punch lines revised.

5. Enrique will look for an employer who offers (*its, his or her*) employees challenging work.

6. All library books that are missing (*their, its*) checkout cards must have new cards typed.

7. Robin invited the new family who just moved into (*his or her, their*) house to join us.

8. Icicles glittered like diamonds that had scattered (*its, their*) crystal fragments along the roof's edge.

9. Uncle Charles was the one who managed not to spend (*their, his*) money.

10. Campers who wander away from (*their, his or her*) tents at night may get lost.

11. Ari and Julia have a friend who will tell us about (*his, their*) experiences as an army nurse.

12. Could someone explain the number system that uses four as (*their, its*) base?

13. Give others who have not gotten (*his or her, their*) room keys some space to line up over there.

14. The picture frame that has cracks in (*their, its*) glass should be recycled for a craft project.

15. In our office, many of the desks that lost some of (*its, their*) parts are being replaced.

16. This is the electric pencil sharpener that needs (*its, their*) cord replaced.

17. For our next meeting, bring a book that has not lost (*its, his or her*) adventure for you.

18. Did you travel to countries that are strict about (*its, their*) customs duties?

19. One of our flight attendants was a woman who had just completed (*her, their*) botany degree.

20. Marlys is someone who is generous toward (*her, his or her*) friends.

Expression of an Amount

5y. An expression of an amount (a measurement, a percentage, or a fraction, for example) may be singular or plural, depending on how it is used.

EXAMPLES   **Four fifths** of the blackberry cobbler is gone, indicating **it** was quite tasty.
Six yards had better be enough fabric because **it** is the last of the bolt.

EXERCISE   For each of the following sentences, underline the pronoun in parentheses that agrees with its antecedent.

Example 1. Half the vendors decided (*it, they*) would reduce prices by 30 percent.

1. Fifteen hundred rocks made a sturdy wall when we stacked (*it, them*) securely.

2. Four pints of blood were requested so (*they, it*) could be used during the emergency surgery.

3. This glass holds eight ounces of cool lemonade; (*it, they*) is enough to be refreshing.

4. Add three cups of flour, and mix (*them, it*) well with the other ingredients.

5. If you put four drops of each scent on the dried leaves in the batch of potpourri, (*their, its*) aroma will spread throughout the entire batch.

6. The diagnostic test might require thirty minutes; (*they, that*) should be plenty of time.

7. Two or three dollars should cover the cost; have you got (*them, it*)?

8. One hundred yards is the length of a football field; (*they, it*) can also be the distance of a race.

9. One third of the employees accepted the overtime workload that was offered to (*it, them*).

10. Hand me three or four inches of tape; I need (*it, them*) to hold this sign in place.

11. Fifty thousand miles are useful if the traveler can convert (*it, them*) to frequent-flyer miles.

12. All hikers carried two liters of water; (*they, it*) would help prevent dehydration.

13. Mom likes to put a half pound of coconut in fruit salad because (*they, it*) can add a nice flavor.

14. Kathy donated one hundred dollars; (*they, it*) will be used to buy coats and gloves.

15. Two yards of fabric is all May will need; we'll buy (*it, them*) for her tomorrow.

16. Since sixty-five percent of the students voted, (*it, they*) should be happy with the results.

17. Five sixths of the cartons of berries quickly sold; (*it, they*) cost much less than normal.

18. Ten cents doesn't buy very much these days; (*it, they*) used to be the price of a phone call.

19. If you put four fifths of those raisins into the dough, you might as well add (*them, it*) all.

20. Weather forecasters had predicted we would get up to three inches of rain; because (*it, they*) fell slowly and could soak in, the vegetation and wildlife benefited greatly.

Review A: **Subject-Verb Agreement**

EXERCISE A   In the following sentences, if a subject and verb do not agree, draw a line through the incorrect verb and write the correct verb above it. If a sentence is already correct, write C next to the number.

Example   **1.** Katherine Anne Porter's *The Days Before* ~~were~~ *was* published in 1952.

1. Her *Flowering Judas,* a 1930 book of short stories, are still read.

2. All but one of her books, *Hacienda: A Story of Mexico,* has been purchased by our library.

3. Not a single one of her books remain on the library shelves very long.

4. Both "Noon Wine" and "Pale Horse, Pale Rider" was praised by critics.

5. There is several possible explanations for her outstanding reputation.

6. Neither poetic sensibility nor psychological insight are in short supply.

7. All but one or two of my relatives admires her.

8. Almost everyone who has read Porter feels she deserved the Pulitzer Prize.

9. A great deal of her insight and talent are apparent in *Ship of Fools.*

10. Porter always cared about human relationships; each of her books prove this point.

EXERCISE B   In the following sentences, if a subject and verb do not agree, draw a line through the incorrect verb and write the correct verb above it. If a sentence is already correct, write C next to the number.

Example   **1.** George R. Stewart's *Names on the Land* ~~describe~~ *describes* how places in the United States were named.

11. Stewart's book about place names are a classic in its field.

12. Place names, which often show a great deal of imagination, has attracted increasing interest.

13. Every small village, stream, and pond needs a name.

14. There is a great many place names that come from American Indian words.

15. Some of the most familiar American Indian names, such as *Utah,* was originally derived from the names of indigenous groups.

16. A list of United States cities show the Spanish influence.

17. Both *Los Angeles* and *San Francisco* comes from Spanish.

18. Each of the two largest cities in Texas is named after a politician.

19. A number of place names in the United States is the same as European place names.

20. Many cities, especially in the East, carries names of European cities such as London or Paris.

Review B: Pronoun-Antecedent Agreement

USAGE

EXERCISE A In the following sentences, if a pronoun and its antecedent do not agree, draw a line through the incorrect pronoun and write the correct pronoun above it. If a sentence is already correct, write C above the number.

                                   his or her

Example 1. Each of the candidates ignored ~~their~~ prepared speech.

1. If anyone has a sure test for political honesty, they should divulge it.

2. It is said that every society gets the politicians it deserves.

3. Everyone planning to vote should be on their guard against glib generalizations and promises.

4. If any of the candidates remained silent before the election, would he do the electorate a disservice?

5. In an election year, all of the voters should think for himself or herself and vote as wisely as possible.

6. Both Cholanda and Dee Dee gave her ten-minute talks on trees.

7. If more of the visitors would like to see an American elm, he or she should go with Cholanda.

8. Not one of the girls identified their gray-birch leaf correctly.

9. If anyone intends to go on a nature hike, they should watch out for poisonous snakes.

10. A poisonous snake can usually be identified by either their color pattern or their head shape.

EXERCISE B In the following sentences, if a pronoun and its antecedent do not agree, draw a line through the incorrect pronoun and write the correct pronoun above it.

                               their

Example 1. Chad, Ricky, Jerry, and Stu brought ~~his~~ baseballs and catcher's mitts to practice today.

11. The movie listings are easier to read since its format was updated.

12. To see which electives she liked, every term Terri took as many courses as they could.

13. New computer technology creates their own market for used equipment.

14. A freezing rain can either help or harm trees and the plants around it.

15. Neither Amy nor Danielle has brought their lunch to school today.

16. Usually, a postmarked envelope will reveal which post office first handled them.

17. Looking around the backyard, Harold thought of a design for their brother's treehouse.

18. Students attending the special lecture on fossils should bring his or her notebooks.

19. Every week Miranda writes several entries in their personal journal.

20. Arlen will no longer be walking everywhere after getting a car of his or her own.

Review C: Subject-Verb and Pronoun-Antecedent Agreement

EXERCISE A In the following sentences, if a subject and verb or a pronoun and its antecedent do not agree, draw a line through each incorrect word and write the correct word above it.

Example 1. A pollster called my friend's family today, but ~~it~~ *they* could not be reached.

1. Neither the questions asked nor the answers given was conclusive or brilliant.

2. When is such attempts to learn national views wholly reliable?

3. Every opinion poll question a small sample of people.

4. These people is considered to be representative.

5. Is my family's opinions better than those of another family?

6. Neither a sample of fifty Democrats nor that of fifty Republicans are representative.

7. Modern sampling techniques tries to guard against biased or unreliable sampling.

8. Even the pollster, a person who conducts polls, admit that polling is an inexact science.

9. Who speaks for the registered voters who may or may not cast his votes?

10. Polls and predictions have its value but also its shortcomings.

EXERCISE B In the following sentences, if a subject and verb do not agree, draw a line through each incorrect word and write the correct word above it.

Example 1. Several of my friends ~~likes~~ *like* to read mystery stories.

11. The author that Juanita and her brother favors is Agatha Christie.

12. Edgar Allan Poe's "The Murders in the Rue Morgue" were the world's first detective story.

13. In fact, Poe's hero C. Auguste Dupin—not Sherlock Holmes or any of his contemporaries— were the original fictional detective.

14. One of Dupin's cases, like some of Miss Marple's, are solved by armchair investigation.

15. Poe introduced elements, such as the locked room, that was used by many later writers.

16. Juanita don't like the later, hard-boiled stories as much as the ones that are more like puzzles.

17. She claims that neither a clever lawyer nor a wisecracking detective are as satisfactory a hero as Miss Marple.

18. It is amazing how many detective heroes has been created over the years.

19. Sherlock Holmes, whose adventures still have appeal, are one of the most popular.

20. Dupin and Holmes, as well as Marple, has a firm place in the history of detective fiction.

Review D: Subject-Verb and Pronoun-Antecedent Agreement

USAGE

EXERCISE A In the following sentences, if a subject and verb or a pronoun and its antecedent do not agree, draw a line through each incorrect word and write the correct word above it.

Example 1. Barbecued chicken, as well as baked potatoes and salad, ~~were~~ *was* served at the dinner.

1. Everyone has their reason for choosing to drive certain models of cars.

2. Her passport, together with her business papers, were taken from her room.

3. In recent years there has been many changes in methods of farming.

4. Five hundred words are a good length for your next writing assignment.

5. Genetics are a branch of biology that deals with the heredity and variation of organisms.

6. My great-great-grandmother were a close friend of a Blackfoot named Mokakin.

7. I heard him say that a pair of scissors were lying on the counter.

8. The news that you told us are quite distressing.

9. The words that someone uses in daily conversation tell a great deal about their background.

10. Each of the players feel that Coach Smith deserves to win the award.

EXERCISE B In the following sentences, if a subject and verb or a pronoun and its antecedent do not agree, draw a line through each incorrect word and write the correct word above it.

Example 1. Neither Alma nor Cobb ~~were~~ *was* at home.

11. There's two notebooks and a backpack lying on the table.

12. If either Theo or Kishi are having difficulty with the trigonometry problems, I can help.

13. Every teacher and student seem to be looking forward to hearing next week's guest speaker.

14. Mathematics, one of my favorite subjects, are not a requirement for this computer course.

15. If you have any questions, remember that either Lili or Roberto know about computers.

16. Neither of the Wilson brothers expect to be drafted by a major-league team this year.

17. All of these computer courses requires a familiarity with the basic functions of a computer.

18. Everyone in the class completed their project on time.

19. Has any of the witnesses been sworn in yet?

20. Asthma, like other respiratory diseases, are made worse when the air quality is poor.

for **CHAPTER 5: AGREEMENT**   *pages 96–117*

Proofreading Application: Movie Review

Good writers are generally good proofreaders. Readers tend to admire and trust writing that is error-free. Make sure that you correct all errors in grammar, usage, spelling, and punctuation in your writing. Your readers will have more confidence in your words if you have done your best to proofread carefully.

PROOFREADING ACTIVITY

In everyday conversation, you probably hear examples of nonstandard English usage, such as "Everyone wants to take their own car." However, in standard English usage, the pronoun *their* should be *his* or *her* to agree with *Everyone*. When you create a formal piece of writing, you should follow the rules of standard English.

In the following rough draft of a movie review, find and correct the errors in agreement. Use proofreading symbols to make your corrections.

Example Watching movies ~~are~~ *is* my favorite pastime.

Probably two thirds of my leisure time are spent at the movies. Now that I've made this confession, aren't every one of you dying to know the best movie I've seen lately?

Well, none of the other adventure movies I've seen was as exciting as *The Adventures of Olaf*. The plot, which features a few twists and turns, are fast paced and captivating. Here's the basics: Many of the Viking warriors wants to prove that their way of fighting is the best. Olaf's own fighting tactics demonstrates how he refuses to accept tradition. Each of his techniques are almost a slap in the face to the old guard. Near the conclusion, it's evident that neither the old style nor Olaf's innovative style are sufficient by themselves to defeat the Vikings' enemies, who is constantly attacking them. The warrior band soon realize that its surest way to victories lie in blending the old and the new.

I have only one more thing to say: Don't miss *The Adventures of Olaf*. You can catch them at the Varsity Theater until March 22.

Language and Sentence Skills Practice

Literary Model: Novel

Moby-Dick was now again steadily swimming forward; and had almost passed the ship— **[1]** which thus far had been sailing in the contrary direction to **[2]** him, though for the present **[3]** her headway had been stopped. **[4]** He seemed swimming with **[5]** his utmost velocity, and now only intent upon pursuing **[6]** his own straight path in the sea. Setting sail to the rising wind, the lonely boat was swiftly impelled to leeward, by both oars and canvas. And at last when Ahab was sliding by the vessel, so near as plainly to distinguish Starbuck's face as he leaned over the rail, he hailed him to turn the vessel about, and follow him, not too swiftly, at a judicious interval.

—Herman Melville, *Moby-Dick*

EXERCISE A   Identify the antecedent of each of the numbered pronouns in the passage.

1. which _____

2. him _____

3. her _____

4. He _____

5. his _____

6. his _____

What pronoun, other than the feminine singular *her*, might Melville have selected for agreement in item 3?

_____

EXERCISE B   Read the final sentence in the passage and identify the antecedent for the pronouns.

1. Who leaned over the rail? _____

2. Who is to be followed? _____

3. Explain whether you think the pronoun antecedents in this sentence are as easily identified as those in the beginning of the passage. _____

_____

4. What impact would familiarity with the previous paragraphs have on antecedent clarity?

_____

Literary Model (continued)

EXERCISE C In a paragraph, describe a scene in which you and a friend are participating in sports or in a performing art, and at which family members are spectators. Attempt to use pronouns, avoiding nouns altogether, to refer to any of these people. Write on every other line, so that you will have room to edit.

_____

_____

_____

_____

_____

_____

_____

_____

_____

_____

_____

_____

_____

_____

_____

EXERCISE D Read the paragraph you just wrote, changing pronouns to nouns where they are needed and double-checking for any new agreement issues.

Explain the reasons for the changes you made to your paragraph. What effect or effects do these changes have on the clarity or the readability of your description? Be specific.

_____

_____

_____

_____

Writing Application: Speech

Most of us use gendered pronouns and indefinite pronouns so casually in speech that we easily slip into agreement problems in writing. You will sometimes hear even professional speakers use the pronoun "they" to agree with an indefinite pronoun like "everybody," but you should avoid this casual and informal habit in formal writing.

INFORMAL	Did somebody forget their car keys?
FORMAL	Did somebody forget his or her car keys?

WRITING ACTIVITY

Parents' night is coming up at your school, and you have been chosen to make a presentation. Your job is to cover, in a speech of three or four minutes, an annual school event that represents your class's interests and abilities. As you speak, you will use pronouns to refer to participating students. Make sure that all the pronouns agree with their antecedents in gender and number.

PREWRITING Review the events of the year thus far so that you can choose the event that best represents your class's spirit. Once you have decided on an event, list details about it. Interview students who participated, or check records, to fill in any gaps in your recollection of the event.

WRITING Preparing a speech requires special attention to your audience. The parents want to know about their students' school experience, but you will need to hold their attention with a quick pace, lively word choice, and perhaps touches of humor. Parents will want to hear their children's names, too.

REVISING Readers can backtrack and re-read a passage that puzzles them, but listeners cannot. Your presentation must be clear. Ask several friends to form a mock audience. Practice your speech two or three times for them, and listen to their feedback. They should be able to follow your speech without having to stop you for clarification.

PUBLISHING Check your speech for errors in spelling and punctuation. Your audience will not see these problems, of course, but the errors may cause you to hesitate in an otherwise smooth speech. Check each pronoun-antecedent pair for correct agreement. Then, with your teacher's permission, present your speech in front of the class.

EXTENDING YOUR WRITING

You may wish to develop your speech into a longer article. You and your classmates could publish a newsletter designed to keep parents informed about school happenings. You could also contact your city's newspaper about publishing your report. Many newspapers have sections devoted to students' achievements and activities, and seeing your own name in print is great inspiration for future writing!

Choices: Exploring Pronouns

The following activities challenge you to find a connection between pronouns and the world around you. Do the activity below that suits your personality best, and then share your discoveries with your class.

ETYMOLOGY

Close Relatives

Look up the word *nominative*. What is its root word? Brainstorm as many words as you can that share this same root word. Use each one in a sentence. Then, create a poster. Write the root word in the center and create a chart showing how each of the words you brainstormed relates to the root word. With your teacher's permission, display your poster in the classroom.

CONTEST

Top This!

Those elliptical clauses can be tricky. Take, for instance, *He liked the movie more than her.* Does this sentence mean that she didn't like the movie as much as he did or that he liked the movie more than he liked her? Oops! These elliptical clauses can be interpreted in a different way than they are intended if the pronouns are in the wrong case. Write a few of these confusing sentences. Then, challenge your classmates to top them! Make a poster out of the best and funniest examples.

RESEARCH

Mi Jamaica!

The beautiful and fascinating language of Caribbean Creole has its own way of handling pronouns. Creole dispenses with nominative and objective case first-person distinctions. It just uses *mi* for both cases and possessive as well. However, in Barbados and Trinidad, Creole speakers still use singular and plural second-person pronouns. Do some research on Caribbean Creole. (*The Oxford Companion to the English Language* would be a good reference. A Caribbean friend would be even better.) If possible, ask a Creole speaker to explain how Creole uses pronouns. Report your findings to your class, and be sure to include a number of written examples of Caribbean Creole's use of pronouns.

SURVEY

The Hit Parade

Which pronoun is most common in ordinary conversation? With the permission of the people involved, tape-record several conversations. Then, count the number of times each personal pronoun is used. Which personal pronoun is used the most often in your experiment? Which pronouns are most often used incorrectly? Which ones are most often used correctly? Present the class with an ordered listing of your results. Include your opinions on why these results may have occurred.

BUILDING BACKGROUND KNOWLEDGE

Thee and *Thine*

Some pronouns that are no longer in general use still retain a special place in the lives of English-speaking peoples. These pronouns may be found in ritual language. Ritual language finds its greatest expression in religious rites and events. Find examples of some of these almost obsolete pronouns. Begin by making a list of them. Then, find texts still used today that feature these special pronouns. Report your findings to your classmates in a short presentation.

BOOK REPORT

Read All About It

Believe it or not, there are quite a few books that discuss the history of the English language. One of them, *The Story of English*, hit the bestseller list a few years ago. There was even a PBS television series based on this fascinating work. Find a copy of this book in a library, and read the parts about pronouns. Then, tell the class what you have learned.

Language and Sentence Skills Practice   **133**

USAGE

Case

Case is the form that a noun or a pronoun takes to show its relationship to other words in a sentence. In English, there are three cases: *nominative, objective,* and *possessive.*

SINGULAR	NOMINATIVE	OBJECTIVE	POSSESSIVE
FIRST PERSON	I	me	my, mine
SECOND PERSON	you	you	your, yours
THIRD PERSON	he, she, it	him, her, it	his, her, hers, its
PLURAL			
FIRST PERSON	we	us	our, ours
SECOND PERSON	you	you	your, yours
THIRD PERSON	they	them	their, theirs

EXERCISE A In each of the following sentences, identify the person and case of the underlined personal pronoun by writing above the pronoun *F* for *first person, S* for *second person,* or *T* for *third person.* Then, write *N* for *nominative case, O* for *objective case,* or *P* for *possessive case.*

                    T–N

Example 1. Paula and she worked together on the Asimov report.

1. Isaac Asimov left Russia as a young child, and he came to the United States.

2. As a boy, Asimov spent a lot of time at his father's candy store.

3. At first, Asimov's father would not let him read the magazines on the candy-store racks.

4. Asimov enjoyed reading them, especially the science fiction magazines.

5. They inspired Asimov to write his own science fiction stories.

6. Later, as an established writer, he wrote more than two hundred books.

7. He wrote *Foundation,* a series of short stories with their plots set in a futuristic society.

8. In my opinion, one of his best stories is "Nightfall."

9. I read that some consider it the best science fiction story of all time.

10. What is your opinion of that story?

EXERCISE B On the line in each of the following sentences, write the pronoun indicated in parentheses.

Example *(third person plural, objective)* **1.** Show _____them_____ where we keep supplies.

(first person plural, possessive) **11.** On Tuesday we will cast _____ votes.

(second person singular, nominative) **12.** Have _____ decided on a film?

(third person singular, possessive) **13.** Anna hasn't made up _____ mind yet.

(third person plural, possessive) **14.** The candidates have made _____ speeches.

(first person plural, nominative) **15.** _____ have many qualified candidates.

Nominative Case A

6a.   The subject of a verb should be in the nominative case.

    EXAMPLES   Indira went to the art museum before **we** did.

                  He, she, and **I** saw an exhibit of paintings by Seurat.

6b.   A predicate nominative should be in the nominative case.

    EXAMPLES   The captain of the team is **he.**

                  Will the winner of the race be Mia or **she**?

EXERCISE A   In each of the following sentences, underline the personal pronoun in parentheses that correctly completes the sentence. Then, identify the pronoun's use by writing on the line provided *S* for *subject of the verb* or *PN* for *predicate nominative*.

Example   _PN_   **1.** Mr. Liu was (*he*, *him*) who explained that story so well.

_____ **1.** Carlos and (*he*, *him*) called last night from Cedar Rapids.

_____ **2.** Either Lola or (*I*, *me*) will be the starting pitcher in tomorrow's game.

_____ **3.** The woman who was awarded the leading role was (*her*, *she*).

_____ **4.** The one who accidentally left the door unlocked may have been (*I*, *me*).

_____ **5.** Neither Sally nor (*he*, *him*) can attend the conference.

_____ **6.** The most successful contestants were (*us*, *we*).

_____ **7.** If the players had been (*they*, *them*), the results would have been quite different.

_____ **8.** The person knocking at the door will probably be (*she*, *her*).

_____ **9.** You and (*me*, *I*) have really contributed to the success of the fund drive.

_____ **10.** In the morning, Dana and (*they*, *them*) will begin the long trip back.

EXERCISE B   In each of the following sentences, replace the underlined word or words by writing an appropriate pronoun above it.

Example   **1.** The person knocking at the door was David. *(he)*

11. Muriel and three other people will meet us at the game.

12. Every weekend, John and the rest of the band practice in a garage.

13. The first speaker will be Tracy.

14. My classmates and I have all signed up to see the touring production of *The Fantasticks*.

15. The team that was awarded the first prize in the tournament was our team.

USAGE

Nominative Case B

| **6a.** | The subject of a verb should be in the nominative case. |

> **EXAMPLES** Lin said that **she** watched two movies this weekend.
> **They** and I finally agreed on a plan of action.

| **6b.** | A predicate nominative should be in the nominative case. |

> **EXAMPLES** The third person from the left in this photograph is **I**.
> Will the next person to receive that offer be Michelle or **she**?

EXERCISE A In each of the following sentences, underline the personal pronoun in parentheses that correctly completes the sentence. Then, on the line before the sentence, identify the pronoun's use by writing S for *subject of the verb* or PN for *predicate nominative*.

Example __PN__ **1.** Is it true that the committee leaders are Johnetta and (*he*, *him*)?

_____ **1.** During the snowstorm, Perry and (*he*, *him*) helped stranded motorists.

_____ **2.** Before long, either Alonzo or (*I*, *me*) will be the master chef of our class.

_____ **3.** Richard or (*she*, *her*) will be elected the student council secretary.

_____ **4.** Would the person you contacted have been Larry or (*I*, *me*)?

_____ **5.** Neither Peggy nor (*he*, *him*) was working behind the counter at the bake sale.

_____ **6.** Among the most satisfied customers at the library benefit were (*us*, *we*).

_____ **7.** If the guests had been (*they*, *them*), would you have responded differently?

_____ **8.** The next time the alarm sounds, the person to turn if off will probably be (*she*, *her*).

_____ **9.** You and (*I*, *me*) will be meeting my favorite author, Virginia Driving Hawk Sneve.

_____ **10.** In two years, Matt and (*they*, *them*) will return to this area to look for fossils.

EXERCISE B On the line provided in each of the following sentences, write a nominative-case personal pronoun that correctly completes the sentence. Then, identify the pronoun's use by writing above it S for *subject* or PN for *predicate nominative*.

Example 1. After a week, the team that had done best was Meg and ____*he*____.

11. In four days, Chris and _____ will be leaving for their first semester at college.

12. The student who finished the chemistry test first was _____.

13. Neither Viola nor _____ had planned to stay after school for so long.

14. It must have been _____ who accidentally left the door unlocked.

15. If the other candidate had been _____ the results would have been quite different.

Objective Case A

6c. A direct object should be in the objective case.

    EXAMPLE After hearing the score, I called Luanne and **them.**

6d. An indirect object should be in the objective case.

    EXAMPLE The doctor gave **her** some good advice.

6e. An object of a preposition should be in the objective case.

    EXAMPLE This is a secret between **us.**

EXERCISE In each of the following sentences, underline the personal pronoun in parentheses that correctly completes the sentence. Then, on the line before the sentence, identify the pronoun's use by writing *DO* for *direct object,* *IO* for *indirect object,* or *OP* for *object of a preposition.*

Example __*OP*__ **1.** The best auto mechanics in town work for (she, *her*).

_____ **1.** Erica brought (*we, us*) a pot of geraniums.

_____ **2.** The play was written by my sister and (*she, her*).

_____ **3.** They invited Rafael and (*he, him*) to the conference.

_____ **4.** The costumes fit Margo and (*she, her*) perfectly.

_____ **5.** Silas bought tickets for you and (*I, me*).

_____ **6.** My parents offered Shanta and (*they, them*) a ride to the game.

_____ **7.** Show (*we, us*) photos of your trip to Puerto Rico.

_____ **8.** To (*she, her*), the best song in the musical was the big production number.

_____ **9.** Please save Gloria and (*I, me*) two seats in the balcony.

_____ **10.** Will the manager employ Dan and (*they, them*) on a part-time basis?

_____ **11.** Freddy has saved (*we, us*) a week's worth of research in the library.

_____ **12.** The center was assisted on the goal by my brother and (*he, him*).

_____ **13.** Would they invite Donetta and (*she, her*) to dinner and a movie?

_____ **14.** That dry cleaner's work pleases Bonita and (*she, her*).

_____ **15.** Nancy saved some of the salad and baked chicken for you and (*I, me*).

_____ **16.** Referees asked the trainers and (*they, them*) for a stretcher.

_____ **17.** Tell (*we, us*) the best place to find CDs and tapes these days.

_____ **18.** For (*she, her*), each moment seemed an eternity as she waited on the snowy sidewalk.

_____ **19.** Mom bought Miriam and (*I, me*) new gloves for our birthdays.

_____ **20.** Each of us asked Serge and (*they, them*) about helping to put up carnival booths.

Objective Case B

6c.	A direct object should be in the objective case.

     EXAMPLE The captain chose **him** for the goalie.

6d.	An indirect object should be in the objective case.

     EXAMPLE The teacher gave Sharon and **him** next week's assignments.

6e.	An object of a preposition should be in the objective case.

     EXAMPLE Have you shown this to **her** for her approval?

EXERCISE A On the line before each of the following sentences, write the correct form of the underlined pronoun if it is incorrect. If the underlined pronoun is already correct, write *C*.

Example __*her*__ **1.** Is this the only letter for she this week?

_____ **1.** Ms. Osaki verified the story for Donald and I.

_____ **2.** Please notify Paula or he about your decision.

_____ **3.** George gave us the idea for the theme of the banquet.

_____ **4.** My uncle told Jim and I the story of his experiences in Korea.

_____ **5.** The coach ordered new uniforms for the halfbacks and we.

_____ **6.** In addition to Pete and she, who helped to set up chairs?

_____ **7.** No one has offered to wash the car in place of they.

_____ **8.** The counselor will see Miyuki and she tomorrow.

_____ **9.** Add Jocelyn, Dirk, and I to your list for the field trip.

_____ **10.** Mr. Gardner congratulated him for answering the most difficult problem.

EXERCISE B On the line provided in each of the following sentences, write an objective-case personal pronoun that correctly completes the sentence. Then, identify the pronoun's use by writing above it *DO* for *direct object*, *IO* for *indirect object*, or *OP* for *object of a preposition*.

Example 1. How do aquifers collect water for us and ___*them*___ in our wells?
                                                 OP

11. Margie and Seth will be going hiking and camping with _____.

12. Please give _____ the first opportunity to buy that car from you.

13. Debate topics had been chosen at random for them and _____.

14. I have an early departure time for tomorrow's trip with _____.

15. Since Jani is our foreign exchange student, Harriet, Jack, and I would like to introduce

     _____ to the class.

USAGE

Nominative and Objective Case Pronouns

6a. The subject of a verb should be in the nominative case.

6b. A predicate nominative should be in the nominative case.

6c. A direct object should be in the objective case.

6d. An indirect object should be in the objective case.

6e. An object of a preposition should be in the objective case.

EXAMPLES **He** and **I** have finished writing our skit. [subjects]

The first one across the line will be either Juana or **she.** [predicate nominative]

For the team leaders, the group selected Tina and **me.** [direct object]

Please send **him** and **her** the invitations. [indirect objects]

Hand your forms to **him** or **her.** [objects of a preposition]

EXERCISE On the line provided in each of the following sentences, write a personal pronoun that correctly completes the sentence. Then, identify the pronoun's use by writing above it S for *subject of the verb,* PN for *predicate nominative,* DO for *direct object,* IO for *indirect object,* or OP for *object of a preposition.*

Example 1. Studying eighteenth-century silversmiths, I discovered that not all of ____*them*____ (OP)

were men.

1. A number of women participated in this trade, as _____ had for hundreds of years.

2. Elizabeth Godfrey applied the popular rococo styling to French tea containers and also gave

_____ a touch of Oriental influence.

3. I wonder how long she worked to decorate _____ with such great detail.

4. One of the three most important female silversmiths to register her mark was _____.

5. Because her family was famous in the silversmith trade, the craft was everywhere around

_____ at home.

6. Among the French Huguenots fleeing to England were her family and _____.

7. Together, _____ exerted great influence on the craft in England during the 1700s.

8. In 1731, Godfrey registered her married name, Elizabeth Buteaux, as her silver mark and

incorporated _____ into her designs.

9. After 1741, she entered the last phase of her career; during that time, _____ was an

independent silversmith.

10. Since her tea containers were both elaborate and elegant, she probably sold _____ to

many of the mid-eighteenth-century gentry.

USAGE

Possessive Case

| **6f.** | The possessive pronouns *mine, yours, his, hers, its, ours,* and *theirs* are used in the same ways that the pronouns in the nominative and objective cases are used. |

SUBJECT	Both Jim's sister and **yours** are in the show.
PREDICATE NOMINATIVE	That coat is **mine.**
DIRECT OBJECT	The waiter brought **hers** right away.
INDIRECT OBJECT	The judge looked at my paper carefully, but only gave **his** a glance.
OBJECT OF A PREPOSITION	Diego's speech comes after Sue's and **theirs.**

| **6g.** | The possessive pronouns *my, your, his, her, its, our,* and *their* are used to modify nouns. |

EXAMPLES   I think **her** story was well written.

Its ending really surprised me.

| **6h.** | A noun or pronoun that precedes a gerund should be in the possessive case. |

EXAMPLE   I praised Leon for **his** editing of my poem. [*His* modifies the gerund *editing*.]

EXERCISE   In each of the following sentences, underline the pronoun in parentheses that completes the sentence correctly.

Example 1. As expected, *(him, his)* singing made quite a bit of difference in our choir.

1. It rained, despite *(his, him)* forecasting fair weather for the weekend.

2. Fred's speech was slightly better than *(my, mine)*.

3. I'm tired of *(you, your)* borrowing my clothes without asking.

4. I saw *(him, his)* sleeping in study hall!

5. My graduation is tomorrow, but I don't know the date of *(her, hers)*.

6. *(You, Your)* shouting really bothers me when I have a headache.

7. I hope that on *(your, yours)* trip to Texas you will have many wonderful experiences.

8. *(Our, Ours)* is the last house on the right, just before the stoplight.

9. You can ride in our car since we still have plenty of room and *(their, theirs)* is full.

10. Please don't keep *(them, their)* waiting by the side of the road.

Case Forms A

Case is the form that a noun or a pronoun takes to show its relationship to other words in a sentence.

	NOMINATIVE	OBJECTIVE	POSSESSIVE
SINGULAR			
FIRST PERSON	I	me	my, mine
SECOND PERSON	you	you	your, yours
THIRD PERSON	he, she, it	him, her, it	his, her, hers, its
PLURAL			
FIRST PERSON	we	us	our, ours
SECOND PERSON	you	you	your, yours
THIRD PERSON	they	them	their, theirs

EXERCISE In each of the following sentences, underline the personal pronoun in parentheses that correctly completes the sentence. Then, on the line before the sentence, identify the function of the pronoun by writing *S* for *subject, PN* for *predicate nominative, DO* for *direct object, IO* for *indirect object, OP* for *object of a preposition,* or *P* for *possessive.*

Example _____*P*_____ **1.** (*Her, Hers*) job, repairing dolls, has certainly made my little sister happy.

_____ **1.** What do the astronauts do when (*they, them*) hear that a mission has been delayed?

_____ **2.** Ellen Walker Craig-Jones served Urbancrest, Ohio, as (*it, its*) first black woman mayor from 1972 to 1975.

_____ **3.** (*Our, Ours*) touring City Hall was an excellent way to see the restoration work.

_____ **4.** All the Spanish club members agree that the person who brought the best dish with the easiest recipe was (*she, her*).

_____ **5.** If you sold Ryan a ticket for the dance, we will certainly see (*he, him*) there.

_____ **6.** We decided to surprise our grandparents and give (*they, them*) a week's vacation at the beach.

_____ **7.** (*I, Me*) helped clean up the meeting hall after the guest speaker had left.

_____ **8.** Many homemakers should thank Howard J. Morgens for (*him, his*) making such helpful products available for their homes.

_____ **9.** Where are the recipes of (*their, theirs*) for Southern-style grits and corn bread?

_____ **10.** Irving Berlin called Bernice Petkere the "Queen of Tin Pan Alley" for (*she, her*) talent for writing song lyrics.

Language and Sentence Skills Practice

USAGE

USAGE

Case Forms B

Case is the form that a noun or a pronoun takes to show its relationship to other words in a sentence.

	NOMINATIVE	OBJECTIVE	POSSESSIVE
FIRST PERSON	I, we	me, us	my, mine, our, ours
SECOND PERSON	you	you	your, yours
THIRD PERSON	he, she, it, they	him, her, it, them	his, her, hers, its, their, theirs

EXERCISE A In each of the following sentences, underline the personal pronoun in parentheses that correctly completes the sentence. Then, on the line before the sentence, identify the function of the pronoun by writing *S* for *subject*, *PN* for *predicate nominative*, *DO* for *direct object*, *IO* for *indirect object*, *OP* for *object of a preposition*, or *P* for *possessive*.

Example __*IO*__ **1.** We asked *(they, them)* three questions.

_____ **1.** *(Her, Hers)* was a job that no one else wanted to attempt.

_____ **2.** The first and last people we see on the commuter train each day are *(they, them)*.

_____ **3.** *(He, Him)* watches the baby for an hour each morning and afternoon.

_____ **4.** Paying bills on time benefits your credit rating; that keeps *(it, its)* in A-plus shape.

_____ **5.** How often have you told *(we, us)* the story about helping stranded motorists?

_____ **6.** Since we talked with *(he, him)*, the weather has gotten much worse.

_____ **7.** What a surprise to learn that the birthday party honorees were *(we, us)*!

_____ **8.** Barbara always treats *(they, them)* as if they are her best buddies.

_____ **9.** Please return these library books for *(I, me)* today.

_____ **10.** The cheerleader said, "Everyone stand up and give *(we, us)* one more 'Win!'"

EXERCISE B On the line provided in each of the following sentences, write a personal pronoun that correctly completes the sentence. Then, identify the pronoun's case by writing above it *N* for *nominative case*, *O* for *objective case*, or *P* for *possessive case*.

Example 1. The opposing band watched ____*us*____ practicing before the competition began.

11. Wild winds whipped tree branches and tore _____ from the tree trunks.

12. Of all my friends, the only one I trust with my secrets is _____.

13. Any time you want to speak up and help _____ explain this, please do.

14. _____ power walking seems to have increased Tim's level of endurance.

15. The voters considered all the candidates and decided that the best one was _____.

USAGE

Pronouns as Appositives

| **6i.** | A pronoun used as an appositive is in the same case as the word to which it refers. |

EXAMPLES   The contestants, **Pete** and **I,** received prizes. [*Pete* and the pronoun *I* are in the nominative case because they identify the subject *contestants*.]

The television quiz show gave prizes to the contestants, **Pete** and **me.** [*Pete* and the pronoun *me* are in the objective case because they identify the object of the preposition, *contestants*.]

The pronouns *we* and *us* are sometimes used with noun appositives.

EXAMPLES   **We players** need new uniforms. [nominative case]

The school committee ordered new uniforms for **us players.** [objective case]

EXERCISE A   In each of the following sentences, underline the pronoun that completes the sentence correctly. Then, identify the pronoun's case by writing above it *N* for *nominative case* or *O* for *objective case*.

Example 1. Which trainers work with the football coaches, Mr. Riley and (they, *them*)?

1. My partners, (she, her) and Garth, will join us in a moment.

2. Reporters asked the team captains, Vance and (he, him), many questions.

3. The parade leaders were two police officers, Sergeant Tsao and (she, her).

4. Refreshments for the conference speakers were donated by (we, us) seniors.

5. It may have been (we, us) outfielders who left the equipment on the bus.

EXERCISE B   In each of the following sentences, draw a line through the pronoun that is used incorrectly. Then, write the correct form of the pronoun above the error.

Example 1. Mrs. Ruiz complimented us, Ted and ~~I~~, *me* on our report.

6. Both actors, Geena Davis and her, deserve to win the award.

7. The choir director gave special attention to we altos.

8. If us citizens don't work together, our efforts will not succeed.

9. Please give we comedians some respect during our performances.

10. Those people may have been your neighbors, Mrs. Wong and him.

USAGE

Pronouns in Elliptical Constructions

| **6j.** | A pronoun following *than* or *as* in an elliptical construction is in the same case as it would be if the construction were completed. |

> **ELLIPTICAL** Katya sings better **than I.**
>
> **COMPLETED** Katya sings better **than I sing.**

In an elliptical construction, be sure to use the case of the pronoun that expresses the meaning you intend.

> **NOMINATIVE CASE** Do you miss Hugo more **than I**? [Meaning: Do you miss Hugo more than *I miss Hugo*?]
>
> **OBJECTIVE CASE** Do you miss Hugo more **than me**? [Meaning: Do you miss Hugo more than *you miss me*?]

EXERCISE A In each of the following sentences, rewrite the elliptical construction to show the complete thought the speaker wishes to convey.

Example 1. You are a faster runner than he. _____*than he is fast*_____

1. She gave him more soup than us. _____

2. Few people have studied that subject as long as they. _____

3. Jewel helped Matt as much as me. _____

4. Did you receive as many valentines as she? _____

5. No one was happier than I. _____

EXERCISE B On the lines provided, change each sentence pair into a single sentence that contains an elliptical construction starting with *than* or *as* and ending with a pronoun.

Example 1. John has four brothers. I have three brothers. _*John has more brothers than I.*_

6. I like Helen. Franz likes Helen even more. _____

_____

7. I sold tickets. He sold fewer tickets. _____

8. He trusts me. He trusts Kathleen more. _____

_____

9. They helped her. We helped her just as much. _____

_____

10. She plays tennis. I play tennis less often. _____

_____

Reflexive and Intensive Pronouns

Reflexive pronouns and intensive pronouns (sometimes called *compound personal pronouns*) are identical in form, although they are used differently.

	SINGULAR	PLURAL
FIRST PERSON	myself	ourselves
SECOND PERSON	yourself	yourselves
THIRD PERSON	himself, herself, itself	themselves

REFLEXIVE	Hassan and Martha helped **themselves** to more soup.
INTENSIVE	I made this chair **myself.**

6k.   A pronoun ending in *–self* or *–selves* should not be used in place of a personal pronoun.

NONSTANDARD	Luisa bought tickets for herself and myself.
STANDARD	Luisa bought tickets for herself and **me.**

EXERCISE A   Complete each sentence below correctly by writing a reflexive or intensive pronoun on the line provided. Then, on the line before each sentence, write *R* for *reflexive pronoun* or *I* for *intensive pronoun.*

Example ____*R*____ **1.** I don't enjoy staying home all by _____*myself*_____.

_____ **1.** I made _____ some lunch.

_____ **2.** Gloria and Tanya made all the scenery _____.

_____ **3.** Please give _____ a pat on the back, Michael.

_____ **4.** If you don't mind, I'd like to walk home by _____.

_____ **5.** Only you, _____, are responsible for your actions.

EXERCISE B   In each of the following sentences, draw a line through the pronoun that is used incorrectly and write the correct form of the pronoun above it. If a sentence is already correct, write *C* after it.

Example 1. Jaime and ~~yourself~~ *you* should see the play tonight.

6. Clarissa and ourselves are holding a party.

7. He gave himself and myself a ride on the new scooter.

8. Don't call the plumber; I'll fix the faucet myself.

9. Thanks to yourself, the fund drive was a huge success.

10. She excused him and myself for being late.

Who and *Whom*

USAGE

Like most personal pronouns, the pronoun *who (whoever)* has three case forms. The form that the pronoun takes depends on its use in a subordinate clause or a question.

NOMINATIVE CASE	who	whoever
OBJECTIVE CASE	whom	whomever
POSSESSIVE CASE	whose	whosever

EXERCISE A In each of the following sentences, underline the pronoun that correctly completes the sentence. Then, indicate how the pronoun is used by writing above it *S* for *subject*, *PN* for *predicate nominative*, *DO* for *direct object*, or *OP* for *object of a preposition*.

Example 1. Do you know (*who, whom*) we should invite to speak during career week?

1. People (*who, whom*) live in glass houses shouldn't throw stones.

2. They were relatives to (*who, whom*) I had not spoken in years.

3. Will the factory manager only hire (*whoever, whomever*) is willing to work long hours?

4. Please come and meet the speaker (*who, whom*) I have hired for tonight's program.

5. Frankly, I'm not sure (*who, whom*) the best candidate for mayor is.

EXERCISE B In each of the following sentences, underline the relative pronoun that completes the sentence correctly. Then, indicate how the pronoun is used by writing above it *S* for *subject of the clause*, *PN* for *predicate nominative*, *DO* for *direct object*, *OP* for *object of a preposition*, or *P* for *possessive*.

Example 1. We should be able to recognize (*who, whom*) the governor is.

6. Eula, (*who, whom*) hadn't seen me in months, gave me a warm welcome.

7. The doctor (*who, whom*) I consulted listened intently as I spoke.

8. To (*who, whom*) did you send the invitation?

9. (*Who, Whose*) jacket is that still draped on the chair?

10. Do you know (*who, whom*) the inventor of the steam engine was?

Special Pronoun Problems

Rules 6i through 6k cover special pronoun problems. You may wish to review these rules before completing this worksheet.

AS AN APPOSITIVE	The winners, Shannon and **he,** move on to the next round.
IN AN ELLIPTICAL CLAUSE	Did Jorge score higher on the test than **I**?
WITHOUT REFLEXIVE PRONOUN	Karen wanted to give these to Fred and **you.** [not *yourself*]
WITH REFLEXIVE PRONOUN	We challenged **ourselves** to finish before dinner.
WHO AS SUBJECT	The man **who owns the store** is Mr. Saks.
WHOM AS OBJECT	A man **whom I know** owns a store.

EXERCISE Write a pronoun that correctly completes each of the following sentences. Then, indicate how the pronoun is used by writing above it *S* for *subject, PN* for *predicate nominative, DO* for *direct object, IO* for *indirect object, OP* for *object of a preposition, P* for *possessive,* or *A* for *appositive.*

Example 1. Have you given ___*them*___ the instructions for the final phase? [*IO* written above blank]

1. _____ might it have been calling so early on a Saturday morning?

2. Mom asked _____ why the hammer and saw were lying by the back door.

3. The coach presented the co-captains, Brad and _____, a special merit award.

4. Don't you think Teresa and I can finish cleaning up the kitchen by _____?

5. No one could have been more surprised by the movie's ending than _____.

6. Have you studied your notes and the chapters as much as _____?

7. Our clean-up day in the park went well because of _____ students participating.

8. To _____ did Chief Sitting Bull say that reservation life would destroy his people?

9. I was just wondering _____ you asked about getting paint for the stage props.

10. _____ is the only person volunteering for the book and magazine drive?

11. The authors of the play, Sharon and _____, are in the audience.

12. Gloria can run faster than _____.

13. We allowed _____ time to get to the airport.

14. The person _____ left the message will call back.

15. To _____ did you send the package?

16. The principal presented the award to the winners, Randall and _____.

17. Would _____ took the stapler from my desk please put it back?

18. Do the Baxters have a larger house than _____?

19. The manager gave the two painters, Jorge and _____, the day off.

20. Do not ask for _____ the bell tolls; it tolls for thee.

Review A: **Pronoun Forms**

EXERCISE A In each of the following sentences, underline the pronoun that completes the sentence correctly. Then, indicate the pronoun's case by writing above it *N* for *nominative case,* *O* for *objective case,* or *P* for *possessive case.*

Example 1. Can't we see the smoke of (*him,* <u>*his*</u>) campfire from here?   [*P*]

1. My friends and (*I, me*) decided to go to the museum.

2. Hisako's aunt drove (*she, her*) and Felicia to the game.

3. Our faculty advisor said that the decision was up to (*we, us*) students.

4. At first I didn't recognize (*her, hers*) float in the parade.

5. In charge of the publicity for the fund-raising dinner were Ms. Platero and (*he, him*).

6. Before the shows went on the air today, the announcer chose (*them, their*) last two contestants.

7. Neither (*we, us*) nor our parents realized what had happened.

8. Everyone except (*he, him*) and Mai arrived on time.

9. The cat seemed to head directly toward Charlene and (*I, me*).

10. Three students—Lani, Judith, and (*he, him*)—have been chosen to represent our school.

EXERCISE B On the line in each sentence, write the correct form of *who, whom,* or *whose,* according to the rules of standard, formal usage. Then, indicate the pronoun's case by writing above it *N* for *nominative case, O* for *objective case,* or *P* for *possessive case.*

Example 1. ___*Whom*___ will the school board hire to replace Mr. Montoya?   [*O*]

11. We were excited that Andre Watts, _____ we admire, was to give a recital.

12. She is the candidate _____ several people have recommended very highly.

13. We do not know _____ will be chosen to take part in the debate.

14. As soon as the tennis match began, everyone realized _____ the winner would be.

15. There was no one at the meeting _____ was willing to serve as chairperson.

16. She could not find anyone _____ face she recognized in the crowd.

17. In those days, a young woman usually had to marry the man _____ her parents had

chosen for her.

18. Kate Jenkins, _____ we had not seen for several months, paid us a surprise visit.

19. _____ did the president appoint to the post?

20. We asked the mayor, _____ answers would be accurate.

Review B: **Pronoun Forms**

EXERCISE A Underline the pronoun that completes each of the following sentences correctly.

Example 1. (We, Us) project leaders chose a topic pertaining to the Amazon region.

1. Either Carmen or (she, her) will star in the play.

2. Has anyone told Kyutaro and (he, him) the news about the varsity football team's win at the regional playoffs?

3. It was not surprising that no one recognized Kim or (I, me) in the library.

4. Ms. Tchong said that (we, us) cheerleaders must practice more.

5. Everyone listened carefully as Dorothea and (he, him) explained.

6. It was (she, her) who made the announcement on the loudspeaker.

7. Our team expected to play a closely matched game against Tranh and (they, them).

8. Cindy said there was a bulletin posted concerning (we, us) band members.

9. Two winners, Paco and (I, me), spoke at the banquet.

10. The group will give you and (she, her) a letter of commendation for your work on behalf of the flood victims.

EXERCISE B On the line in each sentence, write the correct form of who, whom, or whose according to the rules of standard, formal usage.

Example 1. ____Whose____ trucks are the ones parked nearest to the cafeteria?

11. All of us knew _____ had written the letter.

12. With _____ did you leave the package?

13. We never learned _____ nomination Christine had been planning to support.

14. I'd like to thank my parents, without _____ none of this would have been possible.

15. There were thousands of people in the stadium, but no one _____ she recognized immediately.

16. Mr. Yoshira asked _____ would be able to rehearse on Friday.

17. In _____ car are you riding to the football game?

18. Sami asked me _____ I had met at the station.

19. At the end of the trip, I tried to find out to _____ the plaid blanket belonged.

20. Mr. Allende is the person _____ we think should serve on the committee.

Language and Sentence Skills Practice

Review C: **Pronoun Errors**

USAGE

EXERCISE A   Cross out each incorrect pronoun in the following sentences, and write the correct form above it. If the sentence does not contain an error, write *C* on the line provided. Base your answers on the rules of standard, formal usage.

                                        ourselves
Example _____ **1.** We should be able to drive ~~us~~ to this afternoon's soccer game.

_____ **1.** The three of us—Teresa, Rosita, and me—decided to join the chorus.

_____ **2.** Nearly two thirds of the votes were for Kito and myself.

_____ **3.** Although it was not due at the station for another ten minutes, Glen and I thought we heard the train coming.

_____ **4.** The report was written by experts: he and his closest advisors.

_____ **5.** She was surprised to learn about him calling for a new election.

_____ **6.** Our hope is that we can visit you and they in Nebraska this summer.

_____ **7.** The teachers obtained tickets for themselves and we.

_____ **8.** Across the aisle from Corina and I were sitting the mayor and the governor.

_____ **9.** Few can do as good an organizational job as her.

_____ **10.** Several members of the class praised my singing of the national anthem.

EXERCISE B   In each of the following sentences, cross out the incorrect pronoun and write the correct form above it. Base your answers on the rules of standard, formal usage.

                                    whomever
Example **1.** I'm sure we'll approve of ~~whoever~~ you select.

11. Joanne objected to my playing music while us roommates were both studying for the physics test.

12. The two new students, Cindy and him, are both good tennis players.

13. My father and me played catch in our backyard.

14. The agent gave my mother and myself the keys to the summer cottage.

15. You need not be surprised about whom disagrees with you.

16. No one else knows the route as well as her.

17. Do you object to them being with us at the cabin?

18. The applications will be reviewed by she and her staff.

19. Letters were sent to each of us—Nilda, Debbie, and I.

20. Do many of we student council members have project assignments yet?

                                       HOLT HANDBOOK | Fifth Course

Review D: **Pronoun Forms**

EXERCISE A In each of the following sentences, underline the pronoun that completes the sentence correctly.

Example 1. Since (*he, him*) and I now have our licenses, Aunt Sue allowed us to use her car.

1. This afternoon the talent committee will audition Tina and (*myself, me*).

2. (*Who, Whom*) shall I say is calling?

3. The best tennis players in school are my cousin Adele and (*he, him*).

4. The twins, Darren and (*he, him*), have never had a class together.

5. (*Who, Whom*) did you talk to at the information desk?

6. After Alberto and (*he, him*) arrived, we began the game.

7. My math teacher objects to (*me, my*) yelling out answers before I have been called on.

8. I learned about life in post–World War II Cuba from my great-grandmother and (*he, him*).

9. Between you and (*I, me*), I'm glad it's almost lunchtime.

10. When we were young, Ellie always got into more trouble than (*I, me*).

EXERCISE B In each sentence in the paragraph below, underline the pronoun that completes the sentence correctly.

Example   [1] My mother and my uncle decided between (*them, themselves*) to enlist.

[11] In 1991, Mom served in the Persian Gulf Conflict; in fact, both Uncle Tony and (*she, her*) did. [12] When Mom told my brother Pete and (*me, myself*) that she was going to the Persian Gulf, we were worried. [13] However, Pete and (*I, me*) knew that she was well prepared. [14] Mom is a fine officer, and the troops she commands respect no one else as much as (*she, her*). [15] Before Mom left for the Gulf, she, Pete, and (*I, myself*) had several interesting discussions about the U.S. military. [16] Mom thought that (*us, our*) knowing some statistics might make us feel a little better about her safety. [17] For one thing, (*we, us*) boys learned that the average age of the troops in the Persian Gulf was twenty-eight years, whereas those who fought in Vietnam averaged only twenty-one years. [18] Between you and (*I, me*), both my brother and I were glad to hear that Mom would be serving with troops who had more years of maturity and experience. [19] Mom also told Pete and (*I, me*) that, for the first time in U.S. history, a major war was being fought entirely by volunteer troops. [20] I will debate anyone (*who, whose*) says that having a volunteer army didn't improve morale.

for **CHAPTER 6: USING PRONOUNS CORRECTLY**   *pages 124–38*

Proofreading Application: Speech

Good writers are generally good proofreaders. Readers tend to admire and trust writing that is error-free. Make sure that you correct all errors in grammar, usage, spelling, and punctuation in your writing. Your readers will have more confidence in your words if you have done your best to proofread carefully.

The nonstandard use of pronouns is common in informal conversation and writing. Few people would give a second thought to your identifying yourself with "It's me!" However, when you speak and write for formal purposes, as in speeches, you should follow the rules of standard English.

PROOFREADING ACTIVITY

The following is a speech written by a high school student who will present it at a parent appreciation dinner. Find and correct the errors in pronoun usage. Use proofreading symbols to make your corrections.

Parents:

We all know by now that enough money has been raised to pay for an incredible junior-senior prom next month. Us juniors are well aware of the fact that we have arrived at this point because of you having helped us with all the fund-raising.

After the last parent had left the car wash (our last fund-raising event), all the other kids and me spontaneously decided that we needed to publicly express our appreciation to you. Everyone informally chose Rita Mangione and myself as speech-writers. Then, between Rita and I, we decided that I would deliver the speech. So it is me who will have the honor of addressing you great people.

Every mother and father in this room is a busy person to who time is precious. Who knows this better than us, your sons and daughters? And that fact makes us all the more appreciative that you have given so much of your time, money, and effort toward an event that means a great deal to we juniors and seniors at Clifton High School. As we are leaving the prom on May 7, it is you who we will silently thank.

Literary Model: Poetry

Heart! We will forget him!
by Emily Dickinson

Heart! We will forget him!
You and I—tonight!
You may forget the warmth he gave—
I will forget the light!

When you have done, pray tell me
That I may straight begin!
Haste! lest while you're lagging
I remember him!

EXERCISE A

1. Identify all the second-person pronouns in the poem. _____
_____

2. To whom or what do the second-person pronouns refer? _____
_____
_____

EXERCISE B

1. How is Dickinson's use of second-person pronouns unconventional? Explain. _____
_____
_____

2. Why do you think Dickinson uses "you" in this way? What does it help express? Explain.
_____
_____

Language and Sentence Skills Practice

Literary Model (continued)

EXERCISE C   Write a poem in which you use second-person personal pronouns to indicate the one spoken to in the same way that Dickinson does in the poem above. In other words, use *apostrophe,* a technique in which a writer addresses an inanimate object, an idea, or a person who is either dead or absent.

_____

_____

_____

_____

_____

_____

_____

_____

_____

_____

_____

_____

_____

_____

EXERCISE D   How is your use of apostrophe similar to or different from Dickinson's?

_____

_____

_____

_____

_____

_____

_____

_____

_____

_____

_____

_____

_____

_____

Writing Application: Contract

The pronouns ending in–*self* or –*selves* have two specific uses: to show action reflected on the antecedent, and to stress the antecedent. Avoid using them as subjects or personal pronouns, and avoid the nonstandard forms *hisself, theirself,* and *theirselves.*

NONSTANDARD	His mother and hisself delivered the flowers for the wedding.
STANDARD	He and his mother delivered the flowers for the wedding.
STANDARD	He himself delivered the flowers for the wedding.

WRITING ACTIVITY

Every January first, many people make New Year's resolutions. Some students make such resolutions every new semester. Resolutions can focus us on our strengths ("I will continue to exercise daily") and our weaknesses ("I will not procrastinate on my homework"). Decide on several personal strengths that you want to maintain and several personal weaknesses that you want to correct. Write a contract with yourself to help you carry through with each resolution. Use two reflexive pronouns and two intensive pronouns as you remind yourself of your goals.

PREWRITING   A long catalog of resolutions will be hard to keep track of, much less uphold. Brainstorm to produce a list of personal strengths and weaknesses; then, choose the two strengths you most want to maintain and the two weaknesses you most want to correct.

WRITING   Organize your contract so that related strengths and weaknesses appear together. For instance, "exercise more" and "eat more nutritiously" both have to do with health. Success at keeping the first resolution will probably help with success in the second. You might arrange your resolutions from least to most important (emphatic organization) or from easiest to keep to hardest to keep. Whatever strategy you choose, avoid merely listing your resolutions.

REVISING   Resolutions challenge us to do what is difficult. As you write to yourself, choose words that will encourage you. Avoid a tone that communicates the idea "I'll never manage to do this!" Consider dividing each resolution into smaller steps that are easy to take individually.

PUBLISHING   Check your contract for errors in grammar, usage, spelling, and punctuation. You may wish to have a partner to cheer you on as you make changes in your life. Put a copy of the contract where you will see it frequently, and trade copies with a trusted friend.

EXTENDING YOUR WRITING

You may wish to extend this exercise by keeping a journal recording your setbacks and successes as you work to uphold your resolutions. You might eventually write a personal narrative essay describing your efforts and then submit it to a magazine that publishes articles by and for teenagers.

for **CHAPTER 7: CLEAR REFERENCE**   pages 148–54

Choices: Investigating Pronoun Reference

The following activities challenge you to find a connection between pronoun reference and the world around you. Do the activity below that suits your personality best, and then share your discoveries with your class..

Reference Desk

Do some research on the word *reference*. Find out its root, its original meaning, and the language from which it came. Once you've got that information, examine the different meanings of the word. Write a sentence for each of its meanings. You might want to consult more than one dictionary to get the full range of meanings. Then, compile your research into a handout for your classmates.

Context Is All

Are you a person who asks a lot of questions about language? If so, think about this question: Why does English have words, such as pronouns, that can have different referents? In other words, why does it have words that can refer to lots of different things? List five such words, and give at least two different uses of each word. When you present your words to the class (on a visual display of your choice), explain why you think such words exist. Any background information you provide—including examples of such words in other languages or research from books, articles, or online sources—will help the class answer this interesting language question.

The Name of the Game

Precision is the name of the game in mathematics. If an equation doesn't have clear references to specific values, it cannot be solved. Find examples of mathematical equations, and determine what each letter, symbol, or value represents. Write the equations on large note cards with a short paragraph below to explain what the equation means. Share your findings with the class, demonstrating why it is important to know what each value means.

That's Life

For various reasons, song lyricists and poets don't worry much about clear reference. One reason is that they must match their words to a rhythm; they can't waste a beat or two on another word. Another reason is that these writers want to get a general idea, sometimes just an emotion, across to the listener. Consequently, you can find numerous reference errors in song lyrics. Get together with a group of friends and brainstorm a number of lines from songs. What corrections would need to be made to make all the references clear? The corrections will sound awkward in a song. Share your corrections with the class, and if you're feeling brave, sing them!

Crash Test

Pronoun reference errors slip by many a reader. Can they slip by a grammar checker? Find out. Either write a paragraph full of reference errors, or type examples from your textbook into a word processor. Then, run the grammar checker. Make a note of each suggestion that the checker makes. How many reference errors did the checker catch? How many of the checker's corrections were correct? How many were incorrect? Create a table to present your findings to the class.

Riddle Me This

By the time Oedipus walked up to the Sphinx a few thousand years ago, riddles had fascinated, educated, and entertained generations. Riddles often hinge on unclear pronoun references. Beat the Sphinx at her own game. Write a riddle that is based on an unclear reference. If you like, you can illustrate your riddle with a cartoon and post it in the classroom.

Pronouns and Their Antecedents

7a. A pronoun should refer clearly to its antecedent.

> **EXAMPLES** The **man** claimed the rare **vase**, saying that **he** owned **it**. [The antecedent of the pronoun *he* is the noun *man*. The antecedent of the pronoun *it* is the noun *vase*.]
>
> Has **everyone** submitted **his** or **her** questions? [The antecedent of the pronouns *his* and *her* is the pronoun *everyone*.]

EXERCISE A In the sentences below, draw an arrow from each pronoun to its antecedent.

Example 1. The player who has won the grand prize is she, and here it is!

1. Ms. Bluefeather reminded Tony about the book report he was to give today.

2. Roseanne and Daniel said they would make the costumes.

3. Each year, Harvard University's Hasty Pudding Theatrical Society honors performers who have excelled in the entertainment industry.

4. Some students may be asking themselves which career path they should follow after graduation.

5. Once in a while a great song comes along and sets new records with its popularity.

6. Farmers expect to harvest less than they harvested last year.

7. Do the swallows return to their nesting areas at San Juan Capistrano?

8. Each child is saving part of his or her earnings for the future.

9. Perhaps Miranda herself might be the pilot of a hot-air balloon and guide it over the patchwork of towns and fields below.

10. The softball coach told the players, "I have always thought of you as the best team this school has ever had."

EXERCISE B On the line provided in each of the sentences below, write a pronoun that will agree with its antecedent and correctly complete the sentence.

Example 1. Has Stu or Irma ever played baseball? _____*It*_____ is a game _____*he or she*_____ might enjoy.

11. Baseball is played by two teams; _____ of the teams have nine players.

12. We will even up the teams by taking Irma on _____ if Stu may play on yours.

13. Are the umpires here yet? Sara has a question for _____ .

14. Everyone wants to hit a home run, _____ can be an exciting part of the game.

15. After three players on one team strike out, the other team gets _____ turn at bat.

Ambiguous Reference

USAGE

7b.	Avoid an **ambiguous reference**, which occurs when any one of two or more words could be a pronoun's antecedent.

> **AMBIGUOUS** Dora wrote to Anna while she was away. [Who was away?]
> **CLEAR** While Dora was away, she wrote to Anna.
> **CLEAR** While Anna was away, Dora wrote to her.

EXERCISE In each of the following sentences, circle any pronoun with an ambiguous reference. Then, on the line provided, rewrite the sentence to correct the ambiguous pronoun reference.

Example 1. How soon can Maggie take Su Lin (her) history notes?   *How soon can Maggie take her history notes to Su Lin?*

1. After my parents and my friends met, they acted as if they had always known them. _____

_____

2. Once the soprano switched her career from opera to theater, it was never the same. _____

_____

3. Are these pancakes better with the blueberries because of their flavor? _____

_____

4. Connie was glad to give Leta a ride home whenever she did not have play rehearsal. _____

_____

5. The police officer told my brother he could wait for the insurance agent. _____

_____

6. Because the new client's appointment was at the same time as that of the lawyer's regular

client, it was rescheduled. _____

_____

7. Ms. Nguyen went with my aunt to the cakewalk that would benefit her favorite charity. _____

_____

8. Did you sand the frame and put tape over the glass before painting it? _____

_____

9. The robins were almost the size of the blue jays, but they seemed to eat more. _____

_____

10. Dwayne raised his hand at the same time Nigel did, but he didn't have the correct answer. __

_____

USAGE

General Reference

7c. Avoid a *general reference,* which is the use of a pronoun that refers to a general idea rather than to a specific antecedent.

Pronouns commonly used in making general references are *it, that, this,* and *which.*
 GENERAL The storm began at noon. That made commuting difficult.
   CLEAR A storm that began at noon made commuting difficult.

 GENERAL We went to the movies. It was great.
   CLEAR We went to a great movie.

EXERCISE A If a sentence below contains a pronoun causing a general reference error, circle the pronoun. If a sentence is correct, write C above the sentence.

Example 1. Lots of rest and plenty of liquids should help my cold, (which) was always my grandmother's cure.

1. Add extra sunflower seeds to the birdseed; this seems to attract more cardinals.

2. That almost all of our class participated in the recycling drive surprised me.

3. Because we were late, we didn't get tickets for the concert, which really upset us.

4. Bring plenty of forks, knives, and plates. This is essential for our picnic this afternoon.

5. Some club members wanted white T-shirts, others preferred red, while a few held out for blue. It seems like something we should have discussed before we voted.

EXERCISE B On the line after each sentence, rewrite the sentence to correct the general reference.

Example 1. We raised a thousand dollars for the charity, which was good.
That we raised a thousand dollars for the charity was good.

6. My history paper is due tomorrow, which is why I'll be at the library tonight. _____

7. When the pane of glass shattered, it was startling. _____

8. Paper birches exchange carbon (sugar) with Douglas firs. It helps both trees. _____

9. The more the firs grow in the shade, the more sugar they get. That helps them grow faster. _____

10. The alarm didn't go off, which means we'll miss the bus again today. _____

Ambiguous and General References

USAGE

7b. Avoid an *ambiguous reference,* which occurs when any one of two or more words could be a pronoun's antecedent.

7c. Avoid a *general reference,* which is the use of a pronoun that refers to a general idea rather than to a specific antecedent.

AMBIGUOUS	Roberto offered Jaime some advice before he left. [Who left?]
CLEAR	Before Roberto left, he offered Jaime some advice.
GENERAL	We left early, which surprised Celeste. [*Which* has no specific antecedent.]
CLEAR	That we left early surprised Celeste.

EXERCISE   Rewrite the sentences below to correct any ambiguous or general reference errors.

Example 1. Theo reminded Glenn that he should leave for the game soon. *Theo reminded Glenn to leave for the game soon.*

1. The sky grew dark and the winds picked up. That was scary. _____

_____

2. The dog pushed the cat out of its bed. _____

_____

3. Our bank closed early last Friday. This was a problem. _____

_____

4. Then the cup hit the plate, and that made it crack in three different spots. _____

_____

5. As soon as he arrives, Carlos will give Phil a tennis lesson. _____

_____

6. Tim's a great hitter, and that will certainly get him into the record books. _____

_____

7. Sarah saw Maria while she was in Corpus Christi. _____

_____

8. Dave explained to Jared the duties of his new job. _____

_____

9. The dancer told the singer that she needed more practice. _____

_____

10. The white marble statues stood among the magnolia trees. It looked beautiful. _____

_____

160

Weak Reference

7d. Avoid a *weak reference,* which occurs when a pronoun refers to an antecedent that has been suggested but not expressed.

WEAK	After reading the Chinese cookbook, I made some.
CLEAR	After reading the Chinese cookbook, I made **several Chinese dishes.**

WEAK	I'm excited about shop class because he will be teaching us to build tables.
CLEAR	I'm excited about shop class because **the instructor** will be teaching us to build tables.

EXERCISE In the sentences below, circle any pronoun with a weak reference. Then, on the line provided, rewrite the sentence to correct the weak pronoun reference.

Example 1. Rene's report was on the Algonquin legal system and how (they) influenced other tribes.

   Rene's report was on the Algonquin legal system and its influence on other tribes.

1. Our German Club agreed to volunteer at the food bank and to help sort them. _____

_____

2. The volcanic eruption was sudden and violent, throwing it across most of the city. _____

_____

3. Could you tell me what these recycling codes mean and where I can take them? _____

_____

4. The space shuttle mission was postponed while they awaited good weather. _____

_____

5. Belinda talked to the sculptor and then chose several that would make good gifts. _____

_____

6. When Javier translated the poem into Spanish, I appreciated even more the way they rhymed.

_____

7. Mom always prepares my favorite ones for dinner on Saturday nights. _____

_____

8. Stamp collectors and coin collectors often believe that they will increase in value over time.

_____

9. The bookstore is nearby, so I can ride my bike there and buy one. _____

_____

10. We videotaped most of our family reunion. One of these that I wanted was not taped. _____

Indefinite Reference

7e. Avoid an *indefinite reference*—the use of a pronoun that refers to no particular person or thing and that is unnecessary to the meaning and structure of a sentence.

INDEFINITE	In Houston they host a chili cook-off every year.
CLEAR	Houston hosts a chili cook-off every year.
INDEFINITE	Working for this architectural firm, you need to have a college degree.
CLEAR	Employees who work for this architectural firm need to have a college degree.

EXERCISE In each of the following sentences, circle any pronoun with an indefinite reference. Then, on the line provided, revise the sentence to correct the indefinite pronoun reference.

Example 1. In that town, (they) always give the singer a standing ovation.

    That town always gives the singer a standing ovation.

1. In the book *Frontier Children* it describes the lives of American children long ago. _____

_____

2. In the Middle Ages, you didn't expect to live to be very old. _____

_____

3. By changing the value for the *x*-axis, it results in a different answer to this problem. _____

_____

4. Among these events on the time line they show how national alliances shifted in the 1700s.

_____

5. Whenever relatives visited, you were to be very polite and not cause trouble. _____

_____

6. I asked my friend Ruby what you should do to prepare for a career in publishing. _____

_____

7. Each day in the television listings it tells which movies will be broadcast. _____

_____

8. In Brazil, you generally speak Portuguese or a traditional Indian language. _____

_____

9. On my first visit to the optometrist's office, they made me feel at ease with the eye tests. ____

_____

10. In computer programming it requires logical thinking and the ability to plan ahead. _____

_____

USAGE

Weak and Indefinite References

7d. Avoid a *weak reference,* which occurs when a pronoun refers to an antecedent that has been suggested but not expressed.

> **WEAK** After winning the football game, they gave the coach a gift.
>
> **CLEAR** After the football game, the players gave the coach a gift.

7e. Avoid an *indefinite reference*—the use of a pronoun that refers to no particular person or thing and that is unnecessary to the meaning and structure of a sentence.

> **INDEFINITE** In the book, it included spectacular photographs of geese in flight.
>
> **CLEAR** The book included spectacular photographs of geese in flight.

USAGE

EXERCISE A On the lines provided, revise each sentence to correct the weak or indefinite reference.

Example 1. As a photographer you might take many pictures before snapping the perfect one.

A photographer might take many pictures before snapping the perfect one.

1. In a dictionary it tells the meanings of words. _____

_____

2. Doctors must listen carefully to what you say. _____

_____

3. I like wrestling, but I've never seen one. _____

_____

4. Ernest Hemingway was a great writer, and this is one of his best. _____

_____

5. During World War II, you were not always able to buy the goods you wanted. _____

_____

EXERCISE B In the following paragraph, circle the pronouns that have weak or indefinite references.

Example [1] In the book *Drugs and Sports,* it tells about the dangers of taking anabolic steroids.

[6] In athletics they often have injuries and life-threatening illnesses because of steroids. [7] In one chapter it explains how the use of steroids can lead to cancer of the liver, heart disease, or problems with the reproductive organs. [8] Other chapters discuss ways that their muscles get stronger while their tendons and ligaments do not. [9] Athletes may experience tears or ruptures, and you will require a long recovery period. [10] Other athletes report such common symptoms of it as baldness, violent outbursts of anger, and stunted growth.

Review A: Clear Reference

EXERCISE In each sentence below, circle the pronoun with an unclear reference. Then, on the line provided, rewrite the sentence to clarify or correct the pronoun reference.

Example 1. Hank worked with Al in(his)garden.

Hank worked in his garden with Al.

1. When the taxicab hit the car, its radiator cracked. _____

_____

2. Rain clouds are gathering; it might ruin our plans to go hiking this weekend. _____

_____

3. The pot boiled over; it spilled all over the stove. _____

_____

4. At that store they offer shoppers discounts on many products. _____

_____

5. They ran into a beehive, and they stung them. _____

_____

6. The play was sold out, which caused the theater to schedule more performances. _____

_____

7. In the encyclopedia it says that Joseph Conrad was born in Poland. _____

_____

8. The dog rolled in the mud, which amused Marcy. _____

_____

9. We usually listen to the weather forecast, but they're not always right. _____

_____

10. The concert hall was too big, which made hearing the tenor difficult. _____

_____

Review B: **Clear Reference**

USAGE

EXERCISE In each sentence below, circle the pronoun with an unclear reference. Then, on the line provided, rewrite the sentence to clarify or correct the pronoun reference.

Example 1. The garden needs to be watered more often because (they) are wilting.

The garden needs to be watered more often because the flowers are wilting.

1. I dropped the pail, and it splashed all over my feet. _____

_____

2. The puppies' owners were proud that they were housebroken. _____

_____

3. At the law office they were busy with several pending cases. _____

_____

4. During the panel discussion, they brought up several environmental issues. _____

_____

5. The rain started right after the soccer players arrived, so it was called off. _____

_____

6. Archery can be dangerous if you aren't careful. _____

_____

7. I'd give the dog a bone if I could find it. _____

_____

8. Taxes are rising, which makes saving money difficult. _____

_____

9. In the cookbook it says to use fresh herbs for the sauce. _____

_____

10. Several high school seniors have won scholarships, which is exciting. _____

_____

Review C: **Clear Reference**

EXERCISE In the sentences below, circle any pronouns with an unclear reference. Then, on the lines provided, rewrite the sentences to clarify or correct the pronoun references.

Example 1. Only one third of our students voted in this election, (which) is surprising.

That only one third of our students voted in this election is surprising.

1. We searched the room, looking for any clue that might help us solve it. _____

_____

2. Emilio called Seth to ask about the final part of his clarinet solo. _____

_____

3. Playwright Eugene O'Neill once wrote about his dog; it was short but great fun to read. _____

_____

4. Did the article about bookkeeping explain why you should maintain some sort of system

for receipts? _____

_____

5. In Elie Wiesel's memoir, it addresses issues of human rights. _____

_____

6. The opera singer Irra Petina Bussey escaped from Russia, which took great courage. _____

_____

7. Security guards watch transactions carefully to make sure no one steals them. _____

_____

8. At summer camp we had swimming lessons, art lessons, and tennis lessons every morning.

That certainly tired us out. _____

_____

9. Some schools have a dress code that requires you to wear a uniform every day. _____

_____

10. After comparing the writings of Beth E. Brant and Ignatia Broker, I decided that I liked hers

better. _____

_____

USAGE

Proofreading Application: Personal Narrative

Good writers are generally good proofreaders. Readers tend to admire and trust writing that is error-free. Make sure that you correct all errors in grammar, usage, spelling, and punctuation in your writing. Your readers will have more confidence in your words if you have done your best to proofread carefully.

One way to improve your writing is to make sure that every pronoun you have used refers clearly to its antecedent. As you proofread your writing, check for clear pronoun reference.

PROOFREADING ACTIVITY

In the following personal narrative, find and correct the errors in pronoun reference. Use proofreading symbols to make your corrections.

My favorite aunt, Christina, is very talented. Two of these are baking bread and telling stories. That is one of her favorite things to do. My aunt's storytelling became well known around town because everyone loves to hear them.

One Sunday afternoon my aunt called my mom while she was in a particularly exuberant mood. She invited my family over to drink chamomile tea and eat her famous fruitcake, which everyone in my family particularly likes. When we got to her house, she served us some. Aunt Christina then showed us a newspaper clipping and a beautiful trophy. My aunt was obviously very proud of it. She asked my dad to read the newspaper article aloud. In the article it said that Christina von Husen had placed first in the recent statewide storytelling competition. Aunt Christina had told a story about her aging father and his brother on the day he won a piano competition. After we heard the newspaper article, I told Aunt Christina, "I hope to be a good one like you some day."

USAGE | Language in Context: Literary Model

Literary Model: Pronoun Reference in a Poem

from "Magic Island"
by Cathy Song

A collar of water
surrounds the park peninsula
at noon.
Voices are lost
in waves of wind
that catches a kite
and keeps it there
in the air above the trees.
If the day has one color,
it is this:
the blue immersion of horizons,
the sea taking the sky like a swimmer.

The picnickers have come
to rest their bicycles
in the sprawling shade.

EXERCISE A The pronouns used in the excerpt above refer to nouns mentioned in the poem. For each of
the quoted phrases below, underline the pronoun and indicate the noun to which each pronoun refers.

reference

that catches a kite   _____

and keeps it there   _____

If the day has one color,/it   _____

to rest their bicycles   _____

EXERCISE B

1. In the line "that catches a kite," explain how the poet's verb choice helps to clarify the

pronoun's antecedent. What other possible antecedent does the verb exclude? _____

_____

_____

_____

for **CHAPTER 7: CLEAR REFERENCE**   *pages 148–54*

Literary Model (continued)

2. In the line "it is this," what is the antecedent of "this"?

_____

3. Why might it be especially effective to have a powerful image following the line "it is this"?

_____

_____

EXERCISE C   Recall a noontime scene with which you are very familiar. A weekend scene, a work scene, a school scene, or a vacation scene may be among those that come to mind. Describe the scene in a poem. Try including a line that sums up your ideas, such as "What stays in the mind is this:" or "The unforgettable image is this:" followed by specific details.

_____

_____

_____

_____

_____

_____

_____

_____

_____

_____

_____

_____

_____

_____

_____

_____

_____

EXERCISE D   Go back and underline any pronouns that you used in your poem. Then, put parentheses around each antecedent. If you used any pronouns with unstated antecedents, such as *I* or *you;* underline them a second time. Finally, make any revisions needed for clarity.

Writing Application: Report

When people speak, they tend to leave out many words that they expect their listeners to fill in by using contextual clues. In writing, however, it is necessary to include these words. Readers cannot ask writers what they meant, so writers should avoid using general pronouns, especially *it, that, this,* and *which,* alone in a sentence.

UNCLEAR   Jonathan answered, which surprised her. [To what does *which* refer?]

CLEAR   Jonathan's answer surprised her.

CLEAR   That Jonathan answered surprised her.

WRITING ACTIVITY

Speakers rely daily on many words and word groups without thinking about what the words really mean. Why do we say that it is "raining cats and dogs"? What does it mean to "speak off the cuff"? What exactly is a "scapegoat," "right-hand man," or "nerd"? These words and word groups have histories that are lost to many speakers today. Choose a word or word group that intrigues you. Learn its history; then write a brief report of your findings. As you write, avoid unclear pronoun reference.

PREWRITING   You may think of a word or word group to research immediately. If not, spend a day listening to people talk. You are sure to hear some interesting possibilities in the conversations around you. Then, look up your choice in a standard resource, such as *Brewer's Dictionary of Phrase and Fable* or a dictionary that traces words' histories. Your library may have such reference tools; you can also find information on the Internet.

WRITING   You may wish to begin your history by explaining what you guessed about the word or phrase before you researched it. For example, when a promising venture fails, we might say that it "didn't pan out." Does this phrase refer to the old technique of panning for gold? Then, make a transition into what you learned from your sources. Were you surprised by the research, or was your guess correct?

REVISING   Re-read your essay, and revise it to correct any problems in organization, word choice, or transitions.

PUBLISHING   Check your writing for errors in grammar, usage, spelling, and punctuation. Check all pronouns for clear, specific antecedents. Remember to put in quotation marks any quoted materials from your sources and to include a bibliography or Works Cited page. Post your essay where your classmates can see it.

EXTENDING YOUR WRITING

Begin an extended dictionary of words and their histories. You already have one entry for your dictionary. Add two or three more words or word groups to your dictionary, and be sure to arrange them in alphabetical order. You may choose to combine your work with your classmates' work to create a more complete dictionary.

Choices: Investigating Verbs

The following activities challenge you to find a connection between verbs and the world around you. Do the activity below that suits your personality best, and then share your discoveries with your class.

Greetings! You Have Been Selected…

If you have read government publications, newspapers, or business correspondence, you are familiar with passive construction. Find some of these examples. Check the public library for government bulletins and stock reports. If you have access to the Internet, you should be able to come up with a number of examples of passive construction. Paste your examples to poster board, and present them to the class. As you present each example, be prepared to give your explanation of why a passive construction was used in this particular situation.

Living on Paris Time

Consciously or subconsciously, we know the tenses of the English language. What tenses do foreign languages use? Interview someone who speaks a foreign language well, and ask him or her to compare the English tenses to those of another language. Does one language have tenses that the other does not? To what time frames do these tenses refer? While you're at it, ask a few questions of your own. Create a comparison chart, and present it to the class.

As Others See Us

How might a person for whom English is a second language view our tenses? Interview at least two people who are native speakers of a different language. Perhaps members of your class have parents, relatives, or friends who speak Arabic or Vietnamese. Have a list of questions ready before you conduct your interview. What tenses give or gave your interviewees trouble? What tricks do they use? Write a brief biographical sketch of each person you interview, then share their insights with your class.

Moody Clues

Let your classmates listen to the moods of verbs in action. Write a dialogue among three people. One person speaks only in the indicative mood. Another speaks only in the imperative mood. The last speaks only in the interrogative mood. Perform your mini-drama for the class. You could get a discussion going by talking about what limiting a character to a single mood was like and how this limitation affected the development of the character.

Flashback

Films use intriguing techniques to express verb tense. What are some of these methods? Think about the films you have seen. How did they express the future or the past? Make a list of movie scenes that show verb tense in an interesting way. Then, use a technique of your own to express tense in a creative story. Your story can be written in prose or poetry. Before you begin, consider the many options that English verbs offer you.

"Bird Thou Never Wert"

When an old word fades from everyday sight, the word sometimes gains a special place. The word may appear in ritual language, on holidays, or in art. What would everyday speech sound like if a few antiquated words suddenly made a comeback? Find out by using several old verbs to write an essay on one of today's issues. Begin by making a list of verbs that are no longer a part of everyday English. Start your list with *art.* If you end up wanting to use old forms of pronouns, such as *thou,* go ahead! If you have access to a computer, you could print your essay in a font like one of those used at the time these old verb forms were used.

The Principal Parts of Verbs

USAGE

8a. | The principal parts of a verb are the ***base form,*** the ***present participle,*** the ***past,*** and the ***past participle.*** All other verb forms are derived from these principal parts.

BASE FORM	PRESENT PARTICIPLE	PAST	PAST PARTICIPLE
ask	[is] asking	asked	[have] asked
love	[is] loving	loved	[have] loved
burn	[is] burning	burned *or* burnt	[have] burned *or* [have] burnt
sleep	[is] sleeping	slept	[have] slept
put	[is] putting	put	[have] put

When the present participle and past participle forms are used as verbs in sentences, they require helping verbs. All verbs form the present participle by adding *–ing* to the base form; however, not all verbs form the past and past participle by adding *–d* or *–ed* to the base form. Also, some uses of a past participle with a form of *be* are called the *passive voice*.

EXAMPLES   **Is** everyone **looking** at the map on page 46 that we **had looked** at earlier? [*Is looking* uses a present participle; *had looked* uses a past participle.]

Carl **is teaching** school in Tampa now, but he **has taught** in Orlando, too. [*Is teaching* uses a present participle; *has taught* uses a past participle.]

Rescue teams **have been arriving** since dawn and **have been seen** throughout the area. [*Have been arriving* uses a present participle; *have been seen* uses a past participle for the passive voice verb form.]

EXERCISE   For each of the following sentences, write the correct present participle, past, or past participle verb form above the verb in parentheses.

Example 1. All the apples have been *(shake)* from our tree by last night's strong winds.
                   shaken

1. Can you believe our sister's volleyball team is *(play)* the state championship game?

2. In my opinion, that wall shouldn't have been *(paint)* green.

3. Yesterday, Brooke's cat Raven *(jump)* onto the table and knocked over a glass of water.

4. Amanda has *(travel)* all night just to attend this wedding.

5. Before the first week of the new year ended, Ms. Ling had already *(start)* training for next year's marathon.

6. Two weeks ago I *(decide)* that building this bookcase will take longer than I originally thought.

7. For their senior project, Keisha and Jordan are *(write)* a research paper based on the results of their schoolwide survey.

8. In the concert last night, my cousin Amy *(conduct)* the city's largest girls' choir.

9. This year the dance team is *(sell)* candles to raise money for their spring trip.

10. All the recent letters, newspapers, and magazines had been *(stack)* on the desk in the corner.

USAGE

Regular Verbs

8b.   A *regular verb* is one that forms its past and past participle by adding –d or –ed to the base form.

A few regular verbs have alternative past and past participle forms ending in –t.

BASE FORM	PRESENT PARTICIPLE	PAST	PAST PARTICIPLE
use	[is] using	used	[have] used
bake	[is] baking	baked	[have] baked
fry	[is] frying	fried	[have] fried
dream	[is] dreaming	dreamed	[have] dreamed
		or dreamt	*or* [have] dreamt

EXERCISE A   For each of the following sentences, write the correct past or past participle verb form above the verb in parentheses.

Example 1. Henry E. Baker *(work)* worked as a patent examiner in the U.S. Patent Office.

1. In 1900, the U.S. Patent Office *(conduct)* a survey of its inventors' patents.

2. Baker had *(mark)* the patent records of African American inventors.

3. Baker also had *(mail)* numerous letters to many different people.

4. Newspaper editors and company presidents had *(answer)* his queries.

5. Henry Baker *(publish)* a list of African American inventors and their work.

6. All together, they had *(create)* almost four hundred inventions.

7. Baker's list *(include)* Sarah E. Goode's invention of a folding cabinet bed.

8. Thomas L. Jennings was the first African American who *(receive)* a patent for a dry cleaning method.

9. Baker's report was *(present)* as part of the 1900 International Exhibition in Paris, France.

10. In 1913, Baker's second survey *(turn)* up many more inventors.

EXERCISE B   For each of the following sentences, write the correct past or past participle verb form above the verb in parentheses.

Example 1. During last week's cooking class, Robin *(is pounding)* pounded the dough into a flat bread.

11. I should have *(guess)* that telephone call would be important.

12. This morning at dawn, a pair of owls *(call)* to each other.

13. Even when he was a child, Peter seldom *(complains)* about his sister.

14. The ambassadors have already *(are formalizing)* the treaty with their signatures.

15. I could have sworn the bus schedule *(indicates)* four stops between here and Chicago.

Irregular Verbs A

8c. An *irregular verb* forms its past and past participle in some other way than by adding *–d* or *–ed* to the base form.

	BASE FORM	PAST	PAST PARTICIPLE
CHANGING VOWELS	swim	swam	[have] swum
CHANGING CONSONANTS	bend	bent	[have] bent
CHANGING VOWELS AND CONSONANTS	go	went	[have] gone
MAKING NO CHANGE	let	let	[have] let

EXERCISE A   For each of the following sentences, write the correct past or past participle verb form above the verb in parentheses.

bound
Example 1. How has Louis *(bind)* the edges on his book bag?

1. My jeans *(shrink)* in the dryer, and now I can't wear them.

2. Last week the lake *(freeze)*, and we all went skating.

3. Has Carlotta *(ring)* the bell for us to begin the sack race?

4. Arnie and I *(go)* to the boat show on Thursday night.

5. I haven't yet *(begin)* writing my report on recent discoveries in space.

EXERCISE B   In the paragraph below, draw a line through each error in the use of a verb and write the correct past or past participle form above it.

written
Example   **[1]** Many people have ~~wrote~~ stories about pirates, but most pirate tales are largely fictional.

   [6] Little is actually knowed about most pirates. **[7]** The Irish have tolt a story about Grace O'Malley. **[8]** A woman pirate, she was borned in 1530. **[9]** Often she goed to sea on her father's ship. **[10]** In fact, she taked over his ship when he died. **[11]** She begun attacking ships off Ireland's coast. **[12]** One writer saw her as a charming woman with merry eyes; another writed of her carrying a pistol in one hand and a sword in the other. **[13]** As she growed older, she encouraged Irish rebellion against British rule. **[14]** Once her brother and one of her sons were throwed in jail, and she talked Queen Elizabeth I into releasing them. **[15]** After O'Malley's death in 1603, people said that she had hided several tons of treasure during her career.

Irregular Verbs B

8c. An *irregular verb* forms its past and past participle in some other way than by adding –*d* or –*ed* to the base form.

USAGE

	BASE FORM	PAST	PAST PARTICIPLE
CHANGING VOWELS	sit	sat	[have] sat
CHANGING CONSONANTS	lend	lent	[have] lent
CHANGING VOWELS AND CONSONANTS	teach	taught	[have] taught
MAKING NO CHANGE	let	let	[have] let

EXERCISE A For each of the following sentences, write the correct past or past participle verb form above the verb in parentheses.

Example 1. Has Grandpa *(fling)* many horseshoes yet in this game?   *flung*

1. My friend Julio had *(buy)* a new jacket to wear to the dance.

2. None of us *(leave)* before the thrilling end of our band's concert.

3. Anita had *(spend)* a long evening baby-sitting the active two-year-old.

4. Rae shrieked as the movie's monster *(creep)* toward its victims.

5. Someone in this family has *(swing)* on this door once too often and loosened a hinge.

6. We have not *(lose)* any basketball games so far this season.

7. Shouldn't the other team have *(feel)* some sympathy for our player that they injured?

8. I *(seek)* a more recent source for my term paper on cell division.

9. Coby and Hannah successfully *(keep)* Mick's birthday party a secret for the whole week.

10. Sherry had *(think)* she knew the answers to the math test questions.

EXERCISE B In the paragraph below, draw a line through each error in the use of a verb and write the correct past or past participle form above it.

Example [1] Have you ever ~~heared~~ of the aviator Alberto Santos-Dumont?   *heard*

[11] Although he was borned in Brazil, Santos-Dumont received most of his education in France. **[12]** This inventor flied a variety of aircraft. **[13]** One success, an 1898 model, was actually a gas-filled bag that was drived by a single propeller. **[14]** Another model that he himself builded in 1905 looked like a box kite. **[15]** The work of Santos-Dumont becomed influential to European aviation in the early twentieth century.

USAGE

Irregular Verbs C

| **8c.** | An *irregular verb* forms its past and past participle in some other way than by adding *–d* or *–ed* to the base form. |

	BASE FORM	**PAST**	**PAST PARTICIPLE**
CHANGING VOWELS	meet	met	[have] met
CHANGING CONSONANTS	make	made	[have] made
CHANGING VOWELS AND CONSONANTS	leave	left	[have] left
MAKING NO CHANGE	let	let	[have] let

EXERCISE A For each of the following sentences, write the correct past or past participle verb form above the verb in parentheses.

                                              made

Example 1. Deep furrows in the field were *(make)* by the truck's tires.

1. Never had we *(sit)* through such cold weather at a football game.

2. Which of these subjects have you *(teach)* before?

3. Dimitri had *(meet)* with his counselor earlier in the fall.

4. Several of the pinwheels *(spin)* briskly in the evening breeze.

5. Describe the building which has *(stand)* on the Acropolis in Athens.

6. Ernie *(pay)* for the decals showing the school's mascot.

7. The last time a tax issue *(arise)*, the opposition party leader was elected.

8. Many of us were surprised when Ms. Alvarez *(say)*, "No test today."

9. Tammy had *(send)* the packages the quickest way possible.

10. A number of bees had *(sting)* the bear on the nose.

EXERCISE B In the paragraph below, draw a line through each error in the use of a verb and write the correct past or past participle form above it.

Example   [1] Geologists have discovered that the earth, both the land and the oceans, has been

          frozen

          froze at least twice.

    [11] Evidence of these ice ages has came from African rock formations over 500 million years

old. [12] The scientists finded lower carbon levels in the rock layers. [13] They thought the cause

was a lack of weather that could wash carbon from the air into the ground. [14] When the atmos-

phere became warm enough, the ice begun to melt and rain to fall. [15] One theory of how these

cycles started is that an asteroid impact blowed up a cloud of dust that covered the globe.

Irregular Verbs D

| **8c.** | An *irregular verb* forms its past and past participle in some other way than by adding –*d* or –*ed* to the base form. |

	BASE FORM	**PAST**	**PAST PARTICIPLE**
CHANGING VOWELS	sting	stung	[have] stung
CHANGING CONSONANTS	build	built	[have] built
CHANGING VOWELS AND CONSONANTS	seek	sought	[have] sought
MAKING NO CHANGE	let	let	[have] let

EXERCISE A For each of the following sentences, write the correct past or past participle verb form above the verb in parentheses.

shook
Example 1. Frances Gabe (*shake*) up the way her house operated.

1. Tagging along with her father, an architect, had (*give*) Frances Gabe a background in building houses.

2. Gabe's husband had (*be*) an electrical engineer.

3. For thirty-five years, Gabe (*run*) her own building repairs company.

4. With a business to manage and two children to look after, she (*spend*) little time on housework.

5. She (*begin*) to create labor-saving equipment to self-clean her house.

6. To clean each room, she had (*put*) in a ceiling unit that rinsed and dried everything in a room.

7. Because the floors had been (*lay*) at an angle, the water flowed off into a drain.

8. Her dishes were (*set*) in kitchen cabinets in which they were washed, dried, and stored all in one place.

9. Similarly, her clothes had been (*hang*) in closets where they were washed and dried.

10. Frances Gabe has (*hold*) more than sixty-eight patents for the time-saving devices in her house.

EXERCISE B In the sentences below, draw a line through any incorrect verb form and write above it the correct past or past participle. If a sentence is already correct, write *C* after it.

forsook
Example 1. Who ~~forsaked~~ this cabin at the edge of the wilderness?

11. Marcie sanged the baby to sleep with a lullaby remembered from her own childhood.

12. None of us knew why Mr. Hammond weared that expression on his face just now.

13. How quickly that rattlesnake struck at the cowboy's boot!

14. Cecil has ate his lunch in the cafeteria all this year and is ready for a change.

15. In her craft class Caroline has already weaved a small wool rug.

Language and Sentence Skills Practice

Irregular Verbs E

| **8c.** | An *irregular verb* forms its past and past participle in some other way than by adding –*d* or –*ed* to the base form. |

USAGE

EXERCISE A   In the sentences below, draw a line through any incorrect verb form and write above it the correct past or past participle. If a sentence is already correct, write *C* after it.

                          strived
Example 1. Last year, we ~~strive~~ to make the play the best performance that our school had

                  ever seen.

1. Once the steam pipes had bursted, the best thing to do was find a repair service that would

     send help as soon as possible.

2. Nabil has stealed only a minute or two to catch his breath after the fifty-yard dash.

3. We yelled encouragement as Diego hitted the finish line tape and won the relay.

4. Mom has let my brother and me stay up long enough to finish our school projects.

5. Slowly, Ada's shoe sunk to the bottom of the lake, leaving a track of bubbles behind it.

EXERCISE B   On the line in each of the following sentences, write the past or past participle of one of the base form verbs listed below that correctly and sensibly completes a sentence.

break	hide	see	shake
draw	know	~~ride~~	write
go	make	say	

Example 1. Wanda had ____*ridden*____ the bus out to the reservation store to buy Dan's gift.

6. Our tennis team _____ the record by winning three tournaments in a row.

7. The stew will taste better if a little salt has been _____ into it.

8. Modern technology lets archaeologists investigate how artifacts were _____ without

     having to cut open the items.

9. The baby sitter had _____ several toys around the room for the children to find.

10. No one _____ the secret locked away behind the heavy wooden door.

11. At last Ruth had _____ the final frames in her series of cartoons.

12. Can you believe what the meteorologist _____ about the upcoming storm?

13. I wanted to talk to you more since you _____ to the concert Saturday night.

14. Michelle remembered that she had not yet _____ a thank-you note to Brian.

15. Would you order that book for me, the one I _____ in the store window?

Lie and *Lay*

The verb *lie* means "to rest," "to recline," or "to be in a place." *Lie* does not take an object. The verb *lay* means "to put [something] in a place." *Lay* generally takes an object.

BASE FORM	PRESENT PARTICIPLE	PAST	PAST PARTICIPLE
lie	[is] lying	lay	[have] lain
lay	[is] laying	laid	[have] laid

EXERCISE A   In each sentence below, underline the verb form in parentheses that correctly completes the sentence.

Example 1. Whose is this coat that has (<u>lain</u>, laid) in the chair all day?

1. Nicholas will be (*lying, laying*) linoleum tiles today in the shop.

2. The bag of golf clubs now (*lies, lays*) in the corner unused.

3. Records for the victrola (*lay, laid*) in a heap in the attic.

4. Could Lee have (*lain, laid*) out the maps of the county's precinct lines?

5. Until next week, the papers can (*lie, lay*) around where we can reach them.

6. If a hen has been (*lying, laying*) eggs all year, how many eggs has it produced?

7. The cat (*lies, lays*) on top of my feet when I'm asleep at night.

8. In addition to having a headache, Mom felt weak and (*lay, laid*) down to rest.

9. Margaret will be (*lying, laying*) napkins on the table, so would you please arrange the silverware?

10. A good idea sometimes must be (*lain, laid*) aside if it is not accepted by the public.

EXERCISE B   On the line in each sentence below, write the form of *lie* or *lay* that correctly and sensibly completes the sentence.

Example 1. Have you ____*laid*____ the pen and notebook on my desk?

11. Brian _____ the book samples next to the brochures about them.

12. Is there anything _____ around that you would donate to the recycling drive?

13. Russell and Deborah had never _____ carpet before but did a good job.

14. Gretchen has _____ in the hammock all afternoon.

15. This afternoon Dionne will be _____ the seedlings beside these rows.

USAGE

USAGE

Sit and *Set*

The verb *sit* means "to rest in a seated, upright position" or "to be in a place." *Sit* seldom takes an object. The verb *set* means "to put [something] in a place." *Set* generally takes an object.

BASE FORM	PRESENT PARTICIPLE	PAST	PAST PARTICIPLE
sit	[is] sitting	sat	[have] sat
set	[is] setting	set	[have] set

EXERCISE A In each sentence below, underline the verb form in parentheses that correctly completes the sentence.

Example 1. Has anyone (*sit*, *set*) the hands on the clock?

1. Was Oscar (*sitting*, *setting*) on top of the shed so he could repair the shingles?

2. Don't (*sit*, *set*) in the direct sunlight for too long.

3. Uncle Robert (*sat*, *set*) out the tools he would need for the next day's jobs.

4. Should Aunt Beverly (*sat*, *set*) the travel brochures on the kitchen counter?

5. For the first two weeks of class, you may (*sit*, *set*) wherever you wish.

6. Jerrel will be (*sitting*, *setting*) the props in the hall so we will know what we should change or

add for this performance.

7. By the way, Nelda always (*sits*, *sets*) a beautiful table and serves a delicious meal.

8. Albert has (*sat*, *set*) up his own automotive repair shop.

9. I had been (*sitting*, *setting*) for too long, and my foot had become stiff.

10. The county commissioner who (*sat*, *set*) in the center favored the highway's location.

EXERCISE B On the line in each sentence below, write the form of *sit* or *set* that correctly and sensibly completes the sentence.

Example 1. Will Benny be ____*setting*____ the projector at the back of the room?

11. Coral _____ among her college brochures and application forms.

12. Are park rangers _____ the trail route for our hike?

13. Ike and Jacki have _____ higher goals this year regarding their grades.

14. Please _____ the plates, glasses, and silverware on the table.

15. If we had not seen Uncle Jack, we could have still been _____ at the bus station.

Rise and *Raise*

The verb *rise* means "to go up" or "to get up." *Rise* does not take an object. The verb *raise* means "to lift up" or "to cause [something] to rise." *Raise* generally takes an object.

BASE FORM	PRESENT PARTICIPLE	PAST	PAST PARTICIPLE
rise	[is] rising	rose	[have] risen
raise	[is] raising	raised	[have] raised

USAGE

EXERCISE A   In each sentence below, underline the verb form in parentheses that correctly completes the sentence.

Example 1. Who will (*rise*, *raise*) early and go hiking in the cool air?

1. The bread was (*rising, raising*) as the recipe said it should.

2. Claudia would (*rise, raise*) the blinds in her office every morning.

3. Grandma had (*risen, raised*) from the sofa to introduce me to her friends.

4. Sailors across the bay have (*rose, raised*) the bad-weather signal flags.

5. Everyone will now (*rise, raise*) and join in the Pledge of Allegiance.

6. We were (*rising, raising*) funds for the debate team trip and meeting our neighbors, too.

7. The popularity rating of that television program (*rises, raises*) every week.

8. Gerardo (*rose, raised*) his own sign and awnings in front of his bakery.

9. Floodwaters had (*risen, raised*) rapidly during the night.

10. Denise (*rises, raises*) as many different vegetables as her garden will hold.

EXERCISE B   On the line in each sentence below, write the form of *rise* or *raise* that correctly and sensibly completes the sentence.

Example 1. Lou and Isidora had _____*risen*_____ early to go walking.

11. The campfire did not _____ any higher because we did not add more wood.

12. Didn't the supermarket just _____ the prices of oranges and squash?

13. We lost track of the cousins who had been _____ in farming country.

14. The cost of concert tickets has _____ until it is more than I want to pay.

15. Every morning, Lil's puppy wakes her up as soon as the sun has _____.

Language and Sentence Skills Practice

USAGE

Six Troublesome Verbs

BASE FORM	PRESENT PARTICIPLE	PAST	PAST PARTICIPLE
lie	[is] lying	lay	[have] lain
lay	[is] laying	laid	[have] laid
sit	[is] sitting	sat	[have] sat
set	[is] setting	set	[have] set
rise	[is] rising	rose	[have] risen
raise	[is] raising	raised	[have] raised

EXERCISE A In each sentence below, underline the verb form in parentheses that correctly completes the sentence.

Example 1. Everyone will *(sit, set)* the rules for summer vacation.

1. Please *(sit, set)* down over there with the rest of the class.

2. *(Lie, Lay)* the petri dish down on the table.

3. The airplane *(raised, rose)* into the darkening sky.

4. The sleeping baby *(lay, laid)* in the crib.

5. We *(set, sat)* around the computer terminal while Mrs. Toro explained the program.

6. Yesterday, we *(lay, laid)* new tiles on our kitchen floor.

7. Don't *(lie, lay)* around doing nothing.

8. Clothing prices have been *(raising, rising)* for some time.

9. Your dog has *(laid, lain)* in the same spot on the porch for years.

10. The barometer has *(raised, risen)* steadily for the past twenty-four hours.

EXERCISE B In the sentences below, draw a line through any incorrect verb form and write above it the correct form. If a sentence is already correct, write C after it.

Example 1. Have you ever ~~set~~ *sat* and watched a talented designer at work?

11. Please bring me my photography book, which is laying on the coffee table.

12. One Pawnee woman set on the ground with a deer hide.

13. I could not believe how quickly the solo violinist made the notes rise and fall.

14. Now that the laundry has been washed, he has lain it on a clothesline to dry.

15. Will the flag be rised to half-mast today?

182

USAGE

Tense and Form

8d. The *tense* of a verb indicates the time of the action or of the state of being expressed by the verb.

PRESENT	Liz **writes** stories.
PAST	Jibril **wrote** a poem.
FUTURE	Liz **will write** poetry.
PRESENT PERFECT	Jibril **has written** stories.
PAST PERFECT	Before she became a poet, Liz **had written** stories.
FUTURE PERFECT	By the end of next year, Jibril **will have written** a book of poems.

The *progressive form* of each tense consists of the appropriate tense of *be* plus the present participle and is used to show continuing action or state of being. The *emphatic form*, for the present and past tenses only, consists of the appropriate tense of *do* plus the base form and is used to show emphasis.

PROGRESSIVE	The children **are building** a fort made of boxes.
EMPHATIC	Please **do tell** me your secret.

EXERCISE A Above each underlined verb below, write the tense and form of the verb.

past emphatic
Example 1. We always <u>did love</u> to visit Mexico.

1. The cicadas <u>will</u> soon <u>arrive</u>.

2. Vernon <u>had</u> accurately <u>predicted</u> the dreary outcome.

3. By then I <u>will have been teaching</u> for thirty years.

4. By midnight every camper <u>will have retired</u> for the night.

5. Sakiri <u>had been writing</u> her letter of application.

EXERCISE B For each of the following sentences, change the tense of the verb according to the instructions in italics.

did elect
Example 1. The committee ~~will elect~~ a new president. (*Change to past emphatic tense.*)

6. Your math skills impressed me. (*Change to present perfect tense.*)

7. Looking into the distance, we saw our friends. (*Change to past progressive tense.*)

8. Mr. Mora's art class was my favorite subject this year. (*Change to future perfect tense.*)

9. My nine-year-old sister will enjoy your homemade seafood dinner. (*Change to present emphatic tense.*)

10. The museum exhibit really includes dinosaur bones? (*Change to past emphatic tense.*)

Correct Use of Verb Tenses A

USAGE

8e.   Each of the six tenses has its own uses.

(1) The *present tense* expresses an action or a state of being that is occurring now, at the present time.

(2) The *past tense* expresses an action or a state of being that occurred in the past and did not continue into the present.

A past action or state of being may also be shown by using *used to.*

(3) The *future tense* expresses an action or a state of being that will occur. The future tense is formed with the helping verb *shall* or *will.*

(4) The *present perfect tense* expresses an action or a state of being that occurred at an indefinite time in the past. The present perfect tense is formed with the helping verb *have* or *has.*

(5) The *past perfect tense* expresses an action or a state of being that ended before some other past action or state of being. The past perfect tense is formed with the helping verb *had.*

(6) The *future perfect tense* expresses an action or a state of being that will end before some other future occurrence. The future perfect tense is formed with the helping verbs *shall have* or *will have.*

EXERCISE   In each sentence below, circle the verb in parentheses that correctly completes the sentence.

Example 1. Yesterday Jill (*has changed,* (*changed*)) clothes three times before school.

1. Be sure you (*have put, will have put*) the lid on the blender before turning it on.

2. By next Thursday, Aretha (*has been finishing, will have finished*) all the exams for her first semester of college.

3. Last night the toddler (*draws, had drawn*) at least seven pictures by the time the baby sitter said it was time for bed.

4. You may not know it, but the swim team (*had been training, trains*) harder than usual for the meet they won yesterday.

5. Because their star athlete just went into the penalty box, the hockey team (*played, will play*) one person short until he can return to the ice.

6. Do you know that Jeremy Moddes still (*has been, is*) the tallest of the four brothers?

7. Because Stella had outgrown her favorite pair of shoes, she (*gave, gives*) them to her younger sister.

8. My cousin (*collects, has been collecting*) family photographs ever since the reunion.

9. What (*will have been, was*) your favorite scene in the movie last night?

10. Sometimes I accidentally (*do call, will call*) the twins by the wrong name.

Correct Use of Verb Tenses B

8e. Each of the six tenses has its own uses.

EXERCISE A   For each sentence below, write the tense of the underlined verb above it.

present progressive
Examples 1. The Kalispel Indians are living in the northwestern United States.

present perfect progressive
        2. Have any of them been living in Southern Canada?

1. The Kalispel in Montana make their home on the reservation near Flathead Lake.

2. The Kalispel in Montana have made their home on the reservation near Flathead Lake.

3. All Idaho Kalispel did live in the area around Pend Oreille Lake.

4. All Idaho Kalispel were living in the area around Pend Oreille Lake.

5. Some have joined relatives at the Coeur d'Alene Reservation.

6. Some were joining relatives at the Coeur d'Alene Reservation.

7. Others do share reservation land now with the Montana and Washington Kalispel.

8. Others are sharing reservation land now with the Montana and Washington Kalispel.

9. What are the Kalispel going to do this year to continue their traditions?

10. What will the Kalispel have done this year to continue their traditions?

EXERCISE B   For each of the following sentences, write the tense of the verb in parentheses according to the instructions in italics.

will have traveled
Example 1. The Kalispel women (*travel*) several days before they reach the delta. (*future perfect tense*)

11. These women (*gather*) plants that will later become mat coverings for many Kalispel buildings. (*future progressive tense*)

12. The canoe ends (*taper*) to make the craft glide through the marsh. (*present progressive*)

13. An older woman (*sing*) a chant of protection for the gatherers. (*present perfect*)

14. The plants, called bullrushes, (*provide*) both new and replacement coverings for the summer lodges. (*future tense*)

15. The Kalispel women (*follow*) this way of life for many years. (*past perfect*)

Sequence of Tenses

8f. Use tense forms correctly to show relationships between verbs in a sentence. Do not change needlessly from one tense to another.

(1) When describing events that occur at the same time, use verbs in the same tense.
(2) When describing events that occur at different times, use verbs in different tenses to show the order of events.

> **SAME TIME** Lars **dimmed** the lights, and Cassie **opened** the curtain. [past]
> **DIFFERENT TIMES** Lars **had dimmed** the lights, so Cassie **opened** the curtain. [two different points in the past]

8g. Do not use *would have* in *"if"* clauses that express the earlier of two past actions. Use the past perfect tense.

> **NONSTANDARD** If Chet would have asked me, I would have helped him in the student store.
> **STANDARD** If Chet **had asked** me, I would have helped him in the student store.

EXERCISE A   On the line before each sentence below, indicate the time of the action for the underlined verbs by writing *S* for *same* or *D* for *different*.

Example ____*D*____ **1.** Should I need a reference, may I give your name?

_____ **1.** By the time the rain began, we had left the park.

_____ **2.** I become alert once the alarm rings in the morning.

_____ **3.** When Gloria called, she was inviting me to a party.

_____ **4.** After I had lost my key, I called my father.

_____ **5.** If Jiro had arrived ten minutes earlier, he would have seen you.

EXERCISE B   In the sentences below, cross out any verb-tense errors and write correct verbs above them. (Hint: There is more than one way to revise some sentences.)

Example **1.** Jonathan ~~was~~ *is* the new student who ~~is~~ *was* in my class today.

6. This afternoon Mabel answers the phone and told me of the incident.

7. If you would have waited, I could have given you a ride.

8. Because I forgot my lunch at home, I had bought a sandwich at school.

9. Ever since she visits the science museum, my cousin Samantha has dreamed of becoming an astronaut.

10. An hour ago, Mr. Lambert says, "You should choose two classmates to work with on this project."

Using Infinitives and Participles Correctly

USAGE

8h.	The *present infinitive* expresses an action or a state of being that follows another action or state of being.
8i.	The *present perfect infinitive* expresses an action or a state of being that precedes another action or state of being.
8j.	When used as a verbal, the *present participle* or *past participle* expresses an action or a state of being that occurs at the same time as another action or state of being.
8k.	When used as a verbal, the *present perfect participle* expresses an action or a state of being that precedes another action or state of being.

PRESENT PARTICIPLE	**Waking** at five, I heard birds.
PRESENT PERFECT INFINITIVE	Steve claimed **to have heard her.**
PAST PARTICIPLE	**Awakened** earlier than usual, I cannot keep my eyes open.
PRESENT INFINITIVE	Tina wanted **to sing.**
PRESENT PERFECT PARTICIPLE	**Having looked** out the window this morning, we were outside enjoying a picnic all afternoon.

EXERCISE   On the line after each sentence below, revise the sentence to correct the error in the use of tenses. (Hint: There is more than one way to revise some sentences.)

Example 1. Delighted with our test scores, Ms. Chun still had wanted to continue our tutoring.

Delighted with our test scores, Ms. Chun still wants to continue our tutoring. _____

1. Investigators hoped to develop a solid case before now. _____

_____

2. Concerned about the approaching ice storm, city workers will have put sand on the roads.

_____

3. Having served for two months, Owen will become a good choice for class treasurer. _____

_____

4. Worn by years of use, the pages in this book of poetry will have yellowed. _____

_____

5. Rewinding the film, the projector has overheated and stopped running. _____

_____

USAGE

Active and Passive Voice

When the subject of a verb performs the action, the verb is in the *active voice*. When the subject receives the action, the verb is in the *passive voice*.

   ACTIVE   Olivia **bought** a bag of oranges. [The subject, *Olivia*, performs the action.]

   PASSIVE   The bag of oranges **was bought** by Olivia. [The subject, *bag*, receives the action.]

A transitive verb in the active voice often has both an indirect object and a direct object. When such a verb is put in the passive voice, either object can become the subject. The other object may serve as a complement called a *retained object*.

   ACTIVE   Mr. Jenkins read the class a short story.

   PASSIVE   A short story was read to the class by Mr. Jenkins.

   PASSIVE   The class was read a short story.

EXERCISE A On the line before each sentence below, indicate the voice of the verb by writing *A* for *active* or *P* for *passive*. Some passive sentences contain retained objects. Write *RO* above any retained objects.

Example _____P_____ **1.** Which books have been checked out by Leota?

_____ **1.** Maggie admired her classmates' interesting and informative exhibits at the science fair.

_____ **2.** A fierce eagle's face was painted on one of the poles near Ketchikan.

_____ **3.** The volunteer was given a thank-you certificate for all his work and dedication.

_____ **4.** One artist had made a perfectly shaped pot without using a potter's wheel.

_____ **5.** At the end of our hike, we were rewarded by a gorgeous view of the sunset.

EXERCISE B On the line after each sentence below, revise the sentence to make it an active voice sentence. If the performer of an action is not mentioned, leave the sentence as it is and write *Correct*.

Example **1.** The pigs were fed by the farmer. *The farmer fed the pigs.*

6. The letter was signed by the entire class. _____

_____

7. The manuscript was edited by Paulo. _____

_____

8. A large, colorful poster was hung in the window. _____

_____

9. Finally, an understanding was reached by all parties. _____

_____

10. The Purple Heart was presented to the veteran by the President. _____

_____

Using and Revising the Passive Voice

8l. The passive voice should be used sparingly. Use the passive voice in the following situations:

(1) when you do not know the performer of the action
(2) when you do not want to reveal the performer of the action
(3) when you want to emphasize the receiver of the action

EXERCISE   On the line after each sentence below, revise the sentence to make it an active voice sentence. Write *Correct* if the sentence is already in the active voice or if the performer of an action is not mentioned and no change seems necessary.

Example 1. We were given an excellent tour of the shoe museum by her. *She gave us an excellent tour of the shoe museum.*

1. Items in the Bata Shoe Museum have been collected for over fifty years by Sonja Bata. _____

_____

2. The museum was opened in Toronto in May 1995. _____

_____

3. Ms. Bata's hobby was made easier by her husband Thomas, a shoemaker and seller. _____

_____

4. Shoemaking items, in addition to the shoes themselves, have been collected by her. _____

_____

5. Shoes of all sizes, colors, and materials have been put on display by Mrs. Bata. _____

_____

6. Those hot-pink platforms were worn by Madonna. _____

_____

7. A pair of kamiks, or bearded sealskin boots, were made in the traditional way by an Inuit. ___

_____

8. The woman asked for a new set of false teeth in payment for making the kamiks. _____

_____

9. The museum was designed by Raymond Moriyama, a Canadian architect. _____

_____

10. At the entrance to the central exhibit is a plaster cast of footprints discovered by Mary Leakey

in 1978 in Tanzania. _____

Language and Sentence Skills Practice

Mood

Mood is the form a verb takes to indicate the attitude of the person using the verb. Verbs in English may be in one of three moods.

8m. The *indicative mood* expresses a fact, an opinion, or a question.

8n. The *imperative mood* expresses a direct command or request.

8o. The *subjunctive mood* expresses a suggestion, a necessity, a condition contrary to fact, or a wish.

EXAMPLES Tula **translates** articles into Spanish. [indicative]

Show me how it works. [imperative]

Ms. Hena recommended that I **be** in your class. [present subjunctive]

I wish you **were** in chemistry with me. [past subjunctive]

EXERCISE A Indicate the mood of the underlined verb below by writing above it *IND* for *indicative, IMP* for *imperative,* or *SUB* for *subjunctive.*

                                          SUB
Example 1. Is it necessary that I <u>mail</u> this card today?

1. I wish it <u>were</u> Friday instead of Thursday.

2. The sled <u>careened</u> smoothly and quickly down the hill.

3. If I <u>were</u> going sailing, I'd take a sweater.

4. <u>Call</u> me the minute you know the results.

5. Ora wished that the weekend weather <u>were</u> better.

6. Jeanine sang as if she <u>were</u> born to be on the stage.

7. Zoe and my brother <u>were</u> good friends in junior high school.

8. The reporters <u>were pointing</u> to a tiny dot in the sky.

9. <u>Drop</u> off these clothes for me at the dry cleaner.

10. We'd hold the reception outside if it <u>weren't raining</u>.

EXERCISE B In the sentences below, draw a line through any incorrect verb form and write above it the correct one. If a sentence is already correct, write *C* after it.

                            were
Example 1. If Rebecca ~~was~~ living closer to home, her parents would worry less.

11. If I was absent, could you call me with the assignment?

12. It is essential that all passengers are seated.

13. When Eli spoke, he looked as if he was completely confident of his position.

14. One judge suggested that we be given first prize.

15. My grandfather wished he was able to spend more time with us.

190

Modals A

8p.   A *modal* is a helping, or auxiliary, verb that is joined with a main verb to express an attitude toward the action or state of being of the main verb.

(1) The modals *can* and *could* are used to express ability.
(2) The modal *may* is used to express permission or possibility.
(3) The modal *might*, like *may*, is used to express possibility.
(4) The modal *must* is used most often to express a requirement.

> **EXAMPLES**   I think we **can stay** with Aunt Tamiqua for a day or two.
> **Could** you **tell** me when the next bus leaves for Boston?
> Anyone who is interested **may attend** this seminar.
> We **might arrive** around noon tomorrow.
> Dirk **must return** his library book on time to avoid paying a fine.

EXERCISE A   In each sentence below, underline the modal.

Example   1. You <u>must</u> ask Beverly's permission before borrowing her book.

1. Most of us can paddle a canoe well enough to win a race.

2. You say you don't like tuna, but you may find it tasty if you actually try it.

3. Could our principal really have said what I thought he just said?

4. Tonight my brother and I might be cooking dinner for ourselves.

5. May I ask how long you have been standing there?

EXERCISE B   Complete the sentences below sensibly by filling in each blank with one of the following modals: *can, could, might, may,* or *must.*

Example   1. _____*May*_____ we have a moment of your time?

6. Jennifer has worked so hard that she _____ graduate with a straight A average.

7. Chuck _____ have cleaned out the garage last weekend.

8. Since you don't see any leaves, the seeds _____ not have germinated.

9. _____ all of you help me at the senior citizens' game night tonight?

10. If Melanie tells this joke just right, you _____ guess the punch line.

11. Veda _____ not have found that reference book if you had not helped her.

12. I _____ only hope that we have time to rehearse before we go onstage tonight.

13. Will you let me know when I _____ have five minutes to speak with you?

14. Mom or Dad _____ see that the car is inspected before the sticker date expires.

15. _____ you find the happiness and success you seek.

USAGE

Modals B

8p. | A *modal* is a helping, or auxiliary, verb that is joined with a main verb to express an attitude toward the action or state of being of the main verb.

(5) The modal *ought* is used to express obligation or likelihood.
(6) The modals *shall* and *will* are used to express future time.
(7) The modal *should* is used to express a recommendation, an obligation, or a possibility.
(8) The modal *would* is used to express the conditional form of a verb.

EXAMPLES   Clients **ought** to call at least a day in advance for a pet sitter. [obligation]

This **ought** to be a good time to take our vacation. [likelihood]

We **shall be delighted** to take your requests. [future time]

Dean **will be bringing** your food to you. [future time]

We **should take** the earliest flight available. [recommendation]

They **should leave** soon or they'll be late for the soccer game. [obligation]

Several of these rides **should be packed** with thrills. [possibility]

If Ilsa applied for the job, she **would** probably **get** it. [condition]

Do you recall when we **would spend** a week at camp? [repeated past action]

Would you **like** to go to a movie tomorrow afternoon? [invitation]

Would you please **pass** the mashed potatoes? [request]

EXERCISE   Complete the sentences below sensibly by filling in each blank with one of the following modals: *ought, shall, will, should,* or *would.*

Example 1. _____Would_____ you care to join us for dinner?

1. No one _____ forget that reminder to attend the dress rehearsal.

2. _____ you mind bringing me my glasses from the kitchen counter?

3. We _____ enjoy having your company on the drive to the lake.

4. _____ any of you change your minds, please call me.

5. If you had been able to finish the yardwork, I _____ not have called Leon.

6. Moira _____ to do quite well on tomorrow's college admissions test.

7. All of us wondered what Miles _____ do to train for the big race.

8. You _____ always have your doctor check your blood pressure.

9. I _____ be happy to help you train for the track meet next month.

10. Don't you think you _____ have let us know you were going to be so late?

Review A: **Principal Parts of Verbs**

EXERCISE A In each sentence below, identify the form of the underlined verb by writing above it *base form, present participle, past,* or *past participle.*

Example 1. Something with lots of wiggly legs is *creeping* up the screen. *(present participle)*

1. Ms. Suzuki asked whether either of us has ever gone to Mexico.

2. Yesterday we had emptied our canteens by noon, but today we are drinking more sparingly.

3. She gave a report last week on the life of Sojourner Truth.

4. The teams had just begun to play when we arrived.

5. She said that she rang the doorbell only once.

6. She could not have chosen a better day for a picnic.

7. Be careful not to break that delicate plate.

8. By the end of November, the pond may have frozen over, and we could go skating.

9. I can hardly believe no rain is falling for the first day in three weeks.

10. She flew to Toronto in less than two hours.

EXERCISE B On the line in each sentence below, write the correct present participle, past, or past participle of the verb provided in parentheses.

Example 1. (past form of *run*) Barbara ___ran___ four miles every day.

11. (past participle of *see*) The driver had _____ the signal.

12. (past form of *ring*) The bell _____ just before she entered the room.

13. (past participle of *speak*) Ms. Ramirez has not _____ to me about the problem.

14. (present participle of *take*) As we speak, my cousin Julia is _____ the most difficult exam she has ever encountered.

15. (past participle of *try*) Have you ever _____ the appetizer calamari, which is cooked squid?

Review B: Tense, Mood, and Modals

EXERCISE A   In each sentence below, cross out any errors in the use of verb tense and write above them the correct form of each verb. If a sentence is already correct, write *C* after it.

Example 1. Joyce said that she ~~met~~ us at the library at noon, but she got caught in a traffic jam
(would have met)

on the way there.

1. By next August I will be working at this same job for two years.

2. If the directions would have been clearer, I might have done better on the test.

3. I wish I was as talented as you are.

4. This letter is addressed to a woman who has moved out of town three years ago.

5. Last week the letter carrier brought us three packages.

EXERCISE B   On the line before each sentence below, indicate the mood of the underlined verb by writing *IND* for *indicative*, *IMP* for *imperative*, or *SUB* for *subjunctive*.

Example _SUB_ **1.** The governor suggested that his opponent <u>research</u> the issue.

_____ **6.** Is it necessary that you <u>make</u> so much noise in the evenings?

_____ **7.** Trey <u>was handing</u> each student a pep rally button with a ribbon on it.

_____ **8.** <u>Explain</u> the numerical relationship of integers in a base four system.

_____ **9.** We constantly <u>expect</u> to be overrun by junk mail and catalogs.

_____ **10.** If I <u>were</u> independently wealthy, I'd look after my family.

EXERCISE C   On the line in each sentence below, write a modal that will correctly and sensibly complete the sentence. Do not use any modal more than twice.

Example 1. ____Can____ the switch be repaired on this lamp?

11. Any answer _____ be incorrect because a chemical element is missing.

12. _____ I follow the same directions you gave me last week?

13. Some days I _____ not manage without your help.

14. You _____ to see the number of birds sitting on that wire!

15. If you were planning a vacation, where _____ you prefer to go?

Review C: Six Troublesome Verbs

USAGE

EXERCISE In the sentences below, draw a line through any incorrect verb form and write the correct past or past participle above it. If a sentence is already correct, write *C* after it.

Example 1. The branches had ~~laid~~ *lain* by the curb all week.

1. We lain the packages down on the table and left the house.

2. Where was Justina setting when you saw her last?

3. Had the book lain out in the rain all night?

4. The temperature raised to nearly ninety degrees.

5. The examination papers laid on the teacher's desk.

6. She has never once risen her hand in class.

7. Rover was laying peacefully on the front porch, when suddenly a cat ran across the lawn.

8. She started out as soon as the sun had set and the moon had risen.

9. The scarf has laid on the floor all morning.

10. Whenever I laid down, the telephone would ring.

11. The cost of oranges has rose sharply because of the freeze this winter.

12. We had sat in the stadium for more than five hours.

13. Heavy rains have rose the water level of the creek more than a foot.

14. Please sit the vase of flowers over there by the front window.

15. The huge crane sat the steel girder on top of the structure.

16. Strong winds raised from the desert sands and blasted the oasis.

17. My cousins and I set around the dining table and visit while we play games.

18. The caterpillar laid in the shade of the lantana and wildflowers.

19. Fred rose the top off the crate and began unpacking the new CDs.

20. Melting icebergs rumbled and cracked as the temperature raised.

21. Our fan belt was laying on the garage floor in three pieces.

22. How many people do you know who have rose four children?

23. Andy put the checkbook that had been setting on the desk in the top desk drawer.

24. We moved the string that was laying along the side of the board.

25. Looking for a quick meal, the frog had set by the water dish.

Review D: **Correct Use of Verbs**

EXERCISE A For each sentence below, cross out the incorrect verb and write the corrected form above it.

       flew
Example **1.** Dad ~~fly~~ to Boston last week..

1. I cannot believe that batter just swang at the ball and missed!

2. By the time this practice ends, everyone must have swam the length of the pool at least twice.

3. If those two would have done their part in the group project, the group could have received a better grade.

4. Mary McLeod Bethune, a child of former slaves, become a renowned educator.

5. Though this World Cup game is in another country, live TV allows us to watch it right as it has been played.

6. By next Thursday, we will be exercising every day in a row for two weeks.

7. Next semester, our reading assignments include short stories, poems, novels, and plays.

8. Could you have ever predicted that our debate team won the state tournament?

9. This new diva has already became my favorite country singer of all time.

10. Since she still is undecided, had your sister ever considered going out of state for college?

EXERCISE B In the paragraph below, use proofreading symbols to correct any incorrect verb usage. (Hint: There is more than one way to correct the sentences, but your revised paragraph needs to make sense as a whole.)

         had   *would the*
Example **[1]** If you ~~would have~~ mentioned skills that you had used in past jobs, ~~would you~~
    interviewer have hired you
  ~~have been hired by the interviewer~~ for that new job you wanted?

 [11] If you were on a job interview several years ago, skills learned on previous jobs would have been reviewed by a personnel director or manager. **[12]** Nowadays, you will expect to discuss personality and behavioral issues also. **[13]** In the current job market, your abilities have been examined on a questionnaire as well as during one or more face-to-face interviews. **[14]** Some interviewers will have asked you questions about your qualities as a leader. **[15]** Other interviewers may be requesting information about your skill as a team player. **[16]** Still others could rise the issue of your problem-solving ability. **[17]** Knowing your own strengths and weaknesses would prevent your being taken by surprise. **[18]** The secret to successful interviewing lays in self-testing beforehand. **[19]** It is becoming essential that you are prepared for such interviews. **[20]** Keep these hints in mind the next time you set down for an interview.

Proofreading Application: Letter

Good writers are generally good proofreaders. Readers tend to admire and trust writing that is error-free. Make sure that you correct all errors in grammar, usage, spelling, and punctuation in your writing. Your readers will have more confidence in your words if you have done your best to proofread carefully.

When you write any letter, you want to create a good impression and express yourself clearly. If you are writing the letter to a pen pal, particularly to a pen pal whose first language is not English, you especially want to have your writing free of errors, including verb form and tense errors. In addition, to make your writing more direct, you should use the passive voice sparingly.

PROOFREADING ACTIVITY

The following is a letter of introduction to a pen pal. Find and correct the letter's errors in verb forms and tense. One of your corrections will involve changing a passive verb to the active voice. Use proofreading symbols to make your corrections.

Dear Tan,

   My name is Alicia Koslowski. I'am suppose to start a correspon-

dence with a pen pal for a summer project to get extra credit for

the geography class I will take next fall. Actually, for the past

year or so I wanted to find a pen pal; now I will finally have one.

   I am in my second year at O. Henry High School in Austin, Texas.

(If I would have been born two days earlier, I would now be in my

third year.) My favorite subjects are math and biology. I use to

think that I would be a teacher, but now I want to be a research

scientist. I have two brothers and two cocker spaniels.

   Probably by the time you receive this letter, I will finish the

school year. Working hard at my studies for the past nine months, I

am now planning to relax a little during the summer vacation.

   I hope this letter is received by you without any problem. I look

forward to hearing about your life in Vietnam.

Sincerely,

Alicia Koslowski

USAGE | Language in Context: Literary Model

Literary Model: Short Story

In the wan light the faces of the men must have been gray. Their eyes must have glinted in strange ways as they gazed steadily astern. Viewed from a balcony, the whole thing would, doubtless, have been weirdly picturesque. But the men in the boat had no time to see it, and if they had had leisure, there were other things to occupy their minds. The sun swung steadily up the sky, and they knew it was broad day because the color of the sea changed from slate to emerald green streaked with amber lights, and the foam was like tumbling snow. The process of the breaking day was unknown to them. They were aware only of this effect upon the color of the waves that rolled toward them. . . .

from "The Open Boat," by Stephen Crane

EXERCISE A   To help yourself answer the questions on this worksheet, first underline all the verbs in the passage.

1. List two present perfect verbs that appear in the passage. _____

_____

2. List two past tense verbs in the passage. _____

3. What tense is the construction *had had*? _____

4. List two modals that appear in the passage. _____

EXERCISE B

1. What verb tense does Crane use more than any other in this passage?

_____

2. When writers tell a story, their choice of verb tense is deliberate. Some writers use present tense verbs to describe events that have already occurred, while others use past tense verbs to portray past events. Do you think that Crane chose an effective tense to describe this particular morning at sea? Explain your opinion.

_____

_____

_____

Literary Model (continued)

EXERCISE C Using the opener given below, write a paragraph predicting your accomplishments, experiences, or changes in the coming year. Your paragraph should include at least five sentences, each of which includes at least one future tense verb.

By this time next year I will be enjoying a sense of accomplishment. I will have

---

EXERCISE D

1. Re-read your paragraph, and check all your verbs to make sure they are in the future tense. Revise any verbs in the wrong tense.

2. Did you use a variety of verbs in your paragraph? If you have repeated any verbs, replace the duplicates with new verbs.

Language and Sentence Skills Practice

USAGE | Language in Context: Writing Application

Writing Application: Newscast

When we narrate a past event, we usually use past tense verbs to describe the action. Occasionally, however, we speak or write as though the event were happening in the present. Newscasts often use present tense to accompany pictures or videotapes of the event.

PAST TENSE   Fifty-two firefighters and fourteen trucks fought the blaze for six hours before they doused it completely.

PRESENT TENSE   Fifty-two firefighters and fourteen trucks fight the blaze for six hours before dousing it completely.

WRITING ACTIVITY

From a newspaper or magazine, choose and clip a news story of four or five paragraphs. Make sure that the event is reported in the past tense (most printed news stories are). Rewrite the entire story, changing all the verbs to present tense. In the case of irregular verbs, be sure to use the correct form.

PREWRITING   Review verb conjugation in Rule 8e if you are unsure of how present and past tense forms of verbs are formed. Choose a short news story that interests you, and cut it out of its newspaper or magazine, if possible. Then, go through the story and underline all the verbs. Also, start thinking about the best way to organize your description of the story's events.

WRITING   Because news writing is brief and to-the-point, begin your story with a one- or two-sentence introduction. Then, use present tense verbs to explain exactly what happened. Choose short transitions that move readers smoothly through the sequence of events. Many of your transitions should alert readers to causes, effects, and the progress of time. Without effective transitions, any writing—and journalistic writing in particular—can sound choppy.

REVISING   Make a list of the story's facts from the newspaper article. Check your rewrite against the list to see that you have included every fact given in the story.

PUBLISHING   Check your report for errors in grammar, usage, punctuation, and spelling. Then, read the report aloud slowly, listening for consistent use of present tense. You and other students may wish to compare the original stories with your rewrites. Which type of narration do you and your classmates prefer in a news story—past tense or present? Discuss your opinions.

EXTENDING YOUR WRITING

You may wish to develop this exercise into a longer project. For a history class, you and other students could present a "breaking news" newscast to the class, reporting an important historical event as if it had just occurred.

Choices: Exploring the Use of Modifiers

The following activities challenge you to find a connection between modifiers and the world around you. Do the activity below that suits your personality best and then share your discoveries with your class.

ETYMOLOGY

Compare and Contrast

What is the etymology of the word *comparison*? Find its root and original meanings. What other words share the root *–par–* or the prefix *com–*? Prepare a handout that shows the meanings of *comparison*'s prefix, root, and suffix. Include a list of words that share these same origins. Don't forget to give their meanings as well.

BUILDING BACKGROUND KNOWLEDGE

Everyday Use

Adverbs that should have an *–ly* ending sometimes don't in informal usage. For instance, it's not unusual to hear someone say "Walk slow" instead of "Walk slowly." For a day or two, listen to the people around you and compile a list of examples of adjective forms used as adverbs. On your list, clearly note that these expressions should not be used in formal situations. Finally, pass out copies of your list to your classmates.

DRAMA

Your Forecast Today

Stage a newscast to report the changes occurring in the English language. Include a few people in the show. One of them might be a "weather forecaster," predicting changes in English's future. Ask your librarian where you can find information on new modifiers that are entering the language.

BUILDING VOCABULARY

Friendly Persuasion

Some people think only adverbs end in *–ly*. Use friendly persuasion to show them the error of their ways. Not all adverbs end in *–ly,* and some adjectives do end in *–ly*. What are they? Do some research to compile a list. Pass out copies to the class.

OTHER LANGUAGES

What's Your Sign?

What do modifiers look like in American Sign Language? Find out. Also, find out how signers indicate degrees of comparison. If possible, invite a person skilled in signing to come and demonstrate to the class. You might want to ask this person a few questions. For instance, does American Sign Language have irregular modifiers? Are there modifiers that modify only adverbs or verbs? Do modifiers look different from other parts of speech?

DISCUSSION

A Fine Point

In a comparison, adjectives of three syllables or more should be preceded by *more* or *most.* However, is placing *more* or *most* in front of a one-syllable or two-syllable word incorrect? For instance, would *more easy* be incorrect? Why or why not? Would the expression be incorrect in all circumstances? Before you lead a discussion of these issues, find out what the grammar books say and spend several days listening for such expressions and making notes.

LITERATURE

A Far, Far Better Thing

Literature is full of famous lines that use some of the peskiest irregular modifiers. Ask some friends to join you in brainstorming some of these quotations or proverbs. Then, look them up in a good dictionary of quotations. Compile a list of quotations (be sure to highlight the modifiers) and also include the author and the year of publication. Make copies and share your findings with your classmates.

Forms of Modifiers

A *modifier* is a word or word group that makes the meaning of another word or word group more specific. An *adjective* is a modifier that makes the meaning of a noun or a pronoun more specific. An *adverb* is a modifier that makes the meaning of a verb, an adjective, or another adverb more specific. Most, but not all, modifiers that end with *–ly* are adverbs.

ADJECTIVE   The goalie made a **costly** error. [*Costly* makes the noun *error* more specific.]

ADVERB   Lester was humming the song **softly.** [*Softly* makes the verb *was humming* more specific.]

EXERCISE A   In each of the following sentences, circle the word or words modified by the underlined word.

Example 1. How familiar are you with the groundbreaking (work) of Charles Darwin?

1. Charles Darwin wrote his famous book after a trip through South America in 1832.

2. Darwin made a fascinating discovery in Argentina.

3. He discovered some enormous bones that were buried in the clay.

4. The bones were familiar in shape, but they were not very familiar in size.

5. Darwin had apparently uncovered skeletons of extinct creatures.

EXERCISE B   In each sentence below, underline the correct modifier in parentheses. Then, circle the word that it modifies.

Example 1. The golden retriever (clung) to the tennis ball (*stubborn, stubbornly*).

6. Armando looked (*steady, steadily*) for two weeks before finding a summer job.

7. Roberta applied herself (*diligent, diligently*) to her studies.

8. The (*mournful, mournfully*) sound of the violin filled the hall.

9. The foreman explained the jury's decision (*succinct, succinctly*).

10. Jacob glared (*defiant, defiantly*) at his opponent.

11. Miranda poured a glass of (*clear, clearly*) water.

12. Mom (*gentle, gently*) felt my forehead for any fever.

13. The student described the assignment (*accurate, accurately*).

14. A (*cautious, cautiously*) approach to making an important decision is usually best.

15. The trainer urged the runners on with (*loud, loudly*) cheers.

USAGE

Phrases Used as Modifiers

Like one-word modifiers, phrases can also be used as adjectives and adverbs.

ADJECTIVE PHRASE　Tony got a new job **arranging flowers.** [The participial phrase *arranging flowers* acts as an adjective modifying the noun *job*.]

ADVERB PHRASE　That task would be difficult **to accomplish by Friday.** [The infinitive phrase *to accomplish by Friday* acts as an adverb that modifies the adjective *difficult*.]

EXERCISE A　In each of the following sentences, circle the word or words modified by the underlined phrase.

Example 1. Do you ever make (plans) to do special things?

1. Echoing loudly through the room, the alarm clock woke Kim.

2. She was not a person to oversleep on the weekends, and today was special.

3. Kim and her best friend Felicia were going to the big soccer game across town.

4. Kim called Felicia, who was not easy to wake up in the morning.

5. Riding on the crowded bus, the students were eager to get to the stadium.

EXERCISE B　In each of the following sentences, identify the underlined phrase as an adjective or an adverb. Above the phrase, write *ADJ* for *adjective* or *ADV* for *adverb*. Then, circle the word the phrase modifies.

Example 1. Please (place) the book <u>on top of the bookcase.</u>　*ADV*

6. Standing on his head, the clown balanced a tray of cupcakes in his right hand.

7. Mario always comes up with great ideas of things to do on a rainy day.

8. Tara listened to the wind rustling the leaves.

9. I think the calico cat is the one to take home.

10. That is the letter for your mother.

11. After finishing our homework, we will play a game of basketball.

12. Nadia's performance at the state competion impressed the judges.

13. Losing a game is not always easy for my little brother.

14. The quarterback threw the ball to the receiver.

15. Armed with pencil and paper, Brianna readied herself for the test.

Clauses Used as Modifiers

Like words and phrases, clauses may also be used as modifiers.

ADJECTIVE CLAUSE The alligator **that tried to eat the license plate** is the one with the big grin on its face. [The adjective phrase *that tried to eat the license plate* modifies the noun *alligator.*]

ADVERB CLAUSE Rupesh will enter pilot training **after he finishes school.** [The adverb clause *after he finishes school* modifies the verb *will enter.*]

EXERCISE A In each of the following sentences, circle the word or words modified by the underlined clause.

Example 1. If you want to go to college, (think) about your plans.

1. Preparing for college is a task that requires planning and organization.

2. Because many colleges ask for a lot of paperwork, beginning the process early helps.

3. My sister Alicia is one person who worked hard on her applications.

4. She was awarded a scholarship that helps pay for tuition and books.

5. I will be happy when I send off my own applications.

EXERCISE B For each of the following sentences, identify the underlined clause as an adjective or an adverb. Above each, write *ADJ* for *adjective* or *ADV* for *adverb.* Then, circle the word the clause modifies.

Example 1. Whenever we go fishing, we (rise) early in the morning.

6. Jonathan practices the banjo until his fingers begin to ache.

7. The painting of the seascape that we bought is beautiful.

8. Since they were losing the game, the team decided to change strategies.

9. After we wash these shells, we can glue them to the poster board.

10. The dog that chased me was a Chihuahua.

11. Carlos is the one who bakes the best cakes.

12. Before I went to the park this afternoon, I had stared out the window for hours.

13. So that you can recycle them, rinse any cans or bottles you use.

14. Tennis is the sport that impresses me the most.

15. Did you recognize the man who rescued the kitten from the tree?

Uses of Modifiers

9a.   Use an adjective to modify the subject of a linking verb.

A linking verb is often used to connect its subject to a predicate adjective.

    EXAMPLE   The hailstones looked **huge.**

9b.   Use adverbs to modify action verbs.

    EXAMPLE   The man **kindly** offered to help the young children who were lost.

Some verbs may be used as linking verbs or as action verbs.

    ADJECTIVE   The pine tree in my grandmother's yard has grown **taller** since my last visit.
                  [*Has grown* is a linking verb. *Taller* is an adjective modifying *pine tree.*]

    ADVERB   We **primarily** grow herbs in our garden. [*Grow* is an action verb. *Primarily* is an
              adverb modifying *grow.*]

EXERCISE A   In each of the following sentences, circle the word or words modified by the underlined word.

Example 1. You might think that some driving (rules) are elementary.

1. We drive defensively to avoid accidents.

2. You should look around you carefully when merging with traffic.

3. Situations that seem safe may quickly become dangerous.

4. A good driver constantly remains alert.

5. Using your turn signal when turning or changing lanes is highly important.

EXERCISE B   In each sentence below, underline the correct modifier in parentheses. Then, circle the word or words that it modifies.

Example 1. This (fabric) feels (*rough, roughly*) to the touch.

6. Ice cream seems (*strange, strangely*) to eat for breakfast.

7. The editor looks (*close, closely*) at every line of print.

8. Marianna (*quick, quickly*) jumped over the log.

9. Your use of language is (*succinct, succinctly*).

10. The cow stared (*vacant, vacantly*) past the apple tree.

11. This paragraph does not seem (*clear, clearly*) to me.

12. Did Ty (*successful, successfully*) complete the marathon?

13. My dog Spike snores (*loud, loudly*).

14. The child was (*quiet, quietly*) throughout the movie.

15. When I woke up, I felt (*hungry, hungrily*).

Language and Sentence Skills Practice   **205**

USAGE

Bad and *Badly, Good* and *Well*

Bad is an adjective. *Badly* is an adverb. *Good* is an adjective, but *well* may be used as an adjective or as an adverb. The adjectives should be used to follow a sense verb or other linking verb. The adverbs should be used to modify action verbs.

ADJECTIVES   I felt **bad,** so I stayed in and read a book, which was, by the way, quite **good.**

ADVERBS   Although he started the race **badly,** by the first turn Marcus was doing quite **well.**

EXERCISE A In each of the following sentences, circle the word that is modified by the underlined word.

Example 1. After three days of bed rest, (Tamika) finally felt <u>well</u> again.

1. Rachel wanted <u>badly</u> to go on the trip, so she saved up money for the airfare.

2. Miriam sang <u>well</u> in the role of Pitti-Sing in our production of *The Mikado*.

3. Most Americans feel <u>good</u> about the freedoms they enjoy.

4. After the soup boiled over, the kitchen smelled <u>bad</u>.

5. That green shirt looks <u>good</u> with your red hair.

EXERCISE B In each sentence below, underline the modifier in parentheses that is correct according to the rules of formal, standard English.

Example 1. Is there a performer you think is especially (<u>good</u>, *well*)?

6. Celia Cruz used to put on a (*good, well*) show.

7. I feel (*bad, badly*) because I never saw her perform.

8. She sang Cuban music (*good, well*).

9. My cousins wanted very (*bad, badly*) to go to one of her shows.

10. Some entertainers are uncomfortable in front of a large audience; such insecurity can look

    (*bad, badly*).

11. Celia Cruz handled an audience (*good, well*).

12. I missed one of her shows because I didn't feel (*good, well*).

13. Missing the show made me feel as (*bad, badly*) as having the illness.

14. My mother said she was surprised at how (*good, well*) her voice was.

15. Cruz made more than fifty records, and most of them are very (*good, well*).

USAGE

Slow and Slowly, Real and Really

Slow is used as both an adjective and an adverb. *Slowly* is used as an adverb. In most adverb uses, *slowly* is better than *slow*. *Real* is an adjective. *Really* is an adverb meaning "truly" or "actually." Informally, *real* is used as an adverb meaning "very."

ADJECTIVES   That **slow** train is a **real** replica of an old steam engine.

ADVERBS   I was moving so **slowly** after the hike because I **really** needed some water.

EXERCISE A   In each of the following sentences, circle the word or words modified by the underlined word.

Example 1. (Move) the furniture slowly so the pieces don't bump into the walls.

1. Charles really is leaving, isn't he?

2. This elevator is slow.

3. I could not believe that the story she was telling me was real.

4. The dogs seemed really excited to be going to the park.

5. Alex slowly moved his pawns to the center of the chessboard.

EXERCISE B   In each of the following sentences, underline the modifier in parentheses that is correct according to the rules of formal, standard English.

Example 1. I studied (*real, really*) hard until midnight last night.

6. After taking my exams and going to work, I felt (*real, really*) tired.

7. The car began to move (*slow, slowly*), but it soon gathered speed.

8. Is that whole headdress made from (*real, really*) eagle feathers?

9. Denise (*real, really*) wants to attend the symphony's next performance.

10. The lecture was so boring that the time passed very (*slow, slowly*).

11. On the dance floor, Scott's movements are (*slow, slowly*) and his expression is calm.

12. Mr. Nasuma is a (*real, really*) expert on arachnids.

13. Are you sure these pearls are not (*real, really*) valuable?

14. A horse-and-carriage ride is (*slow, slowly*) but certainly provides a wonderful view.

15. Even if you walk (*slow, slowly*), you get cardiovascular benefit.

USAGE

Eight Troublesome Modifiers

The words *bad, good, slow,* and *real* are typically used as adjectives. The words *badly, well, slowly,* and *really* are typically used as adverbs, except when *well* is used to denote good health, as in "I feel well."

ADJECTIVES   I feel **bad** that I missed seeing that **good** movie. I heard the beginning of the film was **slow** but that the action seemed **real.**

ADVERBS   The coach was **badly** mistaken when she thought the game was going **well. Slowly** the team began to tire, and that was when their opponents **really** began to advance.

EXERCISE A   In each of the following sentences, circle the word or words modified by the underlined word.

Example 1. (Do) you <u>really</u> (think) it's going to rain this weekend?

1. Coach Garza believes that physical health and mental exercise are both <u>really</u> important.

2. If you do not exercise physically, you may feel <u>bad</u>.

3. Likewise, your brain also requires some <u>good</u> exercise.

4. Coach Garza feels <u>well</u> when she makes time for both every day.

5. She <u>slowly</u> convinced me of the benefits of exercise.

EXERCISE B   In each of the following sentences, underline the modifier in parentheses that is correct according to the rules of formal, standard English.

Example 1. Being outside on such a beautiful day feels (<u>good</u>, *well*).

6. That pony is not (*real, really*) going to jump the fence, is it?

7. Traffic is moving (*slow, slowly*) today.

8. The concert did not go too (*bad, badly*), though there were some mistakes.

9. I do not think I feel (*good, well*) enough to play basketball today.

10. Mrs. Kung (*slow, slowly*) pruned her rosebushes.

11. The politician felt (*good, well*) about his speech to the audience yesterday afternoon.

12. Tabitha said she saw a (*real, really*) van Gogh painting at her neighbor's house, but I doubt it.

13. George felt (*bad, badly*) that he had missed the goal, but he made several others.

14. Sue landed (*bad, badly*) on her left foot and sprained her ankle.

15. My mother plays piano (*good, well*) for a beginner.

Regular Comparison

9c. Modifiers change form to show comparison.

There are three degrees of comparison: the *positive*, the *comparative*, and the *superlative*.

POSITIVE	COMPARATIVE	SUPERLATIVE
big	bigger	biggest
easy	easier	easiest
cheerful	more cheerful	most cheerful
carefully	more carefully	most carefully
quickly	less quickly	least quickly

EXERCISE A   Identify the degree of comparison that each modifier shows. On the line provided, write *C* for *comparative* or *S* for *superlative*.

Example ___C___ **1.** brighter

_____ **1.** least cautious

_____ **2.** loudest

_____ **3.** more soundly

_____ **4.** most eccentric

_____ **5.** thriftiest

_____ **6.** nicer

_____ **7.** more aggressively

_____ **8.** tiniest

_____ **9.** less energetic

_____ **10.** more competently

EXERCISE B   On the lines provided, write each italicized modifier in the form described in parentheses.

Example 1. I am *less adventurous* than many people I know, but I have traveled to some

interesting places. (*adventurous*, decreasing comparative)

11. Guadalajara has some of the _____ crafts I've seen. (*beautiful*, superlative)

12. This area certainly has a _____ climate than Detroit has. (*warm*, comparative)

13. The city has _____ plazas than most other cities have. (*large*, comparative)

14. People here are _____ about the time. (*worried*, decreasing comparative)

15. One of the _____ events is their local rodeo. (*wonderful*, superlative)

Language and Sentence Skills Practice

USAGE

Irregular Comparison

The comparative and superlative degrees of some modifiers are not formed by the usual methods.

POSITIVE	COMPARATIVE	SUPERLATIVE
bad *or* ill	worse	worst
good *or* well	better	best
many *or* much	more	most
far	farther *or* further	farthest *or* furthest

EXERCISE A Identify the degree of comparison that each word shows. On the line provided, write *P* for *positive*, *C* for *comparative*, or *S* for *superlative*.

Example __*P*__ **1.** much

_____ **1.** furthest   _____ **5.** best   _____ **8.** far

_____ **2.** worse   _____ **6.** less   _____ **9.** farther

_____ **3.** well   _____ **7.** more   _____ **10.** worst

_____ **4.** bad

EXERCISE B On the lines provided, write each modifier in the form described in parentheses.

Example 1. The prosecution offered evidence that _____*further*_____ implicated the accused in

the commission of the crime. (*far*, comparative)

11. That misadventure in Norway was not the _____ experience I have survived.

(*bad*, superlative)

12. Felicia did _____ on the test than she expected. (*well*, comparative)

13. If _____ people recycled, we could better help protect the environment.

(*many*, comparative)

14. We hope her grandmother does not feel _____ today. (*ill*, comparative)

15. You should put _____ salt on your food. (*little*, comparative)

16. The _____ decision I ever made was to attend college. (*good*, superlative)

17. Carlos needs _____ ingredients to make the salad. (*much*, comparative)

18. _____ people would tell you they are excellent drivers. (*many*, superlative)

19. The defendant's story could not be _____ from the truth. (*far*, comparative)

20. The Scout troop rafted _____ down the river than they had planned.

(*far*, comparative)

Regular and Irregular Comparison

To choose the correct form of comparison, first determine whether the modifier is regular or irregular. Then, determine the degree of comparison.

REGULAR   pretty, prettier, prettiest

generous, more generous, most generous

IRREGULAR   well, better, best

bad, worse, worst

EXERCISE A   On the lines provided, write the comparative and superlative forms of each of the following modifiers. Do not include decreasing comparisons.

Example 1. successfully   *more successfully, most successfully* _____

1. plainly _____

2. near _____

3. much _____

4. impatiently _____

5. ill _____

EXERCISE B   On the lines provided, write each italicized modifier in the form described in parentheses.

Example 1. Fruits or vegetables are much _____*better*_____ for you than cookies. (*good*, comparative)

6. _____ kittens are playful. (*many*, superlative)

7. It is _____ to give people constructive criticism than simply to attack their work. (*nice*, comparative)

8. A _____ host you will not find anywhere. (*gracious*, comparative)

9. I felt _____ about breaking the expensive vase than about stepping on her toe. (*bad*, comparative)

10. Earl knows _____ of the best jazz musicians around town. (*many*, superlative)

11. Jerome turned out to be the _____ archer in the class. (*accurate*, superlative)

12. After being teased himself, Todd was _____ to others. (*kind*, comparative)

13. The area in which we pushed our research _____ was in deciphering the symbols on the temple ruins. (*far*, superlative)

14. That is the _____ sweater I have ever seen. (*green*, superlative)

15. The _____ said on the subject, the better. (*little*, comparative)

Comparative and Superlative Forms A

9d.	Use the comparative degree when comparing two things. Use the superlative degree when comparing more than two things.

COMPARATIVE   Carla is the **less talkative** of my two aunts.

SUPERLATIVE   Of all my uncles, Vinnie is the **least talkative.**

EXERCISE A   On the line provided, write the correct form of the italicized modifier.

Example 1. *good*   Friday would be a _____*better*_____ day for me to go than Monday.

1. *friendly*   Louise is one of the _____ people in my school.

2. *nervous*   I felt _____ about my speech than I did about my exam.

3. *young*   My brother is the _____ player on his soccer team.

4. *dark*   My sister's hair is _____ than mine.

5. *interesting*   Of the two books that I read, the first was _____.

6. *thick*   Your dog certainly has a _____ coat than mine has.

7. *shaggy*   I could not say which of the two burros was _____.

8. *wild*   That blizzard is the _____ one I've ever seen!

9. *promptly*   The person who answers the question _____ wins first prize.

10. *active*   That kitten is the _____ one of the litter.

EXERCISE B   On the lines provided, revise the following sentences to correct errors in comparisons.

Example 1. Of the ten players, Tomás is the faster runner.   _Of the ten players, Tomás is the_
fastest runner.

11. It was the rainier weather of any I've ever seen! _____

_____

12. Of all my baseball cards, this one is the more valuable. _____

_____

13. Of the two books, the first book is the longest. _____

_____

14. She is the more famous person to have graduated from my high school. _____

_____

15. The biggest puppy of the litter is also the louder one. _____

_____

Comparative and Superlative Forms B

9d. Use the comparative degree when comparing two things. Use the superlative degree when comparing more than two things.

> COMPARATIVE Tomorrow morning is a **better** time to meet than tomorrow afternoon.
> SUPERLATIVE Tomorrow morning is the **best** time to meet.

USAGE

EXERCISE A On the line provided, write the correct form of the italicized modifier.

Example 1. *happy*   Julio could not have been _____*happier*_____ about our plans.

1. *bad*   Last winter I had the _____ flu of my life.

2. *many*   I heard him say _____ than once that he was leaving.

3. *smart*   My sister says she is the _____ of the two of us.

4. *attractive* I really think that dress is the _____ one you own.

5. *good*   We had a _____ time there than we'd expected.

6. *rich*   The sauce has a _____ flavor than the one you made last week.

7. *early*   Juanita should have thrown the ball _____ .

8. *far*   The _____ place from home we have traveled is San Francisco.

9. *generously* Mr. Katz gave _____ to the charity than his colleague did.

10. *late*   What is the _____ news on that story?

EXERCISE B On the lines provided, revise the sentences below to correct errors in comparisons.

Example 1. What is the more interesting aspect of the book we just read? _What is the most_
interesting aspect of the book we just read?

11. Don't you think the largest of the two trees would provide more shade? _____
_____

12. That pitch was the faster Stacey had ever thrown. _____
_____

13. The worse part about sleeping late on Saturday is that I feel as if I have wasted my whole day.
_____

14. Which is the most important chore to do now, sweeping or washing the dishes? _____
_____

15. The quieter of the three babies fell asleep before the others. _____
_____

Language and Sentence Skills Practice   **213**

Double Comparisons

| **9e.** | Avoid using double comparisons. |

A *double comparison* is the use of two comparative forms (usually *–er* and *more*) or two superlative forms (usually *–est* and *most*) to modify the same word.

DOUBLE COMPARISON   This film is more longer than the last one we saw together.

STANDARD   This film is **longer** than the last one we saw together.

EXERCISE   Revise the following sentences to correct errors in the use of comparisons. Write the revised sentences on the lines provided. If a sentence is already correct, write C.

Example 1. The more I practice, the more better I get at playing the trumpet. *The more I practice, the better I get at playing the trumpet.*

1. Yesterday, Yan and Billy ran more farther than they usually do. _____

_____

2. Jennifer thinks that Beethoven's Ninth Symphony is the most greatest musical

composition ever. _____

_____

3. The most best way to become a better writer is to write as often as possible. _____

_____

4. We waited more longer in line for the first movie than the second. _____

_____

5. The deer ran more faster as the car passed. _____

_____

6. Pedro's skill in tennis is most evident when he serves. _____

_____

7. The quilt Marc's grandmother made for him is the most softest blanket he has. _____

_____

8. Charlie's cat is already huge, and it's only going to get more bigger. _____

_____

9. That was the most best game I've ever seen! _____

_____

10. What is more certainer is that no person can be at two places at the same time. _____

_____

Comparisons Within Groups

9f.   Include the word *other* or *else* when comparing one member of a group with the rest of the group.

NONSTANDARD   Arlo is funnier than anyone in his class.

STANDARD   Arlo is funnier than anyone **else** in his class.

STANDARD   Arlo is funnier than any **other** person in his class.

EXERCISE   Revise the following sentences to correct errors in the use of comparisons. Write the revised sentences on the lines provided.

Example 1. Shawn makes higher grades than anyone in our school.   *Shawn makes higher*
                grades than anyone else in our school.

1. Of all the subjects I have this year, Biology II is better than any class. _____

_____

2. My brother Jim is taller than anyone in his class. _____

_____

3. The queen is better than all the chess pieces. _____

_____

4. Rachel has more saves than any goalkeeper in our district. _____

_____

5. Jane plays the clarinet better than anyone in her band. _____

_____

6. Rafael caught more fish with the top-water lure than with any method. _____

_____

7. Katy has climbed higher mountains than anyone her age. _____

_____

8. Of all my pictures, this framed one is more interesting than any. _____

_____

9. Soccer is better than any team sport. _____

_____

10. Anita performed more volunteer work than any person in her community. _____

_____

USAGE

Clear Comparisons and Absolute Adjectives A

9g. | Be sure comparisons are clear.

Use a complete comparison if an incomplete one could be misunderstood.

UNCLEAR   Juan talks to his sister more than his brother.

CLEAR   Juan talks to his sister more than **his brother does.**

CLEAR   Juan talks to his sister more than **he talks to his brother.**

Absolute adjectives have no comparative or superlative forms; they do not vary in degree. Avoid using absolute adjectives—such as *correct, dead, empty,* and *unique*—in comparisons.

EXERCISE " On the lines provided, revise the sentences below to correct errors in the use of comparisons.

Example 1. The second test will be as hard, if not harder than, the first test.

The second test will be as hard as, if not harder than, the first test.

1. It is more correct to use the word *may* to ask someone's permission than to use *can.* _____

_____

2. The audience enjoyed the music as much as the cast. _____

_____

3. Roland plays with the school rugby team more often than anyone else. _____

_____

4. The parts of a pickup truck are larger than a normal car. _____

_____

5. Alex's drawing of the house was more square than mine. _____

_____

6. Of all the stories told tonight, I thought Tina's was the most unique. _____

_____

7. The bear's paws hit the water more often than the fish. _____

_____

8. My uncle likes that baseball team more than anyone else. _____

_____

9. After eating dessert, I felt even fuller. _____

_____

10. I cannot think of any truer words than "Home is where your heart is." _____

_____

Clear Comparisons and Absolute Adjectives B

9g. Be sure comparisons are clear.

Use a complete comparison if an incomplete one could be misunderstood.

UNCLEAR   Tom likes broccoli more than Janet.

CLEAR   Tom likes broccoli more than **Janet does.**

Absolute adjectives have no comparative or superlative forms; they do not vary in degree. Avoid using absolute adjectives—such as *complete, dead, equal,* and *unique*—in comparisons.

EXERCISE   On the lines provided, revise the sentences below to correct errors in the use of comparisons.

Example 1. With the addition of the sunset, the painting was more complete. *With the addition*
of the sunset, the painting was complete.

1. The quietness was replaced by a deader silence. _____

_____

2. During the debate, Susan offered a more complete set of arguments in favor of her position.

_____

3. I can't think of anything more infinite than the number of stars in the sky. _____

_____

4. The painting was not as unique as the others. _____

_____

5. Marissa made a more perfect drawing of the flowers. _____

_____

6. Patricia gave more food to her dog than her cat. _____

_____

7. Juan and Pilar enjoyed the movie more than anyone else in the group. _____

_____

8. Kara's circle was more round than mine. _____

_____

9. The prospect of the wide ocean was even more endless than the view of a prairie. _____

_____

10. How much more assistance did you give to Mark than Eddy? _____

_____

USAGE

Comparisons Review

9c.	Modifiers change form to show comparison.
9d.	Use the comparative degree when comparing two things. Use the superlative degree when comparing more than two things.
9e.	Avoid using double comparisons.
9f.	Include the word *other* or *else* when comparing one member of a group with the rest of the group.
9g.	Be sure comparisons are clear.

EXERCISE   Revise the following sentences to correct errors in the use of comparisons. Write the revised sentences on the lines provided.

Example 1. He praised Nha as much as Eve.   *He praised Nha as much as Eve did.*

1. The skills of our players were sharper than the other team. _____

_____

2. Of the twins, Gary is the tallest. _____

_____

3. I thought the dog's trick was the most funniest thing I have ever seen. _____

_____

4. Gabe likes broccoli more than any vegetable. _____

_____

5. The explorer said the footprints were bigger than any average alligator. _____

_____

6. Much is to be gained in the struggle for more equal rights for all Americans. _____

_____

7. My aunt has received more college degrees than any member of my family. _____

_____

8. Arturo's second rocket soared more higher than his first. _____

_____

9. Of all the experiences on the trip, Mike thought the wonderfullest was the boat ride. _____

_____

10. Walking across the stage to accept her award was Mia's most happiest moment. _____

Review A: **Forms of Modifiers**

USAGE

EXERCISE Each of the following sentences contains an error in the use of modifiers. Draw a line through each error and write the correct form above it. Base your answers on the rules of standard, formal usage.

carefully
Example 1. Concentrating ~~careful~~, Molly delivered her serve.

1. Her goal as mayor was to treat everyone equal.

2. To avoid accidents, people must drive attentive.

3. The workers handled the explosives very cautious.

4. Recovering quick, Renaldo regained his balance and kept running.

5. In order to play the piano well, one has to practice regular.

6. My brother has been doing his work good ever since his boss spoke to him.

7. The geraniums in the greenhouse looked beautifully.

8. The neighbors' yappy new puppy certainly seems loudly to me.

9. The team lost the first game by a single run, but they won the second game easy, 10–2.

10. The students thought that Ms. Pong's outfits looked elegantly.

11. The members of the team that had just lost the championship felt sadly.

12. The costume fits you perfect.

13. Blowing strong across the hillside, the wind knocked over the tree.

14. Henry felt positively that he was going to be elected to the student council.

15. The squirrel looked anxious for a place to bury the acorn.

16. Summer days in Arizona can get real hot.

17. Ms. Chan and the rest of the golf club ate their early breakfast quick.

18. Drive careful now, George.

19. The president of the club voiced her opinion quite eloquent.

20. Claudia seemed happily about receiving such a good grade.

Language and Sentence Skills Practice **219**

Review B: **Eight Troublesome Modifiers**

EXERCISE   Each of the following sentences contains an error in the use of modifiers. Draw a line through each error and write the correct form above it. Base your answers on the rules of standard, formal usage.

Example 1. Martine sure plays the trumpet ~~good~~ *well*.

1. The plan sounded well, but it did not work very well.

2. Tony's record of wins was only fair, but he pitched good in tough situations.

3. The books that we had ordered were slowly in arriving.

4. I hope An Li feels good enough to go to the recital.

5. The class was real tired after their field trip to the mountains.

6. Nations, like people, can get along good or badly.

7. We agreed that the band had played bad in the parade.

8. The situation in the strife-torn country looked badly.

9. Are you real sure, Ernesto?

10. The butter tasted so badly that we were sure it had become rancid.

11. Running slow, Gina crested the top of the hill.

12. The bus seemed slowly today.

13. The truck climbed the steep hill slow.

14. Her command of the Russian language was bad, but she spoke Polish pretty good.

15. My parents were real glad you could come to the meeting.

16. After two days of fever, Ernie felt good enough to get out of bed.

17. Sonya felt badly for the people who didn't finish their projects on time.

18. When taking up running, start off real slowly.

19. It felt well to be on vacation finally.

20. Tom was not real convinced of the defendant's innocence.

Review C: **Comparison**

EXERCISE A In the following sentences, draw a line through each error in the use of comparisons and write the correct form above it. Base your answers on the rules of standard, formal usage.

Example 1. Of the two books, this one is ~~best~~. *better*

1. People in Paris were more friendlier than I had ever expected.

2. Shalisa's bicycle looked much worser before it was painted.

3. Of all the pianists in the class, Rico was the older and most experienced.

4. Of the two desserts, rice pudding is easiest to prepare.

5. Billy, the youngest of the two cousins, lives in Chattanooga.

6. Last week's snowstorm was the worse blizzard of the decade.

7. The woman in Ward D had more visitors than any patient in the hospital.

8. I think that Pilar is more happier at camp than she thought she would be.

9. She usually makes more higher grades than anyone else in her class.

10. The golfer said she was least happiest when she missed a short putt.

EXERCISE B After each of the following sentences, words appear in parentheses. Rewrite each sentence inserting the words in parentheses at the place indicated by the caret (∧). The added words will require at least one change in the sentence. Write the revised sentences on the lines provided.

Example 1. The casserole looked good ∧. (than any other dish at the picnic) *The casserole* _____
    looked better than any other dish at the picnic. _____

11. Consuelo was certainly happy about the early election returns ∧. (than Pauline was) _____

    _____

12. Dr. Feldman's appointment as dean was recent ∧. (than any other staff changes) _____

    _____

13. Roberto swims fast ∧. (than any other member of the team) _____

    _____

14. The new lawyer was unaware of the facts in the case ∧. (than she should have been) _____

    _____

15. Olga decided that architecture would be a satisfying choice ∧. (of the three careers she was

    considering) _____

    _____

Language and Sentence Skills Practice   **221**

USAGE

Review D: **Problems with Modifiers**

EXERCISE A In the following sentences, draw a line through each error in the use of modifiers and write the correct form above it. Base your answers on the rules of standard, formal usage.

beautiful
Example 1. Utah is the most ~~beautifullest~~ state I've visited.

1. Waving his arms wild, Josh jumped into the water.

2. Jan speaks French really good.

3. Do you think the man's story is truer than the others?

4. Of the pair of birds, the cockatoo is least likely to sing.

5. The committee agreed to investigate the matter more further.

6. Speak slow so that I can understand you better.

7. Do you look worriedly because you are still thinking about the test?

8. After taking the medicine, I felt more better.

9. Nadia felt well about having helped out on the recycling project.

10. Ivan politely asked for a game that would last real long.

EXERCISE B After each of the following sentences, words appear in parentheses. Rewrite each sentence inserting the words in parentheses at the place indicated by the caret (∧). The added words may require changes in the sentence.

Example 1. His sister usually speaks softly ∧. (than he does)   *His sister usually speaks more*

  softly than he does.

11. After a few days' rest, the governor is feeling well ∧. (than she did before) _____

_____

12. Mr. Chang predicted that snowfall this year would be as heavy as ∧ last year's. (if not _____

  heavier than) _____

_____

13. Our drama coach looked happy ∧. (yesterday than he does today) _____

_____

14. Cai's job carries little responsibility ∧. (than yours) _____

_____

15. ∧ The films that we saw in history class were certainly interesting, but we all agreed that the

  first one was the most dramatic. (Both of) _____

_____

Proofreading Application: E-mail

Good writers are generally good proofreaders. Readers tend to admire and trust writing that is error-free. Make sure that you correct all errors in grammar, usage, spelling, and punctuation in your writing. Your readers will have more confidence in your words if you have done your best to proofread carefully.

When you communicate by e-mail with a company about its products or services, your writing should be descriptive, clear, and precise. The correct use of modifiers will help you to achieve this goal.

PROOFREADING ACTIVITY

The following is an e-mail requesting information from a company. Find and correct the errors in the use of modifiers. Use proofreading symbols to make your corrections.

TO: customerservice@HOMEPRODUCTS.com

SUBJECT: Bread Machine Model 68—038

Dear Customer Service Representative:

Yesterday I ate the most perfect bread at my best friend's house. Its taste was superior to any bread I have ever eaten. Since I have been thinking serious about selling baked goods as a way to make extra money for college, I asked my friend's mother how she made the bread. I was real surprised when she told me she had made it in her bread machine. Of course, I told her about my idea and asked her the brand and price of her machine. The price is more higher than I thought it would be. She told me that this machine cooks bread more fast than the other two she has had and that, among the three of them, she likes your model better. She said the bread she bakes in it is as tasty, if not tastier than, the bread her neighbor makes in a machine that cost her twice as much. Please send me very complete information on your bread machine model 68—038; the more sooner the better.

Sincerely,

Literary Model: Drama

from *Macbeth* by William Shakespeare

[Act I Scene 4]

Malcolm. . . . He died
As one that hath been studied in his death
To throw away the <u>dearest</u> thing he owed,
As 'twere a <u>careless</u> trifle.

Duncan. O worthiest cousin!
The sin of my ingratitude even now
Was <u>heavy</u> on me: thou art so <u>far</u> before,
That <u>swiftest</u> wing of recompense is slow
To overtake thee.
Would thou hast <u>less deserved</u>,
That the proportion both of thanks and
  payment
Might have been mine!"

[Act I Scene 5]

Lady Macbeth. Great Glamis! Worthy
  Cawdor!
<u>Greater</u> than both, by the all-hail
  hereafter!

[Act I Scene 7]

Macbeth. We will proceed no <u>further</u>
in this business:
He hath honored me of late, and I have
  bought
<u>Golden</u> opinions from all sorts of people,
Which would be worn now in their <u>newest</u>
  gloss,
Not cast aside so soon.

EXERCISE A For each of the underlined words in these *Macbeth* excerpts, place the modifier in the correct comparison category, and then supply the other two forms of the modifier.

POSITIVE	COMPARATIVE	SUPERLATIVE
1.		
2.		
3.		
4.		
5.		
6.		
7.		
8.		
9.		
10.		

Literary Model (continued)

EXERCISE B   In this play Macbeth's unexpected career advancement only whets his ambition. Explain why comparison forms are likely to abound in literature dealing with themes such as ambition, greed, and envy.

_____

_____

_____

_____

EXERCISE C   Imagine yourself in the shoes of a person who has finished a competition in second place, rather than in the winner's spot. Write a fictional journal entry that explains how the second-place winner feels about the efforts and rewards of the competition. Use at least three modifiers of comparison: one positive, one comparative, and one superlative.

_____

_____

_____

_____

_____

_____

_____

_____

_____

_____

_____

EXERCISE D   Describe the tone of your fictional journal entry. How did you use comparisons to show how your character feels? Use details from your journal in your answer.

_____

_____

_____

_____

Language and Sentence Skills Practice

Writing Application: Campaign Speech

Superlatives can easily be overused. Be careful not to overstate your case, or readers may not take what you say seriously.

   OVERSTATED   J. B.'s Barbecue: It's the Best in the Country!

                He is the greatest teacher you'll ever have!

Readers become so accustomed to reading about "the best," "the greatest," and "the ultimate" that they ignore many superlatives. Careful writers use them sparingly and sincerely so that readers will take the claims seriously.

WRITING ACTIVITY

Your best friend, who is running for office on the student council, has asked you to help with the campaign. You are happy to do so because you sincerely believe that your friend would do well in office. Write a three- or four-minute supporting speech to present at a student assembly and to be published in the student newspaper. Be honest about your friend's qualifications and choose three compelling superlatives that describe him or her.

   PREWRITING   List the attributes that qualify your friend for the office. List also any shortcomings that might be relevant and brainstorm answers to any questions the audience might ask about them.

   WRITING   In prewriting, you listed the candidate's strengths. Simply turning this list into sentences will not provide good organization for your speech. Decide on the most effective order of presentation, remembering that your audience will remember longest whatever you say last.

   REVISING   Read the speech out loud, as you will at the presentation, into a tape recorder if possible. You might also have someone else read it aloud to you. Listen for awkward or incorrect use of modifiers. Also, listen to the speech's tone. Is it confident and enthusiastic? Does it convey your honest beliefs? Or, does it sound overstated and forced?

   PUBLISHING   Check your speech for errors in spelling and punctuation. Be sure that you have used the correct forms of modifiers and placed them near the words they modify. The version of the speech that you submit to the student paper should conform to any editorial requirements. With your teacher's permission, present your speech to the class.

EXTENDING YOUR WRITING

You may wish to develop this exercise into a longer essay. For a civics or government class, you could explore the demands of leadership and which personal characteristics leaders need. For a history class, you could research a well-known leader in a field that interests you.

Choices: Putting Modifiers in the Right Place

The following activities challenge you to find a connection between modifiers and the world around you. Do the activity below that suits your personality best, and then share your discoveries with your class.

CONTEST

Just for Laughs

Misplaced modifiers are often funny, even though the writer may not have intended readers to laugh. Hold a contest to see who can write (and correct) the most hilarious misplaced modifier. You'll need a panel of judges. The winner's entry receives a round of applause and a prize of your choosing.

DEMONSTRATION

Places, Everyone!

You're going to need at least five people for this project. First, write three or four relatively short sentences that each include a misplaced modifier—a word, phrase, or clause. Then, in bold red marker, transfer each misplaced modifier onto its own large piece of paper or poster board. Write the other words in each sentence in black, one to a piece of poster board. In the order of each original sentence, have your group members stand in front of the class and hold up the words. Ask the class where the person holding the misplaced modifier should stand. In how many places can the modifier sensibly fit?

DEMONSTRATION

Bits and Pieces

Divide the class into several small groups. Hand out strips of paper on which you have written three sentences with misplaced modifiers—a prepositional phrase, a participial phrase, and a clause. Tell each group to cut the misplaced modifier out of the sentence. Have groups also cut each of the other words or phrases out of the strip. Then, ask each group to move the strips around until the misplaced modifier finds its proper place. Ask each group for its correction, and write the corrected sentence on the chalkboard. How many different corrections did groups find for each sentence?

MODERN LITERATURE

Avant-Garde

Some modern poets take advantage of the confusion that misplaced modifiers cause. These writers may run two sentences together, make the last word of one sentence the subject of the next, make the last noun in a sentence serve as an adjective in the next, or use only words or phrases rather than sentences. These writers sometimes leave the question of what modifies what up to the reader. The results of these experiments are interesting and often beautiful. Check out a few books of modern poetry and find some examples of these techniques. Show your examples to the class. Be ready to point out modifiers that serve multiple roles in a poem.

TECHNOLOGY

A Wizard of Oz

How much can you depend on that electronic wizard called a grammar checker? Will the Wiz spot a misplaced modifier? It's time to find out. Use a word processor to type a number of sentences with misplaced modifiers. Then, run the grammar checker. How many errors did the program miss? Did it catch any mistakes? Were its corrections appropriate? You be the judge. Report back to the class with a graph charting the program's performance.

CREATIVE WRITING

The Hare and the Tortoise

Write a fable about characters who are misled by a misplaced modifier. If you'd like, read a few of Aesop's fables and use them as a guide for the format of your story. You will need a short moral of the story to place at the end. Illustrate your fable if you like. Then, read your fable to the class.

Misplaced Modifiers A

10a. Avoid using misplaced modifiers.

A *misplaced modifier* is a modifying word, phrase, or clause that seems to modify the wrong word or word group in a sentence. To correct a misplaced modifier, place the modifying word, phrase, or clause as close as possible to the word or words you intend it to modify.

MISPLACED   High up on the wall, I saw a fly. [Was I high up on the wall or was the fly?]

CORRECT   I saw a fly high up on the wall.

EXERCISE A   Some of the following sentences contain misplaced modifiers. In those sentences, underline the modifying clause or phrase that is misplaced. If a sentence is correct, write *C* before the number.

Examples 1. We discussed our trip to Ghana at the neighborhood community center, <u>which we</u>

<u>had wanted to visit for years.</u>

C **2.** Our guide Celia was invaluable during that time.

1. Celia said after her trip she would show slides of Ghana.

2. We took a ferry on the lake called the *Akasombo Queen*.

3. Tourists can stay in guest houses visiting the coast.

4. Years ago the country now called Ghana was known as the Gold Coast.

5. Our tour guide could speak English, Twi, and Nzima in Ghana.

EXERCISE B   On the lines provided, revise the following sentences to correct misplaced modifiers.

Example 1. Felipe saw a giraffe riding his bike down the road next to the zoo. _____

   Riding his bike down the road next to the zoo, Felipe saw a giraffe.

6. Exhausted, the ribbon snapped as the winner of the marathon ran through. _____

_____

7. There is a stereo in the store that is on sale. _____

_____

8. Investigators tested pollution levels equipped with elaborate instruments. _____

_____

9. Mr. Jewesson spotted several moose canoeing down the river. _____

_____

10. Jorge brought a stray puppy to the movie theater, which was too excited to stay quiet. _____

_____

Misplaced Modifiers B

10a. Avoid using misplaced modifiers.

EXERCISE A   Some of the following sentences contain misplaced modifiers. In those sentences, underline the modifying clause or phrase that is misplaced. If a sentence is correct, write *C* next to the item number.

Examples **1.** Ghana is a place that has not been visited by many of my friends at school <u>in Africa</u>.

C **2.** Helping break the language barrier, Trey's dictionary was worth every penny he spent on it.

1. When the Volta River was dammed, Celia said a lake was created.

2. Celia announced in the city of Accra she had contacted the youth hostel.

3. All the spaces had been reserved by local students the week before.

4. When they got off the plane, the beautiful hills awed the tourists.

5. We bought seafood from a local fishing boat that was fresh.

EXERCISE B   Revise the following sentences to correct misplaced modifiers. Write your revised sentences on the lines provided.

Example **1.** The Schulzes will host the party we read about in the newspaper next week. _____

Next week, the Schulzes will host the party we read about in the newspaper.

6. Billy studied strategies used by Confederate generals in the Civil War last summer. _____

_____

7. Running down the field, the football slipped away from Mark. _____

_____

8. Elaine brought a watercolor to her painting class, which was praised by everyone present. ___

_____

9. The dancers twirled to the side of the stage stepping to the beat of the music. _____

_____

10. Roberto rehearsed the melody he would play onstage in practice. _____

_____

Squinting Modifiers A

USAGE

10b. Avoid misplacing a modifying word, phrase, or clause so that it seems to modify either of two words. Such a misplaced modifier is often called a *squinting,* or a *two-way, modifier.*

MISPLACED	Dr. Hena told the man before the operation what to expect.
CORRECT	**Before the operation,** Dr. Hena told the man what to expect.
CORRECT	Dr. Hena told the man what to expect **before the operation.**

EXERCISE Revise the following sentences to correct squinting modifiers. On the lines provided, write each of the two ways the sentences might be revised.

Example 1. Henry and Dat found a pattern in the design they wanted to copy.

In the design, Henry and Dat found a pattern they wanted to copy.

Henry and Dat found a pattern they wanted to copy in the design.

1. The president said when the club met she would announce the next fund-raiser.

2. The coach of the losing side said yesterday the team played as well as it could.

3. June made up her mind after the performance to celebrate with her family.

4. The squirrels hid the pecans they collected at the base of the tree.

5. Ally broke the school record after changing her training regimen last week.

Squinting Modifiers B

10b. Avoid misplacing a modifying word, phrase, or clause so that it seems to modify either of two words. Such a misplaced modifier is often called a *squinting,* or a *two-way, modifier.*

USAGE

EXERCISE A Some of the following sentences contain squinting modifiers. In those sentences, underline the modifying word, clause, or phrase that is squinting. If a sentence is correct, write *C* before the item.

Example 1. Antonio said <u>tomorrow</u> he would visit his aunt.

1. Mr. Jenkins stopped to talk on his way to work with Mr. Kung.

2. The president of our club said yesterday the project was a great success.

3. After the meeting, Juwan and Beverly decided to tabulate their results.

4. Suzanne said she would build a better rocket after she bought new materials.

5. Jeff will start planning the design he intends to enter in the competition tomorrow.

EXERCISE B Revise the following sentences to correct squinting modifiers. On the lines provided, write two ways the sentences might be revised.

Example 1. The woman said when she arrived we could begin.

When she arrived, the woman said we could begin.

The woman said we could begin when she arrived.

6. Alex decided after the movie to work on his own screenplay.

_____

_____

7. The skiers said as soon as the first snow fell they would travel to Colorado.

_____

_____

8. I told Celia yesterday I had seen the new film.

_____

_____

9. The reporter said last night the police had found the suspect.

_____

_____

10. Jill announced at the time of the hearing she was ready to testify.

_____

_____

USAGE

Dangling Modifiers A

10c. Avoid using dangling modifiers.

A *dangling modifier* is a modifying word, phrase, or clause that does not sensibly modify any word in a sentence. To correct a dangling modifier, add or replace words to make the sentence clear and sensible.

> **DANGLING MODIFIER** Startled by the shout, the noise made me look around. [The noise wasn't startled by the shout; the speaker was.]
>
> **CORRECTED FOR CLARITY** Startled by the noise of the shout, I looked around.

EXERCISE A Read each sentence below, and decide whether it has a clear meaning or it contains a dangling modifier. On the line provided, write *C* for *clear* or *DM* for *dangling modifier*.

Examples __C__ **1.** Running across the field, the dog barked at the kite.

__DM__ **2.** Soaked by the heavy rain, it felt good to get inside.

_____ **1.** While jogging along Center Street, an accident occurred.

_____ **2.** Looking out the window, a remarkable sight appeared.

_____ **3.** Taxiing smoothly to a stop, the airplane halted near the terminal.

_____ **4.** Wearing heavy clothing, the hike up the mountain was tiring.

_____ **5.** Alone in the house, Phoebe jumped at every noise.

EXERCISE B Revise each sentence below to correct the dangling modifier. Write your revised sentences on the lines provided.

Example 1. Having chosen a park for the party, the next task was calling Miguel's friends.

Having chosen a park for the party, Miguel next called his friends.

6. Hot and tired, the pool water felt refreshing. _____

_____

7. Having considered all of the evidence, the defendant was found not guilty. _____

_____

8. Kicking a soccer ball every day, the pain in her left knee grew worse. _____

_____

9. Opening my umbrella, the rain stopped almost immediately. _____

_____

10. Slowly approaching the intersection, the traffic signal changed from yellow to red. _____

_____

USAGE

Dangling Modifiers B

| **10c.** | Avoid using dangling modifiers.

A *dangling modifier* is a modifying word, phrase, or clause that does not sensibly modify any word in a sentence.

EXERCISE A   Read each sentence below, and decide whether it has a clear meaning or it contains a dangling modifier. On the line provided, write *C* for *clear* or *DM* for *dangling modifier*.

Example   *DM*   **1.** Stapling the pages in order, the report was ready to be turned in.

_____ **1.** After playing the banjo for several years, Larry's favorite music became jazz.

_____ **2.** To make a good grade in the class, homework will need to be done on time.

_____ **3.** At the top of the slide, the child grinned happily.

_____ **4.** To fix the faucet, a wrench will be needed.

_____ **5.** Having chosen a topic, Juan's paper merely required writing.

_____ **6.** To win this game, our team will need to practice hard and prepare.

_____ **7.** After building a diorama, Eli will show his work to the historical society.

_____ **8.** Cloudy and overcast, the pilots couldn't see the runway from a mile away.

_____ **9.** After taking out the recycling, Maya's next chore was to mow the yard.

_____ **10.** To make an omelet, eggshells will need to be broken carefully.

EXERCISE B   On the lines provided, revise each sentence below to correct the dangling modifier.

Example 1. Looking in the dressing-room mirror, the pants were too big. _____
Looking in the dressing-room mirror, the customer saw that the pants were too big.

11. After rowing across the channel, the water grew less choppy. _____

_____

12. Convinced of the prisoner's innocence, the judgment was that he should be set free. _____

_____

13. While typing on the computer, my cat Riley kept bothering me. _____

_____

14. Applying the final coat, my painting for art class was almost finished. _____

_____

15. To improve the neighborhood, a small park was built. _____

_____

Review A: Modifier Placement

USAGE

EXERCISE A   Each of the following sentences contains a misplaced modifier. Correct each sentence by first circling any misplaced words or word groups and then drawing an arrow to show where they should go in the sentence.

Example 1. She sold the old table to an antique shop (with the marble top).

1. Children scampered after the countless pigeons whose parents kept a watchful eye on them.

2. Flying low over their pasture, the cows were frightened by the noise of the helicopter.

3. The conductor stood with her back to the audience on the podium.

4. In their ballerina costumes the parents thought that all of the little girls looked beautiful.

5. We waited for the mail carrier eager to get your letter.

EXERCISE B   Each of the following sentences contains a dangling modifier or squinting modifier. On the line provided, revise each sentence to make the meaning clear. Some sentences have more than one correct answer but you need to give only one.

Example 1. While eating our lunch, the jukebox played noisily.

    While we ate our lunch, the jukebox played noisily.

6. Stolen by a raccoon, the campers would have to do without their afternoon snack.

_____

_____

7. We decided before the movie we would try out a new restaurant.

_____

_____

8. The student said at the dormitory she had seen a friend of hers from high school.

_____

_____

9. After discussing the problem, two solutions were proposed.

_____

_____

10. While reeling in the fish, my dog jumped out of the boat.

_____

_____

Review B: Modifier Placement

EXERCISE A Each of the following sentences contains a misplaced modifier. Correct each sentence by first circling the misplaced modifier and then drawing an arrow to show where it should go in the sentence.

Example 1. We saw a lamp (in a department store) that cost only ten dollars.

1. Mr. Perez bought tickets to the play about Mozart at the box office.

2. She asked for silence as the howls of protest continued speaking quietly.

3. Paul read a book about trout fishing on the subway.

4. With his back to the camera the photograph of the man was useless to the insurance investigator.

5. My father found a fishing lure on the beach that was caught in some seaweed.

EXERCISE B Each of the following sentences contains a dangling modifier or squinting modifier. On the line provided, revise each sentence to correct the error and to make the meaning clear. Some sentences have more than one correct answer, but you need to give only one.

Example 1. Intending to finish the bookcase, the saw was left on the workbench. _____

Intending to finish the bookcase, I left the saw on the workbench. _____

6. While walking to the office, it began to rain. _____

_____

7. Grasping the carton firmly, one egg somehow became cracked. _____

_____

8. My sister told me last week she had gotten a parking ticket. _____

_____

9. Using computers, the effects that weather systems will have are predicted. _____

_____

10. The teacher said at eight o'clock the science fair would open. _____

_____

Review C: **Modifier Placement**

EXERCISE A   Each of the following sentences contains a misplaced modifier. Correct each sentence by first circling the misplaced modifier and then drawing an arrow to show where it should go in the sentence.

Example   1. Leticia and Evan saw a huge statue of a dinosaur (driving down the highway).

1. We brought the dog home from the pound with the yellow collar.

2. Melissa wore black shoes to the opera that matched her dress.

3. Mr. Gonzalez told us a story in our history class about the Alamo.

4. Climbers scaled the huge icefall equipped with rope, anchors, and aluminum ladders.

5. Homero saw a turtle crawling across the sidewalk on his way to the library.

EXERCISE B   Each of the following sentences contains a dangling modifier or squinting modifier. On the lines provided, revise the sentence in two ways to correct the error and to make the meaning clear.

Example   1. The debate teacher said last week the team did well to place.

    Last week, the debate teacher said the team did well to place.

    The debate teacher said the team did well to place last week.

6. Waiting for the concert to begin, a wallet was found under my seat.

7. The president announced on Tuesday the club had received a generous donation.

8. Mary Sue decided at last she would take golf lessons.

9. Standing on the upper deck, dolphins were seen frolicking alongside the ship.

10. My father told us after the ballet recital we would go eat dinner.

Proofreading Application: Speech

Good writers are generally good proofreaders. Readers tend to admire and trust writing that is error-free. Make sure that you correct all errors in grammar, usage, spelling, and punctuation in your writing. Your readers will have more confidence in your words if you have done your best to proofread carefully. When you compose a speech, you must choose your words carefully. Your audience members will have no text to re-read as they interpret what you say, so your speech needs to be clear and precise. By avoiding misplaced modifiers, you will communicate your intended meaning in an effective way.

PROOFREADING ACTIVITY

The following is an award-acceptance speech presented by a student. Find and correct the errors in the placement of modifiers. Use proofreading symbols to make your corrections.

Example *Recently,* ∧ I was told ~~recently~~ I had won an important award.

The Rose T. O'Connor Award for Excellence among music students in this community is coveted. I am truly delighted to accept this award having aspirations to make music my life.

My parents told me when I was ten years old I was gifted in music. However, realizing that being gifted is not the only require-ment, a great deal of time has been devoted to study and practice. To achieve the music-related goals I have set for myself, much hard work is also required. Having received this award, my career goal to be an orchestra conductor has certainly been energized.

My counselor told me last week the committee had determined the award recipient. Those intervening days have been anxious ones, but now I know the anxiety was worth it. I am absolutely elated. With heartfelt gratitude, please accept my thanks for honoring me with the Rose T. O'Connor Award. Even more determined, my goal is to make a living from my passion for music.

Language and Sentence Skills Practice

Literary Model: Poem

USAGE | Language in Context: Literary Model

Tell all the Truth but tell it slant
by Emily Dickinson

Tell all the Truth but tell it slant—
Success in Circuit lies
Too bright for our infirm Delight
The Truth's superb surprise
As Lightning to the children eased
With explanation kind
The Truth must dazzle gradually
Or every man be blind—

EXERCISE A Begin by reading the poem slowly, picking out subjects, verbs, and modifiers.

1. Circle the phrase modifier "in Circuit." Draw an arrow from "in Circuit" to the word or words it modifies.

2. Circle "Too bright for our infirm Delight." Draw an arrow from that word group to the word or words it modifies.

3. Draw an arrow from the fifth and sixth lines ("As Lightning . . . explanation kind") to the word or words that they, taken together, modify. (Hint: In the fifth line, read *As* as a preposition meaning "like.")

4. Where does Dickinson place the modifiers mentioned in questions 1, 2, and 3, relative to the words they modify?

_____

_____

EXERCISE B

1. Rewrite the poem as a paragraph of declarative sentences. Do not change Dickinson's meaning, but use word order that is natural to you.

_____

_____

_____

_____

_____

2. Did you reposition any modifiers to help make the meaning clearer, more direct? _____

3. Does your paragraph create the same sense of suspense or expectancy that the poem does?

_____

_____

4. How does Dickinson's placement of modifiers reinforce the message of the poem?

_____

_____

_____

Literary Model (continued)

EXERCISE C Write a poem of your own about a mystery, a secret, or some other topic of your own choosing. To create a sense of suspense or expectancy, try placing at least some of your modifiers before the words they modify. See if you can use word order to build toward a revelation or an explanation.

_____

_____

_____

_____

_____

_____

_____

_____

_____

_____

_____

_____

_____

_____

_____

_____

_____

_____

_____

_____

EXERCISE D How did you use modifier placement to influence how the reader interprets your poem? Give specific details in your answer.

_____

_____

_____

_____

_____

_____

_____

for **CHAPTER 10: PLACEMENT OF MODIFIERS** | *pages 230–33*

Writing Application: Personal Essay

Even professional writers sometimes trip up when placing modifiers in sentences, as these newspaper headlines testify.

FAULTY PLACEMENT   New Housing Plans for Elderly Not Yet Dead

Thief Gets Nine Months in Violin Case

As intended, the plans for new housing are "not yet dead"; and the thief in the case of the stolen violin will serve time in prison. As written, however, these headlines tell a very different story. To avoid errors such as these, writers should place modifiers near the word or words they modify.

WRITING ACTIVITY

It can be hard to make it to school on time every morning, and you might like to get an extra fifteen minutes of sleep if you can. Take on the role of efficiency expert to streamline your morning routine. Use five logically placed modifying phrases and clauses as you describe the process of getting ready for school.

PREWRITING   In your mind, review each step of your morning routine. List the steps in order. Break longer steps, such as "get dressed," into smaller steps. Estimate in minutes how much time each step takes you on an average day. Then, if possible, compare your actual morning routine to the routine you estimated. Check your list as you get ready in the morning. Next, examine each step individually, looking for wasted time or unnecessary activities.

WRITING   Write a plan for how to streamline your morning. What will you change? How and in what order will you make the changes?

REVISING   Now that your first draft is finished, organize your material into several logical paragraphs. Be sure that each paragraph covers only one topic at a time. As you develop your paragraphs, remember to include modifiers in at least five of your sentences.

PUBLISHING   Check your paragraphs for errors in grammar, usage, spelling, and punctuation. Pay special attention to placement of modifiers. Then, let your family or friends read your plan, make suggestions, and offer support as you implement your plan.

EXTENDING YOUR WRITING

You may wish to develop this exercise into a longer essay. For a business class, you could explore the many time-management problems that keep people from accomplishing all they could. For a student publication, you could research the widespread problem of procrastination. No matter what time-management problem you choose to explore, be sure to suggest solutions.

Choices: Exploring Common Usage Problems

The following activities challenge you to find a connection between usage and the world around you. Do the activity below that suits your personality best, and then share your discoveries with your class.

ETYMOLOGY

Under the Statue of Liberty

Use a dictionary to research the etymologies of the words *emigrate* and *immigrate*. Then, write a brief report about your findings. In your report, include information about the following: the language from which each word comes, the roots and affixes of each word and what these word parts mean, and examples of other words that use the same roots.

CLASSIFYING

Cause and Effect

The glossary alphabetizes usage errors. However, usage errors may also be divided into categories. For instance, some errors could be seen as the result of faulty listening: *Could have* could easily be heard as *could of*. What other categories do you see in the glossary? Look it over. Then, divide the contents of the glossary into categories. As a study aid, write your categories on a piece of poster board and list several examples beneath each category.

BUILDING BACKGROUND KNOWLEDGE

Even Steven

Gender-specific terms can be found in almost every aspect of society. With your teacher's permission, lead the class in a brainstorming session. List sexist words that you commonly hear or read, and discuss the implications of each word. For example, the word *mankind*, which is supposed to refer to all people, literally refers only to the male gender. For each sexist word you list, supply a substitute nonsexist word.

DISCUSSION

In Plain Words

The vernacular is the everyday, ordinary speech of the streets, of trade, and sometimes of friends. With a small group of classmates, discuss situations for which the vernacular is appropriate. Then, discuss situations that clearly call for formal English. After generating a list of situations, discuss answers to the following questions: What are the possible effects of your using formal or vernacular English in the wrong situation? In what ways could your knowledge of both formal English and vernacular English be beneficial?

INTERNET SEARCH

Surfing Safari

What sources does the Web make available to writers to help them use standard English? Conduct an Internet search to find two or three sites that include information on usage. Jot down their addresses and a summary of the information each site offers. Then, orally report your findings to the class. Be sure to indicate which sites would be the most helpful. Then, give everyone a copy of your findings.

ART

Louder Than Words

Some errors are easy to see but hard to hear. Help everyone see these errors. Illustrate two or three pairs of words in the glossary. For instance, you could draw two cartoons illustrating the words *adapt* and *adopt* or *accept* and *except*. Ask your teacher for permission to post your illustrations in the classroom.

USAGE

Glossary A

Review the glossary entries on pages 242–245 for information on the correct usage of the following terms:

a, an	all the farther, all the faster	and etc.
accept, except	allusion, illusion	anyways, anywheres
affect, effect	a lot	at
ain't	alumni, alumnae	a while, awhile
all right	amount, number	

EXERCISE A In each sentence below, underline the word or word group that is correct according to the rules of standard, formal English.

Example 1. It has been (a while, awhile) since I put my artistic talent to good use.

1. After being involved in a minor traffic accident, my neighbor Esther is (allright, all right).

2. The magician created an (allusion, illusion) with the aid of smoke and mirrors.

3. I saw a large (amount, number) of oilcans in the trash.

4. With sincere gratitude, Mary (accepted, excepted) the gift from her friend.

5. After spending a small fortune at the art auction, Sam learned that good art (ain't, isn't) cheap.

6. (Alot, A lot) of maintenance is needed to keep most cars in proper working condition.

7. Ricky is an (alumni, alumnus) of Louisiana State University.

8. Tracy could not find her keys (anywhere, anywheres).

9. Ms. Berman has assigned (a, an) essay on the Reformation.

10. Sandy is too busy to play golf and tennis (anyway, anyways).

EXERCISE B Revise each of the following sentences to reflect formal, standard English usage by crossing out each nonstandard word and writing the correct word above it. If the sentence is already correct, write C to the left of the number.

Example 1. Gary and Glenda are ~~alumnus~~ *alumni* of the same university.

11. Where is the Holocaust Museum located at?

12. Sixty miles per hour was as fast as the car could travel without shaking violently.

13. Let's stop awhile and rest our tired feet.

14. Catherine plays almost every sport: lacrosse, basketball, volleyball, soccer, and etc.

15. Toshiro's decision to move to Germany will effect his entire family.

USAGE

Glossary B

Review the glossary entries on pages 246–248 for information on the correct usage of the following terms:

because	borrow, lend	done
being as, being that	bring, take	don't, doesn't
beside, besides	bust, busted	emigrate, immigrate
between, among	discover, invent	fewer, less

EXERCISE Revise each of the following sentences to reflect formal, standard English usage by crossing out each nonstandard word and writing the correct word above it. If the sentence is already correct, write *C* to the left of the number.

Fewer
Example 1. ~~Less~~ people are waiting in line for that play tonight.

1. Lester done nothing to embarrass us.

2. When you go to San Francisco, make sure you bring a camera.

3. Besides the driver, four people can easily fit in this spacious luxury sedan.

4. My great-grandparents immigrated from China.

5. On my last French test I made far less mistakes in conjugating verbs.

6. The pipe busted and spewed hot water on the floor.

7. Being as Greg is a good golfer, he easily made the school's golf team.

8. My parents borrowed me the money so that I could go to the dance.

9. When does the family plan to immigrate from Canada?

10. Maya divided the rest of the kibble evenly between the four dogs.

11. Do you know when the Internet was discovered?

12. Tara is going home because she doesn't want to see the rest of the movie.

13. Another reason is because Wally received more votes than Eddy.

14. Explain the differences between a noun, an adjective, and an adverb.

15. One reason to get a tune-up is that it will help your engine run more efficiently.

16. Some say that Mexico, beside being a popular tourist destination, is also a good place to live.

17. Jeff said that he don't like the taste of coconut milk.

18. Cara has vowed to spend less hours in front of the television.

19. Glenda, please bring this book home and read Chapter Five.

20. The force of the earthquake busted windows, damaged buildings, and caused many injuries.

USAGE

Glossary C

Review the glossary entries on pages 252–254 for information on the correct usage of the following terms:

had ought, hadn't ought	**in, into**	**leave, let**
he, she, it, they	**kind of, sort of**	**like, as**
hisself, theirself, theirselves	**kind of a, sort of a**	**like, as if, as though**
hopefully	**kind(s), sort(s), type(s)**	
imply, infer	**learn, teach**	

EXERCISE A   In each sentence below, underline the word or word group that is correct according to the rules of standard, formal English.

Example 1. Countee Cullen *(he was, was)* a writer for both children and adults.

1. The guitar sounds *(like, as if)* it is being played underwater.

2. To avoid a turnover, Marcus, threw *(hisself, himself)* on the football.

3. Because the broken glass from the window lay outside the house, the detective *(implied, inferred)* that no one had actually broken into the house.

4. Last week my neighbor *(let, left)* me borrow one of his books about automotive repair.

5. Today, excellent poems by writers of various cultures are finding their way *(in, into)* literature anthologies.

6. James knew that his paper *(had ought, ought)* to be finished before class on Monday.

7. She was *(kind of, somewhat)* relieved when she learned that practice was canceled.

8. When you write this *(type of, type of a)* paper, be sure to credit your sources accurately.

9. What *(kind of, kind of a)* book do you enjoy reading?

10. Liz *(she is, is)* ready to go on her vacation to Peru.

EXERCISE B   For the sentences below, cross out each nonstandard word and, if necessary, write the correct word above it. If the sentence is already correct, write *C* to the left of the number.

Example 1. Michael ~~he~~ wanted to wrap the present ~~hisself~~.
                                                            himself

11. Whales provide milk for their young just like other mammals do.

12. Gazing up at the expansive night sky, David thought of himself as an amateur astronomer.

13. In fewer than ten days, Kelly learned him to play simple guitar chords.

14. This article implies that these type of foods are not healthful.

15. Although down seven points, the losing team hopefully took the line of scrimmage.

Glossary D

Review the glossary entries on pages 255–257 for information on the correct usage of the
following terms:

of	or, nor	supposed to, used to
off, off of	some, somewhat	than, then

USAGE

EXERCISE   Revise each of the following sentences to reflect formal, standard English usage by crossing
out each nonstandard word and, if necessary, writing the correct word above it. If the sentence is
already correct, write *C* to the left of the number.

Example   **1.**   That crane is ~~suppose~~ *supposed* to lift the beam up to the building's tenth story.

1. Rather than waiting until today, I should of begun shopping for a birthday present last month.

2. The Chinese food I had for lunch was better then any other Chinese food I have eaten.

3. You can get all kinds of useful information off of the Internet.

4. I like reading Shelley somewhat, but I really enjoy reading Keats.

5. Wanda was cheering for neither the home team or the visiting team.

6. The teacher asked Jaime to clear the papers off of the desk.

7. Those people are suppose to be experts in the field of microbiology.

8. Did you say that the density of gold is greater than the density of silver?

9. Helen finished packing the box and then took a well-deserved break.

10. Nicole ought to have copied the notes off the chalkboard.

11. The volunteers faltered some but eventually piled all the bags of sand along the waterline.

12. Carla use to tutor a rambunctious group of third-graders after school.

13. The parakeet must of escaped from its cage sometime during the night.

14. One parachutist jumped off a high cliff.

15. Either Terrell or Kenneth designed the invitations.

16. Mr. James got up from his bed and than began to stretch.

17. Oliver's skill in the javelin throw decreased some after his injury.

18. Neither Felicia or Eduardo will be able to go roller-skating tonight.

19. Raul was suppose to spend the whole day working on the car.

20. I would have waited for you if I had of known you needed a ride.

Glossary E

Review the glossary entries on pages 257–258 for information on the correct usage of the following terms:

them	what
this here, that there	when, where
try and, try to	where
type, type of	who, which, that
ways	

EXERCISE For the sentences below, cross out each nonstandard word and, if necessary, write the correct word above it. If the sentence is already correct, write *C* to the left of the number.

Example 1. We are going to that ~~there~~ circus today with several friends.

1. Tamika is the girl that won at the tournament.

2. Be careful to avoid that type of error in your writing.

3. The man which gave me the maps at the Tourist Board was very helpful.

4. Take that there book and place it on the shelf.

5. I certainly liked the low prices at them shops.

6. Phoebe wants to try and repair the engine.

7. Are those the in-line skates what Herman found in the park?

8. Yesterday, they traveled a long ways to visit our school.

9. He read in the paper where the city council meeting had been canceled.

10. Several of the people which left early did not get to see your grand finale.

11. Stir-frying is where you cook food quickly in a hot pan.

12. Do you know the actor who is in the play we're going to see tonight?

13. This type flower is difficult to identify.

14. Come take a look at this here interesting tarantula.

15. A compulsion is when you have an irresistible, repeated urge to do something.

16. Doreen read where the school was going to have an open house.

17. Although he had a cold, Henry said that he would try to attend the speech tournament.

18. Them athletes won gold medals in the competition.

19. The glove what she bought last week was made of leather.

20. Shelly and Miranda had to drive a long way to buy their uniforms.

The Double Negative and Nonsexist Language

A *double negative* is a construction in which two negative words are used to express a single negative idea. Avoid double negatives, as in the following example:

NONSTANDARD   I couldn't do none of the assignment.

STANDARD   I **couldn't** do **any** of the assignment.

Nonsexist language is language that applies to people in general, both male and female. When referring generally to people, use nonsexist expressions instead of gender-specific ones. For example, use *businessperson* instead of *businessman*, or *mail carrier* instead of *mailman*.

USAGE

EXERCISE A   Read each sentence below, and decide if it contains a double negative. If the sentence contains a double negative, write *DN* for *double negative*, along with the two negative words, on the line provided. If the sentence does not contain a double negative, write *S* for *standard*.

Example _____*DN—hadn't never*_____ **1.** Jane hadn't never seen the movie.

_____ **1.** Since I do not know nothing about woodworking, I took industrial arts.

_____ **2.** He couldn't barely move after his strenuous workout.

_____ **3.** Trevor had heard nothing about the film before he saw it.

_____ **4.** Isn't nobody going to volunteer to go first?

_____ **5.** Haven't you read any books by Gordon Parks?

_____ **6.** It is amazing that scarcely no one has bought tickets to that concert.

_____ **7.** Taking daily piano lessons doesn't hardly leave me any free time.

_____ **8.** I knew nothing about that company until I applied for a job.

_____ **9.** Ms. Chang told me the office wouldn't have no openings this summer.

_____ **10.** Kelly couldn't help laughing when she saw the clown.

EXERCISE B   Revise each of the following sentences by crossing out each gender-specific term and writing an appropriate nonsexist term above it.

Example 1. Right now the company is experiencing a shortage of ~~manpower.~~ *workers*

11. Kwame waved his hand to get the attention of the stewardess.

12. The foreman at the construction site decided to let everyone off work early.

13. Mrs. Miller juggles her duties as a lawyer, mother, and housewife.

14. Yan and I stopped on our way home to watch the firemen battle the blaze.

15. Every employee should bring his own lunch to the company picnic.

Language and Sentence Skills Practice   **247**

Review A: **Glossary**

USAGE

EXERCISE A In each sentence below, underline the word or word group that is correct according to the rules of standard, formal English.

Example 1. The flood victims gratefully (<u>accepted</u>, excepted) the help offered by the Red Cross.

1. The refuse in the dumpster emitted (a, an) awful smell.

2. When the hikers reached the foot of the cliff, their guide explained that this was (as far as, all the farther) they could go without mountain-climbing equipment.

3. The hailstorm had a disastrous (effect, affect) on the alfalfa crop.

4. The prize money was divided proportionately (among, between) the four winners.

5. The judges at the flower show were faced with an unusually large (amount, number) of entries.

EXERCISE B For the sentences below, cross out each nonstandard word and write the correct word above it. Each sentence may have more than one nonstandard word to correct.

Example 1. Who do you think is the person ~~which~~ ~~discovered~~ concrete?
who invented

6. The local YMCA program emphasizes alot of indoor sports—volleyball, basketball, badminton, and etc.

7. Accept for Rolanda, the members of the debate team became nervous during the finals.

8. The reason the editor did not print the article was because it arrived a day too late.

9. Beside raising carrier pigeons, Mrs. Lee, who is a veterinarian, breeds parrots and parakeets.

10. The next time you go to the post office, please bring this package to be weighed and stamped.

11. Paul cannot hardly imagine how so many people mistake luxuries for necessities.

12. We put less discarded soda bottles in the recycling bin than the other class did.

13. As I read the novel, I saw where the author made an illusion to World War II.

14. Jenny hadn't but one reason for looking at the map: to find out where the coliseum was located at.

15. He couldn't scarcely get hisself to begin the difficult task of cleaning his room.

16. Gary said to be careful because all of them glasses are busted.

17. The machine what he discovered revolutionized the industry.

18. Because she was kind of sleepy, Pam knew that she hadn't ought to drive anywhere.

19. Many of the people which left the game early had to wait in traffic for a long time.

20. Carla carefully divided the papers between the twenty students.

Review B: **Glossary**

EXERCISE A   In each sentence below, underline the word or word group that is correct according to the rules of standard, formal English.

Example 1. The meteorologists predict the storm will not (<u>*affect*</u>, *effect*) our area.

1. The volunteers took (*a while, awhile*) to arrive at the disaster site.

2. After (*breaking, busting*) the expensive vase, Todd's little brother felt terrible.

3. In 1975, Gail's grandmother (*immigrated, emigrated*) to the United States.

4. So many interesting magazines were in the rack that I had a hard time choosing (*between,*

   among) them.

5. Suddenly and unexpectedly, the woman jumped (*in, into*) her car and drove away.

EXERCISE B   For the sentences below, cross out each nonstandard word and, if necessary, write the correct word above it. Each sentence may have more than one nonstandard word to correct.

Example 1. That ~~there~~ model airplane did not turn out ~~like~~ ^{as} she had hoped it would.

6. Mrs. Gibbon she done her volunteer work early this morning.

7. He could of pulled more gently on the rope to avoid breaking it.

8. Jon's parents immigrated from Japan decades ago.

9. These kind of novels have always appealed to Robert, an avid reader of science fiction.

10. The mountain climbers which were on the news almost died trying to reach the summit.

11. The quality of that product is suppose to improve some over the next several years.

12. If Sonja don't get to the bus stop soon, she'll have to wait for the next bus.

13. Allright, who is going to try and perform this science experiment at home?

14. She can't hardly doubt that the mystery package contains jewelry.

15. A sandstorm is when a cloud forms from windblown sand.

16. Pablo ain't the player who scored the final goal anyways.

17. After remembering the differences among a participle, a gerund, and a participial phrase,

    Kelly knew that she would do fine on the test.

18. Gary accurately predicted the negative affects of the senator's speech.

19. Being that she felt ill, Ellen took some medicine and called her mother.

20. The dogs who won blue ribbons were supposed to receive their medals on Tuesday.

Review C: **Glossary**

USAGE

EXERCISE A In each sentence below, underline the word or word group that is correct according to the rules of standard, formal English.

Example 1. Most colleges have active (*alumni*, *alumnus*) groups.

1. If there is enough wind, we will (*try and*, *try to*) fly our new stunt kite.

2. Their grandmother always treated them (*as if*, *like*) they were adults.

3. (*Being as*, *Because*) it had rained hard all day, many ticket holders decided to stay home.

4. She wishes she (*could of*, *could have*) been present at the dedication ceremony.

5. Margaret (*taught*, *learned*) her younger brother about fractions.

EXERCISE B For the sentences below, cross out each nonstandard word and, if necessary, write the correct word above it. Also, correct sexist language. Each sentence may have more than one item to correct.

Example 1. It is difficult to tell whether those ~~kind~~ *kinds* of programs will attract large audiences.

6. Mrs. Smith asked that each student bring his book to her desk.

7. Mrs. Holly said that I have come a long ways in my studies.

8. Although we felt like we had been rewarded already, Jack would not leave us go home until he had given each of us a gift.

9. Henry's nervousness increased some when all the stewardesses took their seats and fastened their safety belts.

10. The boy jumped off of them boxes and ran into the house.

11. What equipment, beside a bat and ball, can you borrow me?

12. Martina is a girl which approaches those kind of difficult assignments with a smile.

13. When you come to class tomorrow, remember to take the correct type pencil.

14. Is it true that neither *Moby-Dick* or *Leaves of Grass* was well received when it first appeared?

15. Ms. Simpson's kindly tone and manner inferred that she understood how difficult this kind of a choice was.

Proofreading Application: Book Report

Good writers are generally good proofreaders. Readers tend to admire and trust writing that is error-free. Make sure that you correct all errors in grammar, usage, spelling, and punctuation in your writing. Your readers will have more confidence in your words if you have done your best to proofread carefully.

Different levels of formality exist in communication. Furthermore, language can be standard (grammatically correct in formal and informal situations) or nonstandard (appropriate only in the most casual speaking situations). When you write a formal document, such as a book report, you should follow the rules of standard, formal English.

PROOFREADING ACTIVITY

Find and correct the errors in the use of standard, formal English in the following book report excerpt. Use proofreading symbols to make your corrections.

Example   *Angela's Ashes* had a tremendous ~~affect~~ *effect* on me, and the main
reason is ~~because~~ *that* it is autobiographical.

 Angela's Ashes is so successful because it is subtly poignant.

From the moment the McCourts get off of the boat and step onto Irish

soil, the family's problems seem to grow every day. Being that this

is the situation, you would expect the book to be depressing.

However, it is not. McCourt tells about his childhood and youth with

such innocence that you, the reader, readily except the good with

the bad, just as he did.

 Many authors write like their only goal is to try and put read-

ers' emotions on a roller coaster. Such is not the case for Frank

McCourt. His subtle approach lends to his book a genuine poignancy

that cannot be forced.

Literary Model: Short Story

> "... [T]here was a feller here once by the name of Jim Smiley. ... He ketched a frog one day, and took him home, and said he cal'lated to educate him; and so he never done nothing for three months but set in his back yard and learn that frog to jump. And you bet you he did learn him, too. He'd give him a little punch behind, and the next minute you'd see that frog whirling in the air like a doughnut—see him turn one summerset, or maybe a couple. ... Why, I've seen him set Dan'l Webster down here on this floor—Dan'l Webster was the name of the frog—and sing out, 'Flies, Dan'l, flies!' and quicker'n you could wink he'd spring straight up and snake a fly off'n the counter there, and flop down on the floor ag'in as solid as a gob of mud, and fall to scratching the side of his head with his hind foot as indifferent as if he hadn't no idea he'd been doin' any more'n any frog might do. ..."
>
> —from "The Notorious Jumping Frog of Calaveras County" by Mark Twain

EXERCISE A   Carefully study the excerpt. Then, underline in the excerpt only those errors in standard usage covered in Chapter 11. Ignore creative spellings ("feller," "quicker'n," etc.) that are intended to capture the sound of natural speech. Also, ignore errors in verb usage ("ketched," "set").

EXERCISE B   Throughout much of the 1800's, the dominant force in American literature was Romanticism, a movement that produced characters such as the rugged, heroic, and morally upright Natty Bumppo—James Fenimore Cooper's idealized version of the American frontiersman. However, by the late 1800's, a new creative force in American literature had emerged: Realism. Embraced by writers such as Bret Harte, the followers of this movement sought to represent with clarity characters who acted and sounded like real people.

1. Do you think the excerpt from Mark Twain is an example of Realism? Explain.

_____

_____

_____

2. Describe the character of the narrator of the excerpt above, Simon Wheeler. Does he sound as if he could be a real person? How does Twain's use of nonstandard elements, such as double negatives and creative spellings, affect the way you see Simon Wheeler's character?

_____

_____

_____

for **CHAPTER 11: A GLOSSARY OF USAGE** | pages 241–64

Literary Model (continued)

EXERCISE C Write a brief anecdote told by a colorful narrator like the one in the excerpt by Twain. Employ nonstandard usage, creative spellings, or any other appropriate device to relate to the reader the way your narrator sounds.

_____

_____

_____

_____

_____

_____

_____

_____

_____

_____

_____

_____

_____

_____

_____

_____

_____

EXERCISE D Describe your narrator. What devices did you use to create this narrator? Would your narrator be as believable if you had used standard English?

_____

_____

_____

_____

_____

Writing Application: Dialogue

Formal English usage helps a writer relate a clear, effective message. However, informal usage that has a purpose can also be an effective writing tool. For example, spoken English varies from one region of the country to another and from nation to nation. Many authors have used these varieties of English to create memorable fictional characters.

COLLOQUIAL	We're pumped that y'all could be here.
FORMAL	We are excited that you could be here.

WRITING ACTIVITY

One way to become familiar with the difference between informal and formal English is to study a fictional character who speaks a regional variety of English. For example, many of Mark Twain's and Charles Dickens's characters speak informally. Thumb through novels or other works, and identify a character who speaks informally. Then, find about twenty lines of that character's speech. Rewrite the speech in formal English.

PREWRITING Copy the page or pages on which the character's speech appears so that you can make marks on it. Then, read the lines aloud several times, making sure that you understand each line completely. In this exercise you will change the informal language to formal language, but the essential meaning of the passage should not change.

WRITING Consult your glossary of usage as you rewrite the lines in formal English. You will need, for instance, to eliminate contractions and to replace colloquial words with formal equivalents.

REVISING Read both the original passage and your rewritten version to several listeners. Do both versions contain the same content? Can your audience identify any remaining informal words that need to be changed? Ask your listeners which version they found easier to understand and why. Make sure to jot down their answers. Then, act as the audience for other students.

PUBLISHING Check your rewritten version for errors in spelling and punctuation. Have someone read the passage slowly to you, and listen for any awkward word choices. Your class may wish to compile a booklet including both the original versions and the rewritten versions of the excerpts. The booklets could be shared with younger students to help them understand the difference between formal and informal English.

EXTENDING YOUR WRITING

You may wish to develop this exercise into a longer essay. Readers sometimes complain about the difficulty of reading different characters' speech patterns, but novels, short stories, and even television and movie scripts would be much less interesting and less realistic if everyone used formal English. In an essay for your English class, explore what stories gain when authors have characters speak informally.

Choices: Investigating Capitalization

The following activities challenge you to find a connection between capitalization and the world around you. Do the activity below that suits your personality best, and then share your discoveries with your class.

MATHEMATICS

Boolean Logic

For the most part, mathematics is a singularly impersonal discipline. However, a few people have made such significant contributions to the field that their names are now part of certain aspects of mathematics. Usually, these names have become proper adjectives. Who are these people? Do some research and find out. Then, prepare cards featuring the person's name, the relevant dates, the way the person's name is used in mathematics, and a little bit about the person's discovery. Share your discoveries with your classmates.

HISTORY

Genghis Khan to Colin Powell

Military leaders have been around a long time. Who are these men and women? Make a list of the world's greatest military leaders. Try to include at least one from every continent. Remember that some of these leaders were kings and queens as well as generals and commanders. Use the proper title for each one. Write a short biography for each person, including references to his or her country and most famous battles. Remember to use proper capitalization for titles, proper names, and battles.

DISCUSSION

Seven Wonders of the World

What do you think that people five hundred years from now will point to as the Seven Wonders of the Modern World? A microchip? The transatlantic cable? Satellites? Penicillin? Get together with a few friends and talk about this topic. You might want to do a bit of research in the library. Then, come up with a list of seven items. Be sure that each item on your list is properly capitalized as a specific structure or event. Submit your nominations to the class and defend your reasoning.

HISTORY

Magna Carta

Your book says that historical documents should be capitalized. You've been studying history for a number of years now. What are some of these documents? Create a list of what you consider to be the twenty most important historical documents. Include a broad range of countries and time periods. For each document, prepare a brief description that includes the name of the document, the year of its execution, and a brief description of its contents. By the way, what does "Magna Carta" mean, anyway?

GEOGRAPHY

The Grand Tour

In the nineteenth century, young adults from wealthy families often were sent on a "grand tour," a trip throughout Europe. No doubt, today's grand tours would be a bit different from those of the nineteenth century. Surely, cities and sites from all over the globe would be included. If you were going on a grand tour, where would you choose to go? Get a world map and plot your journey. On the map, label each city or site that you would like to visit. Be sure to use capital letters. For each location, write a paragraph telling why you want to see it.

DESIGN

The Golden Section

If you are interested in drafting, art, or engineering, consider this project. Go to the library and find out how artists design fonts. Engineering a font is a very precise, geometrical, and mathematical process. Using what you have learned, you might even try designing a single capital letter for a font of your own. Make copies of the design process that you find in the library, and use these copies as visual aids when you explain to the class how fonts are designed.

Language and Sentence Skills Practice

First Words, the Pronoun *I*, and the Interjection *O*

12a.	Capitalize the first word in every sentence.

EXAMPLE **S**he thinks that the garden will be a good subject for her photojournalism essay.

Traditionally, the first word of each line of a poem is capitalized.

EXAMPLE **A**lone, alone, all, all, alone,

Alone on a wide, wide sea!

Samuel Taylor Coleridge, *The Rime of the Ancient Mariner*

12b.	Capitalize the first word in both the salutation and the closing of a letter.

EXAMPLES **D**ear Ms. Simmons: **S**incerely,

12c.	Capitalize the pronoun *I* and the interjection *O*.

EXAMPLES After a strenuous bike ride, **I** usually have a cold glass of water and a banana.

René stood to speak to the crowd and thought, "Don't fail me now, **O** voice!"

EXERCISE A In the following sentences, cross out each error in capitalization and write the correct form above it.

                 My   I
Example 1. ~~my~~ classmate Emilio and ~~i~~ spent the entire afternoon doing research for our report.

1. the idea of a pencil with an eraser attached was patented by Hyman L. Lipman in 1858, and

Oh, what a good idea that was.

2. could you remember to bring some pencils to the meeting tonight?

3. Marco read the last line of the poem aloud: "blow mighty wind, o breath of the sky!"

4. The bank where i have my checking account is insured by the FDIC.

5. When i said, "have a nice day," Delia replied, "oh, i certainly will!"

EXERCISE B The following paragraph contains errors in capitalization. Cross out each error in capitalization, and write the correct form above it.

                          I've   oh
Example   George said, "~~i've~~ had some bad days, but ~~Oh~~, was this one the worst."

today didn't start off that badly, unless it bothers you to wear socks that don't match. then i

missed the bus, and my mother had to drive me to school. i was supposed to write a poem in my

English class. "come to me, o muse of poetry," i begged. i couldn't think of anything but the line

"once upon a midnight dreary, while i pondered, weak and weary," which, of course, someone

named Edgar Allan Poe already made famous.

Proper Nouns and Adjectives A

12d. Capitalize proper nouns and proper adjectives.

(1) Capitalize the names of persons and animals. Capitalize initials in names and abbreviations that either precede or follow names.

> **EXAMPLES** Mrs. I. P. Gonzales
> my dog Fred
> Byron McAllister, Jr.

EXERCISE A On the lines provided, correctly capitalize the following names. Write C if a name is already correctly capitalized.

Example 1. f. Scott Fitzgerald _____F. Scott Fitzgerald_____

1. rené descartes _____

2. dr. Martin Luther King, jr. _____

3. gregor johann mendel _____

4. sir edmund hillary _____

5. king henry VIII _____

6. William Du Bois _____

7. grandma moses _____

8. eudora welty _____

9. sir winston churchill _____

10. robert frost _____

EXERCISE B The following paragraphs contain errors in capitalization. Cross out each error in capitalization, and write the correct form above it.

Example Richard and ~~dr.~~ Dr. Scott were talking about their favorite ~~Authors~~ authors.

Dr. Scott began by asking the class to name the authors of books they had recently read. Richard responded by listing several, including hermann hesse, thomas mann, and rainer maria rilke.

"Why, Richard," dr. Scott said, "these are all German authors. Do you read or speak German?"

"My father is Richard T. Gonzalez, sr.," Richard said. "He is a professor of German literature at the university."

Dr. scott laughed. "Maybe I should call you Herr Gonzalez, then."

Proper Nouns and Adjectives B

12d(2). Capitalize geographical names.

> **EXAMPLES**   **I**sle of **W**ight
>
>   **N**inety-second **S**treet
>
>   **P**ioneer **P**ark

12d(3). Capitalize the names of planets, stars, constellations, and other heavenly bodies.

> **EXAMPLES**   the **N**orth **S**tar
>
>   **M**ars, **V**enus, **J**upiter

MECHANICS

EXERCISE A On the lines provided, correctly capitalize the following words and phrases.

Example 1. gulf of California   *Gulf of California*

1. south africa   _____

2. colombia   _____

3. the arabian desert   _____

4. Fifty-First Street   _____

5. Eastern Georgia   _____

6. loch ness   _____

7. andes mountains   _____

8. the west   _____

9. mission san juan capistrano   _____

10. the hawaiian islands   _____

EXERCISE B The following paragraph contains errors in capitalization. Cross out each error in capitalization, and write the correct form above it.

Example   The ~~Sun~~ was bright today.
               sun

    We had an astronomy bee today in science. Mrs. Perez explained the rules to us. She said we could name any celestial body inside or outside the milky way. If you couldn't think of a planet or constellation, such as the big dipper, you were out of the game. Of course, everyone started with the names of the planets: Jupiter, Mars, earth, and so on. Then, people named the constellations: orion, taurus, cancer, and the rest. In the last round, people were giving the names of stars, such as betelgeuse. At the end of the game, only Joe and Yvonne were left. Yvonne couldn't think of anything that had not been named. "Wait a minute," Joe shouted. "We forgot about the Moon!"

Proper Nouns and Adjectives C

12d(4). Capitalize the names of organizations, teams, government bodies, and institutions.

> **EXAMPLES** the **C**onstitutional **C**onvention
> **D**allas **C**owboys
> the **W**hite **H**ouse

12d(5). Capitalize the names of businesses and the brand names of business products.

> **EXAMPLES** the **Q**uickink **C**orporation
> the **Q**uickink **Q**uickwriter 2000

EXERCISE A On the lines provided, correctly capitalize the following words and phrases. Write *C* if a word or phrase is already correctly capitalized.

Example 1. department of Agriculture   *Department of Agriculture*

1. the bureau of american ethnology _____

2. santa maria high school _____

3. the New York yankees _____

4. microsoft word _____

5. Fab Cola _____

6. the red cross _____

7. University of Nebraska Cornhuskers _____

8. national museum of the american indian _____

9. international business machines _____

10. Chock Full Of Grains Cereal _____

EXERCISE B The following paragraph contains errors in capitalization. Cross out each error in capitalization, and write the correct form above it.

Example   My brother Joe just got a job at Mueller's ~~office supply~~. *Office Supply*

Mueller's Office Supply is the shop located across the street from bay college, where I want to go to school. (Go marlins!) The store does a lot of business with the college, especially the office of admissions and records. For standardization purposes, the department uses only one type of pencil, the Yellow barrel #2 by precision pencils. Whenever the Department runs out of stock, someone hurries over to Mueller's to buy a few boxes.

Proper Nouns and Adjectives D

12d(6). Capitalize the names of particular buildings and other structures.

> **EXAMPLES**   Empire State Building
>
> Madison High School

12d(7). Capitalize the names of monuments, memorials, and awards.

> **EXAMPLES**   Nobel Peace Prize
>
> Vietnam Veterans Memorial

EXERCISE A   On the lines provided, correctly capitalize the following words and phrases. Write *C* if a word or phrase is already correctly capitalized.

Example   1. Johnson junior college   *Johnson Junior College* _____

1. St. Stephen's hospital   _____

2. the congressional medal of honor   _____

3. the Lincoln Memorial   _____

4. Reagan high school   _____

5. the golden gate bridge   _____

6. pulitzer prize   _____

7. Old victorian theater   _____

8. the space needle   _____

9. National Book Award   _____

10. washington Monument   _____

EXERCISE B   The following paragraph contains errors in capitalization. Cross out each error in capitalization, and write the correct form above it.

Example   Suzy wants to be the first woman to win best director, best actress, and best film
Academy Awards
~~academy awards~~ for the same movie.

Suzy is currently in a play being performed downtown at the forster center for the performing arts. Last year she won a coveted lifeson award for her stage work. Suzy is very ambitious. After the play finishes its run, she will begin work on a movie that will be filmed near the eiffel tower. When asked if she thought she might win another local award for her work, she said she wasn't sure, but that she was hoping perhaps for a golden globe.

Proper Nouns and Adjectives E

12d(8). Capitalize the names of historical events and periods, special events, holidays, and other calendar items.

EXAMPLES   **V**ictorian **A**ge
Earth **D**ay
Presidents' **D**ay
Fall **H**arvest **F**estival

EXERCISE A   On the lines provided, correctly capitalize the following words and phrases. Write *C* if a word or phrase is already correctly capitalized.

Example 1. Winter   _____*winter*_____

1. Labor day   _____

2. cretaceous period   _____

3. dark ages   _____

4. the cold war   _____

5. autumn   _____

6. the fourth of july   _____

7. the olympic games   _____

8. june   _____

9. Vietnam war   _____

10. halloween   _____

EXERCISE B   The following paragraphs contain errors in capitalization. Cross out each error in capitalization, and write the correct form above it.

Example   My friend Denika is trying to organize the weekly engagement calendar she
received for ~~kwanzaa~~ *Kwanzaa* this year.

We are talking about all the Holidays and events she needs to record. For example, in february

there is groundhog day, valentine's day, and presidents' day.

"Wait a minute," Denika says. "How did a rodent get its own holiday?"

I don't know, but I remind her that this holiday occurs on the same date as forensics fever, a

debate contest that our school is hosting.

"I don't know if I'll be able to concentrate," Denika says. "All I'll be thinking about is that

overgrown rat looking for its shadow."

Proper Nouns and Adjectives F

12d(9). Capitalize the names of nationalities, races, and peoples.

> **EXAMPLES**   **A**frican **A**merican
>
> **C**hristians

12d(10). Capitalize the names of religions and their followers, holy days and celebrations, sacred writings, and specific deities.

> **EXAMPLES**   **M**ormons
>
> **D**ía de **R**eyes

MECHANICS

EXERCISE A   On the lines provided, correctly capitalize the following words and phrases. Write *C* if a word or phrase is already correctly capitalized.

Example 1. buddha _____*Buddha*_____

1. new testament   _____

2. south african   _____

3. southern baptist   _____

4. Inuit   _____

5. christmas   _____

6. episcopalian   _____

7. cajun   _____

8. islam   _____

9. book of mormon   _____

10. hanukkah   _____

EXERCISE B   The following sentences contain errors in capitalization. Cross out each error in capitalization, and write the correct form above it.

Example 1. I am reading the ~~vedas~~ *Vedas*, which are the sacred books of ~~hinduism~~ *Hinduism*.

11. Are there many Holidays Jewish and christian peoples both celebrate?

12. The muslim and buddhist religions have many Followers.

13. I've read parts of the koran, but not all of it.

14. Many Asian Americans in our city celebrate chinese new year.

15. The Norse God of thunder was named Thor.

Proper Nouns and Adjectives G

12d(11). Capitalize the names of ships, trains, aircraft, spacecraft, and any other vehicles.

    EXAMPLES *Spirit of St. Louis*

                     Orient Express

12e. Do not capitalize the names of school subjects, except course names that include a number and the names of language classes.

    EXAMPLES math   English

EXERCISE A On the lines provided, correctly capitalize the following words and phrases. Write *C* if a word or phrase is already correctly capitalized.

Example 1. the shuttle *endeavor*   *the shuttle Endeavor*

1. *niña* _____

2. french II _____

3. the *Titanic* _____

4. Spanish _____

5. *pinta* _____

6. art _____

7. air force one _____

8. Algebra _____

9. old ironsides _____

10. *santa maria* _____

EXERCISE B The following paragraphs contain errors in capitalization. Cross out each error in capitalization, and write the correct form above it.

                                          Titanic

Example   What would he have renamed the ~~titanic~~?

    My brother Terrell is making a soapbox racer as a project for his Physical Science class. It's similar to the solar-powered car project I did last year for chemistry II. He's trying to think of a name for his car, and I want to help him out.

    "I think it should be something exciting," I say, "something like shooting star or lightning bolt or supercarracer, all as one word."

    Terrell thinks for a second. "I'm naming the car bob."

    This stuns me. "Bob? There's nothing exciting about that name."

    "Well," Terrell says, "I want the car to be fast, right? There's no faster name to say than 'bob.'"

Commas with Introductory Elements

13j. Use a comma after certain introductory elements.

(1) Use a comma to set off a mild exclamation such as *well*, *oh*, or *why*. Other introductory words such as *yes* and *no* are also set off by commas.
(2) Use a comma after an introductory participle or participial phrase.
(3) Use a comma after two or more introductory prepositional phrases or after one long one.
(4) Use a comma after an introductory adverb clause.

> **EXAMPLES**   **Oh,** how I love the winter time.   **No,** I don't know how to ice skate.
> **Putting on her skates,** she joined us on the ice.
> **In the corner of the far end of the rink,** she fell.
> **When Hank's cousin offered us a ride,** we were grateful.

EXERCISE A   Add commas where they are needed in each of the following sentences. If a sentence is already correct, write *C* before the item number.

Example 1. Waiting in line for tickets, the tourists became bored and impatient.

1. Entering the store we were greeted by huge crowds.

2. At the beginning of *Raiders of the Lost Ark* Indy outruns a rolling boulder.

3. Rushing to answer the phone Lana tripped over an electric cord.

4. On a clear day you can see the tip of Mt. Monadnock from this field.

5. Nearly blinded by the whirling snow the climbers sought shelter.

6. While we were attending the concert we ran into Maribeth and Tom.

7. Yes I want to compete in the tournament; when you schedule it give me a call.

8. In a church in the center of a small town in Mexico my parents were married.

9. As soon as we entered the exhibition we had to check our packages and cameras.

10. Before my next song I'd like to say a few words about the lyricist, Ira Gershwin.

EXERCISE B   Add commas where they are needed in each of the following sentences. If a sentence is already correct, write *C* before the item number.

Example 1. Once the concert began, the audience fell silent.

11. After the ringmaster completed his introduction the clowns began their show.

12. On the side of the mountain the climbers found a journal from a previous expedition.

13. Gosh that's the biggest pumpkin I've ever seen.

14. Around the corner Annabeth saw the parade coming in her direction.

15. Rolling down the grassy hill the children laughed and shouted.

Commas with Interrupters

13k. Use commas to set off an expression that interrupts a sentence.

(1) Nonessential appositives and appositive phrases are set off by commas.

> **EXAMPLE** Paul Szep, **the political cartoonist,** has won several Pulitzer Prizes.

(2) Words used in direct address are set off by commas.

> **EXAMPLE** **Tanya,** would you like more soup? Thank you, **Jon.**

(3) Parenthetical expressions are set off by commas.

> **EXAMPLES** The younger children, **on the other hand,** stayed at home.
> **Therefore,** I'm going to the hardware store today.

EXERCISE A Add commas where they are needed in the following sentences. If a sentence is already correct, write *C* before the item number.

Example 1. Would you please answer the phone, Leroy?

1. Maine the largest of the New England states has a beautiful coastline.

2. Benjamin Franklin by the way also invented bifocal lenses.

3. Would you like to play tennis or squash Juanita?

4. Kim has decided to major in nursing a course of study that will take five years.

5. Lake Tanganyika is I believe the world's longest freshwater lake.

6. In 1935 George Gershwin wrote *Porgy and Bess* a popular American folk opera.

7. My cousin Frank has signed up for a summer program at Mississippi State.

8. Did you know Larry that lawrencium is the name of a chemical element?

9. Yellow on the other hand is not an attractive color on me.

10. The play was mediocre; we did however enjoy the music and choreography.

EXERCISE B Add commas where they are needed in the following sentences.

Example 1. My first grade teacher, Mrs. Doré, wrote me a letter last week.

11. Brendan are you coming to the dinner tonight?

12. Graham Greene the British novelist wrote screenplays for several films.

13. Consequently the homecoming float will need to be redesigned.

14. The ingredients for vegetarian chili include for instance green peppers, beans, and tomato sauce.

15. Listen to those coyotes howling Brett.

Using Commas Correctly

13f.	Use commas to separate items in a series.
13g.	Use commas to separate two or more adjectives preceding a noun.
13h.	Use a comma before a coordinating conjunction (*and, but, for, nor, or, so,* or *yet*) when it joins independent clauses.
13i.	Use commas to set off nonessential subordinate clauses and nonessential participial phrases.
13j.	Use a comma after certain introductory elements.
13k.	Use commas to set off an expression that interrupts a sentence.

EXERCISE   Most of the following sentences contain a comma error. Insert commas where they are needed, and cross out any commas that are incorrect. If a sentence is already punctuated correctly, write *C* before the item number.

Example 1. Some areas of Alaska are so remote, that they can be reached only by plane.

1. One of the most dangerous assignments for a pilot is flying over the cold barren stretches of snow and ice north of the Arctic Circle.

2. Ellen Paneok, an Inupiat pilot should know.

3. Even before she learned to drive a car Paneok was flying over the tundra far from her hometown of Kotzebue.

4. Traveling in the Arctic a bush pilot must be alert to the dangers of fatigue vertigo and the northern lights.

5. Caught in dense fog or a snowstorm a pilot can easily lose his or her bearings and become a victim of vertigo.

6. Furthermore a pilot, who stares at the northern lights too long, can wind up buried in a snowbank.

7. Paneok therefore keeps a sharp lookout for objects on the ground.

8. A glimpse of a caribou, a patch of brush, or a jutting ice dome will help her regain her sense of direction and will also alleviate her boredom.

9. Soaring over the tundra she provides many rural people with produce, and transportation.

10. Paneok loves to fly and the beauty of Alaska, and the needs of her fellow Alaskans make the risk worthwhile.

MECHANICS

Conventional Uses of Commas

13l. Use commas in certain conventional situations.

(1) Use a comma to separate items in dates and addresses.

> **EXAMPLES** On March 28, 2000, Blake sent the check to 26 Simpson Road, Spring, TX 77034.

(2) Use a comma after the salutation of a personal letter and after the closing of any letter.

> **EXAMPLES** Dear Nikki,   Yours truly,

(3) Use commas to set off a title, such as *Jr., Sr.,* or *M.D.,* that follows a person's name.

> **EXAMPLE** Did you see Henri Pierre Sallé, Jr., when he was in town?

MECHANICS

EXERCISE A Add commas where they are needed in the following sentences.

Example 1. Harold Polk, Sr., still resides in Roanoke, Virginia.

1. Nora's address is 140 Pomeroy Avenue Wichita KS 67208.

2. In 1797, Sojourner Truth was born a slave in Ulster County New York.

3. Teresa Catawba Ph.D. was our guest speaker on Friday January 12 2001.

4. My uncle Guillermo Savilla Rodrigues Jr. was born on 1 June 1976.

5. The poet Emily Dickinson died on May 15 1886 in Amherst Massachusetts.

6. Please forward my mail to 18 Clermont Street Haymarket VA 22069.

7. In September 2003 I hope to enter the University of New Hampshire.

8. Last March we drove from Springfield Ohio to Starkville Mississippi.

9. Odessa Washington M.D. has an office on Oak Street in Downingtown.

10. On Wednesday May 3 2000, a new theater opened at 4 Chestnut Street.

EXERCISE B Insert commas where they are needed in the following letter.

Example [1] Geraldine will move from Seattle, Washington, in February.

[11] January 7 2003

[12] Dear Lorraine

[13] The big exciting day is almost upon us. **[14]** On February 14 2003, my family will be moving to Lancaster Pennsylvania. **[15]** You and I have been friends since August 1996, and I will miss you so much. **[16]** Will you promise to write to me Lorraine? **[17]** My new address will be 1407 Tulane Avenue Lancaster PA 17601. **[18]** As soon as we get to the city I'll write you.

[19] Your friend

[20] Geraldine

Review of Commas

13f.	Use commas to separate items in a series.
13g.	Use commas to separate two or more adjectives preceding a noun.
13h.	Use a comma before a coordinating conjunction (*and, but, for, nor, or, so,* or *yet*) when it joins independent clauses.
13i.	Use commas to set off nonessential subordinate clauses and nonessential participial phrases.
13j.	Use a comma after certain introductory elements.
13k.	Use commas to set off an expression that interrupts a sentence.
13l.	Use commas in certain conventional situations.
13m.	Do not use unnecessary commas.

MECHANICS

EXERCISE Add commas where they are needed in the following sentences. Cross out any unnecessary commas. If a sentence is already correct, write *C* before the item number.

Example 1. Tom, would you prefer a glass of lemonade, or a bottle of water?

1. The sunlight through the leaves cast dark trembling shadows on the ground.

2. I intended to enter my project in the county science fair but I couldn't get it done by the deadline.

3. Say do you know my friend Leora?

4. Send the prize to Marcy Conlon M.D. 2500 Michigan Avenue Ann Arbor MI 48107.

5. The hot-air balloon rose into the bright, blue sky.

6. His given name was John Humphrey Marks Jr. but everybody knew him as Jack.

7. Ms. Compton was offered a position with the fire department but decided to accept the offer from the police department instead.

8. J.R.R. Tolkien who wrote the fantasy trilogy *The Lord of the Rings* was born on January 3 1892 in Bloemfontein South Africa.

9. As soon as he reached the top of the hill the exhausted hiker dropped his pack pulled off his boots and took a long nap under a tree.

10. You can operate Aunt Valerie's new stereo by using the buttons on the front, or you can use the remote control.

Review A: End Marks and Abbreviations

EXERCISE A   Add the appropriate end mark to each of the following sentences. If quotation marks should precede or follow the end mark, write them in the proper place.

Example 1. Ulani shouted, "Watch out for that bus!"

1. The first thing she said to me was, "Where did you get that haircut

2. The tour leader started waving his arms and yelling, "Stop the bus at once

3. Please sit next to me, Juan

4. John Amsterdam is the president of the student council

5. Did Dante Liberato really say, "If Stella wants my ticket, she can have it

6. Hilary, watch out for the falling boulder

7. Come and join me for a sandwich at the diner

8. Alice turned around and said, "Where in the world have you been

9. The police officer blew her whistle and shouted, "Stop that car

10. Then Garnetta stood up and said, "May I add a few thoughts on the issue

EXERCISE B   On the lines provided, rewrite the following sentences to correct any errors in the use of abbreviations.

Example 1. Rick P Avrile may be reached at 1409 Falco Avenue, Newark, New Jersey 07101.

Rick P. Avrile may be reached at 1409 Falco Ave., Newark, NJ 07101.

11. Sen. Chen of Calif. serves on the committee that oversees the Corporation for Public

Broadcasting. _____

_____

12. Doctor Martin Luther King, Junior, was born in Atlanta, GA. _____

_____

13. Dr. Billy Franklin, M.D., may be reached at 3414 Hill Crest Dr., Mobile, Ala. 36609. _____

_____

14. The A.M.A. will be holding its annual convention this year in Chicago, Ill. _____

_____

15. The Roman presence in Britain lasted from BC 55 to the early fifth century AD. _____

_____

Review B: **Commas**

EXERCISE Most of the following sentences contain a comma error. Insert commas where they are needed, and cross out any commas that are incorrect. If a sentence is already punctuated correctly, write *C* before the item number.

Example 1. Would you please repeat the question for Seth, and me, Ms. Miles?

1. She spent a week in Los Angeles California, but she did not visit Hollywood or Beverly Hills.

2. Although the patient announced that she felt well and strong her doctor insisted that she stay in the hospital a little longer.

3. The essay contest is open to any student, who is taking an American history course.

4. No we have not heard from Mrs. Whittaker since she moved to Iowa City.

5. On a bright day in October walking in the autumn woods can be pleasant and exhilarating.

6. Crater Lake, which occupies the crater of a dead volcano is known for its deep-blue color.

7. Three of the largest species of deer are the moose, the elk, and the caribou.

8. Having discussed the matter for several hours the committee finally decided to hold the spring prom on Saturday, May 27.

9. When the machine finally broke down, we called Mr. Smith the local electrician.

10. I think, that you can find that information in our supplementary textbook, *A History of the Original Colonies*, on page 76.

11. The tour guide expected us to bring, jackets, raincoats, gloves, and extra shoes.

12. Senator Gutiérrez spoke eloquently but few of his colleagues were listening.

13. The limerick, which is a light or humorous five-line verse is named after a county in Ireland.

14. Chief Tecumseh of the Shawnee argued that the land belonged to everyone, and could not be bought and sold.

15. Realizing that a delay might be costly, Emilia continued to work after the others had left.

16. The handsome adventurous hero was young and foolhardy.

17. No I doubt that either Kimiko or her sister will attend the band concert tomorrow.

18. Molly Pitcher whose real name was Mary McCauly, won fame at the Battle of Monmouth in the Revolutionary War.

19. After our meeting in the conference room on the second floor we went directly to the auditorium.

20. Although most of the team protested the franchise moved out of state.

Review C: Using End Marks and Commas Correctly

EXERCISE A Add end marks and commas where they are needed in the following sentences.

Example 1. Is María R. Sanchez, M.D., the staff doctor for Talmadge & Co.?

1. When the presentation was over Ella and Bob met with the mayor.

2. She grew her flowers from seeds young seedlings and cuttings from my garden

3. In June 1982 the offices of that company moved to Akron Ohio

4. I'm not sure that a big shaggy sheepdog would be my first choice as a pet

5. He wanted to do well on the test so he carefully studied all the chapter reviews

6. On Saturday 11 April 1998 my older sister was married in Miami Florida

7. Jeremy who is my next-door neighbor wants to go to Connecticut College

8. When you finish reading that book may I borrow it

9. No I've never seen a mockingbird; if you spot one please point it out to me

10. Irene hoping to get a job as a lifeguard took the Red Cross senior lifesaving course

EXERCISE B Add end marks and commas where they are needed in the following sentences.

Example 1. On 15 March 1990, my sister Tish was born in Waco, Texas.

11. Is Harold P. Stockwell Jr still the treasurer of United Products

12. Oskar while training for the regional meet dislocated his shoulder

13. After you return from vacation let's get together to plan the picnic

14. Their meatless meal consisted of macaroni and cheese asparagus and a salad

15. The afternoon sun filtered light through the tall stately red cedars

16. Nick Nolte once an ironworker has become an acclaimed actor

17. Students who complete all their credits will graduate in May 2003

18. The plane from Casper Wyoming landed at noon

19. Ms. Chung who graduated from Purdue University has recently joined our faculty

20. On June 1 1982 Western Gas Company opened a plant in Ames Iowa

for **CHAPTER 13: PUNCTUATION**   *pages 294–315*

Proofreading Application: Script

Good writers are generally good proofreaders. Readers tend to admire and trust writing that is error-free. Make sure that you correct all errors in grammar, usage, spelling, and punctuation in your writing. Your readers will have more confidence in your words if you have done your best to proofread carefully.

With the appropriate use of commas and end marks, writers can communicate where pauses and certain types of expression should occur. People who are reading a script must pay special attention to commas and end marks as they deliver their lines.

PROOFREADING ACTIVITY

The following is the script of a skit to be performed in a high school history class. Find and correct the errors in the use of end marks and commas. Use the proofreading symbols to make your corrections.

Mark: Believe it or not the early history of our fair city of Boise is really interesting.

Luz: Why should I believe you.

Cassie: Its history includes Native Americans gold and the Oregon Trail.

Luz: Since you haven't convinced me yet you'd better keep talking.

Mark: In the first part of the nineteenth century French-Canadians who were fur trappers attempted to start a settlement in what is now Boise but the Shoshone people thwarted them. It wasn't until 1863 following the discovery of gold that a permanent white settlement was established.

Cassie: A U.S. military base Ft. Boise was built. Considering the Shoshone attacks it seemed wise to build Boise City next to it.

Luz: So what made it grow!

Mark: There were several reasons. The Oregon Trail and routes to the gold mines passed through it. Also, many Chinese immigrants who came to mine gold near Boise decided to settle here. Becoming farmers merchants and restaurant owners they outnumbered white miners by 1870.

Language and Sentence Skills Practice

MECHANICS | Language in Context: Literary Model

Literary Model: Persuasive Writing

> Do unto all men as you would men should do unto you? Is it not enough that we are torn from our country and friends, to toil for your luxury and lust of gain? Must every tender feeling be likewise sacrificed to your avarice? Are the dearest friends and relations, now rendered more dear by their separation from the rest of their kindred, still to be parted from each other, and thus prevented from cheering the gloom of slavery with the small comfort of being together, and mingling their sufferings and sorrows?
>
> —from *The Interesting Narrative of the Life of Olaudah Equiano*

EXERCISE A

1. Equiano, an African sold into slavery in North America, makes a strong case against slavery. In the passage above, Equiano uses an unusual but effective strategy. Rather than using declarative sentences to make his point, Equiano uses interrogative sentences. Is this a choice that you would have expected? Why or why not?

_____

_____

_____

2. The passage is full of rhetorical questions, but one sentence is different: It has the word order of an imperative sentence. Identify that sentence by writing it on the line below. What effect was achieved when Equiano turned this well-known imperative sentence into an interrogative sentence?

_____

_____

_____

EXERCISE B

1. Why is Equaino's use of rhetorical questions effective in this passage?

_____

_____

2. How would your reaction to this passage have been different if Equiano had used declarative sentences to make his point?

_____

_____

Literary Model (continued)

EXERCISE C Have you ever given a speech on an issue that you felt strongly about? Write an introduction to a speech you might make on a subject such as animal rights, water conservation, safe driving, or graduation requirements. Using the Equiano passage as a model, use rhetorical questions in your introduction.

_____

_____

_____

_____

_____

_____

_____

_____

_____

_____

_____

_____

_____

_____

EXERCISE D

1. Did using interrogative sentences work for you, or do you think your introduction would have been stronger if you had used other sentence types? Explain.

_____

_____

_____

2. Look over your introduction, and choose the sentence that you feel is most effective. Why did you choose the sentence you did?

_____

_____

MECHANICS | Language in Context: Writing Application

Writing Application: Invitation

Punctuation marks often cue readers. When writers use certain punctuation marks, they clarify written language that might temporarily confuse readers.

UNCLEAR   My brother just finished his MEd at Baylor University.

CLEAR   My brother just finished his M.Ed. at Baylor University.

Readers of the first sentence would figure out that "MEd" is an abbreviation for "master of education," but they might perceive the word "med" at first. The periods prevent this misreading.

WRITING ACTIVITY

You are on the committee organizing the junior prom. Your job is to write the text for formal invitations that will be printed and mailed to all juniors and to the faculty who will attend. Because part of the junior prom budget will be spent on these invitations, all the information you write must be accurate and correctly punctuated. Every letter costs money, so use all abbreviations and punctuation marks appropriately.

PREWRITING   With other committee members, brainstorm to decide what information must appear on the invitation. Remember that space is limited! Gather and check the needed facts.

WRITING   The text for this invitation will be minimal: only a few well-chosen words. You may want to read other invitations—from weddings, graduations, and so on—to get a feel for the formal language of such texts.

REVISING   Now that you have written the invitation, put yourself in the place of a student reading it. Given the information, could you make plans to attend the event? Given the tone and word choice, do you want to go? Get feedback from other readers, too.

PUBLISHING   Check the invitation for errors in grammar, usage, spelling, and punctuation. Check information about time, date, location, and so on carefully. (After the invitations are printed is certainly no time to catch an error!) Then, make an attractive mock-up version of your invitation. You can use neat handwriting or a computer printout for the text, using paper and script that fits the occasion.

EXTENDING YOUR WRITING

You may wish to develop this exercise into a longer essay. For a sociology class, you could write a paper on the history of proms. *Prom* is a shortened form of "promenade": How did this American tradition get started, and how has it changed over the years? For an English class, you could write a personal narrative about a formal event you attended recently. You might even wish to work with other students on a short, comic play about a formal occasion gone awry. Choose one of these activities to add to your anthology.

for **CHAPTER 14: PUNCTUATION** *pages 322–54*

Choices: Investigating Punctuation

The following activities challenge you to find a connection between punctuation marks and the world around you. Do the activity below that suits your personality best, and then share your discoveries with the class.

ETYMOLOGY

Dig Deep

The word *apostrophe* has an interesting root. Look up the meaning of this root. While you've got the dictionary open, look around and find a meaning of *apostrophe* that doesn't involve punctuation. Finally, do a bit of research and see if you can find out when apostrophes were first used as marks of punctuation. When you've dug up as much information as you can about apostrophes, summarize the information that you have found in the form of a brief report. Make copies and pass them out to your classmates.

LITERATURE

In Other Words

Writers sometimes use apostrophes in dialogue to re-create the sound of regional dialects. The apostrophes indicate missing letters, as they do in contractions such as *don't.* Find some examples of this use of apostrophes in literary works and share them with your class. Then, lead the class in a discussion of this technique. What is its effect? Does it successfully re-create the intended dialect? Does it make the dialogue seem more or less realistic? Does it add regional flavor to the work? Is it demeaning to the group whose dialect is being imitated?

WRITING

X Marks the Spot

Ellipses mark a mystery. They make a reader wonder and in doing so spark the imagination. Write ten sentences that could each function as the first line in a story. End each of your sentences with ellipses. Make copies of your sentences and hand them out to your classmates. Then, they can use your sentences as the opening lines and inspiration for their own creations.

DISCUSSION

Why's and *Wherefore*'s

Lead a discussion of the reasons for hyphenation and the results of bad hyphenation. To prepare for your presentation, write a paragraph in which you break each hyphenation rule in this chapter. Each of your "mistakes" should trip a reader up, making him or her mispronounce the word. Be sure to omit a hyphen, too.

VIEWING AND REPRESENTING

Decisions, Decisions

Create a flowchart showing the decision-making process involved in choosing whether to use a semicolon or a comma between words in a sentence. Include each step of the process and make your chart as simple and clear as possible so that someone who doesn't know how to punctuate a sentence could do so. Display your flowchart in the form of a colorful, visually interesting poster.

MUSIC

Top-Ten List

Create your own top-ten lists. Brainstorm two lists: your top-ten CDs and your top-ten songs of all time. Rank the items on each list, with number one being the favorite. As you make the final copy of your lists, make sure you have used italics and quotation marks correctly. Then, share your lists with classmates. Are their musical tastes similar to yours?

LOGIC

New : Old :: Good : ?

Analogy questions often use colons to indicate relationships between words. Find out what the colons and double colons in analogy questions mean. Then, write a few incomplete analogies for your classmates to complete.

Semicolons A

| **14a.** | Use a semicolon between independent clauses that are closely related in thought and that are not joined by a coordinating conjunction *(and, but, for, nor, or, so,* or *yet).* |

                 EXAMPLE   I was happy about the trip; Nepal had always appealed to me.

| **14b.** | Use a semicolon between independent clauses joined by a conjunctive adverb or a transitional expression. |

        CONJUNCTIVE ADVERB   I was tired; **therefore,** I stopped to rest.
    TRANSITIONAL EXPRESSION   Pang is a great runner; **in fact,** he's unbeatable.

EXERCISE   Insert semicolons where they are needed in the following sentences.

Example 1. The elevator is full; would you like to use the stairs?

1. One side was willing to negotiate however, the other side refused.

2. Ms. Kyung is a fantastic teacher that is, she's my favorite.

3. Adjust the dial carefully the mechanism is sensitive.

4. Guadalupe ran toward home plate her run tied the game.

5. I was disappointed in the play in other words, it was terrible.

6. The novel is set in my hometown indeed, I recognized several places.

7. That shrub has a strong scent it smells like grape drink.

8. Kelly wanted a better job as a result, she started polishing her résumé.

9. We were all bored to tears nevertheless, we kept working.

10. The fax machine beeped the computers buzzed the phones jangled.

11. My grandfather was a code talker during WWII in fact, he got a medal for his work.

12. Turn up the television the news is on.

13. The film broke the audience groaned in disappointment.

14. The play's cast was frightened even so, they put on a good performance.

15. Bring us our check, please we'd like to go.

16. The dog lay down in the sun for a nap the cat joined him soon after.

17. Carl bumped the glass with his elbow the glass hit the floor milk sprayed in all directions.

18. Today is Mara's birthday therefore, she gets to pick the video.

19. I read the book I was not impressed.

20. Please set the table it is time to eat.

Semicolons B

14c. A semicolon (rather than a comma) may be needed before a coordinating conjunction to join independent clauses that contain commas.

> **EXAMPLE** The painting, which had once adorned the vestibule, lay in the attic for decades; and when it was rediscovered, the church promptly sold it.

14d. Use a semicolon between items in a series if the items contain commas.

> **EXAMPLE** The ushers will be Anthony Morales, brother of the groom; George Rosada, cousin of the bride; and Hershel Webber, friend of the groom.

EXERCISE Insert semicolons where they are needed in the following sentences. Some commas should be changed to semicolons.

Example 1. The present, a concertina, was for my sister, Irene; but Igor, who isn't good at keeping secrets, told her what it was half an hour before the party.

1. I lent him *The Adventures of Tom Sawyer*, by Mark Twain, *Call of the Wild*, by Jack London, and *Their Eyes Were Watching God*, by Zora Neale Hurston.

2. The hailstones, which were the size of marbles, fell for at least five minutes, but still, despite the chance of damage to the floats, they did not cancel the parade.

3. Mr. Magruder, the engineer, Ms. Lipscombe, the sheriff, Mr. Jones, the pastor, and Ms. Blank, the secretary, were all suspects.

4. The frog, whose name is Steve, likes to swim, dive, and float but, as you know, he also frequently hides inside the small, plastic castle.

5. I have blue, green, and black socks but I don't have any maroon, gold, or rust ones.

6. Aunt Bea, who loves photography, has pictures of deer, antelope, and other wild beasts but she has never photographed a lion, tiger, or bear.

7. Virginia, who wants to be a doctor, has been studying hard, but, in my opinion, Mark, her brother, studies even harder.

8. I have visited Paris, Texas, Paris, Idaho, Paris, Kentucky, and Paris, Illinois.

9. Cyrus mowed the grass, raked the leaves, fertilized the flower beds, and watered the plants and he also made chicken soup for Maddie, who had been feeling ill.

10. I felt immense relief when I finished the exercise, which had taken hours to complete, but much to my dismay, there was yet more to be done.

Language and Sentence Skills Practice

301

MECHANICS

Semicolons C

MECHANICS

14a.	Use a semicolon between independent clauses that are closely related in thought and that are not joined by a coordinating conjunction (*and, but, for, nor, or, so,* or *yet*).
14b.	Use a semicolon between independent clauses joined by a conjunctive adverb or a transitional expression.
14c.	A semicolon (rather than a comma) may be needed before a coordinating conjunction to join independent clauses that contain commas.
14d.	Use a semicolon between items in a series if the items contain commas.

EXERCISE Insert semicolons where they are needed in the following sentences. If a sentence is correct, write *C* before the numeral.

Example 1. Gujarat, India, includes wet, fertile regions; however, it also includes arid deserts of salt.

1. The Nal Sarovar Bird Sanctuary in India attracts cranes, ducks, pelicans, ibises, and storks and the Rann of Kachchh, a vast Indian salt marsh, is the nesting ground of flamingos.

2. Both offshore and inland fishing are good; salmon, tuna, and pomfret can all be caught.

3. A variety of ethnic groups can be found in Gujarat indeed, the region includes Indic, Dravidian, and aboriginal peoples.

4. Hinduism is prevalent however, Islam, Jainism, and Zoroastrianism are also practiced.

5. Staple food crops include wheat, millet, and rice and cash crops include cotton, peanuts, and oilseeds.

6. Gujarat is also famous for art and craft products in fact, craft guilds are among its most important cultural institutions.

7. The history of Gujarat dates from around 250 B.C. that is, the known history dates from that time.

8. Gujarat has had Arabic Muslim, Mughal, Maratha, and British rulers.

9. The Gujarati language is derived from Sanskrit it was the first language of Mohandas Gandhi.

10. The places in India I would most like to visit include the Rann of Kachchh, in the state of Gujarat, Srinagar, in the state of Kashmir, Varanasi, in the state of Uttar Pradesh, and Dharmsala, in the state of Himachal Pradesh.

Colons A

14e.   Use a colon to mean "note what follows."

(1) Use a colon before a list of items, especially after expressions such as *as follows* and *the following*.

> **EXAMPLE**   Items you will need are as follows: hiking boots, heavy socks, and rain gear.

(2) Use a colon before a long, formal statement or quotation.

> **EXAMPLE**   The campaign manager began by thanking all the volunteers: "On this glorious day of victory, I'd like to thank each one of you for your unfaltering devotion to our cause."

(3) Use a colon between independent clauses when the second clause explains or restates the idea of the first.

> **EXAMPLE**   His report was clear: The committee knew exactly what he meant.

EXERCISE   Insert colons where they are needed in the following items.

Example 1. The Iroquois Confederacy was a union of several peoples: Senecas, Cayugas, Onondagas, Oneidas, and Mohawks.

1. This confederacy became a formidable power By 1750, it consisted of approximately fifteen thousand people.

2. The Iroquois Constitution, regarded as the oldest living constitution, provides for the following equal voice for member tribes, a system of checks and balances, and religious and political freedom.

3. The constitution also grants considerable power to women "Women shall be considered the progenitors of the Nation. They shall own the land and the soil."

4. Leaders of the original U.S. colonies studied the Iroquois Constitution They studied its democratic and federalist principles.

5. In 1988, Congress passed a resolution that stated the following "The confederation of the original Thirteen Colonies into one republic was influenced by the political system developed by the Iroquois Confederacy, as were many of the democratic principles which were incorporated into the Constitution itself."

MECHANICS

Colons B

14f.   Use a colon in certain conventional situations.

(1) Use a colon between the hour and the minute.

EXAMPLES   7**:**45 in the morning   the 11**:**15 flight

(2) Use a colon between chapter and verse when referring to a passage from the Bible.

EXAMPLES   Genesis 3**:**2   James 3**:**7–11

(3) Use a colon between a title and subtitle.

EXAMPLE   *Scrapbooks***:** *The Artistic Approach*

(4) Use a colon after the salutation of a business letter.

EXAMPLES   Dear Senator Specter**:**   Dear Sir or Madam**:**

EXERCISE   Insert colons where they are needed in the following items.

Example 1. The 8**:**15 flight was full, so I reserved a seat on the 9**:**10.

1. Mary remembered that we had already read Luke 1 1–7.

2. I just finished *Undaunted Courage Meriwether Lewis, Thomas Jefferson, and the Opening of the American West.*

3. Since I didn't know the editor's name, I began the letter by writing, "To Whom It May Concern Thank you for accepting my poem for publication."

4. Class begins promptly at 7 45.

5. Have you seen the new movie entitled *Star Battle 8 The Return of the Mutants*?

6. I had gotten as far as Genesis 2 6 when I fell asleep.

7. "Dear Mr. Traub Thank you for sending my refund check," was how I opened the letter.

8. Priscilla wakes between 6 00 and 6 05 each morning and begins her day by reading a few pages of *Go Get Them Your Guide to Success in Business.*

9. Read Proverbs 1 1–8 and then decide.

10. I began with "Dear Sir or Madam I am interested in working in Spain this summer."

Colons C

| **14e.** | Use a colon to mean "note what follows." |
| **14f.** | Use a colon in certain conventional situations. |

EXERCISE A Insert colons where they are needed in the following items.

Example 1. The time for the cookout is finally set. Everyone should be at the pavilion by 12:30.

1. Please bring the following items to the screening a notebook, fresh paper, and two pencils.

2. The plane was scheduled to depart from O'Hare Airport at 10 42.

3. The exam will cover unit materials as follows Chapters 8, 9, and 10.

4. Her book was titled *Charles Drew Pioneer in Health and Medicine.*

5. The Biblical reference of the rabbi's talk was Joshua 14 1–15.

6. The guide's instructions were explicit Stay with the group and walk slowly.

7. If the bus is on time, Pierre should be home by 10 30.

8. One reason for her success is evident She's willing to work long hours.

9. I enjoyed Mr. Coker's article, "The Civil War The States Divide."

10. Take the following trains the 4 22 from Penn Station and the 5 07 from Newark.

EXERCISE B Insert colons where they are needed in the following business letter, and cross out any colons that are incorrect.

Example [1] The editor has an opening in her schedule at 2:30 on Thursday afternoon.

[11] Dear Ms. Rodrigues

[12] After reviewing the manuscript for your article, "Santa Fe Yesterday and Today," I am happy to inform you of the magazine's interest in publishing your work. **[13]** I have one major piece of feedback for you What an informative, engaging article! **[14]** I would love to meet with you on Monday morning, around 9 45, to discuss a few minor changes. Let me know if this time will be convenient for you. **[15]** You'll need to bring: one copy of the manuscript, your research notes, and your signed contract.

Yours truly,

Melanie Fong

Language and Sentence Skills Practice

305

Parentheses

14g.	Use parentheses to enclose informative or explanatory material of minor importance.

Be sure that the material enclosed in parentheses can be omitted without changing the meaning of the sentence.

> **EXAMPLES**   The platypus (*Ornithorhynchus anatinus*) is a small, aquatic, carnivorous mammal found in Australia and Tasmania.
>
> The Comoro Islands (see the map on page 64) lie off the southeastern coast of Africa.

EXERCISE A   Insert parentheses where they are needed or would be helpful in the following items.

Example 1. Several of Mark Twain's works are considered classics of American literature. (Have you read any of them?)

1. *Mark Twain* is the pseudonym of Samuel Langhorne Clemens 1835–1910.

2. He is probably most famous for *The Adventures of Tom Sawyer* 1876 and *The Adventures of Huckleberry Finn* 1884.

3. The young Samuel Clemens worked as a delivery boy, a grocery clerk, a blacksmith's helper, and a compositor for a newspaper the *Hannibal Journal*.

4. For a time he wrote humorous travel letters under another pseudonym Thomas Jefferson Snodgrass; in these he used misspellings and bad grammar for comic effect.

5. It wasn't until the publication in 1865 of "The Celebrated Jumping Frog of Calaveras County" a short story that Clemens became famous as "Mark Twain."

EXERCISE B   Above each of the following items, write *C* if parentheses are used correctly or *IN* if they are used incorrectly.

Example 1. Decorative carvings called cameos are made from hard or precious stones or glass *C* imitations of these stones (called pastes).

6. Cameos are commonly made from gems (agate, onyx, and sardonyx) that have layers of different colors.

7. The figures are carved in one layer to stand out against (the background of) the other layer.

8. Many cameos that date from the early Sumerian period (*c.* 3100 B.C.) have been found.

9. Roman cameos were often (very expertly carved) with mythological subjects.

10. Portraits of Queen Elizabeth (1533–1603) graced many English cameos.

Dashes

14h. Use a dash to indicate an abrupt break in thought or speech.

EXAMPLES   Building model airplanes—now, where did I put that glue?—has always been a great way for me to relax.

My surprise gift for Mom is going to be—no, I'd better not tell you yet.

14i. Use a dash to mean *namely, in other words,* or *that is* before an explanation.

EXAMPLE   The special assembly will be open only to select students—those who have taken advanced courses in the physical sciences.

EXERCISE   Insert carets to show where dashes are needed in the following items.

Example 1. The dancer you should have seen how high she leapt was amazing.

1. You won't believe what I heard Yasmina was voted Homecoming Queen!

2. Be careful don't slip on that ice.

3. Her kimono one of the most beautiful things I've ever seen featured a pattern that reminded me of goldfish swimming beneath the surface of a pond.

4. Nobody least of all me wanted to be the one to tell him he'd lost.

5. For her bouquet, she requested at least I think she did a mix of roses, petunias, daisies, and lilies.

6. The Río Grande known as the Río Bravo in Mexico is the border between Texas and its neighbor to the south.

7. Pablo has mastered the major concepts of Chapter 3 I think they include photosynthesis and transpiration.

8. Tito Puente he's my favorite Latin music percussionist produced more than 100 albums.

9. To make my quiche recipe, you'll have to buy all the ingredients on the list oh wait, it looks as though you've already got a few of them.

10. Class, today you will complete the first two sections of Dennis, please wait until I finish the instructions before you begin.

MECHANICS

Brackets

14j. Use brackets to enclose an explanation within quoted or parenthetical material.

EXAMPLES   The article states, "The Downtown Revitalization Project [introduced by Mr. Logan in 1998] has been a disappointment to many businesspeople in the area."

The AEG Turbine Factory (designed by Peter Behrens [1868–1940]) was one building that significantly influenced the development of modern architecture.

EXERCISE A   Above each of the following items, write *C* if brackets are used correctly or *IN* if they are used incorrectly.

Example 1. The article begins, "A brief outline of Emily Dickinson's life [1830–1886] reads like the plot of a story destined to become a legend."

1. It goes on to say that "no one doubted that she [Dickinson] would grow gracefully into womanhood, make a good marriage, and settle into a village life of churchgoing, holiday gatherings, and neighborly harmony."

2. However, she did not marry, but instead secluded herself [kept to herself and always dressed in white] and began writing poems.

3. Dickinson sent a few of her poems to Thomas Wentworth Higginson (the editor of the *Atlantic Monthly* [a well-respected magazine]).

4. Dickinson later gave up on finding readers other than her friends and relatives [she often sent her poems to them as Valentine notes or birthday greetings].

5. Eventually, a collection of her poems (*The Poems of Emily Dickinson* [1955]) was published.

EXERCISE B   Above each of the following items, write *C* if brackets are used correctly or *IN* if they are used incorrectly.

Example 1. Referring to the "American dream," the writers assert that *"The Great Gatsby* by F. Scott Fitzgerald [1896–1940] mirrors both its failures and its promises."

6. We are told that "the novel's title character [Gatsby] is a dreamer on a grand scale."

7. The article emphasizes the importance of the novel's setting [the Roaring Twenties].

8. Earlier, the Transcendentalists (including Ralph Waldo Emerson [1803–82]) had championed a different aspect of the dream—individualism.

9. In my term paper, I wrote that "Emerson also embodied optimism, another aspect of it [the American Dream]."

10. I also pointed out that the Great Depression [of the 1930s] extinguished some of this optimism.

Parentheses, Dashes, and Brackets

14g.	Use parentheses to enclose informative or explanatory material of minor importance.
14h.	Use a dash to indicate an abrupt break in thought or speech.
14i.	Use a dash to mean *namely, in other words,* or *that is* before an explanation.
14j.	Use brackets to enclose an explanation within quoted or parenthetical material.

EXERCISE A On the line provided before each sentence, write *D* if the underlined words or numerals should be set off by dashes, *P* if they should be enclosed by parentheses, or *B* if they should be enclosed by brackets.

Example ____*B*____ **1.** The article begins, "The great American pastime baseball has been around longer than many of us might have thought."

_____ **1.** For years, people thought that Abner Doubleday 1819–1893 had invented baseball.

_____ **2.** However, American colonists in the 1700s did they have time for games? played it.

_____ **3.** George Herman Ruth (commonly called "Babe Ruth" 1895–1948) was a great player.

_____ **4.** Early in his career he was known for one great talent he was quite a pitcher.

_____ **5.** During his career twenty-two seasons he had a lifetime batting average of .342.

EXERCISE B For each of the following items, write on the line provided a sentence that uses punctuation marks in the way indicated.

Example 1. Use a dash to indicate a break in speech. *We were cold—our teeth were chattering, in fact—as we stood on the dock.*

6. Use a dash to indicate *in other words*. _____

_____

7. Use parentheses to enclose explanatory material of minor importance. _____

_____

8. Use brackets to enclose an explanation within parenthetical material. _____

_____

9. Write two sentences, the second of which stands by itself in parentheses. _____

_____

10. Use a dash to indicate an abrupt break in thought. _____

_____

Italics A

14k. Use italics (underlining) for the titles and subtitles of books, plays, long poems, periodicals, works of art, movies, radio and TV series, videos, video games, long musical works and recordings, computer games, and comic strips.

BOOKS	*A Tale of Two Cities*	*Football for Dummies*
PLAYS	*A Raisin in the Sun*	*Othello*
PERIODICALS	*USA Today*	*Cat Fancy*
MOVIES	*Twister*	*Life Is Beautiful*
COMIC STRIPS	*Calvin and Hobbes*	*Peanuts*

Do not use italics for titles of religious texts or for titles of legal or historical documents.

EXERCISE A   For each of the following categories, list five titles, either real or made-up.

Example 1. long poems   *The Waste Land, Beowulf, Gilgamesh, Paradise Lost, Rubáiyát*

1. movies _____

2. books _____

3. long musical works and recordings _____

4. television series _____

5. periodicals _____

EXERCISE B   Underline any titles that should be italicized in the following sentences. If a sentence is already correct, write *C* before the item number.

Example 1. In Madrid, I saw Guernica, a fascinating painting by Pablo Picasso.

6. In London, we saw Oscar Wilde's play The Importance of Being Earnest.

7. In Tokyo, I played one of the earliest computer games, Space Invaders.

8. At a cafe in Paris, I pretended to read the French newspaper Le Monde.

9. In Germany, we went to hear a performance of Mozart's Mass in C Minor.

10. While in Istanbul, Turkey, I looked at a copy of the Islamic religious text, the Koran.

11. Giuseppe Verdi's most popular opera, Aïda, was first performed in Cairo.

12. Sundiata: An Epic of Old Mali is a legend about a thirteenth-century leader in Mali.

13. In the summer Ramona likes to watch reruns of I Love Lucy.

14. In the 1940's, Langston Hughes wrote a column for the New York Post in which a character called Simple voiced the thoughts of young black Americans.

15. You should read the novel The Joy Luck Club by Amy Tan.

MECHANICS

Italics B

14l. Use italics (underlining) for the names of trains, ships, aircraft, and spacecraft.

   EXAMPLES   *Best Friend of Charleston* (train)   *Titanic* (ship)
   Spruce Goose (airplane)   *Columbia* (space shuttle)

14m. Use italics (underlining) for words, letters, symbols, and numerals referred to as such, and for foreign words that have not been adopted into English.

   EXAMPLES   What is the symbol for the Greek letter *pi*?
   The word *Briton* begins with a capital *B.*

MECHANICS

EXERCISE   Underline any words, letters, symbols, or numbers that should be italicized in the following sentences.

Example 1. The name of the spaceship in *Star Trek* is the Enterprise.

1. The word care is derived from the Old English word caru, meaning "sorrow."

2. Orient-Express was the name of a luxury train that ran between Paris and Constantinople.

3. I know that numeral looks like a 9, but actually it is a 7.

4. People often confuse the words imply and infer.

5. I spell my name with a k, not a c.

6. The symbol < in the dictionary means "derived from."

7. The only Japanese word I remember is nekko, "cat."

8. My aunt named her airplane Penelope.

9. The price tag read $5.

10. Mark Twain learned to navigate on the steamboat the Paul Jones.

11. Charles Lindbergh's airplane was named the Spirit of St. Louis.

12. How many times did the speaker say um during his talk?

13. There are four i's and four s's in Mississippi.

14. In the film business, the term trailer means "a preview of a forthcoming film."

15. We rode the train the City of New Orleans to Memphis.

16. I christen this ship the Endurance.

17. The French for "I don't know what" is je ne sais quoi.

18. Does the van in van Gogh start with a capital v?

19. In *Star Wars*, Han Solo's ship is the Millennium Falcon.

20. The answer has four 6's in a row.

Language and Sentence Skills Practice   **311**

Italics: Review

14k. Use italics (underlining) for the titles and subtitles of books, plays, long poems, periodicals, works of art, movies, radio and TV series, videos, video games, long musical works and recordings, computer games, and comic strips.

Do not use italics for titles of religious texts or for titles of legal or historical documents.

14l. Use italics (underlining) for the names of trains, ships, aircraft, and spacecraft.

14m. Use italics (underlining) for words, letters, symbols, and numerals referred to as such, and for foreign words that have not been adopted into English.

EXERCISE A Underline all words, letters, symbols, and numerals that should appear in italics.

Example 1. The Ingrid Bergman Festival will feature the films Notorious and Gaslight.

1. Our neighbor, Kim Wong, was a contestant on Jeopardy.

2. Do you ever get the words to, too, and two confused?

3. Composer Andrew Lloyd Webber wrote the music for Cats and The Phantom of the Opera.

4. The adjective jumbo is derived from the Gullah word jamba, meaning "elephant."

5. The Philadelphia Inquirer is a morning newspaper.

6. Schubert died before finishing one of his greatest musical compositions; today it is known as The Unfinished Symphony.

7. The Spirit of St. Louis is the plane in which Charles Lindbergh made the first nonstop solo flight from New York to Paris.

8. The Spanish word alcalde means "mayor."

9. In Italian the vowel i is pronounced like the English letters ee in the word see.

10. The English word atlas comes from the name of the Greek god who supported the heavens on his shoulders.

EXERCISE B Underline all words, letters, symbols, and numerals that should appear in italics.

Example 1. Milton's long poem Paradise Lost contains many allusions to the Bible.

11. I based my book, titled Land of the Free: The Rights of Teenagers, on the Bill of Rights.

12. My name is spelled with an n, as in Nancy.

13. The name of Captain Ahab's whaling ship in the novel Moby-Dick is the Pequod.

14. The French word for "yes" is spelled oui but is pronounced like we.

15. I named my cat Gatsby after the title character in Fitzgerald's The Great Gatsby.

MECHANICS

Quotation Marks A

14n. Use quotation marks to enclose a *direct quotation*—a person's exact words.

(1) A direct quotation generally begins with a capital letter.

> **EXAMPLE** Jane said, "The cat looks like a statue on top of the piano."

(2) When an expression identifying the speaker divides a quoted sentence, the second part begins with a lowercase letter.

> **EXAMPLE** "You will find," Angela said, "that this course is challenging."

(3) A direct quotation can be set off from the rest of the sentence by a comma, a question mark, or an exclamation point, but not by a period.

> **EXAMPLES** "Let's go to the film festival," said Mingan.
>
> "Why are you so upset?" asked Annie.
>
> "Hold that line!" shouted the spectators.

(4) When used with quotation marks, other marks of punctuation are placed according to the following rules:

- Commas and periods are placed inside the closing quotation marks.
- Semicolons and colons are placed outside the closing quotation marks.
- Question marks and exclamation points are placed inside the closing quotation marks if the quotation itself is a question or an exclamation. Otherwise they are placed outside.

> **EXAMPLES** "I'd like a banana," I said, "but please make sure it's ripe."
>
> He said that he was "too tired"; I, on the other hand, felt just fine.
>
> What do you mean by "I don't want to talk about it"?

EXERCISE Add quotation marks, commas, and end marks where they are needed.

Example 1. "How many dogs do the Durands have?" asked Elston.

1. Are you staying late at the library again? asked Daniel.

2. Your first responsibility the colonel told her troops is to your country.

3. Who said Let's walk instead of riding in the car?

4. If you listen carefully remarked Dvori you can hear the sound of the doves' wings.

5. My days begin each dawn, wrote the mountain climber, when I awaken to the loneliness that crowds my soul.

6. Encore shouted the enthusiastic crowd.

7. Pilar said My potato salad is the best; most of us agreed with her.

8. Are you finished asked Mrs. Traub, or do you need more time

9. She writes, I am having the time of my life; she also says that she misses us.

10. In his speech, the mayor warned We must all do our part in preserving the environment.

Language and Sentence Skills Practice

Quotation Marks B

14n. Use quotation marks to enclose a *direct quotation*—a person's exact words.

(5) When quoting a passage that consists of more than one paragraph, put quotation marks at the beginning of each paragraph and at the end of only the last paragraph of the passage.

EXAMPLE   "We must learn to appreciate the beauty around us. We can see miracles if we keep our eyes open. How many times have we awakened to a magnificent sunrise and yet not noticed it? Did you see the sunrise this morning? What colors filled the sky?

"Do you remember what the moon looked like last night? What stage was it in? How visible was it? Jot down a few sentences about a view of the moon that you clearly recall."

(6) When writing *dialogue* (a conversation), begin a new paragraph every time the speaker changes, and enclose each speaker's words in quotation marks.

EXAMPLE   "Are you suggesting we leave right now?" asked Petra. "I'm not sure Roger is completely ready."

"It's always best to arrive early," advised Suzi.

(7) Use single quotation marks to enclose a quotation within a quotation.

EXAMPLE   "When Arnold said, 'I'll be back,' the whole theater laughed," said Jill.

EXERCISE   On the lines provided, rewrite the following dialogue, correcting any errors in the use of quotation marks and other marks of punctuation and beginning a new paragraph wherever necessary.

Example **[1]** Didn't you just have a birthday asked Marcia.   _"Didn't you just have a_

birthday?" asked Marcia.

[1] What did Steve give you for your birthday? asked Marcia. **[2]** A pet frog replied Greg, and I named it after him. **[3]** A frog named Steve asked Marcia. **[4]** What does Steve think about having a frog named after him? she pondered. **[5]** Well said Greg when I told him he said, Wow, that's great!

_____

_____

_____

_____

_____

_____

_____

_____

_____

MECHANICS

Quotation Marks C

14o. Use quotation marks to enclose titles (including subtitles) of short works such as short stories, poems, essays, articles and other parts of periodicals, songs, episodes of radio and TV series, and chapters and other parts of books.

SHORT STORIES	"Miss Awful"	"Marriage Is a Private Affair"
ARTICLES	"Hills of Green"	"People of the Valley"
SONGS	"La Bamba"	"Gloria"

Use single quotation marks for the titles of short works within quotations.

EXAMPLE   "My favorite song on that album is 'Hey, Jude,' " said Hernando.

14p. Use quotation marks to enclose slang words, invented words, technical terms, dictionary definitions of words, and any expressions that are unusual in standard English.

EXAMPLES   Charlie calls everybody "dude," even girls.

My sister has created a special, enormous version of the chalupa that she calls the "supalupa."

The French expression *raison d'être* means "reason for being."

MECHANICS

EXERCISE   Add quotation marks and single quotation marks where they are needed in the following sentences.

Example 1. Mr. Tate assigned "Shelling Corn by Moonlight" and "Pedro the Hunter," two selections from the book *Among My People*.

1. In W. B. Yeats's poem A Coat, what does the coat symbolize?

2. Chapter 5, which is called In the Woods, was pretty frightening.

3. According to my Spanish dictionary, the word *escudo* means shield.

4. Galen Rowell's article Along the High, Wide Sierra: The John Muir Trail appeared in *National Geographic*.

5. Isn't *burrah sahib* a Hindi phrase meaning a person of importance?

6. "Hand me the whatsamadoodle," said Latanya.

7. Modern dancers often talk about being grounded, a term that refers to the dancer's center of gravity.

8. "I loved last night's episode of *Time Travels*, called Alien Alert," said Todd.

9. Chi wrote an article titled Aprons Can Be Fashionable.

10. "Those shoes are really fly," said Marcus's older brother, who still uses slang from the nineties.

Quotation Marks: Review

MECHANICS

14n. Use quotation marks to enclose a ***direct quotation***—a person's exact words.

> **EXAMPLE**   "Did you hear that strange noise?" asked Jeremy.

14o. Use quotation marks to enclose titles (including subtitles) of short works such as short stories, poems, essays, articles and other parts of periodicals, songs, episodes of radio and TV series, and chapters and other parts of books.

> **POEM**   "The Whisper of the Wind"
>
> **SONG**   "Kathy's Song"
>
> **TITLE OF ARTICLE**   "The Secret Lives of Bees"

14p. Use quotation marks to enclose slang words, invented words, technical terms, dictionary definitions of words, and any expressions that are unusual in standard English.

> **EXAMPLE**   Roberto said that his new suit was "groovy."

EXERCISE   Add quotation marks and single quotation marks where they are needed in the following sentences. Be careful to show the correct position of quotation marks in relation to other marks of punctuation.

Example 1. "Have you read the short story 'Speaking of Courage'?" wondered Durga.

1. Felipe cleared his throat and then said, Reading the Declaration of Independence has given me a new understanding of my country's history.

2. Louisa was known as Louloubelle in her home town.

3. According to the dictionary, the word *betroth* derives from an Old English word, *treowth*, meaning truth.

4. Ms. Finch said that she had read an article titled Dreams of Flying that might interest Dan.

5. When the pine cone fell onto the crown of his head, Richard asked, What was that?

6. My brother coined the term slubberfritz to refer to anyone who leaves clothes lying on the floor.

7. She could be heard humming the tune Greensleeves while she worked.

8. I will now read Sylvia Plath's poem Mirror, declared Sophie.

9. What did she mean when she said she felt woogie?

10. That, said Manessa, was the best work I've ever done.

Italics and Quotation Marks: Review

14k.	Use italics (underlining) for the titles and subtitles of books, plays, long poems, periodicals, works of art, movies, radio and TV series, videos, video games, long musical works and recordings, computer games, and comic strips.
14l.	Use italics (underlining) for the names of trains, ships, aircraft, and spacecraft.
14m.	Use italics (underlining) for words, letters, symbols, and numerals referred to as such, and for foreign words that have not been adopted into English.
14n.	Use quotation marks to enclose a **_direct quotation_**—a person's exact words.
14o.	Use quotation marks to enclose titles (including subtitles) of short works such as short stories, poems, essays, articles and other parts of periodicals, songs, episodes of radio and TV series, and chapters and other parts of books.
14p.	Use quotation marks to enclose slang words, invented words, technical terms, dictionary definitions of words, and any expressions that are unusual in standard English.

MECHANICS

EXERCISE   In the following sentences, underline any words that should be in italics, and insert quotation marks where they are needed. Be careful to show the correct position of quotation marks in relation to other marks of punctuation.

Example 1. "Are you sure," Jalen asked, "that the dog is not injured?"

1. The passage that he quoted was from Ralph Waldo Emerson's lecture The American Scholar.

2. Margaret Walker's first book, For My People, included a tribute to grandmothers in a poem titled Lineage.

3. Barbara said to the librarian, I'm looking for a volume of short stories by Katherine Anne Porter.

4. Jan told us that she had seen the article in yesterday's edition of the Daily News.

5. The song Maria from the musical West Side Story was very popular.

6. My friend Corrine's essay, Terra Firma, appeared in the literary magazine Puerto del Sol.

7. Guillermo asked the clerk, Do you know if you have last month's Scientific American?

8. When you go to the library, I said, remember to find out who wrote the line And now there came both mist and snow.

9. Dorotea said, I believe you mispronounced the word epitome.

10. Have you learned, she asked, who wrote Beware the Jabberwock, my son!?

Ellipsis Points

14q. Use ellipsis points (. . .) to mark omissions from quoted material.

> **EXAMPLES**   "A rushing wind **. . .** made its way through the village."
>
> Connie wrote, "I found it difficult to learn how to enter numbers in the ledger book. **. . .** The work I had to do to learn the process, however, was well worth my time."

14r. Use three ellipsis points to indicate a pause in dialogue.

> **EXAMPLE**   "Well **. . .** I guess I'm not sure," admitted the defendant in a low voice.

MECHANICS

EXERCISE On the lines provided, rewrite the following quoted passages, omitting the parts that appear in italics. Use ellipsis points to indicate where words have been omitted.

Example 1. Francine got home early. *The play was a short one.* She even had time to finish her painting.   Francine got home early. . . . She even had time to finish her painting.

1. Güler said, "I really enjoy ice-skating, *but I can't stand the cold.*" _____

_____

2. Send your finest thoughts out into the world. Let them beam *like the rays of the sun* into the lives of others. _____

_____

3. The years of a tree are measured in rings.

   And so it is with all of nature.

   The years of the human heart are measured in courage.

_____

_____

_____

4. Mr. Clayton called. *He's going out.* Call him back at 4:30. _____

_____

5. Love, *even that which springs naturally from the heart,* is often hard work. _____

_____

Apostrophes and the Possessive Case A

The *possessive case* of a noun or a pronoun shows ownership or possession.

14s. Use an apostrophe to form the possessive forms of nouns and indefinite pronouns.

(1) To form the possessive of most singular nouns, add an apostrophe and an *s*.

EXAMPLES   a cat's bed   Doris's coat   the company's policy

When forming the possessive of a singular noun ending in an *s* sound, add only an apostrophe if the noun has two or more syllables and if the addition of an apostrophe and an *s* will make the noun awkward to pronounce.

EXAMPLES   axe's blade   Hermes' message

(2) To form the possessive of a plural noun ending in *s*, add only the apostrophe.

EXAMPLES   the musicians' chairs   citizens' votes   Dalmatians' spots

The few plural nouns that do not end in *s* form the possessive by adding an apostrophe and an *s*.

EXAMPLES   the women's team   the mice's nest   children's literature

EXERCISE   On the line provided, write the possessive form of each of the nouns below.

Example ____leaves'____ **1.** leaves

_____ **1.** ostrich   _____ **11.** men

_____ **2.** Bob   _____ **12.** dogs

_____ **3.** today   _____ **13.** Philoctetes

_____ **4.** oxen   _____ **14.** deer

_____ **5.** books   _____ **15.** writer

_____ **6.** theater   _____ **16.** fish

_____ **7.** people   _____ **17.** bees

_____ **8.** fields   _____ **18.** house

_____ **9.** Cornelius   _____ **19.** Hercules

_____ **10.** houses   _____ **20.** Ross

MECHANICS

Apostrophes and the Possessive Case B

14s.   Use an apostrophe to form the possessive forms of nouns and indefinite pronouns.

(3) Do not use an apostrophe with possessive personal pronouns or with the possessive pronoun *whose*.

> **EXAMPLES**   That backpack isn't **his.**   **Whose** stories do you prefer?
> Their Web site is phenomenal.   **Its** paw is hurt.

(4) To form the possessive of an indefinite pronoun, add an apostrophe and an *s*.

> **EXAMPLES**   no one**'s** explanation   someone**'s** lunchbox

EXERCISE   On the lines provided, rewrite the following possessive forms correctly. If an item is already correct, write *C*.

Example   _no one's sermon_   **1.** no ones' sermon

_____   **1.** someone's lunch

_____   **2.** whose's vote

_____   **3.** it's worth

_____   **4.** my voyage

_____   **5.** nobodys' fault

_____   **6.** it's fur

_____   **7.** Is that yours'?

_____   **8.** our town

_____   **9.** hers desk

_____   **10.** somebody house

_____   **11.** its surface

_____   **12.** whose sock

_____   **13.** ones' time

_____   **14.** its luster

_____   **15.** their's eggs

_____   **16.** to each his' own

_____   **17.** That is his's.

_____   **18.** our names

_____   **19.** yours' book

_____   **20.** it's food

320

MECHANICS

Apostrophes and the Possessive Case C

14s. Use an apostrophe to form the possessive forms of nouns and indefinite pronouns.

(5) Generally, in compound nouns, in names of organizations and businesses, and in word groups showing joint possession, only the last word is possessive in form.

> **EXAMPLES** mother-in-**law's** book   the National Park **Service's** brochure
> Randall and **Stacy's** discussion

(6) Form the possessive of each noun in a word group showing individual possession of similar items.

> **EXAMPLES** the veterinarian's and groomer's fees

(7) When used in the possessive form, words indicating time, such as *minute, hour, day, week, month,* and *year,* and words indicating amounts in cents or dollars require apostrophes.

> **EXAMPLES** two weeks' vacation   a month's salary   five dollars' worth

EXERCISE A Insert apostrophes where they are needed in the following items.

Example 1. the ex-senator's mansion

1. my only brother-in-laws CD collection

2. Medgar and Roths accounting firm

3. the United Nations aid programs

4. a days work

5. the president-elects speech

EXERCISE B Each of the following phrases expresses a possessive relationship. On the lines provided, revise each word group so that a possessive noun or pronoun expresses the same relationship.

Example 1. eyes of Rob and Katie *Rob's and Katie's eyes*

6. headquarters of the FBI _____

7. favorite song of Jorge and Terry _____

8. photograph of her great-uncle _____

9. essays of Emerson and essays of Thoreau _____

10. law office of Chang, Johnson, and O'Reilly _____

11. worth of five cents _____

12. opinion of the ex-mayor _____

13. paintings of Renoir and paintings of Picasso _____

14. pay of one week _____

15. science project of Lydia and me _____

MECHANICS

Possessive Case: Review

14s. Use an apostrophe to form the possessive forms of nouns and indefinite pronouns.

EXAMPLES	monster's eyes	Glenn's uniform	human beings' physiology
	geese's feet	no one's business	editor in chief's idea
	Dawna and Fred's mom	Yoshi's and my project	fifty cents' worth
	Dove's and Walker's poems	a day's notice	

Do not use an apostrophe with possessive personal pronouns (*my, mine, our, ours, your, yours, his, her, hers, its, their, theirs*).

EXERCISE On the lines provided, rewrite the following phrases and short sentences so that the possessive forms are correct. If an item is already correct, write *C*.

Example 1. Casey's and Marcos grades _____ *Casey's and Marcos's grades* _____

1. that areas geographical regions _____

2. anybodys' guess _____

3. the CIAs history _____

4. mens' suits _____

5. Whose' book is it? _____

6. Chris and Lindas' conversation _____

7. Those poems are hers'. _____

8. the three drummer's shoes _____

9. todays weather forecast _____

10. twelve month's salary _____

11. Socrates's philosophy _____

12. It's name is Toby. _____

13. Ellis's report card _____

14. the rabbis writings _____

15. a towns's reputation _____

16. fifty cents worth _____

17. the governor's-elect policies _____

18. The shoes are theirs. _____

19. each ones' efforts _____

20. both electricians' bills _____

MECHANICS

Apostrophes and Contractions

14t. Use an apostrophe to show where letters, numerals, or words have been omitted in a contraction.

EXAMPLES	they have—they've	let us—let's
	she is—she's	1999—'99
	would not—wouldn't	cannot—can't

Do not confuse contractions with possessive pronouns.

CONTRACTIONS	POSSESSIVE PRONOUNS
It's [It is] time to go.	The dog ate **its** bone.
Do you know **who's** [who is] playing center?	**Whose** basketball is this?
They're [They are] leaving now.	Is that **their** car?

EXERCISE A On the line provided after each item, write the contracted form, using apostrophes correctly.

Example 1. will not _____won't_____

1. who has _____
2. they are _____
3. I would _____
4. is not _____
5. have not _____
6. 1998 _____
7. he had _____
8. who is _____
9. does not _____
10. let us _____

11. you will _____
12. he is _____
13. you are _____
14. could not _____
15. of the clock _____
16. she would _____
17. they have _____
18. I am _____
19. should have _____
20. was not _____

EXERCISE B Underline the choice in parentheses that will complete each of the following sentences correctly.

Example 1. (*Who's, Whose*) is the report with the colorful cover?

21. These are (*their, they're*) homework assignments.

22. (*Who's, Whose*) coming to the meeting?

23. (*You're, Your*) phone is ringing.

24. (*It's, Its*) the most beautiful painting I've ever seen.

25. (*Their, They're*) buying the tickets now.

MECHANICS

Language and Sentence Skills Practice

Apostrophes and Plurals

14u. Use an apostrophe and an *s* to form the plurals of lowercase letters, symbols, numerals, some uppercase letters, and some words referred to as words.

> **EXAMPLES**   The word *occasion* contains two *c*'s.
>
> Fill in each column with +'s and −'s to indicate the trial results.
>
> Lorraine's street address has three *8*'s in it.
>
> Wow! I've never had so many A's on my report card before!

EXERCISE   In each sentence below, place a caret (∧) to indicate where an apostrophe should be inserted.

Example 1. Write *0*∧s with a slash through them to distinguish them from the letter *O*.

1. Most of the students made 80s and 90s on the last biology exam.

2. Davey, you need to learn that *thank you*s sometimes have an almost magical effect.

3. Akiro's latest report card included three Ds.

4. Grandmother Lee claims that 3s and 7s are lucky numbers.

5. Please write your +s and *x*s more carefully so that I can tell them apart.

6. Half dozing by the pool, Mr. Ferlinghetti listened with nostalgia to the *Marco*s and *Polo*s the children shouted as they played.

7. Does the phrase "mind your *p*s and *q*s" have an equivalent in Finnish?

8. Now that Janie knows how to write Xs and Os, you can teach her how to play tic-tac-toe.

9. In Spanish, *d*s and *t*s are pronounced more softly than in English.

10. Your next step is to write ✓s in the appropriate column.

MECHANICS

Contractions and Plurals: Review

14t.   Use an apostrophe to show where letters, numerals, or words have been omitted in a contraction.

Do not confuse contractions with possessive pronouns.

14u.   Use an apostrophe and an *s* to form the plurals of lowercase letters, symbols, numerals, some uppercase letters, and some words referred to as words.

EXERCISE A   On the line provided after each item, write the contracted form, using apostrophes correctly.

Example 1. were not _____*weren't*_____

1. they will _____

2. he would _____

3. will not _____

4. you would _____

5. it is _____

6. she will _____

7. there has _____

8. cannot _____

9. did not _____

10. where is _____

EXERCISE B   Underline the choice in parentheses that completes each sentence correctly.

Example 1. *(You're, Your)* hair looks lovely today.

11. *(It's, Its)* leg is wounded.

12. *(Who's, Whose)* at the door?

13. *(You're, Your)* a great dancer.

14. *(Their, They're)* home at last!

15. *(You're, Your)* making a list.

16. *(Their, They're)* sleeping.

17. *(Its, It's)* been great to see you.

18. *(Whose, Who's)* whispering?

19. *(Their, They're)* car won't start.

20. *(Whose, Who's)* pen is this?

EXERCISE C   In each sentence below, place a caret (∧) to indicate where an apostrophe should be inserted.

Example 1. Any student making all As will receive an award.

21. This would be a perfect example of penmanship if all the *i*s had been dotted.

22. A chorus of *yea*s was heard at the conclusion of the ambassador's speech.

23. Scores of 6s and 8s were predominant in the data.

24. Is your sister's name spelled with one or two *r*s?

25. Many third graders still confuse <s and >s when solving inequalities.

Apostrophes: Review

14s. Use an apostrophe to form the possessive forms of nouns and indefinite pronouns.

> **EXAMPLES** kitten's ears   Roberto's cap   bunnies' fur
>
>   men's coats   someone's mittens   a week's rest

14t. Use an apostrophe to show where letters, numerals, or words have been omitted in a contraction.

> **EXAMPLES** he is—he's   has not—hasn't   who is—who's

14u. Use an apostrophe and an *s* to form the plurals of lowercase letters, symbols, numerals, some uppercase letters, and some words referred to as words.

> **EXAMPLES** How many *c*'s are in the word *circumstance*?
>
>   Mark the most important items with *'s for now.

EXERCISE A On the lines provided, write the possessive form of each of the nouns and pronouns below.

Example 1. family _____*family's*_____

1. dentists _____

2. Mr. Schertz _____

3. geese _____

4. you _____

5. anyone _____

6. OPEC _____

7. father-in-law _____

8. M.D. _____

9. civilians _____

10. Joneses _____

EXERCISE B The following sentences contain errors in the use of apostrophes. In each sentence, draw a line through each incorrect word and write the correction above it.

Example 1. My ~~dogs~~ *dog's* ears were too long; its tail was too short.

11. In a few weeks time, everyones' worries will be over.

12. Dont the twins understand that they're fathers work is respected internationally?

13. The Laughlins house is the only two-story structure on our block.

14. Twenty *please*s later, Mr. Abernathy gave in to his sons request to join the Little League team.

15. Both T. S. Eliot and E. E. Cummings's poems evoke unusual images in the mind.

16. The childrens' suffering has been somewhat alleviated by the fifteen volunteer's efforts.

17. Someones' essay—who's it is I can't say—is lying on the floor of the main corridor.

18. During the treasurer's-elect speech, the club's members listened attentively.

19. Juanito, please try to make the top and bottom parts of your *8*s touch each other.

20. What do you think about MTVs voter registration drives?

Hyphens A

14v. Use a hyphen to divide a word at the end of a line.

> **EXAMPLES** Lillian Hellman is one of my favorite play-
> wrights.
> Hellman's characters always seem real-
> istic and interesting.

MECHANICS (side tab)

EXERCISE A On the line provided, write each of the following words, using hyphens to show how the word could be divided at the end of a line. If a word should not be divided, write *do not divide*.

Example 1. frankly _____ *frank-ly* _____

1. fifty-four _____
2. mid-September _____
3. baseball _____
4. alarm _____
5. plunge _____
6. thirty-five _____
7. insure _____
8. pre-October _____
9. brunch _____
10. bluebird _____

11. willingness _____
12. thought _____
13. alive _____
14. foresight _____
15. dangerous _____
16. dense _____
17. goldfish _____
18. rebate _____
19. cozy _____
20. well-intentioned _____

EXERCISE B Some of the numbered words at the end of lines in the following paragraph are incorrectly divided. If a word is incorrectly divided, write the word, correctly divided, in the blank to the right of the line. Hint: Some words can be correctly divided in more than one way. You need to give only one answer for each item.

Example You can never **[1]** pred- _____ *pre-dict* _____

ict what my relatives are going to do.

At seventy years old, my aunt Elaine **[21]** dec- _____

ided to learn to paint. She took a few **[22]** beginn- _____

er courses to learn some techniques. Her first **[23]** wo- _____

rk was a surprisingly well-executed **[24]** self-por- _____

trait, remarkable for her use of colors. They were **[25]** a- _____

stonishingly subtle, yet bold at the same time.

Hyphens B

14w. Use a hyphen with compound numbers from *twenty-one* to *ninety-nine* and with fractions used as modifiers.

    EXAMPLES   **thirty-seven** people   **one-half** cup of milk

14x. Use a hyphen with the prefixes *ex–*, *self–*, *all–*, and *great–*; with the suffixes *–elect* and *–free;* and with all prefixes before a proper noun or a proper adjective.

    EXAMPLES   **ex**-senator   **self**-confident   **all**-important
                     senator-**elect**   **pro**-Arab

14y. Hyphenate a compound adjective when it precedes the noun it modifies.

    EXAMPLES   a **well-defined** rule   a rule that is well defined

Do not use a hyphen if one of the modifiers before a noun is an adverb ending in *–ly*.
    EXAMPLE   a **clearly stated** argument

EXERCISE   In each item below, place a caret (∧) to indicate where a hyphen should be inserted. If an item is already correct, write *C* before the item number.

Example 1. a well∧groomed dog

1. a tender hearted man
2. one fourth cup of water
3. a storm in the mid Atlantic
4. the new president elect
5. a finely tuned instrument
6. a world renowned tenor
7. one third cup of rice
8. a clearly expressed point
9. a pro Mexican statement
10. one half of the class

11. thirty four states
12. post World War II
13. three quarters of the water
14. eighty two years old
15. a time honored tradition
16. an anti American slogan
17. one half teaspoon of salt
18. a highly dangerous sport
19. a germ infested bandage
20. sugar free gum

MECHANICS

Hyphens: Review

14v.	Use a hyphen to divide a word at the end of a line.
14w.	Use a hyphen with compound numbers from *twenty-one* to *ninety-nine* and with fractions used as modifiers.
14x.	Use a hyphen with the prefixes *ex–*, *self–*, *all–*, and *great–*; with the suffixes *–elect* and *–free;* and with all prefixes before a proper noun or a proper adjective.
14y.	Hyphenate a compound adjective when it precedes the noun it modifies.
14z.	Use a hyphen to prevent awkwardness or confusion.

EXERCISE   On the line provided, write a sentence according to each of the following guidelines. In your sentences use a variety of subjects and verbs.

Example 1. Write a sentence in which you divide a word at the end of the line.

_____ At the antiques store we saw a type- _____

_____ writer that was probably eighty years old. _____

1. Write a sentence containing a word with double consonants; at the end of a line, correctly

   divide that word. _____

   _____

2. Write a sentence in which you divide an already hyphenated word at the end of a line. _____

   _____

   _____

3. Write a sentence containing a compound adjective that precedes the word it modifies. _____

   _____

   _____

4. Write a sentence containing a word with the prefix *all-*. _____

   _____

5. Write a sentence containing a fraction used as an adjective. _____

   _____

MECHANICS

Review A: Using Punctuation Correctly

EXERCISE A In most of the following sentences, a comma or no mark of punctuation at all has been used where the writer should have used a semicolon (**;**) or a colon (**:**). For each error, cross out the incorrect punctuation mark (if any) and insert the semicolon or colon. If a sentence is already correct, write *C* before the item number.

Example 1. Latasha is quite serious about cooking, she intends to become a master chef.

1. Jack was supposed to meet me at the station at noon, he was fifteen minutes late, however.

2. Rainy days at camp were discouraging there was nowhere to go and almost nothing to do.

3. The three parts of a composition are the introduction, the body, and the conclusion.

4. Nevada borders the following states, California, Oregon, Idaho, Utah, and Arizona.

5. The reasons for her leaving are clear, She is overworked, underpaid, and bored.

EXERCISE B The following sentences contain errors in punctuation. Write each sentence, deleting incorrect punctuation and inserting correct dashes, parentheses, and brackets as necessary. Make sure that any parenthetical material is properly capitalized and punctuated.

Example 1. Rory is fascinated by any branch of the natural sciences physics, biology, zoology.

Rory is fascinated by any branch of the natural sciences—physics, biology, zoology.

6. The Impressionist art movement [see Chart A (page 12) for a list of the major artists] developed in reaction to the sentimentality of previous art. _____

_____

7. I resent your implication that I had something to do with oh, you're never going to believe the truth anyway. _____

_____

8. A. J. Foyt [born in 1935 in Houston, Texas] was the first person to win the Indianapolis 500 four times. _____

_____

9. The report stated, "In that year (1977) the town's population increased 20 percent." _____

_____

10. Leon Hatcher [Do you remember him from high school?] was named Engineer of the Year.

MECHANICS

Review B: **Using Punctuation Correctly**

EXERCISE The following expressions involve the use of parentheses, dashes, hyphens, and apostrophes. Each item consists of three expressions. Two of the expressions are punctuated correctly; one is incorrect. Circle the letter of the incorrect expression, and then write that expression correctly on the line provided.

Example 1. [a] Its not too late. **[b]** Jody's and my correspondence **[c]** pre-Reformation events

     It's not too late.

1. [a] the womens' hats **[b]** a well-known actor's signature **[c]** each girl's score

_____

2. [a] looking for its owner **[b]** her sister-in-law's car **[c]** either our car or your's

_____

3. [a] Mayor-elect Smith's speech **[b]** Peg's twenty-fourth birthday **[c]** does'nt cross her *t*'s

_____

4. [a] Very few students—only two—failed the test. **[b]** See the definitions in the first column (Column A). **[c]** Gina is well-liked by everyone.

_____

5. [a] She had left the manuscript—a year's work—in the taxi. **[b]** Tamara borrowed the self help book I bought last week. **[c]** The last chapter (pages 67–91) is the best.

_____

6. [a] the Thomases' driveway **[b]** the carton and it's contents **[c]** last month's payment

_____

7. [a] Frank and my project **[b]** those girls' paintings **[c]** one's choice of college

_____

8. [a] mid-October sale **[b]** re-covered the worn sofa **[c]** softly-packed snow

_____

9. [a] She ca'nt hear the speaker from this distance. **[b]** His father-in-law's car was parked at the curb. **[c]** One third of the money went to charity.

_____

10. [a] My letter (could it be?) was printed on page one. **[b]** Claude McKay [1890–1948] wrote poems about Harlem. **[c]** That singer is well respected locally.

_____

Language and Sentence Skills Practice

MECHANICS

Review C: Using Punctuation Correctly

EXERCISE A   On the lines provided, rewrite the following dialogue, correcting any errors in the use of quotation marks and other marks of punctuation and capitalization. Begin a new paragraph wherever necessary.

Example   What did you think of the talk? Antonia asked.

"What did you think of the talk?" Antonia asked.

After hearing the health teacher talk about heart disease, Suzy told her friend Antonia, I *know* I need to get more exercise. Same for me, replied Antonia. I usually don't even want to walk from the car to the mall entrance. What are we going to do about the situation, asked Suzy. We can't start out running a marathon. We've got to make changes gradually, Antonia suggested. Let's start by taking a walk after school, exclaimed Suzy. _____

_____

_____

_____

_____

_____

_____

_____

EXERCISE B   In the following sentences, place a caret (∧) to indicate where quotation marks are missing, and underline any words or groups of words that should be italicized.

Example   1.   Have you read Frank McCourt's second novel, called 'Tis?

1. The Italian phrase la dolce vita translates as the good life.

2. A movie was made about President John F. Kennedy's World War II experience aboard PT Boat 109.

3. The Rodgers and Hammerstein song My Favorite Things is from the movie The Sound of Music.

4. Reading the chapter called Myth and the Modern World from Joseph Campbell's book The Power of Myth will help you get started on your essay.

5. Grandfather Daigle says that the Bible is the greatest book ever written and that Emerson's Self-Reliance is the greatest essay ever composed.

Proofreading Application: Research Paper

Good writers are generally good proofreaders. Readers tend to admire and trust writing that is error-free. Make sure that you correct all errors in grammar, usage, spelling, and punctuation in your writing. Your readers will have more confidence in your words if you have done your best to proofread carefully.

When you write a research paper, the words you use are the principal part of your communication with readers. However, a secondary component of that communication is punctuation. Punctuation marks help you to establish relationships between the words you use and the ideas you wish to convey. Consider punctuation marks tools to use to construct a precisely and clearly written research paper.

PROOFREADING ACTIVITY

The following is an excerpt from a research paper. Find and correct the errors in the use of semicolons, colons, italics (underlining), quotation marks, ellipses, apostrophes, hyphens, dashes, parentheses, and brackets. Use proofreading symbols to make your corrections.

The passing of time is a fascinating experience for human beings. Marcus Aurelius Antoninus A.D. 121–180 said, "Time is a sort of river of passing events. . . . ; no sooner is a thing brought to sight than it is swept by and another takes its place, and this too will be swept away." Equally as fascinating is the lack of uniformity with which human beings perceive the passing of time. When I asked my great aunt Mathilda born in 1910, two years before the Titanic sank what the passing of time was like for her as a child, she responded, The first part of my childhood seemed to go on forever. Similarly, the three months of summer vacation in actuality only one-fourth of a year passed by so lazily as to seem longer than the remaining nine months. She paused, then continued, Why do you think children nowadays never perceive time as passing by lazily"? My aunts thought provoking question encouraged me to ask my eight year old cousin about her perception of time. Leticia said Theres too much to do every day, like dance class and gymnastics and playing video games.

Literary Model: Punctuation in Dialogue

> "I want some poison," she said.
> "Yes, Miss Emily. What kind? For rats and such? I'd recom—"
> "I want the best you have. I don't care what kind."
> The druggist named several. "They'll kill anything up to an elephant. But what you want is—"
> "Arsenic," Miss Emily said. "Is that a good one?"
> "Is ... arsenic? Yes, ma'am. But what you want—"
> "I want arsenic."
>
> —from "A Rose for Emily" by William Faulkner

EXERCISE A   From the excerpt above, list one example of each of the following.

1. comma placement before the quotation marks: _____

2. period placement before the quotation marks: _____

3. question mark before quotation marks: _____

4. apostrophe to indicate contraction: _____

5. dash to indicate interruption: _____

6. ellipses to indicate a pause: _____

EXERCISE B

1. How does Faulkner's use of dashes help convey a contrast between the characters in their

level of authority? _____

_____

_____

_____

_____

2. Consider Faulkner's line *"I want arsenic."* Explain the different effect of a line such as *"I want

arsenic!" shrieked the woman.* _____

_____

_____

Literary Model (continued)

EXERCISE C Compose your own dialogue between two people of contrasting personalities or authority levels. Use a scenario of your own invention or one of the following: a conversation between a new salesperson and an irritated customer, an interviewer and a job applicant with few skills, a hairdresser in a hurry and a timid client. Use punctuation marks to indicate differences between the characters.

_____

_____

_____

_____

_____

_____

_____

_____

_____

_____

_____

_____

_____

_____

_____

_____

EXERCISE D What punctuation marks did you use to indicate differences in personality or levels of authority between your characters? How do they affect your meaning? Be specific.

_____

_____

_____

_____

MECHANICS | Language in Context: Literary Model

Writing Application: Essay

Writers italicize or set in quotation marks a word or word group to cue readers that there is something unusual about it: Perhaps it is foreign or is slang, or perhaps the writer is referring to the word itself.

> **EXAMPLES**   When you say she's "cool," what exactly do you mean?
>
>   The slang use of the word *cool* is about fifty years old.

WRITING ACTIVITY

Like *cool,* many words' meanings have changed over the years. Slang words and intensifiers especially change in terms of popularity, usage, and meaning; but every word has a past. The history of a word is called its etymology and is found in good dictionaries. The *Oxford English Dictionary (OED)* traces the entry into English of vast numbers of words and is available in good libraries and online. Choose a word that intrigues you and use a good dictionary to find out its history. Write up your findings to share with your classmates, being sure to italicize the word you are writing about and any foreign words that are its ancestors.

PREWRITING   When investors are optimistic, they speak of a "bull" market; but when stock values fall, they refer to a "bear" market. Why? Listen to yourself and others speaking throughout the day to find a commonly used word that intrigues you. Then, go to one or more dictionaries, and to the *OED* if possible, and find the entry for that word. Write down all of the information you can find on the history of your word.

WRITING   As you write up your findings in a paragraph, do not simply report the information you have gleaned. Tell the story of the word as you have reconstructed it through your research. A straightforward chronological organization, beginning with the word's earliest use, seems an obvious choice. However, talking about the word's current use first might be more interesting; alternately, you could focus on recent changes in meaning.

REVISING   As you read over your paragraph, look for information on the word's language of origin, roots and affixes, and various uses. Many words carry multiple meanings. *Cool,* which was mentioned above, has many uses, all with different meanings, some positive and others negative: a cool car, a cool glass of water, a cool relationship. If your etymology has gaps, consult another dictionary.

PUBLISHING   Check your etymology for errors in grammar, usage, punctuation, and spelling. Make sure to italicize words appropriately. Compile your findings with your classmates' in a notebook or on a bulletin board.

EXTENDING YOUR WRITING

You may wish to develop this exercise into a longer essay. Though many people do not think of scientists as writers, writing is an important part of all scientific endeavors, such as naming. For a science class, you could write an essay on naming—naming a newly discovered element, life form, star, method, or phenomenon. Consider interviewing a working scientist in the field of your choice.

Choices: Exploring Spelling

The following activities challenge you to find a connection between spelling and the world around you. Do the activity below that suits your personality best, and then share your discoveries with your class.

LINGUISTIC HISTORY

Treffef

If you were to read the word *treffef* in an old-timey book, what would you think? Is it another language? No, it's English, all right, and it's a word you know well—*tresses*. Find out why *tresses* was spelled this way. See if you can find a copy of an actual document from the eighteenth century that shows this now unusual practice of using an *f* for an *s*. Then, photocopy the page and show it to your classmates.

DISCUSSION

Back Home

Because of television and radio, everyone has an opportunity to hear standard pronunciation. Some people believe that American English is becoming less regional and that accents are smoothing out a bit. Because pronunciation affects spelling, standard pronunciation should make spelling easier, shouldn't it? Or, are people clinging to and even emphasizing their accents to retain their regional identities? Lead a discussion of these questions with your classmates.

COMPUTER

Check It Out

Spellcheckers are great, aren't they? However, not all spellcheckers are equal. Some are better than others. Check out this year's computer magazines, and find some reviews of spellcheckers. Get the facts on the best ones—number of words, price, ease of use, and anything else that's important. Present your findings to the class.

HISTORY

Private Investigator

Who was or is James Murray, and what does he have to do with spelling? Find out, and make appropriate notes on a time line. Then, give a short speech to your class or write a few pages explaining his relationship to spelling.

COMPUTER TECHNOLOGY

Hear Say Evidence

Pronunciation is half the battle when it comes to triumphing over misspelled words. Yet, as you get older, you'll find yourself learning more words that you have never heard said. It's tough to pronounce a word you've never heard and tougher still to spell it. Technology can help you. There are computer dictionaries (some that are quite inexpensive) that will pronounce a word for you! You can ask the program to say the word over and over. Try out one of these programs and learn to pronounce ten difficult and unfamiliar words.

HISTORY

A First Time for Everything

Get this: Once upon a time, dictionary entries were not written in alphabetical order. Yikes! Of course, that was a long time ago. By the way, when and where was the first English dictionary written? Find out. While you're in the library and looking at a book about dictionaries, find out a little about them. Tell your classmates what you have discovered, and make appropriate notations on a time line.

GAME

Amaze Everyone

If you misspell more words than you spell correctly, here's a project for you. Create a maze game. The only correct way through the maze is to follow the correctly spelled words. Most of the words will be misspelled and will lead nowhere. Use some graph paper to compose your maze. Write the correct words first, then anything goes! Words can go up, down, or sideways. When you've written all the words in, you can draw walls for the maze if you like.

Good Spelling Habits

To learn the spelling of a word, pronounce it, study it, and write it.

(1) Pronounce words carefully. Mispronunciation can lead to misspelling.

(2) Spell by syllables. A *syllable* is a word part that is pronounced as one uninterrupted sound.

(3) Use a dictionary. By using a dictionary, you will become familiar with the correct pronunciations and divisions of words.

(4) Proofread for careless spelling errors.

(5) Keep a spelling notebook.

EXERCISE A On the line provided, write the number of syllables each word has. Check a dictionary if you are unsure of a word's division.

Example 1. opportunity _____5_____

1. tournament _____

2. description _____

3. incident _____

4. recommend _____

5. sufficient _____

6. discipline _____

7. aisle _____

8. unnecessary _____

9. fiery _____

10. schedule _____

EXERCISE B On the line provided, write each word syllable-by-syllable. Draw a vertical line between syllables. Check a dictionary if you are unsure of a word's division.

Example thoroughly _____thor | ough | ly_____

11. calendar _____

12. parallel _____

13. etiquette _____

14. propaganda _____

15. guarantee _____

MECHANICS

ie and *ei*

15a. Write *ie* when the sound is long *e*, except after *c*.

EXAMPLES	shr**ie**k	ch**ie**f	gr**ie**ve	dec**ei**t	rec**ei**ve
EXCEPTIONS	n**ei**ther	l**ei**sure	s**ei**zure	prot**ei**n	**ei**ther

15b. Write *ei* when the sound is not long *e*.

EXAMPLES	for**ei**gn	sl**ei**gh	th**ei**r	counterf**ei**t	r**ei**gn
EXCEPTIONS	suffic**ie**nt	v**ie**w	fr**ie**nd	misch**ie**f	anc**ie**nt

EXERCISE A Underline the correctly spelled word in each of the following pairs.

Example 1. <u>ceiling</u>, cieling

1. feind, fiend

2. reveiw, review

3. decieve, deceive

4. neither, niether

5. heifer, hiefer

6. freight, frieght

7. height, hieght

8. cheif, chief

9. consceince, conscience

10. soceity, society

EXERCISE B In each of the following sentences, a word is underlined. If the word is misspelled, write it correctly on the line provided. If the word is already spelled correctly, write *C*.

Example _____*believe*_____ **1.** I <u>beleive</u> I have just seen the first robin of the spring.

_____ **11.** What are your favorite hobbies during your <u>liesure</u> time?

_____ **12.** The <u>biege</u> carpet was being replaced with something more colorful.

_____ **13.** Several of us wondered if the new student was <u>concieted</u> or just shy.

_____ **14.** Exchange papers with your <u>nieghbor</u>, and we'll correct them.

_____ **15.** After a <u>breif</u> rest, the caravan resumed its journey.

_____ **16.** Jason displayed his collection of <u>foriegn</u> currency.

_____ **17.** The insignia on the knight's <u>shield</u> identified him as a friend of

the kingdom.

_____ **18.** Have you <u>received</u> the phone call you were expecting?

_____ **19.** During the <u>riegn</u> of King John, the Magna Carta was signed.

_____ **20.** Wasn't that the <u>wierdest</u> movie you've ever seen?

–cede, –ceed, and –sede

15c. The only English word ending in –*sede* is *supersede*. The only English words ending in –*ceed* are *exceed, proceed,* and *succeed*. Most other words with this sound end in –*cede*.

EXAMPLES   con**cede**   inter**cede**   pre**cede**   re**cede**

EXERCISE A   Underline the correctly spelled word in each pair below.

Example 1. <u>supersede</u>, supercede

1. exceed, excede

2. interceed, intercede

3. seceed, secede

4. proceed, procede

5. acceed, accede

6. preceed, precede

7. succeed, succede

8. conceed, concede

9. receed, recede

10. anteceed, antecede

EXERCISE B.   In each of the following sentences, a word is underlined. If the word is misspelled, write the word correctly on the line provided. If the word is already spelled correctly, write C.

Example _____*exceed*_____ **1.** Don't <u>excede</u> the specified quantities, or the experiment will

not work.

_____ **11.** The marching band will immediately <u>precede</u> the seniors' float in the parade.

_____ **12.** Was the judge willing to <u>intercede</u> on your behalf?

_____ **13.** The dog finally <u>succeded</u> in its effort to dig up the entire yard.

_____ **14.** <u>Procede</u> with caution.

_____ **15.** If the water does not <u>recede</u> soon, this area will be evacuated.

MECHANICS

Prefixes

15d. When adding a prefix, do not change the spelling of the original word.

> **EXAMPLES**   dis + similar = dis**similar**   re + elect = re**elect**
>   in + competent = in**competent**   mis + step = mis**step**

EXERCISE A   For each item, add the prefix to form a new word. Write your answer on the line provided.

Example 1. re + arrange = ___*rearrange*___

1. sub + atomic = _____

2. in + eligible = _____

3. mid + morning = _____

4. de + classify = _____

5. un + forgettable = _____

6. mal + function = _____

7. in + convenience = _____

8. milli + liter = _____

9. im + mobile = _____

10. bi + valve = _____

EXERCISE B   On the line in each sentence below, write the word formed by adding the word parts shown in the parentheses.

Example 1. The ___*irregular*___ marks on the rock indicated that it was a tool. (*ir + regular*)

11. The weather report said that rain was _____ this weekend. (*un + likely*)

12. I hope you were not _____ with the final results. (*dis + pleased*)

13. The label _____ washing the sweater in cold water. (*re + commends*)

14. When the king _____ from war, he found that his brother had usurped the

throne. (*re + turned*)

15. Are the effects of the chemical reaction _____ ? (*ir + reversible*)

Language and Sentence Skills Practice

Suffixes A

15e. When adding the suffix –*ness* or –*ly*, do not change the spelling of the original word.

EXAMPLES	total + ly = **total**ly	open + ness = **open**ness
	actual + ly = **actual**ly	vague + ness = **vague**ness
EXCEPTIONS	For most words ending in *y*, change the *y* to *i* before adding –*ly* or –*ness*.
	angry + ly = angr**ily**	happy + ness = happ**iness**

EXERCISE A   For each item, add the suffix to form a new word. Write your answer on the line provided.

Example 1. safe + ly = _____*safely*_____

1. awkward + ness = _____

2. kind + ness = _____

3. awful + ly = _____

4. persuasive + ness = _____

5. weary + ly = _____

6. decided + ly = _____

7. busy + ness = _____

8. accurate + ly = _____

9. necessary + ly = _____

10. weird + ness = _____

EXERCISE B   On the line provided in each sentence, write the word formed by adding the word parts shown in parentheses.

Example 1. This will _____*definitely*_____ be the final performance of the play. (*definite* + *ly*)

11. That artist always includes her _____ hidden somewhere in the

painting. (*like* + *ness*)

12. The materials required for this project are _____ available. (*ready* + *ly*)

13. Your _____ during the past year will not go unrewarded. (*conscientious* + *ness*).

14. The machine puttered _____ in the background. (*constant* + *ly*)

15. Vicky's _____ to assist her classmates made her popular. (*willing* + *ness*)

Suffixes B

15f. Drop the final silent *e* before adding a suffix that begins with a vowel.

    EXAMPLES   date + ing = **dat**ing   scare + ed = **scar**ed

    EXCEPTIONS notice + able = **notice**able   dye + ing = **dye**ing

15g. Keep the final silent *e* before adding a suffix that begins with a consonant.

    EXAMPLES   brave + ly = **brave**ly   hope + ful = **hope**ful

    EXCEPTIONS awe + ful = **aw**ful   argue + ment = **argu**ment

MECHANICS

EXERCISE A Spell each of the following words, adding the suffix that is given.

Example 1. taste + ful = _____*tasteful*_____

1. future + ist = _____

2. realize + s = _____

3. emote + ive = _____

4. determine + ation = _____

5. date + ed = _____

6. arrange + ment = _____

7. adverse + ary = _____

8. true + ism = _____

9. continue + ous = _____

10. apprentice + ship = _____

EXERCISE B On the line provided in each of the following sentences, spell the word in parentheses, adding the suffix that is given.

Example 1. Have they perfected their new apparatus for _____*breathing*_____ underwater?

        (*breathe + ing*)

11. Scientists have not yet discovered if that substance has _____ value. (*medicine + al*)

12. Class rings should be less _____ this year than they were last year. (*expense + ive*)

13. Even Aaron's _____ poetry was surprisingly moving. (*nonsense + ical*)

14. Everyone arrived at _____ on time. (*rehearse + al*)

15. Playing chess can improve both your _____ and your analytical skills.

    (*concentrate + ion*)

Suffixes C

MECHANICS

15h. For words ending in *y* preceded by a consonant, change the *y* to *i* before any suffix that does not begin with *i*.

    EXAMPLES   bounty + ful = bount**iful**   messy + est = mess**iest**   fry + ing = fr**ying**

15i. For words ending in *y* preceded by a vowel, keep the *y* when adding a suffix.

    EXAMPLES   play + ful = pla**yful**   employ + ment = emplo**yment**
                boy + ish = bo**yish**   annoy + ing = anno**ying**
    EXCEPTIONS   day + ly = da**ily**   pay + ed = pa**id**

EXERCISE A   Spell each of the following words, adding the suffix that is given.

Example 1. necessary + ly = _necessarily_

1. ordinary + ly = _____
2. lonely + ness = _____
3. joy + ful = _____
4. auxiliary + es = _____
5. shiny + er = _____
6. injury + ous = _____
7. pay + ment = _____
8. play + ing = _____
9. quantify + able = _____
10. marry + age = _____

EXERCISE B   On the line provided in each of the following sentences, spell the word in parentheses, adding the suffix that is given.

Example 1. What is the _scariest_ sound you've ever heard? (*scary + est*)

11. Kevin _____ that he always goes straight home after school. (*say + ed*)

12. Both _____ will hold their conventions in July. (*party + s*)

13. When Sharon finishes _____ her sources, her paper will be complete. (*verify + ing*)

14. The study will seek to confirm the _____ benefits of the new energy source. (*ecology + cal*)

15. The panel will make recommendations about the _____ of the security guards. (*deploy + ment*)

Suffixes D

15j. Double the final consonant before a suffix that begins with a vowel if the word both (1) has only one syllable or has the accent on the last syllable and (2) ends in a single consonant preceded by a single vowel.

> **EXAMPLES**   spin + ing = spi**nning**   clip + er = cli**pper**   hem + ed = he**mmed**
> commit + ing = commi**tting**   control + ed = contro**lled**   expel + ed = expe**lled**

EXERCISE A   Spell each of the following words, adding the suffix that is given.

Example 1. forget + able = ___*forgettable*___

1. compel + ing = _____

2. omit + ed = _____

3. appoint + ment = _____

4. occur + ing = _____

5. forfeit + ing = _____

6. begin + ing = _____

7. control + ing = _____

8. design + er = _____

9. regret + able = _____

10. villain + ous = _____

EXERCISE B   On the line provided in each of the following sentences, spell the word in parentheses, adding the suffix that is given.

Example 1. At midnight, power was officially ___*transferred*___ to the new president.
(*transfer + ed*)

11. A _____ from an important person is the best way to get an interview. (*refer + al*)

12. That was an _____ workout. (*exhaust + ing*)

13. Nick _____ to finish his project over the weekend. (*plan + ed*)

14. Carla has never _____ her choice of careers. (*regret + ed*)

15. The design of the _____ has been modified to be more efficient. (*propel + er*)

MECHANICS

Suffixes E

15e.	When adding the suffix –*ly* or –*ness*, do not change the spelling of the original word.
15f.	Drop the final silent *e* before adding a suffix that begins with a vowel.
15g.	Keep the final silent *e* before adding a suffix that begins with a consonant.
15h.	For words ending in *y* preceded by a consonant, change the *y* to *i* before any suffix that does not begin with *i*.
15i.	For words ending in *y* preceded by a vowel, keep the *y* when adding a suffix.
15j.	Double the final consonant before a suffix that begins with a vowel if the word both (1) has only one syllable or has the accent on the last syllable and (2) ends in a single consonant preceded by a single vowel.

EXERCISE A   On the line provided, spell each of the following words, adding the suffix given.

Example 1. base + ing _____*basing*_____

1. manage + able _____

2. final + ly _____

3. trace + ed _____

4. life + less _____

5. plenty + ful _____

6. pray + er _____

7. stop + ing _____

8. occur + ed _____

9. noisy + ly _____

10. empty + ing _____

EXERCISE B   On the line provided in each of the following sentences, spell the word in parentheses, adding the suffix that is given.

Example 1. What type of bird is that _____*gliding*_____ across the sky? (*glide* + *ing*)

11. Which _____ has gained the most yards? (*play* + *er*)

12. Gretchen's older cat is _____ than the younger one. (*friendly* + *er*)

13. Will such a slight change in the rules make a _____ difference? (*notice* + *able*)

14. The contributor _____ to remain anonymous. (*prefer* + *ed*)

15. You can't make a problem go away just by _____ its existence. (*deny* + *ing*)

MECHANICS

Plurals A

15k. Remembering the following rules will help you spell the plural forms of nouns.

  (1) For most nouns, add *s*.
  (2) For nouns ending in *s, x, z, ch*, or *sh*, add *es*.
  (3) For nouns ending in *y* preceded by a vowel, add *s*.
  (4) For nouns ending in *y* preceded by a consonant, change the *y* to *i* and add *es*.

EXAMPLES	secret—secret**s**	donkey—donkey**s**	Daly—Daly**s**
	glass—glass**es**	dish—dish**es**	tax—tax**es**
	delay—delay**s**	turkey—turkey**s**	Saturday—Saturday**s**
	puppy—pupp**ies**	county—count**ies**	fly—fl**ies**

EXERCISE A On the line provided, write the plural for each of the following words.

Example 1. trophy _____*trophies*_____

1. inventor _____

2. convoy _____

3. Anna _____

4. suffix _____

5. crutch _____

6. dish _____

7. pastime _____

8. derby _____

9. Mackintosh _____

10. genius _____

EXERCISE B Above each of the underlined words in the following sentences, write the plural of the word.

             students   *plays*
Example 1. Several <u>student</u> bought tickets to see all four <u>play</u> at the renovated theater.

11. Do you select your schedule based on the <u>professor</u> or the <u>class</u>?

12. The <u>attorney</u> had to choose which of the two <u>case</u> they would argue.

13. Both coaches' <u>strategy</u> will be adjusted according to the other team's <u>move</u>.

14. This company offers terrific <u>guarantee</u> on both their <u>box</u> and their packing materials.

15. Of all the <u>surprise</u> last season, the two <u>loss</u> to their rivals were the most frustrating.

MECHANICS

Plurals B

15k.   Remembering the following rules will help you spell the plural forms of nouns.

(5) For some nouns ending in *f* or *fe,* add *s.* For others, change the *f* or *fe* to *v* and add *es.*
(6) For nouns ending in *o* preceded by a vowel, add *s.*
(7) For nouns ending in *o* preceded by a consonant, add *es.*

For proper nouns ending in o preceded by a consonant and for some common nouns, especially those referring to music, add only s.

EXAMPLES		
roof—roof**s**	fife—fife**s**	knife—kni**ves**
patio—patio**s**	stereo—stereo**s**	video—video**s**
veto—veto**es**	tomato—tomato**es**	echo—echo**es**
Mercado—Mercado**s**	alto—alto**s**	photo—photo**s**

EXERCISE A   Write the plural for each of the following words on the line provided.

Example 1. wife   *wives*

1. tornado _____   **6.** flamingo _____

2. trio _____   **7.** belief _____

3. calf _____   **8.** leaf _____

4. Guillermo _____   **9.** cello _____

5. wharf _____   **10.** potato _____

EXERCISE B   For each underlined word in the following sentences, write the plural above the word.

Example 1. A popular program on many people's <u>radio</u> *(radios)* is the one about everyday <u>hero</u> *(heroes)*.

11. Did you and Dario write the <u>script</u> <u>yourself</u>?

12. Among the <u>motto</u> the company considered was "No one gets into our <u>safe</u>."

13. The four <u>calf</u> were the most popular <u>buffalo</u> on the ranch.

14. When the marching band played their <u>piccolo</u>, their <u>scarf</u> kept getting in the way.

15. For the rest of their <u>life</u>, none of the boys would forget the <u>echo</u> they heard in the canyon

that day.

MECHANICS

Plurals C

15k. Remembering the following rules will help you spell the plural forms of nouns.

(1) For most nouns, add *s.*
(2) For nouns ending in *s, x, z, ch,* or *sh,* add *es.*
(3) For nouns ending in *y* preceded by a vowel, add *s.*
(4) For nouns ending in *y* preceded by a consonant, change the *y* to *i* and add *es.*
(5) For some nouns ending in *f* or *fe,* add *s.* For others, change the *f* or *fe* to *v* and add *es.*
(6) For nouns ending in *o* preceded by a vowel, add *s.*
(7) For nouns ending in *o* preceded by a consonant, add *es.*

EXERCISE A   Write the plural for each of the following words on the line provided.

Example 1. opinion _____*opinions*_____

1. beach _____   **6.** telephone _____

2. tomato _____   **7.** video _____

3. company _____   **8.** guess _____

4. parley _____   **9.** contralto _____

5. life _____   **10.** Antonio _____

EXERCISE B   For each underlined word in the following sentences, write the plural above the word.

Example 1. The Lunt, a famous husband and wife acting team, performed in many
        Lunts

        plays
        play together.

11. Lori spent her time sketching the giraffe, while Scott photographed the wolf.

12. The candidate from both party spoke at the town hall last week.

13. Students must provide their own lunch but will not be allowed to eat while the bus

are moving.

14. How many day are left before all the leaf have fallen from the trees?

15. Stereo began replacing hi-fi system in the 1960s.

MECHANICS

Plurals D

15k. Remembering the following rules will help you spell the plural forms of nouns.

(8) The plurals of a few nouns are formed in irregular ways.
(9) For a few nouns, the singular and the plural forms are the same.

EXAMPLES	man—m**e**n	goose—g**ee**se	child—child**ren**	louse—**lice**
	sheep—sheep	Chinese—Chinese	species—species	ficus—ficus

EXERCISE A Write the plural for each of the following words on the line provided.

Example 1. child _____*children*_____

1. Sioux _____

2. aircraft _____

3. mouse _____

4. woman _____

5. scissors _____

6. deer _____

7. fowl _____

8. salmon _____

9. Japanese _____

10. louse _____

EXERCISE B For each underlined word in the following sentences, write the plural above the word.

Example 1. How many *trout* <u>trout</u> did the anglers bring home?

11. Eric no longer trips over his own <u>foot</u> when he dances.

12. The flock of <u>goose</u> were tremendously noisy passing overhead.

13. Danielle is helping design the next three <u>spacecraft</u> that will orbit Jupiter.

14. The next unit of study will cover the <u>Aztec</u> and their art.

15. Have you ever wondered what <u>fish</u> think about all day?

MECHANICS

Plurals E

15k. Remembering the following rules will help you spell the plural forms of nouns.

(10) For most compound nouns, form the plural of only the last word of the compound.

  EXAMPLES football—football**s**   ten-year-old—ten-year-old**s**   heat pump—heat pump**s**

(11) For compound nouns in which one of the words is modified by the other word or words, form the plural of the noun modified.

  EXAMPLES father-in-law—father**s**-in-law   justice of the peace—justice**s** of the peace

EXERCISE A Write the plural for each of the following words on the line provided.

Example 1. airline _____*airlines*_____

1. boathouse _____   **6.** African American _____

2. post office _____   **7.** snowboard _____

3. spot-check _____   **8.** attorney general _____

4. daydream _____   **9.** bird-watcher _____

5. lipstick _____   **10.** soapbox _____

EXERCISE B For each underlined word in the following sentences, write the plural above the word.

Example 1. The four of you have been assigned as *aides-de-camp* for the *major generals* stationed

   in this area.

11. Both of my sister-in-law have joined car pool.

12. How many landlord have you heard of that help tenants care for their houseplant?

13. Aaron practiced by shooting basketball into wastebasket.

14. Jessica searched her notebook for the research she had done on historic boardinghouse.

15. Are sea horse related to shellfish?

Language and Sentence Skills Practice   **351**

MECHANICS

Plurals F

15k. Remembering the following rules will help you spell the plural forms of nouns.

(12) For some nouns borrowed from other languages, the plural is formed as in the original languages.

   EXAMPLES   criterion—criter**ia**   alumnus—alumn**i**   phenomenon—phenomen**a**

A few nouns borrowed from other languages have two plural forms.

   EXAMPLES   index—index**es** *or* ind**ices**   formula—formula**s** *or* formul**ae**

EXERCISE A   Write the plural for each of the following words on the line provided. You may use a dictionary if necessary.

Example 1. addendum   *addenda*

1. synopsis _____   6. ellipsis _____

2. stimulus _____   7. phenomenon _____

3. axis _____   8. synthesis _____

4. curriculum _____   9. focus _____

5. nucleus _____   10. datum _____

EXERCISE B   For each underlined word in the following sentences, write the plural above the word.

Example 1. Who can explain the physics of auror*a*?   *auroras or aurorae*

11. Next, examine the insect's antenna through your magnifying glass.

12. Aki searched the index of three books before she found the information she needed.

13. The judges will consider several criterion before they render a decision.

14. The map clearly indicated the oasis along the trail.

15. Maria's hobby is photographing octopus in their natural habitat.

MECHANICS

Plurals G

15k. Remembering the following rules will help you spell the plural forms of nouns.

(13) To form the plural of numerals, most uppercase letters, symbols, and words used as words, add either an *s* or both an apostrophe and an *s*.

> EXAMPLES 7—7**s** or 7**'s**   1990—1990**s** or 1990**'s**   &—&**s** or &**'s**
> however—however**s** or however**'s**   then—then**'s**

EXERCISE A   Write the plural for each of the following numerals, letters, symbols, or words used as words.

Example 1. @ _____@'s_____

1. *d* _____   **6.** *$* _____

2. 1600 _____   **7.** *Q* _____

3. *3* _____   **8.** *oops* _____

4. *or* _____   **9.** * _____

5. *uh* _____   **10.** ? _____

EXERCISE B   For each underlined item in the following sentences, write the plural above the item.

Example 1. Too many *but̲* in your persuasive essay may weaken its impact. (*but's*)

11. Would you rather have lived in the 1200̲ or the 1600̲?

12. Some e-mailers use *̲ to emphasize words in their letters, while others prefer #̲.

13. When David writes too fast, his *cannot̲* begin to look like *cannon̲*.

14. Nina's first college report card showed three A̲ and two B̲.

15. Here's a hint: The sum should contain four 3̲ and four 8̲.

MECHANICS

Plurals H

15k. Remembering the following rules will help you spell the plural forms of nouns.

(8) The plurals of a few nouns are formed in irregular ways.

(9) For a few nouns, the singular and the plural forms are the same.

(10) For most compound nouns, form the plural of only the last word of the compound.

(11) For compound nouns in which one of the words is modified by the other word or words, form the plural of the noun modified.

(12) For some nouns borrowed from other languages, the plural is formed as in the original languages.

(13) To form the plural of numerals, most uppercase letters, symbols, and words used as words, add either an *s* or both an apostrophe and an *s*.

EXERCISE On the line provided, write the plural form of each of the following nouns.

Example 1. passerby _____*passersby*_____

1. belief _____

2. pony _____

3. radio _____

4. hero _____

5. calf _____

6. wish _____

7. lunch _____

8. president-elect _____

9. theory _____

10. woman _____

11. mouse _____

12. sister-in-law _____

13. potato _____

14. wife _____

15. loyalty _____

16. eighty-year-old _____

17. tooth _____

18. law of the land _____

19. decoy _____

20. Japanese _____

MECHANICS

Writing Numbers

15l.	Spell out a *cardinal number*—a number that shows how many—if it can be expressed in one or two words. Otherwise, use numerals.
15m.	Spell out a number that begins a sentence.
15n.	Spell out *ordinal numbers*—numbers that express order.
15o.	Use numerals to express numbers in conventional situations.

> **EXAMPLES** **seventy-five** students   **213** students   **one hundred** miles   **1,145** miles
>
> **One hundred twenty-six** runners finished the marathon.
>
> Marisha was the **fifteenth** [not 15th] student from our school to win the award.
>
> Chapter **28**   lines **5–10**   **44** degrees   **1.5** ounces   **334** Park Lane
>
> Denver, CO **80217-4007**   January **25, 2000**   **9:00** A.M.

MECHANICS

EXERCISE Read each sentence and decide if the underlined number should be spelled out. If it should, write the spelled-out form above it. If the number is already correct, write *C* above it.

One hundred fifty-two

Example 1. <u>152</u> students auditioned for the marching band.

1. Imala saw <u>6</u> different species on her first day of bird-watching.

2. The temperature should not drop below <u>32</u> degrees tonight.

3. <u>25</u> new titles have just been added to the library.

4. Ruben is currently <u>3rd</u> on the school's all-time scoring list.

5. I want you to polish all <u>88</u> keys on that piano.

6. The study group will meet at Sam's house, <u>17</u> Park Circle.

7. The next rest area is <u>100</u> miles away.

8. Mai needs to be at the auditorium by <u>6:00</u> P.M. for rehearsal.

9. Did you notice that the rhyme scheme in lines <u>7–12</u> is different from that of the first stanza?

10. Felicia came in <u>4th</u>, which was her best finish yet.

Words Often Confused A

Review the glossary entries on pages 375–376 of your textbook for information on the correct usage of the following terms:

all ready, already	*ascent, assent*
all right	*born, borne*
all together, altogether	*brake, break*
altar, alter	*capital, capitol*

EXERCISE   Underline the word or word group in parentheses that correctly completes the sentence.

Example 1. They had (*born*, <u>*borne*</u>) that burden for many years.

1. When the choir finally sang (*all together, altogether*), they sounded beautiful.

2. The house was (*all ready, already*) except for the paint on the trim.

3. What is the (*capital, capitol*) of Wisconsin?

4. The movie was so long they had to include a fifteen-minute (*brake, break*).

5. A catalyst will (*altar, alter*) other chemicals without itself changing.

6. If it's (*all right, allright*) with you, I'll leave a little early today.

7. Will all of them (*ascent, assent*) to the new rules?

8. The audience was (*all together, altogether*) swept away by the stirring speech.

9. The kittens were (*born, borne*) just three weeks ago.

10. If we gather our resources (*all together, altogether*), we can have a much greater impact.

11. The start-up company is raising (*capital, capitol*) to expand their production facilities.

12. The balloon's (*ascent, assent*) was an awe-inspiring sight.

13. They have always (*born, borne*) their troubles with dignity.

14. If your car has anti-lock (*brakes, breaks*), you may be eligible for an insurance discount.

15. Have they (*all ready, already*) announced the teams in the tournament?

16. The board of directors gave their (*ascent, assent*) to the proposal.

17. (*All right, Allright*), I'll trade topics with you.

18. Justin was (*born, borne*) on February 29, so he's only had four birthdays.

19. When you tour the (*capital, capitol*), be sure to take pictures of the dome.

20. The couple wanted to be photographed in front of the (*altar, alter*).

MECHANICS

Words Often Confused B

Review the glossary entries on pages 376–378 of your textbook for information on the correct usage of the following terms:

clothes, cloths	*councilor, counselor*
coarse, course	*desert, dessert*
complement, compliment	*formally, formerly*
consul, council, counsel	*ingenious, ingenuous*

EXERCISE Underline the word in parentheses that correctly completes the sentence.

Example 1. Thank you for the *(complement, compliment)*; yes, it is a new hairstyle.

1. The amendment proposed by the *(councilor, counselor)* from District 3 was rejected.

2. Then, underline the *(complement, compliment)* of the transitive verb.

3. Mr. Garza, *(formally, formerly)* a state representative, is running for governor.

4. Toshio has signed up for a *(coarse, course)* in calligraphy.

5. Harry would never *(desert, dessert)* us in our time of need.

6. The foreign *(consul, council, counsel)* will have to sign the papers.

7. Diego's *(ingenious, ingenuous)* idea solved the problem immediately.

8. Everyone looked forward to the main *(coarse, course)* of the dinner.

9. By the time *(desert, dessert)* was served, Pat was already full.

10. Wipe the surface with lint-free *(clothes, cloths)* to avoid scratches.

11. Jared is looking for a small table to *(complement, compliment)* the furnishings in that room.

12. The next meeting of the *(consul, council, counsel)* will concern property taxes.

13. The costume designer sorted through the *(clothes, cloths)* that had been donated to the theater.

14. Schedule changes must be approved by your *(councilor, counselor)*.

15. Sarah looked at the *(ingenious, ingenuous)* faces of the children and told them the truth.

16. Begin with *(coarse, course)* sandpaper and gradually switch to a finer grade.

17. A wide variety of creatures can survive in a *(desert, dessert)*.

18. A *(complement, compliment)* will often produce better results than an insult.

19. Red kangaroos, *(formally, formerly)* known as *Macropus rufus*, generally search for food

    at night.

20. Ms. Kerrigan would be happy to *(consul, council, counsel)* you about career choices.

MECHANICS

Words Often Confused C

Review the glossary entries on pages 378–380 of your textbook for information on the correct usage of the following terms:

its, it's	*miner, minor*
later, latter	*moral, morale*
lead, led	*passed, past*
loose, lose	*peace, piece*

EXERCISE   Underline the word in parentheses that correctly completes the sentence.

Example 1. Both dogs and cats make wonderful family pets, but I prefer the *(later, <u>latter</u>)*.

1. Jamal *(passed, past)* his sister the corn bread.

2. The *(miners, minors)* were searching for gold or silver.

3. During the hurricane, many of the shingles were torn *(loose, lose)*.

4. After the fourth defeat in a row, the team's *(moral, morale)* reached a low point.

5. "*(Its, It's)* a beautiful day for a picnic at the lake," Dwayne announced.

6. I've been this way before; let me *(lead, led)*.

7. This is the last *(peace, piece)* of the puzzle.

8. The silly dog was chasing *(its, it's)* own tail.

9. After the storm had *(passed, past)*, the birds began singing again.

10. Given those two options, I guess I'll choose the *(later, latter)*.

11. Paula fixed the *(loose, lose)* wheel before beginning her bike trip.

12. The *(peace, piece)* was greatly appreciated after the noise of the children's party.

13. Just as Karen was finishing, her mechanical pencil ran out of *(lead, led)*.

14. It turned out to be only a *(miner, minor)* inconvenience.

15. You'll love this book; *(its, it's)* the best one in the series!

16. The *(later, latter)* you arrive, the longer you'll have to stay.

17. Reviewing your *(passed, past)* essays will help you improve your writing.

18. Don't you dare *(loose, lose)* that key!

19. If we both want *(peace, piece)*, why are we still fighting?

20. Our opponents *(lead, led)* at halftime, but we came back strong.

Words Often Confused D

Review the glossary entries on pages 381–383 of your textbook for information on the correct usage of the following terms:

personal, personnel	*rout, route*
plain, plane	*stationary, stationery*
principal, principle	*straight, strait*
quiet, quite	*than, then*

EXERCISE Underline the word in parentheses that correctly completes the sentence.

Example 1. Using a reliable road map, we carefully planned our (*rout, route*) to the park.

1. A business letter should be written on (*plain, plane*) white paper.

2. Uranium is heavier (*than, then*) mercury, isn't it?

3. He sent his application for employment to the (*personal, personnel*) department.

4. The reporters were (*quiet, quite*) as they waited for the president.

5. Are you going (*straight, strait*) home after softball practice?

6. Kelly explained the (*principal, principle*) of osmosis to me.

7. Before the game became a (*rout, route*), the coach put in the second team.

8. Try to remain (*stationary, stationery*) so you don't scare the hummingbird away.

9. As he gazed out over the (*plain, plane*), Tomás felt very peaceful.

10. This building is not (*quiet, quite*) fifteen years old.

11. Let the dough rise for thirty minutes; (*than, then*), knead it thoroughly.

12. A tunnel under the (*straight, strait*) was rejected as impractical.

13. (*Personal, Personnel*) business should be taken care of on your own time.

14. Has the school board hired a new (*principal, principle*) yet?

15. Smooth the surface with a (*plain, plane*) before you sand it.

16. Did you buy that fancy (*stationary, stationery*) for Mike's birthday?

17. If you plan the (*rout, route*) carefully, the trip is much more pleasant.

18. The monument is (*quiet, quite*) a bit larger than I imagined it to be.

19. Is a (*straight, strait*) line really the shortest distance between two points?

20. Tim is actually fifteen minutes younger (*than, then*) his twin brother, Tom.

Words Often Confused E

Review the glossary entries on pages 383–384 of your textbook for information on the correct usage of the following terms:

their, there, they're	*weather, whether*
theirs, there's	*who's, whose*
to, too, two	*your, you're*
waist, waste	

EXERCISE Underline the word in parentheses that correctly completes the sentence.

Example 1. For this project, you must split up into *(to, too, two)* groups.

1. When you get *(their, there, they're)*, say hello to Aunt Judy for me.

2. Tim, *(who's, whose)* family moved here from Arizona, isn't used to the cold weather.

3. Have you been *(to, too, two)* the new museum yet?

4. That should go in the recycling bin, not the *(waist, waste)* container.

5. *(Theirs, There's)* is the newest house on the block.

6. The *(weather, whether)* has been a factor in the golf tournament all week.

7. All three wet dogs shook *(their, there, they're)* coats at the same time, spraying water around the room.

8. Mark had added *(to, too, two)* much water to the bread dough.

9. An obi is worn around the *(waist, waste)*, not the head!

10. If *(your, you're)* finished with your project, will you help me with mine?

11. Have you decided *(weather, whether)* to continue your after-school job?

12. Michelle asked the chess club members when *(their, there, they're)* meeting next.

13. No one is sure why *(theirs, there's)* no practice tonight.

14. Have you heard *(who's, whose)* been cast as Romeo?

15. Ask *(your, you're)* sister what she thought of that book.

16. Is the last float in the parade *(theirs, there's)* or ours?

17. The forecast may determine *(weather, whether)* the spring carnival is held indoors or outdoors.

18. *(Who's, Whose)* turn is it to wash the dishes?

19. *(To, Too, Two)* many squirrels have been eating from the bird feeder.

20. *(Your, You're)* next!

Review A: **Spelling Rules**

EXERCISE A Underline the word that is spelled correctly in each of the following pairs.

Example 1. emptyness, <u>emptiness</u>

1. desireable, desirable
2. precede, preceed
3. pityful, pitiful
4. supercede, supersede
5. reccommend, recommend
6. keeness, keenness
7. begining, beginning
8. changeable, changable
9. ninteen, nineteen
10. receipt, reciept

11. sillyness, silliness
12. argument, arguement
13. procede, proceed
14. wierd, weird
15. refered, referred
16. definitely, definitly
17. peirce, pierce
18. patrolling, patroling
19. achievment, achievement
20. disappear, dissappear

EXERCISE B On the line provided, write the plural form of each of the following nouns.

Example 1. solo _____solos_____

21. journey _____
22. witch _____
23. gulf _____
24. curio _____
25. cupful _____
26. piano _____
27. spoonful _____
28. tragedy _____
29. ten-year-old _____
30. buoy _____

31. son-in-law _____
32. flurry _____
33. thief _____
34. tomato _____
35. lens _____
36. leaf _____
37. lieutenant governor _____
38. waltz _____
39. alumnus _____
40. glass _____

MECHANICS

Review B: Words Often Confused

EXERCISE   Underline the correct word or word group in parentheses in each of the following sentences.

Example 1. I must (*complement*, *compliment*) the chef for this delicious (*desert*, *dessert*).

1. I am (*altogether*, *all together*) sure he is honest.

2. Sometimes the trail followed a longer but more level (*rout*, *route*).

3. We were (*already*, *all ready*) to play, but our fans (*deserted*, *desserted*) us.

4. The senators began their (*ascent*, *assent*) up the steps of the (*capital*, *capitol*).

5. The (*clothes*, *cloths*) can be used to dust the furniture.

6. A (*moral*, *morale*) person stands up for the (*principal*, *principle*) of equality.

7. The rough surface of that wood can easily be smoothed with a (*plain*, *plane*).

8. After the (*principal's*, *principle's*) speech, school (*moral*, *morale*) was high.

9. He stated an (*ingenuous*, *ingenious*) and practical solution.

10. Certainly the committee will (*ascent*, *assent*) to the proposal.

11. Tighten (*your*, *you're*) necktie slightly; (*its*, *it's*) too (*lose*, *loose*).

12. This scarf (*complements*, *compliments*) many of your winter (*cloths*, *clothes*).

13. Please let us know (*weather*, *whether*) you plan to be there.

14. Interviewing is done by the (*personal*, *personnel*) department.

15. I hope we won't (*lose*, *loose*) because of the catcher's (*miner*, *minor*) error.

16. Jessica received excellent (*council*, *counsel*) from the hospital staff.

17. (*Your*, *You're*) welcome to use my (*stationary*, *stationery*) for your letter.

18. Who has been chosen to (*lead*, *led*) the orchestra?

19. Some presidents have (*born*, *borne*) the strain of office better than others.

20. The storm forced the airline pilot to (*altar*, *alter*) her course.

MECHANICS

Review C: **Spelling Words Correctly**

EXERCISE A In each of the groups of words below, underline the misspelled word. On the line provided, write the word correctly.

Example ___*traceable*___ **1.** succeed, friend, <u>tracable</u>, toying

_____ **1.** careful, dryly, usually, hopless

_____ **2.** decieve, niece, receipt, height

_____ **3.** confidential, sheild, ceiling, easily

_____ **4.** speechs, science, guidance, useful

_____ **5.** precede, ticklish, playful, procede

_____ **6.** definitely, ninty, copies, wolves

_____ **7.** awesome, leadder, precedes, either

_____ **8.** mispell, leisure, supersede, readily

_____ **9.** chief, cupfuls, sieze, sombreros

_____ **10.** monkeys, stories, potatos, radios

EXERCISE B Many of the following sentences contain errors in the use of words often confused. Draw a line through each incorrect word, and write the correct word in the space above it. If a sentence is already correct, write *C* before the item number.

Example 1. Many fine stories have a theme but no obvious ~~morale.~~ *moral*

11. Your not going to run until later, Joanna.

12. We had past the house without noticing it.

13. Who is the principal of the school for the hearing impaired?

14. Most golfers are to cautious to play during a thunderstorm.

15. The grassy planes of the western states make excellent grazing land.

16. The quarterback has lead his team to victory again.

17. Despite the bad weather, she refused to altar her plans.

18. If you arrive latter than seven o'clock, you may not get a seat.

19. How much waist can be eliminated by these budget cuts?

20. At the press conference, she formally announced her candidacy for governor.

MECHANICS

Review D: Spelling Words Correctly

EXERCISE A Proofread the following sentences. Draw a line through each misspelled or misused word, and write the correct spelling in the space above it. If a sentence contains no spelling errors, write C before the item number.

> **Example 1.** There were several students in class who ~~planed~~ *planned* to do ~~they're~~ *their* reports on Isaac Bashevis Singer.

1. Isaac Bashevis Singer was borne in Poland in 1904.

2. The son of a rabbi, Singer went to a religious school, hopeing at first to become a rabbi also.

3. However, he left the rabbinical seminary in Warsaw to become a journallist instead.

4. In 1935, Singer moved to the United States; their, he wrote articles and serializzed novels for New York's *Jewish Daily Forward.*

5. This newspaper, like the paper for which Singer had written in Poland, was printed in the Yiddish language.

6. Singer wanted too write in Yiddish because he beleived an author should work in his native language.

7. He began writing children's storys because, he said, "Children are the best readers of genuine literature."

8. He wrote stories in Yiddish and than supervised there translation into English.

9. Singer won many awards, includeing the National Book Award and the Nobel Prize in literature, the most distinguished award a writer can recieve.

10. One of his stories, "Yentl, the Yeshiva Boy," was made into a movie staring Barbra Streisand.

EXERCISE B Most of the following sentences contain errors in the use of words often confused. Draw a line through each incorrect word, and write the correct word in the space above it. If a sentence is already correct, write C before the item number.

> **Example 1.** When the overhead light is on, ~~it's~~ *its* glare disturbs me.

11. She bought new cloths—a coat and two dresses—with her earnings.

12. The girls are proud of they're mother's success as a television broadcaster.

13. The first busload of students has already arrived.

14. What are your principle objections to our suggestion?

15. She wisely counseled me to let bygones be bygones.

MECHANICS

for **CHAPTER 15: SPELLING**   *pages 361–84*

Proofreading Application: Letter

Good writers are generally good proofreaders. Readers tend to admire and trust writing that is error-free. Make sure that you correct all errors in grammar, usage, spelling, and punctuation in your writing. Your readers will have more confidence in your words if you have done your best to proofread carefully.

When you write a letter asking for financial support for your organization, make sure that it does not contain misspelled and misused words. An error-free document leaves a much different impression on a potential sponsor than one that contains careless mistakes.

PROOFREADING ACTIVITY

The following is a letter written by a student to the representative of a potential financial supporter. Find and correct the errors in spelling. Use proofreading symbols to make your corrections.

Example The club has al̲l̲ ready had to cut some activit*ie*ys.

Dear Ms. Wei:

   Elizabeth Cantrell, my high school councilor and a close freind of the family, sugested that I contact you about the organization of which I am president, the Junior Optimist Club. I am writting in refference to the club's current financial situation. This year, we have recieved fewer donations from alumnuses than in the passed, and we unfortunatly find ourselves with a budget problem.

   Ms. Cantrell informed me that you are head of community relations of the Worthington Busyness Assosiation and that their might be a posibility of your group's making a substantial contribution to the Junior Optimists.

   I apreciate your even considering a contribution to the Junior Optimist Club. It is a truely worthy organization.

Sincerely,

Tom Ávila

MECHANICS | Language in Context: Literary Model

Literary Model: Poetry

Much Madness is divinest Sense
by Emily Dickinson

Much Madness is divinest Sense—
To a discerning Eye—
Much Sense—the starkest Madness—
'Tis the Majority
In this, as All, prevail—
Assent—and you are sane—
Demur—you're straightway dangerous—
And handled with a Chain—

EXERCISE A

1. In your own words, what does the word *assent* mean?

_____

_____

2. In your own words, what does the word *ascent* mean?

_____

_____

EXERCISE B   How would your understanding of the poem above have been different if *assent* had been misspelled as *ascent*?

_____

_____

_____

_____

for **CHAPTER 15: SPELLING**   *pages 361–84*

Literary Model (continued)

EXERCISE C   Write a poem using one of the words often confused, such as *born, borne, break, brake, coarse, course, desert,* or *dessert.*

_____

_____

_____

_____

_____

_____

_____

_____

_____

EXERCISE D   How would the meaning of your poem be different if the word you used had been spelled like the word with which it is often confused? How might you avoid confusing your readers in future writing projects?

_____

_____

_____

_____

_____

_____

Writing Application: Newspaper Column

With the largest vocabulary of any known language, English has many homonyms—words, like *scene* and *seen*, that sound alike but have different meanings. Homonyms can trip up even careful writers.

EXAMPLES   Some dogs' coats improve when treated with moose.

Janelle mustard up her courage and stepped out on to the stage.

"Mousse," of course, is the hair treatment that the writer had in mind; and "mustered," not the popular hot dog condiment, makes much more sense in the second sentence. Such errors can be humorous, unless they occur in *your* writing.

WRITING ACTIVITY

You have heard the saying "There's strength in numbers." It is true that no one person can know everything or be an expert in every field. Think of a skill that you have mastered and that your peers would benefit from learning. Write a column, to be published in the school newspaper, in which you explain the skill. Persuade your peers to consider mastering it themselves by explaining how your knowledge has made your life easier or more interesting. Use correctly five words from the list of frequently misspelled words.

PREWRITING   You have many skills, but you may need to spend some time thinking about what you do well and how it benefits you before you begin writing. Remember that hidden skills make good, less obvious topics. For instance, knowing how to keep conversation flowing in social settings is a valuable skill, as people who lack that skill know. After you have chosen your topic, recall how you developed your skill, what is required to master it, and how it helps you.

WRITING   Because your purpose is in part to persuade readers that the skill is valuable, relate it to their lives—their problems, their needs, their goals. You could interview several peers and incorporate their answers into your column.

REVISING   This column is informative and persuasive, but it is not intended to explain how to master the skill. It is not a process analysis. If you find yourself slipping into a "how-to" explanation, focus your thoughts through more prewriting.

PUBLISHING   Check your column for errors in spelling and punctuation. Check especially the words you used from the list in Chapter 15 of your textbook. Consult the newspaper's editor for any submission requirements, and follow them closely. Submit the article for publication.

EXTENDING YOUR WRITING

You may wish to extend this exercise into a longer essay. In the column, you had no time to discuss learning the skill you wrote about. In a longer essay, you could teach your peers how to master the skill. Process analyses are very popular with readers, but they are useful only when they are thorough and accurate. Review this mode of writing before you undertake this essay.

Choices: Avoiding Common Errors

The following activities challenge you to find a connection between usage and mechanics and the world around you. Do the activity below that suits your personality best, and then share your discoveries with your class.

REFLECTION

Your Worst Critic

If you are like many people, you are your own worst critic. Don't fight it. Sit down and make a list of criticisms you have about your own writing. Then, go through your list point by point. Strike every general statement and make it specific. Most importantly, for every criticism, think of a corrective action. Then, choose three corrective actions that you feel would help the most in improving your writing. Write them down, and form a plan for incorporating them into your writing.

PEER-ASSESSMENT COMMITTEES

Constructive Critics

Don't you wonder what your classmates think of your writing? Well, here's your chance to find out. Divide the class evenly into Group A and Group B. Then, students from one group can submit to the other group typed papers in plain envelopes with numbers on them. Numbers should be known only to each student submitting a manuscript. Each group can then individually read the papers and make honest and fair comments. Comments may be written in the margins or on a separate sheet of paper. Later, the groups can leave manuscripts on a table where people can simply pick them up and take them home.

STUDY AID

Tense Moments

Declare war on verb tense errors. Ask your teacher to give you a list of the most common verb tense errors that your class made on its last test. Your job is to make copies of this list and to give a copy to everyone in the class. Then, get together with some friends and compose a song, rap, or other mnemonic device to help you remember how to avoid these verb tense errors.

MEDIA

No-No's

As you read newspapers, magazines, and books, you may come across errors in usage or mechanics. Collect as many of these errors as possible. Then, neatly copy each error onto a sheet of paper. Be sure that you highlight the error, explain the nature of the error, and provide a suggestion for correcting the error. With permission, display the errors on the class bulletin board.

INTERVIEW

In the Business World

Interview three business people who frequently write and read business communications. Ask these people what kinds of errors bother them most. Find out what impresses them when they read a business letter. During the interview, either take careful notes or use a tape recorder. Then, share your findings with your class.

PUBLISHING

Final Edition

What is it like to be an editor in chief? Find out by publishing a collection of your class's writings. Have each class member submit a favorite piece of writing from this year, and then compile these works into a newsletter or Web site. Write a "Letter from the Editor" to introduce the compilation.

ANALYSIS

Hitch Your Wagon to a Star

Identify and write down ten characteristics of your favorite kind of writing. For example, do you like a certain vocabulary, a lot of dialogue, or informal usage? Thumb through novels, poems, articles, or stories to get ideas. When your list is complete, pull out some of your own writing and compare it to your list. Does your writing display the characteristics you enjoy most?

Sentence Fragments and Run-on Sentences A

EXERCISE Identify each word group below by writing to the left of the item number *F* for *sentence fragment*, *R* for *run-on sentence*, or *S* for complete *sentence*.

Example *F* **1.** Whether to go camping or spend our vacation at the beach.

1. If you ask me, he didn't seem to be having much fun at the amusement park.

2. Roller coasters are my favorite ride, my sister, however, has never enjoyed them.

3. Especially being upside-down.

4. At the water park near the amusement park, giant water slides and a wave pool.

5. Sunscreen is a necessity for a long day in the sun, good sunglasses and a hat with a brim are also recommended.

6. The park is expensive, but we try to go once or twice every summer.

7. We went tubing on the river, it's a pleasant way to spend a hot summer day.

8. First, we'll set up the tent, then we can go on a hike.

9. The deer, startled by the headlights of the pickup truck.

10. The refreshing sound of water spilling over the rocks.

11. At dawn, the eastern sky was filled with soft yellow and pink light.

12. By the time we reached the spring creek, we were weary, nothing could have felt better than that cold water on our tired feet.

13. Gliding silently through the water, the kayakers.

14. I wonder whether kayaking lessons are available locally.

15. Probably takes some practice to learn how to right the boat when it turns over in the water.

16. Wearing helmets and wet suits for protection, approached the rapids cautiously.

17. We can rent a canoe at the city park, perhaps that's a good place to begin.

18. These old aluminum canoes are heavy, but they are well-balanced and easy to maneuver.

19. Stop spinning us in circles!

20. Remarkably, we didn't tip over, I was sure we would at some point, since we were both so inexperienced.

COMMON ERRORS

Subject-Verb Agreement A

EXERCISE A In each sentence below, underline the verb in parentheses that agrees in number with its subject.

Example 1. Either Fred or Ned *(is, are)* the oldest of the three brothers.

1. Both the pasta and the broiled fish *(is, are)* good choices at this restaurant.

2. Unfortunately, not one of the desserts *(appeal, appeals)* to me.

3. Don't you think the prices on the dinner menu *(look, looks)* reasonable?

4. My mother and I usually *(have, has)* a salad, but my father always orders soup.

5. Which one of the soups *(is, are)* being served tonight?

6. The proprietor and her husband *(know, knows)* most of the people who eat here regularly.

7. Both of them *(cooks, cook)*, but she develops most of the recipes.

8. *(Do, Does)* either of them have formal training as a chef?

9. I believe she does, but he just *(enjoy, enjoys)* cooking.

10. My family *(eat, eats)* here on special occasions, especially birthdays.

EXERCISE B In each sentence below, cross through any verb that does not agree with its subject and write the correct form of the verb above the incorrect form. If all the verbs in a sentence are already correct, write *C* to the left of the item number.

Example 1. Either my brother or one of my parents ~~feed~~ *feeds* the dogs in the evening.

11. My job, unless I have a practice that run late, is to walk the dogs daily.

12. Whose responsibilities includes bathing the dogs?

13. Bathing the dogs are a shared responsibility in our house; we take turns.

14. The dogs like to go on long walks, but unfortunately, one of them are not very well trained.

15. While one dog walk by my side obediently, the other always pulls and strains on the leash.

16. Surprisingly, our big dog—Teeny, the Great Dane—is content to do whatever she is asked.

17. You're not telling me that Tiger, your terrier, cause any trouble?

18. Believe me, Tiger is stronger than a lot of dogs twice her size is!

19. Tiger and Teeny, despite the difference in size, really gets along very well.

20. Many people are cautious around Teeny, especially, but neither of these two dogs has ever bitten anyone.

COMMON ERRORS

Sentence Fragments and Run-on Sentences B

EXERCISE On the short lines provided, identify each numbered word group in the following paragraph as a sentence fragment (F), a run-on sentence (R), or a complete sentence (S). Then, on the long lines, correct each sentence fragment and run-on sentence.

Example ____R____ **[1]** You might think mythology and folklore are just a bunch of stories from the past these stories, however, are alive today.

1. *You might think mythology and folklore are just a bunch of stories from the past. These stories, however, are alive today.*

_____ **[1]** Do you know any Norse mythology, if you know the days of the week, you do.

_____ **[2]** Two days named for Norse gods: Wednesday was originally "Odin's day" and Thursday was "Thor's day." _____ **[3]** Saturday, however, is named after Saturn, a Roman god.

_____ **[4]** Folklore and mythology have influenced common words as well, the word *panic* comes from the Greek god Pan, who played scary noises on his pipes. _____ **[5]** The word *tantalizing* originated from the Greek king Tantalus, who was punished in Hades by never being able to reach the water at his feet or the fruit above his head. _____ **[6]** The word *titanic* refers to the ancient Titans, these huge figures, according to classical mythology, ruled the universe before being deposed by Zeus. _____ **[7]** One word you may not know is *protean*, it comes from the name of a mythological god who could change his shape. _____ **[8]** Can you guess what the word means?

_____ **[9]** Mythology and folklore have also given us sayings, one is about "the goose that lays the golden eggs." _____ **[10]** A goose that lays golden eggs found in stories from many of the world's cultures.

_____

_____

_____

_____

_____

_____

_____

_____

_____

COMMON ERRORS

Subject-Verb Agreement B

EXERCISE A For each of the following sentences, decide whether the underlined verb agrees in number with its subject. If the verb form is incorrect, write above it the correct form. If the verb is already correct, write *C* above the verb.

                                                    brings

Example **1.** Each of the children in the preschool <u>bring</u> his or her own lunch.

 1. The jam that we made from my grandfather's strawberries <u>is</u> delicious.

 2. He sometimes borrows his brother's bicycle, especially if his own <u>need</u> work.

 3. Neither Curtis nor his younger sisters, Sarah and Sydney, <u>belongs</u> to any service club.

 4. <u>Do</u> either of his sisters have any interest in joining a club this year?

 5. Both my mother and my aunt Teresa, my mother's younger sister, <u>enjoys</u> reading biographies.

 6. <u>Has</u> Michael or Jason remembered to tell the team about the canceled practice?

 7. Oletha, together with Karen and Sid, <u>have</u> agreed to bring the refreshments for the meeting.

 8. The pattern on those sheets and curtains <u>is</u> really overwhelming in this small room.

 9. Ninety-eight dollars <u>are</u> too much for most families to pay for a hotel room.

 10. Most of the kittens, including Boots and Whiskers, <u>are</u> very playful.

EXERCISE B In each of the following sentences, circle the subject of the underlined verb. Then, if the verb does not agree in number with its subject, write the correct form of the verb above the incorrect form. If the verb agrees, write *C* above the verb.

Example **1.** The assistant principal is concerned because ⟨one⟩ of the students in my homeroom
                  arrives
                  <u>arrive</u> late almost every day.

 11. Do you think she <u>sleep</u> late every morning?

 12. Many students in my class <u>works</u> part-time, sometimes late into the evening.

 13. What will she do when basketball practices <u>start</u>?

 14. I know she is saving for college, but I think she also <u>want</u> to buy a car.

 15. The assembly will not begin until the last class <u>comes</u> into the auditorium.

 16. Only thirty-seven percent of the class <u>want</u> to go to Philadelphia for our senior trip.

 17. All of the coaches at our school, including Coach Jackson, <u>teach</u> academic classes.

 18. We might have to change our plans unless someone in the class <u>have</u> a sure-fire way to raise

     money.

 19. The main attractions of the city <u>are</u> the historical sites.

 20. He returned his band uniform because the pants <u>was</u> too short.

Language and Sentence Skills Practice

Pronoun-Antecedent Agreement A

EXERCISE A   In each of the following sentences, circle the antecedent of the pronoun in parentheses. Then, underline the pronoun or pronouns in parentheses that agree with the antecedent.

Example 1. Every (citizen) has the freedom to express *(his or her, their)* opinion.

1. One of the boys who was working on the scenery injured *(his, their)* thumb.

2. Students in Biology II will meet briefly after school to discuss *(their, its)* field trip.

3. In *(its, their)* effort to please everyone, the family members agreed to spend three days at the beach, three days in the mountains, and one day at the art museum.

4. Did the United States welcome *(its, their)* fiftieth state, Hawaii, in 1959 or 1960?

5. Anyone who has experience with sound or lighting equipment should come to the backstage area if *(he or she, they)* would like to help on this production.

EXERCISE B   In each sentence below, cross through any pronoun that does not agree with its antecedent. Then, write the correct pronoun above the incorrect pronoun. If a sentence is already correct, write *C* to the left of the item number.

Example 1. The new high school in our county has chosen ~~their~~ *its* colors and team name.

6. The Hawaiian Islands, which make up the state of Hawaii, are well known for its natural beauty.

7. Melissa, who is one of my oldest and best friends, is admired and liked by most of their peers.

8. When they were younger, Rhiannon and Emrys didn't like the names his or her parents had given them.

9. I can't wait for the news to come on tonight; they should have a story about our winning the district championship.

10. "Waste not, want not" is a saying my frugal grandmother used almost every day; I don't think I have to explain what it means.

11. Harriet, alone among all the children in that family, is determined to keep her room neat.

12. Many of the participants did not mind spending his or her time at the out-of-state tournament.

13. If she carefully reads the map, she should be able to use it to find her way out of the woods.

14. Every person in the room raised their hand when the teacher asked a question about the philosopher Socrates.

15. Either the tomato or the bell pepper plants reseed itself, I think.

Pronoun-Antecedent Agreement B

EXERCISE In each sentence below, circle the antecedent of the pronoun in parentheses. Then, underline the pronoun or pronouns in parentheses that agree with the antecedent.

Example 1. I know that we need cumin, cinnamon, and coriander, but does the (recipe) also have

garlic in (*it*, *them*)?

1. Not one of the students in my class would admit that (*he or she*, *they*) needed a tutor.

2. During the fire drill, students are expected to leave (*its*, *their*) classrooms in an orderly manner.

3. Each of the teachers establishes (*their*, *his or her*) own homework policies.

4. I think that the coupons were returned; did you count (*it*, *them*) again?

5. When the band brought home two trophies from the state competition, the school had to make

room in the display case for (*it*, *them*).

6. Does everyone who is working on this experiment understand that (*their*, *his or her*) lab notes

will have to be turned in tomorrow?

7. If you want to buy that book, you'll need sixteen dollars and twelve cents; do you have

(*them*, *it*), or do you need to borrow some money?

8. Both Terrell and Dan are proud that (*his*, *their*) fathers are in public service.

9. Each of the neighbors has agreed to trim (*his or her*, *their*) own trees.

10. Please ask those women if one of them has forgotten (*their*, *her*) coat.

11. Ed makes tasty chicken and dumplings; I always eat two helpings of (*them*, *it*).

12. After the judge signed the summons, the constable delivered (*them*, *it*) to the witness.

13. You'd better bring slacks; you'll need (*it*, *them*) later this afternoon.

14. Neither Kristin nor Mattie can borrow (*their*, *her*) parents' car this Saturday.

15. One of the horses had gotten out of (*their*, *its*) stall.

16. Both of these suits appear to fit well; do you like either of (*it*, *them*)?

17. I prefer the news on Channel 12, but I wish (*they*, *it*) didn't come on so late at night.

18. Guadalupe and Marisa didn't do as poorly on the test as (*she*, *they*) originally thought.

19. Anyone who thinks that the United States is the largest nation in the world doesn't know

(*their*, *his or her*) geography very well.

20. She didn't like the author's short stories as much as she liked his novel, but she read a lot of

(*them*, *it*) anyway.

COMMON ERRORS

Pronoun Forms A

EXERCISE A In each of the following sentences, underline the correct pronoun in parentheses.

Example 1. It may have been (*her, she*) who broke the world record in the long jump.

1. The bookstore gave discount coupons to Emily and (*he, him*).

2. The best team won the award, but the people who had the most fun were (*we, us*).

3. The principal gave (*her, she*) a special citation for her attendance.

4. The story may focus on (*whoever, whomever*) you choose.

5. Marco and (*he, him*) went on a camping trip last weekend.

6. The person who took the photograph of the comet is (*he, him*).

7. Amir, (*who, whom*) you recommended to me, is an excellent tutor.

8. Either Debby or (*I, myself*) will volunteer to lead the school's recycling program.

9. The magician asked Ronaldo and (*they, them*) to come onstage.

10. I hope (*us, we*) new choir members will have a chance to try out for solos.

EXERCISE B In each sentence below, draw a line through the incorrect pronoun and write the correct pronoun above it. If a sentence is already correct, write *C* to the left of the item number.

Example 1. He and ~~me~~ *I* are the only members of the team who haven't bought uniforms yet.

11. The doctor showed my father and I the X-rays of my knee.

12. Do you know who is driving to the regional track meet?

13. I hope you'll invite some of we new students to join the yearbook staff.

14. My cousin Gary and me are going fishing at the coast during spring break.

15. We would prefer to do that ourselves, but we would not mind advice from he.

16. Two students, Todd and her, were assigned the most difficult chapters.

17. Whomever leaves the room last should turn off the lights.

18. Bring Krystal and me some lemonade when you come back outside, please.

19. Sherry is a better singer than him.

20. I'd like to apply for that internship; to who should I send my application?

COMMON ERRORS

Pronoun Forms B

EXERCISE In each sentence below, underline the correct pronoun in parentheses. Then, identify the function of the pronoun by writing above it *S* for *subject*, *PN* for *predicate nominative*, *DO* for *direct object*, *IO* for *indirect object*, *OP* for *object of a preposition*, or *A* for *appositive*.

Example 1. Our neighbors, *(her, she)* and Mrs. Stinson, are always thoughtful and pleasant.

1. *(Who, Whom)* will be bringing the refreshments for the meeting?

2. Whoa, *(we, us)* little kids need a chance to catch up with you!

3. Four of my friends, Kara, Michelle, Emma, and *(her, she)*, will be working as camp counselors this summer.

4. Don't forget to clean out Fluffy's litter box after you give *(her, she)* the food.

5. The first person in line for tickets was *(he, him)*.

6. My mother invited my younger brother's friends—Keith, Kevin, and *(he, him)*—to join us for supper.

7. The drama teacher taught Carol and *(I, me)* how to use a hammer correctly.

8. Cecil didn't see the nails in the middle of the street, so he rode right over *(they, them)*.

9. I'm sure neither *(himself, he)* nor his father planned to spend an hour fixing the tires.

10. If my mother calls their parents, I'm sure their parents will bring *(they, them)*.

11. What Jerome and *(me, I)* intend to do with all that string is a surprise.

12. When the dog caught up with the little boy and girl, it trotted next to *(him and her, them)*.

13. Are the brothers who own the appliance repair shop *(them, they)*?

14. *(Her, She)* and my sister have been best friends since elementary school.

15. Did your father write down the recipe for Matt and *(her, she)*?

16. The author whose writing you enjoy most is *(who, whom)*?

17. Lisa, Mark, and Dieter are some of the people *(who, whom)* I have invited to the party.

18. The best dancer in the talent show was certainly either *(he, him)* or one of those twins.

19. Show Katerina and *(me, I)* the pictures from your vacation.

20. Brian sat between Ramona and *(I, me)*.

COMMON ERRORS

Clear Pronoun Reference A

EXERCISE On the lines provided, rewrite each of the following sentences, correcting the unclear or inexact pronoun references. You may need to add or rearrange words to make the sentences clear and meaningful.

Example 1. On the fence by the backyard, it read, "Keep Out." *The sign on the fence by the backyard read "Keep Out."*

1. On the news, they said that the blizzard had paralyzed the state's transportation systems.

2. Katherine began by asking the class rhetorical questions. This made the students feel relaxed.

3. The ranger talked to the young scout about his fire-making skills.

4. When Ira returned to get the plant in the garage, he discovered that it had vanished.

5. At Natalie's house, they eat dinner together every Tuesday, Wednesday, and Thursday.

6. Before Eduardo went to Garrett's house, he called his parents.

7. Whenever he pinches the bridge of his nose, it means that he's getting a headache.

8. My best friends and I like to skate. We believe it is the best way to spend a Friday night.

9. On the invitation, it did not say whether we should bring anything to the surprise party.

10. The police officers told my grandparents that they could not tow the car to the body shop.

COMMON ERRORS

Clear Pronoun Reference B

EXERCISE On the lines provided, rewrite each of the following sentences, correcting the unclear or inexact pronoun references. You may need to add or rearrange words to make the sentences clear and meaningful.

Example 1. Nha shook hands with Stephen when he presented the award.

When Stephen presented the award, he shook hands with Nha.

1. According to an article in this magazine, they say pasta dishes are both easy to make and

nutritious. _____

_____

2. The girl reached up and took her mother's hand so that she could help her cross the street.

_____

3. My mother reminded Kelly that she had homework to do. This made Kelly reconsider her

weekend plans. _____

_____

4. My neighbor Shelly jogs every morning and considers it to be a relaxing activity.

_____

5. If Harold wants to get up at 5:30 A.M. and work out for an hour before school, it means he'll

have to go to bed at 9:30 P.M. to get eight hours of sleep. _____

_____

6. In my history classroom, they like to pull the desks into a circle. _____

_____

7. Neither of us wants to walk to school this morning, which Dad doesn't seem to understand.

_____

8. Jim said that it doesn't make sense to shower before going to the gym. _____

_____

9. It says in the ad that if you buy two half-gallons of milk, you get one free. _____

_____

10. After the teacher gave Clarice an award, she returned to her desk. _____

_____

COMMON ERRORS

Verb Forms A

EXERCISE A In each of the following sentences, underline the correct verb form in parentheses.

Example 1. In class yesterday, we heard that our science teacher had (*speaked,* <u>*spoken*</u>) about the

    Alvarez hypothesis on a TV show last year.

1. Evidence from the Yucatán Peninsula indicates that an asteroid that (*struck, striked*) there 65

 million years ago might have killed the dinosaurs.

2. Many more people in Western countries have (*beginned, begun*) to try acupuncture to treat pain

 and disease.

3. Before the bell (*had rang, had rung*) on the last day of school, we had already taken all our

 books out of our lockers.

4. Hakiko (*had written, had wrote*) the computer program that calculated population statistics.

5. I know metal contracts when cold, but could an object (*have shrinked, have shrunk*) that much

 when frozen in ice?

6. Amy said that Alexander Graham Bell, inventor of the telephone, (*gave, gived*) much of his

 time to developing electronic hearing devices.

7. Ralph Nader burst onto the national scene in the 1960s, when he (*breaked, broke*) the news that

 many U.S.-made cars were unsafe.

8. Had you ever (*went, gone*) to a meeting of your city council before you arrived here today?

9. After he had driven his go-cart into their prize-winning rose bushes, Zeke finally (*weared, wore*)

 out his welcome with the neighbors.

10. Unfortunately, he hadn't (*seed, seen*) the curb in time, and he had turned the wheel too hard to

 the right.

EXERCISE B In the following paragraph, most of the verb tenses are inconsistent or illogical. If an underlined verb is incorrect, write the correct form above it.

      will be giving
Example My friend Leah <u>gave</u> a report on Harriet Tubman next Thursday.

 Leah <u>had</u> researched her subject at the library for many days now. Yesterday, she <u>tells</u> me that

Harriet Tubman <u>serves</u> as a scout and a nurse for the Union army during the Civil War. That work

<u>is</u> in addition to helping hundreds of slaves escape to freedom. Leah has organized her information

and notes on cards so that her report is easy to give.

Verb Forms B

EXERCISE In each of the following sentences, write the correct verb form above the underlined verb.

Example 1. Meiko suddenly remembered where she <u>see</u> the painting. *had seen*

1. Some kind of animal has <u>dig</u> holes in my flower beds again.

2. By the time we arrived at their house, they had already <u>leave</u>.

3. Please don't <u>sit</u> that vase on the wooden shelf; it will leave a stain.

4. When they were ready to assemble the tricycle, they realized they had <u>lose</u> the instructions.

5. We should have saved our money and <u>buy</u> a plane ticket.

6. John says he has <u>visit</u> twenty-one countries.

7. When she plugged in the space heater, a fuse <u>blow</u>.

8. Before the young girl had <u>eat</u> the sandwich, her mother had removed the crust.

9. Although we spent three hours in the library, we could not find the books we <u>seeked</u>.

10. We should have <u>bring</u> our coats and gloves.

11. As of today, Charles has <u>work</u> for the company a total of three years.

12. Although the lake was <u>freeze</u>, we didn't go skating.

13. When you <u>meet</u> him, did he tell you that he knows your brother?

14. Our English teacher gave us our assignments last week, when you <u>are</u> absent with the flu.

15. Malcolm had <u>eat</u> the peach before Anna came home.

16. My family had <u>drive</u> in the mountains two weeks before the avalanche occurred.

17. If you had written down the time and the place, we would not have <u>miss</u> the party.

18. My grandfather told us about the time he <u>speak</u> to President Truman.

19. She <u>tear</u> the bread in pieces and feeds some to the ducks.

20. After we had <u>build</u> the scenery, we painted it.

Comparative and Superlative Forms

EXERCISE A In the following sentences, correct the errors in the use of the comparative and superlative forms of modifiers. If the sentence is already correct, write *C* to the left of the number.

                                            more carefully

Example 1. Please wash the glasses ~~carefuller~~ next time.

1. Which of the two dogs have you had longest?

2. We can finish the job more quickly if we work together.

3. She has some of the elegantest clothes I've ever seen.

4. Of gold and platinum, which is most valuable?

5. Of the two paintings, I like that one most.

6. I performed my routine more better this time than I did last time.

7. All of the ripe strawberries have been picked already.

8. Of the two dancers, she is certainly more graceful.

9. I really doubt I could feel any more tired than I do now.

10. Of all the kittens in the litter, that one is the cuter.

EXERCISE B In the following sentences, correct the errors in the use of the comparative and superlative forms of modifiers. If the sentence is already correct, write *C* to the left of the number.

                                    any other place

Example 1. The Marianas Trench is deeper than ~~any place~~ in the ocean.

11. The water in the pool was more warmer than the outside air.

12. Between a hurricane and a tornado, which do you think is most dangerous?

13. Of my two brothers, Felipe is least patient.

14. Rupesh says that baseball is more easier to play than cricket is.

15. The wrestler had won more trophies than anyone.

16. Of all my teammates, Shelly is better at taking penalty kicks.

17. The angrier the child became, the calmer his mother grew.

18. The ruby in this display may be worth more than any gemstone in the exhibition.

19. Of all the poems she entered in the contest, she felt sure that the sonnet was the better.

20. Both Raul and Clara have brown hair, but Clara's is darkest.

Misplaced and Dangling Modifiers A

EXERCISE On the lines provided, rewrite each of the following sentences to correct any misplaced or dangling modifiers. You may have to add or rearrange words to make a sentence meaningful.

Example 1. She displayed her sculpture at the gallery, which was formed from scrap metal.

She displayed her sculpture, which was formed from scrap metal, at the gallery.

1. We are planning to go to the carnival we heard about tomorrow. _____

   _____

2. Cold and refreshing, the girl swam in the waters of the spring creek. _____

   _____

3. With these apples, we will make a delicious applesauce that we bought at the roadside stand.

   _____

4. While on a field trip to the natural history museum, the curator showed us many remarkable

   fossils. _____

   _____

5. Having left the windows open, the floor got wet when the rain started. _____

   _____

6. The boy put down his oar to feed the swan who was rowing the boat. _____

   _____

7. The old bicycle had two flat tires he found in the shed. _____

   _____

8. Sitting on a grassy hillside above the town, the fireworks lit up the night sky. _____

   _____

9. The flowers will be beautiful in this vase from my uncle's garden. _____

   _____

10. Wrapped in a warm bathrobe and sitting in front of a blazing fire, the blizzard howled outside.

   _____

   _____

COMMON ERRORS

Misplaced and Dangling Modifiers B

EXERCISE   On the lines provided, rewrite each of sentence below to correct any misplaced or dangling modifiers. You may have to add or rearrange words to make a sentence meaningful.

Example 1. Danika zipped up her winter jacket shivering in the cold.   *Danika, shivering in the cold, zipped up her winter jacket.*

1. Searching through a dictionary, numerous Latin roots may be found. _____
_____

2. Only stop and chat if you have plenty of time to get to class. _____
_____

3. To complete the driving test, parallel parking is required. _____
_____

4. The school counselors collected schedule requests who were helping us sign up for classes.
_____

5. After adding some fresh vegetables, the stir-fry dish cooked for a couple more minutes.
_____

6. To meet the requirements, a change in plans may be needed. _____
_____

7. The baseball player waved at the spectators running toward home plate. _____
_____

8. The experienced campers found several signs of animals in the woods that are rarely sighted.
_____

9. Having practiced for weeks, the game went well. _____
_____

10. While hiking in the high mountain meadows, the wildflowers in full bloom are a sight not to
be missed. _____
_____

Correct Use of Modifiers A

EXERCISE On the lines provided, rewrite the following sentences to correct any errors in the use of modifiers. You may need to add or rearrange words to make a sentence meaningful.

Example 1. The events happened in the late eighteenth century on which the novel was based.

The events on which the novel was based happened in the late eighteenth century.

1. That was certainly the most delightful of the two movies that I watched this weekend.

   _____

2. I bought a wallet at that store that was expensiver. _____

   _____

3. Our plans are more definiter now that we've gotten our tickets. _____

   _____

4. While reading that new poetry collection, one poem reminded me of an event in my own life.

   _____

5. The man stopped to pet a puppy who was carrying a bag of groceries. _____

   _____

6. Concentrating hard on finishing the project, the hours slipped by. _____

   _____

7. As heard on the radio, the concert was canceled. _____

   _____

8. The pumpkins will be perfect for pie in that field. _____

   _____

9. I only want you to join us if you think you would enjoy the play. _____

   _____

10. Rising out of its banks, the rescue team surveyed the raging river. _____

   _____

Correct Use of Modifiers B

EXERCISE On the lines provided, rewrite the following sentences to correct any errors in the use of modifiers. You may need to add or rearrange words to make a sentence meaningful.

Example 1. Watching the clock, time can seem to pass slowly. *Time can seem to pass slowly when you're watching the clock.*

1. To learn the positions and names of the constellations, a star chart will be quite helpful.
   _____

2. Buzzing angrily around its head, the bear tried to swat away the bees. _____
   _____

3. Working late into the night, the costume for the play was finished. _____
   _____

4. Between Rick and Dave, which boy can jump farthest? _____
   _____

5. Dozens of stars appeared in the darkening sky that hadn't been visible a few minutes earlier.
   _____

6. Last night, while playing chess with my brother, all the dogs in the neighborhood started
   howling. _____
   _____

7. Of all the cars you have tested, which was less reliable? _____
   _____

8. Few things taste gooder than cool water on a hot day. _____
   _____

9. In the Pacific Ocean, my brother and I read about the violent origin of the Hawaiian Islands.
   _____

10. Scoring ninety-two percent, the most highest mark in the class went to Jane's report.
    _____

Standard Usage A

EXERCISE A In each of the following sentences, underline the correct word or words in parentheses.

Example 1. (*Set*, *Sit*) the books on the counter, please.

1. (*Can, May*) I have another helping of mashed potatoes, please?

2. The rabbits (*who, that*) live in the hedge near our shed are not bothered by the cat.

3. (*Lying, Laying*) on the grass in the shade of the giant elms, he closed his eyes and quickly

fell asleep.

4. (*These kinds, This kind*) of shell is not common in this area.

5. In this article I read (*that, where*) the city council has agreed to build a new park.

6. At that store I couldn't find (*no one, anyone*) to help me.

7. The (*affects, effects*) of the storm were minimal.

8. Mr. Harrington pays honest wages for (*a, an*) honest day's work.

9. The soccer players talked (*among, between*) themselves.

10. The colors in this wallpaper pattern look (*well, good*) with the upholstery fabric.

EXERCISE B In each of the following sentences, determine whether the underlined word or word group is correct according to standard English usage. If the usage is incorrect, revise the sentence to show the correct usage. If the usage is correct, write *C* to the left of the item number.

Example 1. I ~~must of~~ accidentally given my biology paper to my English teacher.
must have

11. The student council hasn't decided yet <u>where</u> the meeting will be <u>at</u>.

12. One <u>reason</u> the streets are so clean <u>is because</u> the people take pride in their neighborhood.

13. Tranh is going to the local college, <u>as</u> his older sister did.

14. Since Cedric cannot join the new team, think of someone <u>beside</u> him to invite.

15. I was hoping that you would join us for lunch <u>somewheres</u>.

16. Have you heard how <u>good</u> Jimmy performed at the music contest?

17. He's hiked in those mountains so many times that he <u>doesn't need no</u> map.

18. You <u>ought not to of</u> brought your dog to the restaurant.

19. This <u>type of</u> fax machine requires special paper.

20. Don't you think <u>this here</u> car needs to go to the shop?

COMMON ERRORS

Standard Usage B

EXERCISE On the lines provided, rewrite each of the following sentences, correcting any errors in standard, formal usage.

Example 1. Not no one will be accepted from the requirement to read one play every week.

No one will be excepted from the requirement to read one play every week.

1. If I drink alot of water, I'll feel alright in a few minutes. _____

_____

2. She looked for her keys for several minutes, but she couldn't find them anywheres. _____

_____

3. My mother and father they have a kind of a family business. _____

_____

4. The boy couldn't hardly explain why he done that. _____

_____

5. Do you mean to infer that I ought to of left my dog at home? _____

_____

6. I wish Martina, whom I've known for several years, wouldn't act like she's never met me.

_____

7. The crew of the yacht congratulated theirselves on there victory. _____

_____

8. If we expect to be at the camp by sundown, than we should hurry; we have a long ways to go.

_____

9. Quentin wanted to know who's jacket was laying on the ground. _____

_____

10. Being as he wants to learn hisself Spanish, he bought some language tapes off of the Internet.

_____

_____

Capitalization A

EXERCISE A   In each of the following sentences, circle any letters that should be capitalized but are not.

Example 1. Did you know that ⓓr. ⓒrandall lives at 123 ⓣwenty-ninth ⓢtreet?

1. Would you prefer french or russian dressing on your salad?

2. Did you know that your mother's uncle charles was a roman catholic priest?

3. The city council will dedicate the monument at Bass drive and forty-seventh street.

4. some of ellen's family came from ireland in the eighteenth century.

5. "Meredith," julie began, "will you lend me the notes you took on the french revolution?"

6. My summer ends on august 12, when my latin class begins.

7. At the u.s. capitol, you can tour the original chambers of the supreme court.

8. My brother's friend max studied the painting *american gothic*.

9. Hey, mom, does aunt louisa live in kansas city, kansas, or kansas city, missouri?

10. Most of my father's family lives in the south, but Aunt Jo lives in new england.

EXERCISE B   In the following paragraph, circle each letter that should be capitalized but is not, and draw a slash (/) through any letter that is capitalized but should not be.

Example   **[1]** In my ⓜusic I class, which is taught by ⓓr. Julie ⓜcBride, we learned that Ṛock

music is an ⓐmerican invention.

[11] Rock-and-roll developed in the 1950s and 1960s from the combination of many different

american styles, especially Gospel music and Rhythm and Blues music. [12] These forms, in turn,

were developed in the united states by african Americans, from a tradition of Spirituals—hymns

to god—from the south that dates back to before the civil war. [13] one famous spiritual is the

song "when the saints go marching in." [14] Important musicians in the early development of

rock-and-roll include chuck berry, buddy holly, and the beatles. [15] The beatles especially had

great success in the late sixties, with such songs as "I want to hold your hand." [16] Rock music

has also been influenced by jazz, which grew out of another african american tradition. [17] you

have probably heard of the jazz artists louis armstrong and ella fitzgerald. [18] People all around

the world today listen to rock music. [19] In my Music class, i have studied many different types

of music, such as reggae from jamaica and polkas from eastern europe. [20] I have even enjoyed

listening to some Classical music; so far, mozart is my favorite composer.

COMMON ERRORS

Capitalization B

EXERCISE In each of the following sentences, circle any letter that should be capitalized but is not, and draw a slash (/) through any letter that is capitalized but should not be.

Example 1. Jen's Mother, who speaks both french and Spanish, says that the Arabic Language is not difficult to learn.

1. Last Summer i went to the rodeo and livestock show at memorial coliseum.

2. Is majorca, one of the balearic islands, in the mediterranean sea off the Coast of Spain?

3. Ryan's full name is ryan merrill green II, not jr.; he was named after his Grandfather.

4. the senior class will hold its annual Class dinner at the Graver hotel, which is downtown.

5. My mother gave dad a dozen roses for valentine's day.

6. Baker, Beaton & Bettis, inc., is an old accounting firm in our city; grandfather Bettis was one of the founding partners.

7. The Capital City of germany is no longer bonn, but berlin.

8. if my niece katie plays "Mary had a little lamb" one more time, I think I'll scream.

9. Built during the great depression, Hoover dam is still an engineering marvel.

10. Did you see Mayor-Elect Simpson at the opening day of the Legislative session?

11. Send your application to 447 Fifty-Fifth street, Calabash, south Carolina 33045.

12. The U.S. postal service issues commemorative stamps; check your local Post Office.

13. Every school child knows the names of Columbus's Ships, the *niña*, the *pinta*, and the *santa maria*.

14. "Ida," Morgan asked, "Do you like new england clam chowder or manhattan clam chowder?"

15. When you reach the intersection of Reynolds avenue and Macon street, turn East.

16. Mary, an Architect who loves to study roman buildings, visited the flavian amphitheater.

17. Congress established the united states department of agriculture (usda) in 1862.

18. Our Team, the hamilton hornets, beat the madison high school meteors in the last few seconds of the game.

19. "Please call aunt Jane and ask her how to make irish soda bread," mother said.

20. When is a newly elected president's family allowed to move into the white house?

COMMON ERRORS

Commas A

EXERCISE In each of the following sentences, draw a caret (∧) to show where any missing commas should be inserted.

Example 1. Oh boy∧I forgot to renew my library books again∧but I'm already late for class.

1. Diego would you please give a copy of this announcement to Doug Rina Cathy and Leighton?

2. No although I wish I could join you at the ballpark tomorrow I told my father I would help him around the house.

3. She could call you tomorrow evening to remind you or you could just write yourself a note.

4. On Thursday Friday and Saturday evenings the curtain will go up at eight o'clock but the Sunday performance begins earlier at seven.

5. Do you remember where you were and what you were doing at midnight on January 1 2000?

6. Antonio and Eduardo my cousins on my mother's side are coming to visit us.

7. Still singing softly she laid the baby in the crib and covered him with a fine cotton blanket.

8. "Well boys you could just spend the whole day lying around eating popcorn and watching TV" Mom said with a certain edge to her voice.

9. I have studied studied and studied some more and now I think I'm really ready for the test.

10. "Did the woman who left these keys on the counter ever call?" asked the manager his brow furrowed with concern.

11. Bring sunscreen a hat and good sunglasses or you might not have much fun on the hike.

12. Take the elevator to the third floor turn right go to the end of the hallway and turn right again.

13. Mr. Caswell are the chairs that we need in the storage room or in the closet?

14. The meeting in case you didn't know was canceled at the last minute.

15. My great-grandmother who was born in Colorado at the end of the nineteenth century knew how to ride a horse rope cattle fix fences and mend a wagon wheel.

16. If you have a minute I could use help with these math problems especially the third one.

17. Meredith mailed the letter to 900 Congress Avenue Suite 1400 Houston TX 77002.

18. In that long narrow building is the office of Carol McGinnis M.D.

19. Near the revolving door of the gigantic skyscraper Jerry paused to look at the face of his battered worn wristwatch.

20. Unfortunately Cindy we can't afford to fly to Los Angeles so we'll have to drive.

COMMON ERRORS

Commas B

EXERCISE In the following letter, draw a caret (∧) to show where any missing commas should be inserted and circle any unnecessary commas.

Example   **[1]** On Monday of last week∧Martina∧who was unhappy∧with the order she

received∧decided to write a complaint letter to the company.

[1] 412 Callahan St. Apt. 16

[2] Lemon Grove CA 99771

[3] April 14 2003,

Rittenberg's Fine Clothing for Women

[4] 9490, Avenue C 10th Floor

[5] Donivan WY, 87007

To Whom It May Concern:

[6] I am returning almost everything, I ordered from your catalog last month and I am writing

to explain why. **[7]** In the past everyone in my family, who has done business, with your company

including my mother my three sisters and my aunt has been pleased with the quality cut and fit of

the clothes. **[8]** However the items I recently received, were very disappointing. **[9]** For example

item no. 53007 the blue sweater was missing three buttons. **[10]** Item no. 53008 the skirt which was

supposed to match the sweater was a completely, different color. **[11]** The pants item no. 54433

were neither the size, nor the color, I ordered. **[12]** The only satisfactory item in my entire order,

was the soft luxurious sweat suit which fits perfectly.

[13] I was quite disappointed when I opened the box, and looked at the clothes. **[14]** If your

company continues to cut corners you will lose my business. **[15]** In fact I had planned to order a

new suit but now I'm not sure, that I will.

[16] Like many people these days I do not have money, to waste on return postage. **[17]** Your

company I believe should reimburse me for this expense. **[18]** To return the items I spent $14.33.

[19] Please mail my refund to the address, above.

[20] Sincerely

Martina Maniscalco

COMMON ERRORS

Semicolons and Colons

EXERCISE In each of the following sentences, show where the correct punctuation marks should be inserted by underlining any word that should be followed by a colon and by drawing a caret (∧) to show where a semicolon should be inserted instead of a comma.

Example 1. The camp has no laundry facilities∧be sure to bring all of the following <u>items</u> six complete changes of clothing, two pairs of sturdy shoes, a lightweight jacket, a hat, and a swimsuit.

1. My brother will not be able to join us tomorrow, he has basketball practice.

2. If you are going to the store this afternoon, please pick up the following for me two cans of Italian tomatoes, parsley, and a three-pound bag of white onions.

3. Maybe we should go to the Lincoln Theater, the movie there doesn't start until 7:45.

4. She wanted to spend the afternoon at the park, however, the weather did not cooperate.

5. Nan wrote out a list of supplies she needed for school notebook paper, pens, pencils, a protractor, a three-ring binder, six spiral notebooks, and a box of diskettes.

6. Last summer we drove to visit my uncle in Charleston, West Virginia, my aunt in Scotch Plains, New Jersey, and my grandparents in Jacksonville, Florida.

7. We always leave a dish of water outside for the cats, one of them, unfortunately, will not drink from a dish.

8. Your mouth will feel a little sore this afternoon please eat soft foods for the rest of the day.

9. My grandmother, who is almost eighty, is still very active she does all her own yard work, volunteers at the library, and is learning how to use the computer.

10. On Saturday morning I completed many chores I mowed the front and back yards, trimmed all the hedges, including the one by the driveway, and bundled up all the newspapers that had been stacked in the garage.

Quotation Marks with Other Punctuation A

EXERCISE On the lines provided, rewrite each of the following sentences, correcting errors in the use of quotation marks, other marks of punctuation, and capitalization.

Example 1. Britta asked Have you read the short story To Build a Fire. *Britta asked, "Have you read the short story 'To Build a Fire'?"*

1. "Beth" Harry said "Doesn't want any watermelon" _____
_____

2. Our class read A Day's Wait, a short story by Ernest Hemingway. _____
_____

3. It's Dr. Martin Luther King, Jr.'s birthday tomorrow said Jane. Are you going to the parade?
_____
_____

4. The verb *abhor* means to detest. _____
_____

5. In an essay titled What a Character! Jason describes Dickens's ability to create interesting
believable characters. _____
_____

6. Rosa exclaimed "Watch out for that tree"! _____
_____

7. The Star-Spangled Banner is the national anthem of the United States. _____
_____

8. Please turn to Poe's poem The Raven, said Mr. Butler. _____
_____

9. "By the way", remarked Li "the car needs to be washed". _____
_____

10. "Do you know who said A penny saved is a penny earned?" asked Veronica. _____
_____

Quotation Marks with Other Punctuation B

EXERCISE Revise the following dialogue, inserting quotation marks and other punctuation as necessary. Be sure to indicate a new paragraph (¶) every time the speaker changes.

Example [1] "Would you prefer a table in the corner or one nearer the window?" the hostess asked.

[1] Well, I like window tables, but a table in the back corner would be more private my sister said. [2] Why don't you decide. [3] No, I answered. This is your favorite restaurant. You decide. [4] My sister looked up when she realized the hostess was tapping her foot impatiently. Okay, said my sister. A window table will be fine. [5] It's nice of you to treat me for my birthday I told my sister as the hostess was leading us to our table. [6] Order anything you like. Dinner is on me my sister said. [7] What may I get you to drink, the waiter, who seemed to have come out of nowhere, asked me. [8] Just water for me. [9] I'll have the lemon tea my sister replied. Could you also bring us two spinach salads? [10] I don't want a salad I put in quickly. [11] I'd rather have the pasta al dente. [12] Do you know what *al dente* means? asked my sister. *Al dente* means "cooked until firm". [13] I know, I said. That's what I want. [14] Okay, make that one salad and one pasta al dente, she said to the waiter. [15] My, you certainly are a picky eater. [16] No, I began through gritted teeth, I am not a picky eater. [17] Didn't you just say "You can order anything you like?" I asked. [18] Yes, I did say that, said my sister, but I just want you to enjoy your food. [19] I know you do, said I. [20] Maybe I'll try some of your salad, and you can try some of my pasta.

Apostrophes

EXERCISE In each of the following sentences, draw a caret (∧) to show where an apostrophe should be inserted.

Example 1. Melissas brothers friend just moved here from Cleveland.

1. Theyll try to get a good nights rest first.

2. The days program includes workshops in the morning, lunch at twelve o clock, and a general meeting in the afternoon.

3. Shouldnt you try to call Bills and Bettys mothers?

4. The grandchildrens names are Ella, Edna, Everett, and Elliott; in that family, everyones name begins with *E*.

5. The note my brother's teacher had written on his term paper read, "Youve used too many *howevers*. Please revise."

6. This winters coldest temperature was only 25°F; its usually much colder in January.

7. Hes never on time; you can always count on at least an hours delay.

8. Felicias fathers family moved from California to Massachusetts.

9. Phylliss favorite vegetables are carrots and peas.

10. The crusts too hard, and its difficult for a person with braces to chew.

11. Doesnt anyone in this class know someone whos interested in geology?

12. Lets unpack our clothes, get out the map, and start exploring the citys sights.

13. In the summers of 98 and 99, he spent hours at the pool every day.

14. Whats the name of the dog that broke its leash?

15. Isnt it true that every writers dream is to be published?

16. The Katzes restaurant wont be open until five o clock today.

17. Its hard to read her writing because her *t*s look like *l*s and her *r*s look like *n*s.

18. Martas and Janices horses saddles are hanging in the tackroom.

19. Do you think shell find a shell she likes in the shop thats near the beach?

20. Lets bring the refreshments; Ill ask Sara and Lee to handle the decorations.

All Marks of Punctuation Review A

EXERCISE A   On the lines provided, rewrite each of the following sentences, inserting or deleting commas, semicolons, colons, quotation marks, and apostrophes where necessary.

Example 1. Leona doesnt the color of this paint asked Mother complement the fabric?

"Leona, doesn't the color of this paint," asked Mother, "complement the fabric?"

1. I cant understand the contract, it has too many *if*s *but*s and *wherefore*s in it. _____

_____

2. Weve built a house for the purple martins but no birds have moved into it yet. _____

_____

3. Kim asked Did Ms Fletcher really say No homework this week? _____

_____

4. Well Im not sure how to explain this, Jan replied, but I think he left at 430 P.M. _____

_____

5. On the shelf in the garage you will find an old rusty hammer. _____

_____

EXERCISE B   On the lines provided, rewrite each of the following sentences, inserting parentheses, brackets, hyphens, and dashes where necessary. Underline any words that should be italicized.

Example 1. The two well behaved boys specifically, Roger and Trey were allowed to leave

before lunch. *The two well-behaved boys—specifically, Roger and Trey—were allowed*

to leave before lunch.

6. The painting Anatomy Lesson of Professor Tulp was painted by Rembrandt 1606–1669.

_____

7. My great grandfather read to me the novel Anne Frank: The Diary of a Young Girl.

_____

8. The team's captain I can't remember his name knew that the statue was called The Thinker.

_____

9. "During the student sponsored coat drive March 10–13, we collected 265 well made coats."

_____

10. The man approached the ex mayor with one goal to ask her for an autograph. _____

_____

COMMON ERRORS

Punctuation Review B

EXERCISE Revise the following minutes from a photography club meeting. Insert necessary commas, semicolons, colons, parentheses, quotation marks, apostrophes, hyphens, and dashes. Underline any words that should be italicized.

Example [1] Twenty—two members of the Photography Club, thats a majority of the clubs

membership, met this week.

[1] The Photography Club met on Tuesday March 14 2002 at 430 P.M. in room 432.

[2] In the absence of the clubs president Jessica Farwell Mark Combs the vice president called the meeting to order. [3] Mark asked the members to sign in and he announced that a majority of the membership was present.

[4] According to the vice presidents report of the clubs finances as of February 28 the date of the most recent bank statement we have a balance of $1,426 in our account.

[5] Mark announced that the members would discuss the following items which were listed on the meetings agenda the cost of another enlarger the current one needs repairs the field trip to Crenshaws Art Gallery and the clubs school wide photo contest.

[6] Meredith Jones Nicki Furth and Cedric Johnson volunteered to research current prices for a new enlarger. [7] After volunteering Cedric stood up and said, My uncle owns a photo supply store. He'll probably give us a good deal. [8] As for the field trip, a three fourths majority agreed that club members should meet in the school parking lot at 1000 A.M. on Saturday. [9] Nicoles parents have offered to drive more cars as needed.

[10] The vice president went over the rules for the photo contest photos must be original either black and white or color shots are acceptable entrants must pay a fee $1.00 per photo and the club sponsors Mr Stefanik and Ms Sedgwick will screen all entries before the photos are displayed.

COMMON ERRORS

Spelling A

EXERCISE A On the lines provided, write the plural form of each of the following words.

Example 1. adversary   *adversaries*

1. moose _____
2. waltz _____
3. Jackson _____
4. attorney general _____
5. formula _____
6. hero _____
7. banana _____
8. loaf _____
9. roof _____
10. tooth _____
11. piano _____
12. ox _____
13. half _____

14. cactus _____
15. alumna _____
16. potato _____
17. Ph.D. _____
18. buzz _____
19. fox _____
20. runner-up _____
21. *3* _____
22. Nash _____
23. sheep _____
24. deity _____
25. leaf _____

EXERCISE B In each of the following sentences, draw a line through each misspelled word. Then, write the correct spelling above the misspelled word.

Example 1. This year's Thanksgiving Day parade ~~proceded~~ *proceeded* right ~~thru~~ *through* downtown.

26. My aunt's puppies have always prefered not to make mischief.

27. How many sister-in-laws does the office manager have?

28. Her dayly wage exceded Demetria's expectations.

29. Gail's fellow alumni also enjoyed the girls' reunion.

30. The stunt pilot beleives in the value of good judgment.

31. Our team conceeded defeat after eight more goals were scored.

32. We postponed our plans because of our arguement.

33. Henry percieved that he had paid the full price even though he had a coupon.

34. Dr. Chan refered to a similar occurence.

35. We called the hostel and made arrangments for overnight accomodations.

COMMON ERRORS

Spelling B

EXERCISE In each of the following sentences, draw a line through each misspelled word. Then, write the correct spelling above the misspelled word.

              accidentally   *tacos*

Example **1.** I ~~accidentaly~~ put too much cheese in the ~~tacoes~~.

1. She was completly disatisfied with the service she recieved at the store.

2. Most athletes will tell you that to succede, you need hard work and practice.

3. She didn't reconize Marvin when she saw him on 12th Avenue.

4. He was more than happy to show us his trophys.

5. My teachers say that mispelled words are inexcusable.

6. After the performance we asked about the singer's accompanyment.

7. Fortunatly, although the traffic was terrible, we arrived on time.

8. Our conversation about our mother-in-laws was barely peacable.

9. She wasn't able to catch either salmons or trouts.

10. I have exactly—and this is no exaggeration—one hundred books on my shelfs.

11. The hotel lobby was, in all likelyhood, the most luxurious room he had ever seen.

12. In my experience, indexes can be very useful referrences.

13. In school we didn't study busyness.

14. The staff had discovered five new specieses.

15. The drummers rehearsed their soloes for hours.

16. Didn't you think that letter was truely lovly?

17. My younger brother constantly interseded, making helpful comments every two or

three minutes.

18. The greenish light above the swamp was a phenomena we could not explain.

19. The bookeeper's formulae were quite complicated.

20. A baseball game superseded my favorite comedys.

Words Often Confused

EXERCISE A In each of the following sentences, underline the correct word in parentheses.

Example 1. Don't (*alter*, *altar*) a single word of this essay; (*its*, *it's*) perfect!

1. When did the climbers begin the (*assent*, *ascent*) to the summit?

2. The team has (*born*, *borne*) (*its*, *it's*) defeats gracefully.

3. The (*personnel*, *personal*) office is down the hall, the second door on the right.

4. Although we have (*passed*, *past*) the correct exit, I'm sure we can find an alternate (*rout*, *route*)
   to the stadium.

5. The (*moral*, *morale*) of the team was at an all-time low.

6. This (*plain*, *plane*) stops in Midland and El Paso and (*than*, *then*) goes on to Albuquerque.

7. Freedom of speech is a (*principle*, *principal*) upon which true democracy is based.

8. (*Theirs*, *There's*) no good reason to let all that food go to (*waste*, *waist*).

9. Those (*too*, *two*) insist on going with us, (*too*, *two*).

10. She wasn't (*quiet*, *quite*) finished with the research paper.

EXERCISE B In each of the following sentences, draw a line through each incorrect word and write the
correct word above it. If all the words in a sentence are correct, write *C* above the sentence.

Example 1. ~~Whose~~ (*Who's*) planning to have ~~desert~~ (*dessert*)?

11. The Straight of Magellan is near the southern tip of South America.

12. After the cave-in, the moral of the miners was lower then it had been in months.

13. Karl was formerly with a big law firm, but now he has his own practice.

14. Of the two ideas, the later is the more ingenuous.

15. Don't loose the instructions, or we'll never be able to assemble this stationery bike.

16. Did you know that our principal has her pilot's license and keeps her plain at the private
    airport near Georgetown?

17. Although they ascented to the plan, we could tell that they were not all together happy
    about it.

18. All right, now turn the wheel and ease off the break—slowly!

19. The counselor complemented him on the cloths he wore to the interview.

20. That peace of music is well known, of coarse, but I can't remember its name.

COMMON ERRORS

Spelling and Words Often Confused

EXERCISE In each of the following sentences, draw a line through each misspelled or misused word. Then, write the correct word above the misspelled or misused word.

        already   *intercede*
Example 1. She had ~~all ready~~ decided to ~~interceed~~ on the boy's behalf.

1. My 4th-grade teacher retired last year; he plans to spend his retirment raising beagles.

2. Carl waited to long to decide weather or not to go.

3. My whole family occasionally stays up late to watch a movie altogether.

4. One of the blades on these scissors isn't strait any longer.

5. I need to learn to accept complements.

6. Ladys and gentlemen, its my priviledge to introduce to you Dr. Marilyn Butcher.

7. The old man took a handkercheif from his back pocket, wiped the sweat from his forhead, and looked at the setting sun.

8. How many tomatos and potatos are here?

9. The house had been altared considerably since he had last seen it.

10. At the embassy's holiday party, the guests waited to be formerly introduced to the counsel.

11. Do you want desert now or later?

12. Nelson, the only hiker who didn't loose his head during the crisis, lead us out of the woods.

13. Tonight he will explain his ingenuous plan to the mayor and counselors.

14. Is Garrett as mischieveous as his brothers were when they were his age?

15. We have been studying the meanings and orgins of suffixs and prefixs.

16. The candidates have born a lot of criticism during this campaign.

17. Please put the too loafs of bread in the oven; than you should rake the leafs.

18. If you start argueing again, I may loose my temper, too!

19. Don't assume that a state's largest city is also it's capitol.

20. As the hours past without any word from the missing ship, the moral of the sailors' families plummeted.

Review A: Usage

EXERCISE A   In each of the following sentences, draw a line through each verb that does not agree with its subject and any pronoun that does not agree with its antecedent. Then, write the correct form of the verb or pronoun above the incorrect form.

Example 1. Some of the stories in the book *The Arabian Nights* ~~involves~~ *involve* the characters Ali Baba

and Aladdin.

1. Each of the five girls have given their opinion on what the word *quixotic* means.

2. Buddhists believe that following strict spiritual and physical rules are the key to achieving

nirvana, a state of peacefulness.

3. Few of the first women pilots had her abilities taken seriously.

4. One of the students in the Geography Club will win a prize for their map of the Middle East.

5. Everyone should know their American history well enough to define "flapper."

EXERCISE B   On the lines provided, rewrite each of the following sentences, correcting the errors in usage. You may need to rearrange or add words to make a sentence meaningful.

Example 1. Laying across the ocean like a blanket, Katy stared vacantly at the fog.

Katy stared vacantly at the fog, which was lying across the ocean like a blanket.

6. In this newspaper story, they said that a actor was hit by an car who was riding a bicycle.

_____

7. Jimmy and him did not want no one to read the story he had wrote last week. _____

_____

8. The grade I got on this math test tells me that I should of studied thorougher. _____

_____

9. Clapping and cheering wildly, the pitcher whom stood on the mound waved to the crowd in

the stands. _____

_____

10. Jason and her carefully planned his vacation in the kitchen. _____

_____

COMMON ERRORS

Review B: Mechanics

EXERCISE Revise the following letter, correcting any errors in capitalization, adding or deleting punctuation marks, and correcting any misspelled or misused words.

Example [1] The team agreed to ~~meat~~ *meet* at 8.00, however, some members were late.

[1] 109 cunningham lane

[2] hilltown mi 32333

[3] January 22 2001

[4] Dear sir or Madam

  [5] Ive been a longtime fan of your granola bars for many reasons there taste there freshness and there nutritional value. [6] However I never would have imagined they would save my life what a shock! [7] If you need to verify the following story you can look up the newspaper story titled Granola bars Win Bears Stamp of Approval in the January 19 edition of The hilltown gazette. [8] The story by the way is also available on the Internet.

  [9] During a vacation to Hiawatha national forest this Fall my father my sister and I went camping. [10] Of course we took with us, a supply of Arthur's Granola Bars for the trip. [11] As we were hiking we noticed shapes following us among the trees, they were black bears. [12] We were frightend but we quickly assumed that they were attracted by the smell of our granola bars. [13] After we tossed the bars on the ground the bears left us alone.

  [14] After we returned the Park Ranger said You should be very careful when hiking. "Weve had many bear sitings this season. [15] Anyway, human food is not good for bears bears usually eat small animals such as mice, and squirrels, insects such as ants and grubs, or fruits, nuts, and roots". [16] We thought maybe you could put a warning on the label of your packages that reads Warning Do not take these granola bars on a camping trip into bear country." [17] Seriously we mean this story as a complement to your product not as a criticism and we hope youve enjoyed it

  [18] Next time well either pack our desert in an airtight container or leave it behind.

[19] Thank's for making such a great product.

[20] Sincerly

Al Dinte

COMMON ERRORS

Review C: Usage and Mechanics

EXERCISE Proofread the following sentences, correcting any errors in usage and mechanics. Underline any words that should be italicized.

Example 1. London, ~~england~~ england, is one of Jills most favorite ~~citys~~ *cities* in the world.

1. All of the students accept Rudy was able to attend the nieghborhoods labor day celebration.

2. Henry and her had wrote a article for the schools newspaper The Paper Panther but they submited there article to late for publication in next weeks edition.

3. Sally's Super Sports are having a spectacular Fall sale in fact each one of the cities four franchise locations including the original store in the crosshill mall will stay open until 10 00 P.M. throughout the weekend.

4. The woman in charge of savings accounts at fairfield bank speaked to the woman about her financial strategy.

5. All of the team members is eligible to win the award however the reason Kathy will probably win is because she recieved less deductions on her test then anyone on the team.

6. Began by William the conqueror 1027?–1087 the tower of london now houses the Crown Jewels crowns, scepters and other treasures and an amazing collection of armor and weapons.

7. Peter who's apartment is on the second floor saw the sleek stylish car peering from his second story window.

8. Although he dont know nothing about the history of the empire state building he thinks its a inspiring building.

9. Theres even a sherlock holmes museum located at as you fans of the great detective will have all ready guessed 221 B baker street.

10. If you go to england Gena said Dont forget to see the Domesday Book the first official record of the land owners living in england.

COMMON ERRORS

Proofreading Application: Directions

Good writers are generally good proofreaders. Readers tend to admire and trust writing that is error-free. Make sure that you correct all errors in grammar, usage, spelling, and punctuation in your writing. Your readers will have more confidence in your words if you have done your best to proofread carefully.

Experienced writers sometimes use intentional sentence fragments or run-on sentences to create a certain style, particularly in works of fiction. However, in a set of directions, you should avoid using fragments and run-ons, as these may confuse your reader.

PROOFREADING ACTIVITY

The following set of directions contains several run-on sentences and sentence fragments. Revise each sentence fragment to make it a complete sentence. Revise each run-on sentence to make at least one complete sentence. Use proofreading symbols to make your corrections.

TO: Roland Camacho

RE: Directions to Party

   Janie's parents giving her a surprise party this Saturday. Since you already plan to see *The Maltese Falcon* at the Great Classics Film Festival earlier that afternoon. Here are the directions you will need.

   To get from the North Hills movie theater to Janie's house. You should leave from the parking lot on the west side of the theater, turning right onto Bessette Avenue. Take the first left. You will then be traveling west on Davies Parkway, continue on this road for six blocks. Until you see the Modern Art Museum on your right. Just past the museum is Constitution Street, after you turn right on Constitution, travel approximately one mile. Look for the subdivision called Lost Maples there is a sign at the entrance. Janie's home two-story with a brick façade and a large front lawn.

Literary Model: Narration

> She looked down to see that her hand lay upon a pile of silk stockings. . . .
>
> "Do you think there are any eights-and-a-half among these?"
>
> There were any number of eights-and-a-half. In fact, there were more of that size than any other. Here was a light blue pair; there were some lavender, some black, and various shades of tan and gray. Mrs. Sommers selected a black pair and looked at them very long and closely. She pretended to be examining their texture, which the clerk assured her was excellent.
>
> "A dollar and ninety-eight cents," she mused aloud. "Well, I'll take this pair." She handed the girl a five-dollar bill and waited for her change and for her parcel. What a very small parcel it was!
>
> —from "A Pair of Silk Stockings" by Kate Chopin

EXERCISE A As the passage above demonstrates, commas can function many ways in literature. As you complete the items below, notice Chopin's varied use of commas.

1. Underline one of the sentences that uses a comma after an introductory element.

2. Circle the sentence that uses a comma to introduce a nonessential clause.

3. Underline twice the sentence that uses commas to separate items in a series.

EXERCISE B

1. Of the four semicolon rules listed below, circle the one that applies to the fifth sentence of the passage.

Use a semicolon between independent clauses that are closely related in thought and that are not joined by a coordinating conjunction.

Use a semicolon between independent clauses joined by a conjunctive adverb or a transitional expression.

A semicolon may be needed before a coordinating conjunction to join independent clauses that contain commas.

Use a semicolon between items in a series if the items contain commas.

Literary Model (continued)

2. In your opinion, which sentence in the passage contains a punctuation mark that is the most effective? Explain why this punctuation mark was necessary for communicating a certain meaning.

_____

_____

_____

EXERCISE C   Using Chopin's passage as a model, write a narrative paragraph in which a person is making a decision about something. In your paragraph, include at least one example of each of the following punctuation marks: comma, semicolon, quotation marks, question mark, exclamation point.

_____

_____

_____

_____

_____

_____

_____

_____

_____

_____

_____

_____

_____

_____

EXERCISE D   Read over your narrative paragraph, and decide which punctuation mark contributed to your story the most effectively. Explain how this punctuation mark helped you communicate your ideas.

_____

_____

_____

Writing Application: Description

Confusing *it's* and *its* is a very common problem. *It's* is a contraction meaning "it is." *Its* is a possessive pronoun that shows ownership. Remember that possessive pronouns—such as *yours*, *his*, and *theirs*—never have apostrophes. If you are unsure of which spelling is correct, try this test: "When in doubt, spell it out."

   EXAMPLE   The dog buried its bone.

"The dog buried it is bone" makes no sense, so the possessive pronoun *its* is correct. This test works with other confusing pairs, too, such as *your* and *you're* and *their* and *they're*.

WRITING ACTIVITY

For an earth sciences class, students are studying habitats—not exotic, faraway habitats, but habitats that surround us. Choose a small habitat in your neighborhood, perhaps even in your backyard, to describe in detail. You will combine your description with other students' descriptions to produce a clear, specific description of your environment.

PREWRITING   Observation is a key skill in science. Examine the area around your house or neighborhood for some small habitat. Do not rule out the very small. For instance, you could write about insect life in your backyard. Write about what you see. Sketch what you see. You know what life needs from a habitat: food, shelter, protection from predators, and the opportunity to procreate. Identify the source of these requirements in the habitat you choose to describe.

WRITING   Consider organizing your report spatially. You could also organize your report in logical order by discussing in separate paragraphs each of the requirements for survival. Do not forget to describe the life form as well.

REVISING   Because you are describing a real-world scene, you must help readers see, hear, feel, smell, and perhaps even taste the scene. Use vivid, specific sensory details as you write.

PUBLISHING   Check your report for grammar, usage, spelling, and punctuation. Pay special attention to your use of contractions, possessive pronouns, and possessive nouns. Then, combine your report with the reports of your classmates to create a panoramic description of your local environment.

EXTENDING YOUR WRITING

You may wish to develop this exercise into a longer essay. Beginning with the report you wrote, continue to investigate the habitat. What do the habitat and the creatures that live in it contribute to the larger environment? What environmental influences threaten the habitat? How can our awareness of the habitat help protect it, if it is in need of protection? This essay could eventually become a project that results in some sort of environmental action.

COMMON ERRORS | Language in Context: Writing Application

Selecting Appropriate Conjunctions

EXERCISE A For each of the following sentences, choose an appropriate coordinating or subordinating conjunction to fill in the blank. The hint in parentheses tells you what kind of relationship the conjunction should express.

Example 1. The teacher distributed sample questions yesterday _____*so that*_____ the students could prepare for the test. *(purpose or result)*

1. We planned to attend the state championship in New Orleans, _____ the game was postponed due to rain. *(contrast)*

2. Our elm tree had to be cut down _____ it had Dutch elm disease. *(cause or reason)*

3. _____ Alfredo was reading a novel by Gary Soto, he was reminded of some of his own experiences. *(time)*

4. We did not go back to Laos for many years, _____ we wanted to. *(condition)*

5. _____ our English class finished reading *Hamlet*, we attended a performance of the play. *(time)*

6. _____ most people know the answer to it, an enduring trivia question is "What are the names of the five Great Lakes?" *(condition)*

7. Several birds splashed about in the bird bath _____ it had been refilled with water. *(time)*

8. _____ we do not win the game tomorrow, we will not be able to play in the finals. *(condition)*

9. _____ you have a topographical map, it is very easy to get lost while hiking in the Wasatch Mountains. *(condition)*

10. _____ you pull out of the driveway, be sure that your seat belt is securely fastened. *(time)*

SENTENCES

Selecting Appropriate Conjunctions (continued)

EXERCISE B   For each of the following sentences, choose an appropriate coordinating or subordinating conjunction to fill in the blank. The hint in parentheses tells you what kind of relationship the conjunction should express.

Example 1. _____*Unless*_____ the drought ends soon, many of the crops will be ruined. *(condition)*

11. _____ there was a leak under the sink, we had to call a plumber. *(cause or reason)*

12. The city council approved funding for the construction of a new community center,

     _____ they have not selected the site yet. *(contrast)*

13. _____ she was a comparative newcomer to state politics, her talent and poise quickly

     gained her recognition. *(condition)*

14. The members of the expedition went to bed at sundown _____ they could get an

     early start the next morning. *(purpose or result)*

15. _____ people camp or hike in the woods, they should leave no trace of their passing.

     (place)

16. Do not volunteer for this assignment _____ you are willing to work at least four

     hours a week. *(condition)*

17. _____ the Erie Canal opened, an enormous number of barges began to use it. *(time)*

18. Many people wanted to see the exhibit, _____ the art gallery extended its hours.

     (purpose or result)

19. They did extensive research _____ they began working on the science project. *(time)*

20. The leaf landed in the stream, _____ it was carried away by the current. *(coordination)*

SENTENCES

Subordinating Ideas by Using Adjective Clauses

EXERCISE A Change the emphasis in each of the following sentences. Emphasize the idea that is now in the subordinate clause, and subordinate the idea that is now in the independent clause. You may have to delete words, change the word order, or use a different word to begin the new subordinate clause. Write your revisions on the lines provided.

Example 1. The person who is riding his dirt bike behind our house is our new neighbor, Desmond Parilla. *Desmond Parilla, who is our new neighbor, is riding his dirt bike behind our house.*

1. My father, who loves the outdoors, taught me to fish. _____
_____

2. The professor, who was a mathematical genius, was well liked by many students.
_____

3. The play, which got great reviews, is sold out. _____
_____

4. Flowers that must be planted every year are called annuals. _____
_____

5. Rachel, who volunteers at the hospital, wants to be a pediatrician. _____

6. Carmen Tafolla, who writes popular children's stories, is also well known for her essays.
_____

7. The outdoor amphitheater, where many concerts and plays are held, will be renovated next
year. _____
_____

8. The car show, which comes here every spring, displays cars from the twentieth century.
_____

9. Hummus, which I love, isn't always easy to find in grocery stores. _____
_____

10. Marcy, who has relatives in Vermont, spends her summers there. _____
_____

SENTENCES

Subordinating Ideas by Using Adjective Clauses (continued)

EXERCISE B   Change the emphasis in each of the following sentences. Emphasize the idea that is now in the subordinate clause, and subordinate the idea that is now in the independent clause. You may have to delete words, change the word order, or use a different word to begin the new subordinate clause. Write your revisions on the lines provided.

Example 1. I thought the documentary, which was about the American Revolution, was

fascinating. *The documentary, which I thought was fascinating, was about the*

American Revolution.

11. Ms. Dimarco, who teaches American history, delivered an amazing lecture.

_____

12. We reviewed our notes in the library, where our study group meets. _____

_____

13. The American troops, who had a certain advantage, were familiar with the terrain.

_____

14. The British commanders, who had been trained in traditional military strategies, were not

prepared to fight an American war. _____

_____

15. The British soldiers, who fought in tight formations, were used to standing in rows.

_____

16. In 1775, the British lost the battle at Concord, where colonists used guerrilla tactics.

_____

17. General Washington, who transformed the Continental Army, sought experienced military

officers. _____

_____

18. The soldiers of the Continental Army, who used guerrilla tactics, did not fight in formation.

_____

19. Friedrich von Steuben, who was a Prussian general, helped train the American troops.

_____

20. American soldiers, who incorporated European battle tactics into their fighting style, were able

to defeat the British through closed combat. _____

_____

HOLT HANDBOOK | Fifth Course

Revising Sentences by Using Parallel Structure

EXERCISE A Some of the following sentences are out of balance. Bring balance to them by putting the ideas in parallel form. You may need to delete, add, or move some words. If a sentence is already correct, write *C*. Write your answers on the lines provided.

Example 1. The mechanic suggests changing the oil and to rotate the tires every three months or three thousand miles. *The mechanic suggests changing the oil and rotating the tires every three months or three thousand miles.*

1. Every morning, my grandmother walks around her neighborhood, works in her garden, and then reading the paper occupies the remainder of the morning. _____

_____

2. Each book should be cataloged, labeled, and returned to the shelf. _____

_____

3. It's always a good idea to exercise as well as monitoring your sugar and fat intake. _____

_____

4. For their art project, Jamal and Jordan will create clay models of their cartoon characters, or painting several cells for an animated short feature is what they'll do. _____

_____

5. To enjoy nature and to see awe-inspiring sights are reasons why some Americans visit National Parks. _____

_____

6. The job duties include filing, answering phones, and to make photocopies. _____

_____

7. Two things we learned in Mr. Quadri's chemistry lab were to wear safety goggles and making careful measurements. _____

_____

8. Decide which healthful dishes you enjoy and keep the ingredients in your pantry. _____

_____

9. Building these bookshelves required less effort than to build the desk. _____

_____

10. The ducks at the park are usually swimming in the pond or sit along the shore. _____

_____

Revising Sentences by Using Parallel Structure (continued)

EXERCISE B Some of the following sentences are out of balance. Bring balance to them by putting the ideas in parallel form. You may need to delete, add, or move some words. If a sentence is already correct, write C. Write your answers on the lines provided.

Example 1. I prefer hearing music performed live, but to listen to recorded music is sometimes my only option. *I prefer hearing music performed live, but listening to recorded music is sometimes my only option.*

11. Listening to a variety of music and to get to know different musical techniques are two ways to fully appreciate music. _____

_____

12. Is classical music or playing jazz music more difficult? _____

_____

13. As lovers of jazz music know, jazz requires skill and that musicians be disciplined. _____

_____

14. Jazz fans admire a great horn player's improvisational ability and having technical skill. _____

_____

15. Not only jazz trumpet players but also musicians who play classical violin profit from a sound knowledge of music theory. _____

_____

16. In a symphony orchestra, the musicians must not only read music with great facility but also follow the directions of the conductor. _____

_____

17. In a marching band, having stamina is as important as to play an instrument well. _____

_____

18. Being an orchestra conductor requires a knowledge of music and that one have good pitch. _____

_____

19. Critics praise a musician's technical skill and to applaud his or her charisma. _____

_____

20. Even people who don't play an instrument can appreciate music and benefit from it. _____

_____

SENTENCES

Revising Paragraphs for Clarity

EXERCISE A Faulty coordination and subordination and faulty parallelism make the following paragraphs confusing. Using proofreading symbols, revise the paragraphs to make each faulty sentence
clear and smooth. You may need to add, delete, or rearrange some words in the sentences. Remember
to check the placement of correlative conjunctions.

Example   Discussing animal migration and ~~to~~ explain~ing~ certain animal behaviors are the two

purposes of my oral report. *I believe that* My report will be informative. ~~I believe.~~

Many animals migrate long distances with the changing of the seasons. Some travel in search of

food and water. Others travel to breeding grounds. Scientists believe. Many animals originally

migrated to America from Asia across the land bridge.

There are now many barriers to animal migration. These not only are cities and dams, but also

roads and highways. Because of these barriers, most migrations now involve animals, such as

whales and bats, that swimming or fly. Baleen whales spend the summer in the polar seas eating

plankton. Then they migrate thousands of miles to temperate or tropical seas for winter. Whales

have excellent vision. They also use echolocation, a sort of natural sonar. It helps them find their

way. Bats also use echolocation to navigate and finding insects to eat. Several kinds of bats in

Europe and Asia migrate with the changing of the season. The red bat, the large hoary bat, and the

silver-haired bat fly from Canada to as far south as Georgia and South Carolina. They also fly to

Florida.

How do migrating animals know exactly where to go? This question fascinates people. They

study animal behavior. Perhaps migratory animals can smell the trails laid down by previous gen-

erations. Or perhaps they respond to environmental cues such as cold weather.

SENTENCES

Revising Paragraphs for Clarity (continued)

EXERCISE B   Faulty coordination and subordination and faulty parallelism make the following paragraphs confusing. Using proofreading symbols, revise the paragraphs to make each faulty sentence clear and smooth. You may need to add, delete, or rearrange some words in the sentences. Remember to check the placement of correlative conjunctions.

Example   At the end of a long day of going to classes, ~~to~~ study*ing*, and working part time at a
local restaurant, Jason relaxes. *and* ~~He~~ enjoys an hour of solitude.

Fortunately, Jason lives only a short walk from a small lake. Sometimes he takes a book or his CD player. At other times, he just walks over to the lake and sitting on a rock that juts out over the water. He watches birds flying overhead. He listens to the water lapping against the shore. Sometimes he lies back on the rock, which is smooth and that is comfortable. He watches clouds move slowly across the sky. The shadows grow longer as evening arrives. Time seems to slow down. His mind and body relax.

At first, he felt guilty about just sitting. Most of his friends do not take time just to be alone and doing nothing. They worry that he is unhappy. He reassures them that he is not unhappy. He likes spending time alone. He can clear his mind and enjoying the sights and sounds of nature. It is refreshing and which relaxes him, so he plans to go on doing it even though nobody else seems to understand.

Identifying and Revising Sentence Fragments

EXERCISE A Decide which of the following word groups are sentences and which are fragments. If an item contains a fragment, revise the fragment to make it a complete sentence. If the item contains only complete sentences, write *C*. Write your answers on the line provided.

Example 1. Many tasks must be completed. Before a film, TV show, or play can be produced.

Many tasks must be completed before a film, TV show, or play can be produced.

1. Every object that an audience sees in a play, TV show, or movie is called a prop, or property. The property master is responsible for finding the props. _____

_____

2. A property master has to be a good scavenger. Because props can be found in odd places.

_____

3. First, the property master reads the script. Then, talks to the designer and the director.

_____

4. The property master makes a detailed list of props. Thinks about where props might be found.

_____

5. The budget always a concern in the theater. The property master must be aware of the budget.

_____

6. For science fiction movies, the property master sometimes has to build expensive props.

_____

7. The property master has lists. The "pull" list a list of props that the theater or studio might already own. _____

_____

8. The "buy" list is another kind of list. Includes things that have to be purchased.

_____

9. The property master ensures that the props are on the stage. Checks that they are ready to be used by the actors. _____

_____

10. In the theater, sometimes have to be placed or moved in full view of the audience. In these cases, the property master wears black to be less noticeable. _____

_____

Identifying and Revising Sentence Fragments (continued)

EXERCISE B Decide which of the following word groups are sentences and which are fragments. If an item contains a fragment, revise the fragment to make it a complete sentence. If the item contains only complete sentences, write C. Write your answers on the line provided.

Example 1. An Englishman, Peter Durand, invented the first tin can in 1810. Was invented to preserve food used to supply sailors. *It was invented to preserve food used to supply sailors.*

11. For forty-four years, there were cans but no can openers. The lack of an opener a problem.

   _____

12. In 1812, British soldiers their bayonets or shot at the cans to open them.

   _____

13. Some historians believe that the bayonet was originally intended as a can opener.

   _____

14. Explorers to the Arctic in 1824 were instructed to open cans of food with a chisel and a hammer.

   _____

15. In 1858, Ezra J. Warner of Waterbury, Connecticut, invented the first can opener. Was large, unwieldy, and even dangerous. _____

   _____

16. Although tin cans had been invented in 1810. They did not become popular in the United States until 1861. _____

   _____

17. By 1895, canned food was common in America. Life more convenient for busy families.

   _____

18. Despite the introduction of frozen food. Canned food has remained popular.

   _____

19. Many people use electric can openers. Open cans of all sizes in just a few seconds.

   _____

20. Multi-purpose pocketknives, which often include can openers, are also popular.

   _____

Revising to Eliminate Sentence Fragments

EXERCISE A   Some of the following items contain complete sentences; others contain fragments. If an item contains a fragment, revise the fragment to make it a complete sentence. If the item contains only complete sentences, write *C*. Write your answers on the line provided.

Example 1. Hollywood is a center of the entertainment industry in the United States. Along with New York City and Nashville. *Hollywood, along with New York City and Nashville, is a center of the entertainment industry in the United States.*

1. New York City is known as the home of live theater in the United States. Television shows are produced there. And a large number of movies, also. _____

_____

2. Nashville, Tennessee, is home to the booming country-western music business. _____

3. In 1853, the first house was built in Hollywood. Which is northwest of Los Angeles. _____

4. Horace Wilcox laid out a subdivision in 1887. An immigrant from Kansas. _____

5. After making the first movies on the East Coast. Producers decided to move to Hollywood. _____

6. These early moviemakers liked Hollywood because of its mild climate. Also because of its diverse terrain. _____

_____

7. In Hollywood's early days. Movie moguls such as D. W. Griffith and Samuel Goldwyn started and managed the big studios. _____

_____

8. With the growing popularity of television in the 1950s, fewer movies were made. Hollywood adapted, becoming the center for television production. _____

_____

9. Today, the movie and television businesses coexist. In sunny Hollywood. _____

_____

10. Nashville remains famous for its country-music hits. And for the stars that perform the hits. _____

_____

SENTENCES

Revising to Eliminate Sentence Fragments (continued)

EXERCISE B Some of the following items contain complete sentences; others contain fragments. If an item contains a fragment, revise the fragment to make it a complete sentence. If the item contains only complete sentences, write C. Write your answers on the line provided.

Example 1. When ranchers came to Texas. They dreamed of owning their own land.

When ranchers came to Texas, they dreamed of owning their own land.

11. In 1810 farmers and ranchers to Texas from the eastern United States.

_____

12. There were a few small towns, but no cities. Practically no roads. _____

_____

13. Moses Austin got permission from Spain in 1820. To take settlers into the area.

_____

14. In the early years. Texas was part of the Spanish colony of New Spain.

_____

15. Mexico gained independence from Spain in 1821. Many settlers became Mexican citizens.

_____

16. Who died in 1821. Moses Austin never saw his dream become reality.

_____

17. However, his son, Stephen F. Austin, assumed leadership of the early settlers.

_____

18. The year 1835 was a turning point in Texas history. Although some adventurous settlers

wanted independence from Mexico, most wanted only to tend their farms and ranches.

_____

_____

19. In order to preserve the rights granted to settlers by the Mexican Constitution of 1824. Many

settlers fought the Mexican army. _____

_____

20. In 1836, General Santa Anna, the president of Mexico. Decided to march north and settle the

dispute. The result was the Battle of the Alamo. _____

_____

Revising Run-on Sentences

EXERCISE A Revise each of the following run-on sentences by using the method given in parentheses. If you add a conjunction, make sure your revised version shows the appropriate relationship between the ideas. Be sure to check your revised version for correct punctuation and capitalization. Use proofreading symbols to show your changes.

Example 1. Mysterious rocks are found in California's Death Valley, they move across the

surface of the desert in peculiar ways. *(two sentences)*

1. Some of the rocks weigh only a few ounces others are more than seven hundred pounds.

   (semicolon, conjunctive adverb, and comma)

2. The area where they are found is an old lake bed, it is almost perfectly flat. *(semicolon)*

3. A few of the rocks move in straight paths others move in curving paths. *(comma and

   coordinating conjunction)*

4. Nobody has ever seen one of the rocks move, scientists are actively studying the phenomenon.

   (subordinating conjunction)

5. No one knows for sure why the rocks move perhaps their movement requires the perfect

   combination of wind, ice, and slick clay. *(semicolon)*

6. One scientist believes that the rocks are moved by ice sheets blown by wind over water others

   think that wind alone might be responsible. *(comma and coordinating conjunction)*

7. Some scientists survey and record the tracks of the rocks, others study the force needed to

   move a rock. *(semicolon, conjunctive adverb, and comma)*

8. One theory is that dust devils—small but powerful tornadoes—make the rocks move one

   geologist flew a plane over the area to see how the wind from the propeller affected the rocks.

   (two sentences)

9. I am interested in unexplained phenomena, I have collected information on the rocks in Death

   Valley. *(subordinating conjunction)*

10. I have also collected information on another odd area it is called the Bermuda Triangle.

    (semicolon)

SENTENCES

Revising Run-on Sentences (continued)

EXERCISE B Revise each of the following run-on sentences by using the method given in parentheses. If you add a conjunction, make sure your revised version shows the appropriate relationship between the ideas. Be sure to check your revised version for correct punctuation and capitalization. Use proofreading symbols to show your changes.

Example 1. Art forgery is a serious crime forgers paint a picture, supposedly created by a famous artist, well enough to fool the experts. (*two sentences*)

11. Elmyr de Hory was a skilled and versatile painter, he was able to pass his work off as that of Picasso, Chagall, Cézanne, and others. (*subordinating conjunction*)

12. He was clever he was caught when he tried to sell two "original" Matisse paintings before the paint was dry. (*comma and coordinating conjunction*)

13. He could no longer create forgeries he began to sell "paintings in the manner of" famous artists. (*subordinating conjunction*)

14. A writer named Clifford Irving wrote a biography of de Hory de Hory soon became famous beyond art circles. (*semicolon*)

15. Jean de Sperati was another famous forger, he created "rare" postage stamps that could fool the experts. (*two sentences*)

16. The stamps he created were forgeries he sold them as the real thing. (*comma and coordinating conjunction*)

17. He was never caught for creating his "rare" stamps de Sperati's great skill got him into trouble. (*semicolon, conjunctive adverb, and comma*)

18. He was accused of exporting capital in the form of genuine stamps from France he convinced the authorities to charge him with the lesser offense of forgery by creating a fake stamp for them. (*subordinating conjunction*)

19. Other types of forgery include forging signatures and forging currency both types involve the use of artistic skill. (*two sentences*)

20. These forgeries may be wonderful examples of the artist's skill the artists have robbed themselves of the pleasure of displaying their skill openly in the art world. (*subordinating conjunction*)

Revising to Eliminate Fragments and Run-ons

EXERCISE A Revise the following paragraphs to eliminate fragments and run-ons. Add or delete words wherever necessary. Be sure to check your revised version for correct capitalization and punctuation. Use proofreading symbols to show your changes.

Example   While researching a topic for my history paper, I found some fascinating facts about an island. That is on the east coast.

Ellis Island sits. In New York City's harbor with one of the most spectacular views in the United States. Visitors can see New York City and the Statue of Liberty. Which is a popular attraction. The island has had an interesting past. History records show. That the Dutch originally named it Oyster Island. The government used the island to store weapons in the nineteenth century. It became well known. As one of the major gateways for immigrants to America. People came to America from many places. Such as Europe, Africa, Asia, and Latin America. Between 1892 and 1943. Sixteen to seventeen million immigrants first set foot on American soil at Ellis Island.

Many immigrants were unable. To speak English when they arrived. They had just taken a long and sometimes hazardous sea voyage they had very little money in their pockets. What they did have was a sense of adventure and a strong desire to make a new life for themselves and their families. These bold people spread out. Across the country. Some sought communities made up of their former compatriots others established new towns throughout the country.

Revising to Eliminate Fragments and Run-ons (continued)

EXERCISE B   Revise the following paragraphs to eliminate the fragments and run-ons. Add or delete words wherever necessary. Be sure to check your revised version for correct capitalization and punctuation. Use proofreading symbols to show your changes.

Example   When I was at my uncle's house last weekend, He told me about some unusual aspects of the human body. here are a few of the facts.

If you were to live all by yourself on a deserted island. You would still not be alone. Because living on your body are thousands of invisible microorganisms. One square inch of your shoulder may contain hundreds of bacteria millions more may live on your arm.

A somewhat ugly creature. A follicle mite is one kind of microorganism. For the most part. The follicle mite lives in the hairs of your eyelashes and nose. It crawls down the shaft of a hair, it climbs down but it does not come back up. With its head down. It gathers fluid from skin cells. There are about ten mites per follicle, each one is about a hundredth of an inch long. Four of them would fit in the period. At the end of a sentence. They are harmless scrubbing and taking medicine cannot remove them. It is even possible. That they may be beneficial to humans.

Other kinds of microorganisms that live on the human body are funguses and viruses. Humans provide homes and meals for creatures. Such as fleas, lice, and ticks. These and other organisms that inhabit humans do sometimes cause diseases. Which are more widespread in developing countries. It is hard to become used to the idea. That the human body is a kind of ecosystem. Humans are a source of life. For millions of creatures that cannot be seen. There is nothing you can do. To be completely free of these tiny organisms.

SENTENCES

Inserting Single Words and Prepositional Phrases

EXERCISE A   Combine each group of short, related sentences into one sentence. Insert adjectives, adverbs, or prepositional phrases. If needed, change the forms of the words before you insert them. Add commas where they are necessary. Write your new sentences on the lines provided.

Example 1. More than ten thousand species have been identified. These are species of butterflies and moths. The species were found in North America. The butterflies and moths had been identified by 1993. _By 1993, more than ten thousand species of butterflies and moths had been identified in North America._

1. When you see butterflies, notice the patterns and the antennae. The patterns are on their wings. The antennae are on their heads. _____

_____

2. Butterflies and moths have two pairs of wings. The wings are large. All butterflies and moths have this characteristic. _____

_____

3. Butterflies have threadlike antennae. This type of antennae is not like moth antennae. Butterflies' antennae are scaleless. _____

_____

4. The antennae on moths are varied. Some may appear feathery. _____

_____

5. Male moths respond to chemical signals. The signals come from female moths. The signals are powerful. _____

_____

6. Have you ever wondered about the markings? The markings are on butterflies' wings.

_____

7. Wing color and patterns play a part. They play a part in the mating of butterflies. The part they play is key to the mating process.

_____

8. The wings of some butterflies and moths draw the attention of predators. The wings have spots. The wings draw attention away from more vital body parts. _____

_____

Language and Sentence Skills Practice

427

Inserting Single Words and Prepositional Phrases (continued)

9. Butterflies with similar markings may fly together. This is for mutual protection. The

butterflies are of different species. _____

_____

10. Some butterflies have red, orange, or yellow markings that indicate they are poisonous. The

butterflies are poisonous to predators. The markings appear on a dark background.

_____

_____

EXERCISE B Combine each group of short, related sentences into one sentence. Insert adjectives,
adverbs, or prepositional phrases. If needed, change the forms of the words before you insert them.
Add commas where they are necessary. Write your new sentences on the lines provided.

Example 1. Eugene O'Neill attained a goal of writing autobiographical works. It was a lifelong

goal. He realized his desire with his last plays. *With his last plays, Eugene O'Neill*

attained a lifelong goal of writing autobiographical works.

11. O'Neill wrote plays. His plays won many awards. His plays are about tragic relationships and

conflicts. _____

_____

12. O'Neill's play *Bound East for Cardiff* was first staged by the Provincetown Players. The play

was staged in 1916. It was presented on Cape Cod in Massachusetts. _____

_____

13. O'Neill joined the theater group. It was an experimental group. O'Neill joined the group after

studying at Harvard. _____

_____

14. O'Neill used European techniques. He used these techniques in many of his plays. The

techniques were experimental. _____

_____

15. O'Neill helped make theater an art form. He helped make theater an art form in the United

States. He made it more respected. _____

428 HOLT HANDBOOK | Fifth Course

Inserting Participial and Absolute Phrases

EXERCISE A Combine each of the following sentence pairs. Reduce one sentence to a participial or an absolute phrase. Change the form of the verb if necessary. Insert the phrase into the other sentence. Be sure to place a participial phrase next to the noun or pronoun it modifies. Write your new sentences on the lines provided.

Example 1. I saw dozens of paperbacks. I looked at my bookshelves.

Looking at my bookshelves, I saw dozens of paperbacks.

1. Paperbacks became a very popular book format in the mid-twentieth century. They cost less than hardcover books. _____

    _____

2. The book has taken many forms over the centuries. It was developed as a portable tool of communication. _____

    _____

3. Ancient Egypt's papyrus roll is probably the book's ancestor. It dates to around 3000 B.C.

    _____

4. Books in ancient China were valued as tools of education. They were created from wood or bamboo strips bound together. _____

    _____

5. The parchment leaves of the Romans represented a significant change in bookmaking. They carried text on both sides. _____

    _____

6. Manuscript books were made by monks in the Middle Ages. They were copied by hand.

    _____

7. Printing spread rapidly in the late fifteenth century. It sparked a revolution in learning.

    _____

8. Women became a part of the reading public. This change began in the seventeenth century.

    _____

9. Machines began to be used extensively for printing in the nineteenth century. The demand for books increased. _____

    _____

SENTENCES

Inserting Participial and Absolute Phrases (continued)

10. Book collectors are aware of the value of old and rare books. They buy and trade books as one

would deal in valuable art. _____

_____

EXERCISE B Combine each of the following sentence pairs. Reduce one sentence to a participial or an absolute phrase. Change the form of the verb if necessary. Insert the phrase into the other sentence. Be sure to place a participial phrase next to the noun or pronoun it modifies. Write your new sentences on the lines provided.

Example 1. Hungry mosquitoes buzzed around the scientists' bodies. They collected specimens

for study. *Hungry mosquitoes buzzing around their bodies, the scientists collected*

specimens for study.

11. Malaria cases are increasing again. Many malaria-carrying mosquitoes have developed a

resistance to insecticides. _____

_____

12. Malaria is a serious disease. It infects about 250 million people a year worldwide.

_____

13. A parasite causes malaria in humans. The parasite is carried by the female anopheles mosquito.

_____

14. Malaria-carrying mosquitoes transmit a form of the parasite. The mosquitoes infect people

with a bite. _____

_____

15. Malaria is most common in tropical and subtropical regions. The climate there is favorable for

the mosquitoes that transmit the disease. _____

_____

Inserting Appositive Phrases

EXERCISE A Combine each pair of sentences by turning one of the sentences into an appositive phrase. You may see several ways to create the appositive; choose the combination that sounds best to you. Be sure to set off the appositive phrase with commas. Write your new sentences on the lines provided.

Example 1. Patricia Espinoza is trying out for the track team. Patricia is my best friend.

Patricia Espinoza, my best friend, is trying out for the track team.

1. Many high school athletes need a physical examination. The exam is a requirement for

   competitive sports. _____

   _____

2. During an exam the physician can explain the cardiovascular system. The physician is often

   the school doctor. _____

   _____

3. The cardiovascular system includes the heart, the arteries, the veins, and the capillaries. The

   cardiovascular system is a vital part of the body. _____

   _____

4. The heart is a hollow muscle in the chest. The heart is one of the body's main organs.

   _____

5. Oxygen-rich blood flows to the heart from the lungs. The lungs are part of the respiratory

   system. _____

   _____

6. The heart pumps the blood to all parts of the body through the arteries. The arteries are a

   network of tubes with thick walls. _____

   _____

7. Blood returns to the heart through veins. Veins are a network of tubes similar to arteries but

   with thinner walls. _____

   _____

8. Capillaries connect the arteries and veins. Capillaries are tiny blood vessels.

   _____

9. In the capillaries, oxygen and carbon dioxide pass between the blood and body cells. Oxygen

   and carbon dioxide are gases inhaled and exhaled through the lungs.

   _____

Inserting Appositive Phrases (continued)

10. Nutrients and waste products are also exchanged between the blood and body cells. Nutrients are substances needed for life and growth. _____

_____

EXERCISE B Combine each pair of sentences by turning one of the sentences into an appositive phrase. You may see several ways to create the appositive; choose the combination that sounds best to you. Be sure to set off the appositive phrase with commas. Write your new sentence on the lines provided.

Example 1. The history class outing included a tour of several historical aircraft. The class outing was a field trip to the sea-air-space museum. *The history class outing, a field trip to the sea-air-space museum, included a tour of several historical aircraft.*

11. Aircraft carriers allow airplanes to take off and land at sea. They are essentially mobile airfields.

_____

12. The USS *Intrepid* served as an aircraft carrier in World War II and during the conflict in Vietnam. It is now part of a sea-air-space museum in New York Harbor. _____

_____

_____

13. Planes were launched from the flight deck by a catapult. A catapult is a device that gives the extra thrust planes need to take off from a carrier's short runway. _____

_____

_____

14. Planes landed with the help of a tailhook. The tailhook is a hook near the tail of the plane.

_____

15. The hook catches a steel cable stretched across the flight deck's aft end. The aft end is the part of the runway toward the back of the ship. _____

_____

_____

Coordinating Ideas

EXERCISE A Combine each of the following sets of sentences by forming a compound element. Choose a coordinating conjunction that expresses the correct relationship between the ideas. Add punctuation where necessary. Use proofreading symbols to show your changes.

Example 1. The distinctive art of Diego Rivera is well known *and* ~~by many art enthusiasts. It is also~~ well loved by many art enthusiasts.

1. Diego Rivera created large, bold murals. His work revived Latin American fresco painting.

2. Rivera studied painting in Europe between 1907 and 1921. He became friends with famous artists there.

3. The simplified forms and bold colors used by some European painters influenced him. Rivera did not develop his own style until he returned to Mexico.

4. Rivera wanted to create a new art based on national themes. David Alfaro Siqueiros, another Mexican artist, also wanted to create a new art based on national themes.

5. Rivera believed that art should be available to all people. He began painting murals on public buildings.

6. His murals depict farmers, factory workers, American Indians, and Spanish soldiers. Many relate to Mexican history.

7. The traditions of native Mexican artists can be seen in much of Rivera's work. The designs of native Mexican artists can be seen in much of Rivera's work.

8. Rivera's largest mural portrayed the history of Mexico. He died before he could finish it.

9. Like writers, artists often cause controversy with their work. Artists often cause heated debate with their work.

10. Rivera's paintings caused controversy in the United States. Rivera's paintings caused controversy in Mexico.

SENTENCES

Coordinating Ideas (continued)

EXERCISE B   Combine each of the following sets of sentences by forming a compound element. Choose a coordinating conjunction that expresses the correct relationship between the ideas. Add punctuation where necessary. Use proofreading symbols to show your changes.

Example 1. Dian Fossey worked for a while as an occupational therapist. She became famous for her study of mountain gorilla behavior.

11. Dian Fossey worked as a zoologist. She studied the mountain gorilla.

12. Jane Goodall was always interested in animal behavior. She became famous for her research on chimpanzees.

13. Fossey was not satisfied to learn about animal behavior from books. Goodall was not satisfied to learn about animal behavior from books.

14. In Africa, Fossey studied animals in their natural habitats in Rwanda's Virunga Mountains. Goodall studied animals in their natural habitats in the Gombe Stream Game Reserve.

15. Fossey examined the social structure, communication, and habits of the mountain gorilla. Goodall learned about the complex social behaviors and intellectual abilities of the chimpanzee.

16. Goodall wrote many books, most notably *In the Shadow of Man* in 1971. Fossey published her findings in her only book, *Gorillas in the Mist*, in 1983.

17. Fossey worked to protect mountain gorillas from hunters and other threats. She put herself in danger by doing so.

18. Fossey was killed in 1985 at her campsite, possibly by poachers. Goodall has remained the foremost expert on chimpanzees for many years.

19. These two woman worked in remote locations in foreign countries. They have inspired many students in schools around the world.

20. The influences of many great scientists continue to be felt for generations. The inspiration of these scientists is felt as well.

SENTENCES

Subordinating Ideas

EXERCISE A Combine each of the following pairs of sentences by turning one sentence into a subordinate clause. Write your new sentences on the lines provided.

Example 1. This book brings life to people and events related in history books. The book documents the cultures of various North American peoples.

This book, which documents the cultures of various North American peoples, brings life

to people and events related in history books.

1. The Chickasaw lived in Mississippi and Alabama. They spoke a Muskogean language.

_____

2. At first, the Chickasaw traveled over a huge area. They finally settled within this area.

_____

3. Many American Indians lived close together in villages. The Chickasaw spread out along a

river or stream. _____

_____

4. The Chickasaw lived in the woods. They used forest materials to build pole-frame structures.

_____

5. The Chickasaw had an interesting way of catching fish. It involved poisoning the water.

_____

6. They put a mild poison into a lake or pond. The poison was made of green walnut husks.

_____

7. The poison took effect. The Chickasaw could gather the fish. _____

_____

8. The Chickasaw also hunted deer. Fish could not supply all their needs. _____

_____

9. The Chickasaw's first contact with Europeans was probably in 1540. Hernando De Soto's expe-

dition arrived in their region. _____

_____

10. In the 1830s, the Chickasaw were forced to move to Oklahoma. Several groups of displaced

American Indians lived there. _____

_____

SENTENCES

Subordinating Ideas (continued)

EXERCISE B Combine each of the following pairs of sentences by turning one sentence into a subordinate clause. Write your new sentence on the lines provided.

Example 1. The lift has been a part of architecture for centuries. The lift is an elevator.

The lift, which is an elevator, has been a part of architecture for centuries.

11. The Romans were already using hoists, or lifting platforms, in the first century B.C. We think of the elevator as a fairly recent invention. _____

_____

12. In the early nineteenth century, steam power was used for lifts. Lifts previously had been run by human, animal, or water power. _____

_____

13. Elevator machines in operation before the 1850s were mainly for hoisting freight. The ropes used on lifts broke easily. _____

_____

14. An important development occurred in 1853. The development guaranteed passenger safety. _____

_____

15. That year, Elisha Otis introduced a safety hoist. It was an elevator with a safety device. _____

_____

16. At a public show, Otis gave a demonstration. The demonstration showed how the device prevented an elevator from falling. _____

_____

17. A hoist lifted Otis high above the ground. Then he asked someone to cut the lifting rope. _____

_____

18. The rope was cut. Clamps grabbed the elevator platform guide rails. _____

_____

19. The elevator did not fall. People present at the demonstration were astonished. _____

_____

20. In 1857, Otis installed the first safety passenger elevator in a New York City department store. It would serve many people there. _____

_____

SENTENCES

Review A: **Coordinating and Subordinating Ideas**

EXERCISE A Use either coordination or subordination to combine each of the following pairs of sentences. You may see more than one way to combine a sentence pair. Write the combination that sounds best to you. Write your new sentences on the lines provided.

Example 1. My hobby is model railroads. I study information on old railway systems.

Since my hobby is model railroads, I study information on old railway systems.

1. The Baltimore and Ohio Railroad was completed in 1827. Baltimore grew rapidly in the following years. _____

_____

2. Baltimore was established in 1729. Today it is a financial, industrial, and shipping center.

_____

3. Baltimore's port opens to the sea through the Chesapeake and Delaware Canal. It also opens to the sea through Chesapeake Bay. _____

_____

_____

4. Visitors to Baltimore admire its harbor. They also explore its historical sites.

_____

5. The original fifteen-star flag was sewn in Baltimore by Mary Young Pickersgill. Few people are aware of this. _____

_____

6. Baltimore is the birthplace of Babe Ruth. It is a destination for many baseball fans.

_____

7. Lacrosse is popular in this city. Baltimore's Lacrosse Hall of Fame shows this popularity.

_____

8. Visitors to the city should recognize another fact. Baltimore has a great literary tradition.

_____

9. Edgar Allan Poe lived in Baltimore. He wrote the poem "The Raven." _____

_____

10. The famous essayist H. L. Mencken lived in Baltimore. He described it in glowing terms as an especially civilized city. _____

_____

SENTENCES

Review A: **Coordinating and Subordinating Ideas** (continued)

EXERCISE B Use either coordination or subordination to combine each of the following pairs of sentences. You may see more than one way to combine a sentence pair. Write the combination that sounds best to you. Write your new sentences on the lines provided.

Example 1. Have you seen the docks and factories? They huddle on many lakefronts.

Have you seen the docks and factories that huddle on many lakefronts?

11. Grant Park is on the shores of Lake Michigan. It has been called Chicago's "front yard."

_____

12. The park provides a dramatic setting for outdoor concerts. It attracts people from all over Chicago.

_____

13. Grant Park occupies many acres of lakefront land. This land is prime real estate.

_____

14. The park is on a landfill. It was created when tons of rock and dirt were dumped into Lake Michigan. _____

_____

15. The land might have been used for commercial purposes. The city planners decided it should be a park. _____

_____

16. A lakefront lined with docks and factories would be like the waterfronts of other cities. The city planners were aware of this. _____

_____

17. The natural beauty of the lakefront would not be compromised. Most Chicagoans were pleased to hear this. _____

_____

18. Elaborate plans for the park were drawn up. The process of filling in part of the lake began.

_____

19. The plans included designs for boulevards and beaches. The city also planned yacht basins.

_____

20. Today, Chicagoans are grateful. Their city officials created a beautiful park for them to enjoy.

_____

SENTENCES

Review B: **Revising a Paragraph by Combining Sentences**

EXERCISE A   Using all the sentence-combining skills you have learned, revise each of the following paragraphs for style. Use your judgment about which sentences to combine and how to combine them. Do
not change the meaning of the original paragraphs. Use proofreading symbols to show your changes.

Example 1. Although Roman architecture used many Greek elements, The Romans developed structural

forms of their own.

1. The forms developed by Romans include the vault. A vault is an arched ceiling. The outer

    walls of a vaulted structure held up the roof. Columns were no longer needed as support. A

    vault created a lofty, open space. The space was in the interior of a building. The Baths of

    Caracalla are one example of a vaulted design. The Baths of Caracalla were built in A.D. 217.

    The ruins of the baths are impressive. It is still possible to imagine the height and magnificence

    of the original structure.

2. The eruption of Tambora caused a large number of deaths. It was the largest number of deaths

    since the late eighteenth century. Tambora was a volcano on an Indonesian island. Tambora

    exploded in April 1815. Tambora coughed up huge amounts of magma. It left a thick layer of

    ash everywhere. A good part of its summit cone was destroyed during the eruption. Tambora

    all but disappeared. In its place was a gigantic hollow. The hollow extended for miles in all

    directions. The explosion and tidal waves killed about 10,000 people. The tidal waves were a

    result of the explosion. An additional 82,000 people died from famine and disease. Ash

    deposits on the land caused famine and disease.

SENTENCES

Review B: Revising a Paragraph by Combining Sentences (continued)

EXERCISE B   Using all the sentence-combining skills you have learned, revise each of the following paragraphs for style. Use your judgment about which sentences to combine and how to combine them. Do not change the meaning of the original paragraphs. Use proofreading symbols to show your changes.

Example 1. The Sahara ̶i̶s̶ a formidable desert̶.̶ I̶t is a barren expanse of sand in North Africa.

3. The Sahara is dotted with oases. The oases are sunbaked. Taghaza was in one such oasis. It was called "the salt city." An early world traveler reported on Taghaza. He visited Taghaza in the mid-1300s. He said that the houses and mosques were built of blocks of salt. The buildings were roofed with camel skins. Taghaza had large salt deposits. The inhabitants of Taghaza dug for salt. They found thick slabs of salt. The slabs were lying on top of each other. Taghaza's mines provided traders with salt. Salt was one of the most important commodities in North Africa. It was worth its weight in gold. It was worth that in the marketplace.

4. The original diary of Anne Frank is on display at the Anne Frank House. The Anne Frank House is in Amsterdam. Anne wrote her diary over a two-year period. The diary is a record of her life in hiding during World War II. To escape the Nazis, Anne went into hiding in the annex of her father's office building. Seven other people went into hiding in the annex. Anne and the others went into hiding in July 1942. They could not leave the building. Friends brought them food and other supplies. Unfortunately, the hiding place was discovered in 1944. It was discovered by the Nazis. Anne and the others were taken to the concentration camps. Anne's diary was found later. Today the building is a museum. The building looks the way it did when Anne lived there.

SENTENCES

Varying Sentence Beginnings

EXERCISE A Revise the following sentences by varying their beginnings. The hint in parentheses tells you which type of beginning to use. Write your new sentences on the lines provided.

Example 1. Soccer is played in countries around the world and is popular with men and women alike. *(participial phrase)* _Played in countries around the world, soccer is popular with men and women alike._

1. Soccer has a long history as a fast-moving and popular sport. *(single-word modifiers)*

_____

2. People since ancient times have played games involving two teams moving a ball toward opposite goals. *(prepositional phrase)* _____

_____

3. One team must move the ball beyond the other team's goal line to score in these games. *(infinitive phrase)* _____

_____

4. A game similar to soccer was being played in China by 206 B.C. *(prepositional phrase)*

_____

5. *Harpaston* was played by the ancient Greeks and was related to soccer. *(participial phrase)*

_____

6. Roman soldiers spread the game, which they called *harpastum*, eventually to England and throughout continental Europe. *(single-word modifier)* _____

_____

7. Melees, or large group ball games, were held by competing towns in medieval Europe and included as many as a hundred players. *(participial phrase)* _____

_____

_____

8. Melees continued to be held for centuries in England although they were periodically banned by the king. *(adverb clause)* _____

_____

SENTENCES

Varying Sentence Beginnings (continued)

9. Soccer became a recognized sport when rules for the game began to be established in Great

Britain in the mid-1800s. *(adverb clause)* _____

_____

10. Soccer is now popular all over the world, and the World Cup soccer championship has

become an international event. *(adverb clause)* _____

_____

EXERCISE B Revise the following sentences by varying their beginnings. The hint in parentheses tells
you which type of beginning to use. Write your new sentences on the lines provided.

Example 1. The tree we planted one Arbor Day is growing majestically in the front yard.

(prepositional phrase)

In the front yard, the tree we planted one Arbor Day is growing majestically.

11. Many festivals throughout the world celebrate the recurring seasons of the year. *(prepositional*

phrase) _____

_____

12. Women in many parts of ancient Greece held a festival honoring Demeter, the goddess of

agriculture. *(prepositional phrase)* _____

_____

13. The Romans made offerings to the goddess Juno on March 1 every year to honor married

women. *(infinitive phrase)* _____

_____

14. Schoolchildren plant trees on a Jewish festival day to commemorate the conversion of desert to

farmland. *(infinitive phrase)* _____

_____

15. Japanese children may ask for blessings on an important November festival day if the girls are

three or seven years of age and the boys are five. *(adverb clause)*

_____

_____

SENTENCES

Revising a Paragraph to Vary Sentence Structure

EXERCISE A Revise the paragraph below. Decide which sentences would be better with compound, complex, or compound-complex structures. Use sentence-combining techniques such as appositives, adverb and adjective clauses, and coordinating conjunctions to vary the sentence structure. Write your new paragraph on the lines provided.

Example 1. A caravan is a group of people traveling across the desert together for protection. Often the people are merchants or pilgrims. *A caravan is a group of people, often merchants or pilgrims, traveling across the desert together for protection.*

1. Camels and donkeys are most often used to carry people and supplies in caravans in Africa and Asia. Llamas are usually used in South America. The animals traditionally travel in single file. Larger caravans may extend for miles. In the past, Muslim pilgrims formed traveling groups for the annual journey to the holy city of Mecca. Their caravans sometimes included several thousand people and more than ten thousand camels. Trade caravans are still a familiar sight in parts of Africa and Asia. Camels and donkeys are being replaced by motor vehicles. These animals were an essential part of the traditional caravan.

_____

_____

_____

_____

_____

_____

_____

_____

_____

_____

_____

_____

_____

_____

_____

_____

SENTENCES

Revising a Paragraph to Vary Sentence Structure (continued)

EXERCISE B   Revise the paragraph below. Decide which sentences would sound better with compound, complex, or compound-complex structures. Use sentence-combining techniques such as appositives, adverb and adjective clauses, and coordinating conjunctions to vary the sentence structure. Write your new paragraph on the lines provided.

Example 1. The Fahrenheit temperature scale is named for the eighteenth-century German physicist Gabriel Fahrenheit. He devised the scale.

The Fahrenheit temperature scale is named for the eighteenth-century German physicist

Gabriel Fahrenheit, who devised it.

2. The freezing point of water is 32° on the Fahrenheit scale. The boiling point is 212°. The term *centigrade* is derived from the Latin words *centum* and *gradus*. *Centum* means "hundred." *Gradus* means "step" or "degree." The name reflects the degrees between the freezing and boiling temperatures of water. Water freezes at 0° and boils at 100° centigrade. The centigrade scale is the metric scale for temperature. It was officially renamed the Celsius scale in 1948 after the Swedish astronomer Anders Celsius. Celsius had developed the scale two centuries earlier. Many people still refer to it as the centigrade scale.

_____

_____

_____

_____

_____

_____

_____

_____

_____

_____

_____

_____

_____

SENTENCES

Reducing Wordiness

EXERCISE A Some of the following sentences are wordy. Revise each wordy sentence to make it straightforward and concise. If a sentence does not need revision, write *C* for *correct*. Write your answers on the lines provided.

Example 1. Everyone who lives in the United States has probably heard of the baseball player Babe Ruth, a famous baseball player. *Everyone in the United States has probably heard of the famous baseball player Babe Ruth.*

1. George Herman "Babe" Ruth was one of baseball's most talented players.

_____

2. He began playing minor-league baseball in the year 1914 in the city of Baltimore.

_____

3. Ruth, who had a long and impressive career that spanned many years, played with the Boston Red Sox, the New York Yankees, and the Boston Braves. _____

_____

4. When Yankee Stadium opened in 1923, it was nicknamed "The House that Ruth Built."

_____

5. Although he came from poor, humble beginnings, Babe Ruth's skills and talent would earn him a salary of eighty thousand dollars a year for both of the years 1930 and 1931.

_____

_____

6. Ruth hit a lifetime total of 714 home runs during his life.

_____

7. Ruth, who was also known to be a remarkable pitcher, struck out many batters.

_____

8. He once pitched twenty-nine consecutive scoreless innings in a row. _____

_____

9. Ruth also was one of the best and premier fielders to be mentioned in baseball history.

_____

10. A member of the Baseball Hall of Fame, Babe Ruth is a great American sports hero.

_____

SENTENCES

Reducing Wordiness (continued)

EXERCISE B Some of the following sentences are wordy. Revise each wordy sentence to make it straightforward and concise. If a sentence does not need revision, write *C* for *correct*. Write your answers on the lines provided.

Example 1. One of the people who are my friends, who is a Native American, told me about the heritage that belongs to her.

One of my friends, who is a Native American, told me about her heritage.

11. The Alabama, who are one of the most ancient of American Indian peoples, now live mostly in the states of Texas and Oklahoma. _____

_____

12. When first encountered by European explorers, they lived in what is now known as the state of Alabama, to which they gave their name. _____

_____

13. The French who settled in the area fought the Alabama, who joined together with additional other groups, in the early 1700s. _____

_____

14. As settlers invaded their homeland, the Alabama were forced to move to Texas. _____

_____

15. The Alabama merged with the Coushatta, who were close relatives of the Alabama, to become the Alabama-Coushatta; more than five hundred members of the group live in Texas at this time. _____

_____

_____

SENTENCES

Revising Sentences to Improve Style

EXERCISE A Revise each sentence below as suggested in the parentheses. Write your new sentences on the lines provided.

Example 1. I saw the book on Tikal. I eagerly pulled it from the shelf. *(adverb clause beginning)*

When I saw the book on Tikal, I eagerly pulled it from the shelf.

1. Tikal is located in the rain forests of northern Guatemala and is an important archaeological landmark. *(phrase beginning)* _____

_____

2. Tikal was only a minor center in ancient Mayan civilization, but it is one of the most significant of all Mayan ruins. *(adverb clause beginning)* _____

_____

3. Archaeological evidence discovered by archaeologists shows that the first residents to live in Tikal arrived in the location around 700 B.C. *(reduce wordiness)* _____

_____

4. Those who first inhabited Tikal probably were attracted by its position above the surrounding swamps, and there was an abundance of flint available that they could use to make tools. *(reduce wordiness)* _____

_____

5. The first buildings appear to have been erected around 500 B.C. The settlement seems to have included ceremonial structures by about 200 B.C. *(compound sentence)*

_____

6. Tikal was abandoned. This happened when the Mayan civilization collapsed by the end of the tenth century A.D. *(complex sentence)* _____

_____

7. Tikal's enormous temples were covered with tropical plant life when the first photographs of the ruins were taken in 1881. *(adverb clause beginning)* _____

_____

8. Tourists and archaeologists take buses or planes to reach this popular site. *(phrase beginning)*

_____

SENTENCES

Revising Sentences to Improve Style (continued)

9. Five granite pyramids that are steep and sheer rise 130 feet (39 m) above thousands of smaller structures. (*single-word modifiers*) _____

10. Many of the numerous people who tour this area enjoy taking photographs of this magnificent site. (*reduce wordiness*) _____

EXERCISE B Revise each sentence below as suggested in the parentheses. Write your new sentences on the lines provided.

Example 1. Diamonds are a traditional wedding gemstone; diamonds are popular in the United States. (*phrase beginning*)
   A traditional wedding gemstone, diamonds are popular in the United States.

11. Rough diamonds can be cut and polished as gemstones after they are mined from volcanic pipes deep within the earth. (*adverb clause beginning*) _____

12. Diamond is made of closely packed carbon atoms and is the hardest natural substance known. (*phrase beginning*) _____

13. Only a small percentage of the diamonds mined are made into gems because diamonds used in jewelry must have certain qualities. (*adverb clause beginning*) _____

14. A diamond expert considers a diamond's color, clarity, cut, and carat weight to determine its market value. (*phrase beginning*) _____

15. T'__ __'d's most productive diamond mines are located in Africa and Asia. Diamonds have ___ in the United States. Arizona, Nevada, and Montana are the leading diamond-____ound-complex sentence*) _____

Revising Paragraphs to Improve Style

EXERCISE A   Revise the paragraphs below. As you revise, remember to vary sentence beginnings and sentence structure and to eliminate wordiness. Use proofreading symbols to show your changes.

Example   Hairstyles are a matter of taste. ~~They are also a matter of~~ tradition, and convenience.

People style and arrange their hair in many different ways to look attractive and to fit their ways of life. They might also style their hair in certain ways just to make a statement or convey some kind of message. A kind of art, hairstyling involves cutting, curling, braiding, coloring, and oiling. Ornaments might be added. Examples of ornaments are barrettes, ribbons, and beads. For centuries, people have been experimenting with different hairstyles. Hairstyling has continued to change with the times since.

The ancient Egyptians, for example, shaved their heads to stay cool. They also sometimes wore black wigs or cones of perfumed oil. The upper-class nobility of ancient Mesopotamia and Persia curled, dyed, and wove their hair and beards into braids. They added gold dust or gold and silver decorations. Early tribes in northern Europe also wore hair and beards that were long due to the fact that short hair was a sign of punishment or social rank of a low level.

Simpler styles have also been common. They have been common in different places. They have been common in different times. It is traditional for women in many places in the Middle East and the East, for instance, to hide their hair under head coverings. It is traditional for men in these regions to do the same. These coverings include scarves, turbans, or veils. Chinese and Japanese men once followed a tradition. They used to shave the front of their heads and gather the remaining hair that was left over in back in a pigtail.

Revising Paragraphs to Improve Style (continued)

EXERCISE B   Revise the paragraphs below. As you revise, remember to vary sentence beginnings and sentence structure and to eliminate wordiness. Use proofreading symbols to show your changes.

Example   Epilepsy is a disorder ~~that affects brain function. It is~~ characterized by sudden
                attacks, ~~which are~~ known as seizures.

It is a fact that about or approximately one in every two hundred people has epilepsy. This makes it a fairly common condition. Most people with epilepsy experience their first seizure early in life during childhood. Seizures seem to happen for no apparent reason. An electrical charge is released suddenly by the brain. That makes them occur. That is what doctors believe.

A *grand mal* seizure is an especially serious and dramatic type of attack. It is especially serious and dramatic because a person experiencing a *grand mal* seizure becomes unconscious suddenly, falls down, and shakes with convulsions. The person usually falls into a deep sleep after the seizure. A *petit mal* seizure is a less noticeable kind of attack of epilepsy. The person remains conscious during a *petit mal* seizure but is unaware of his or her surroundings for a moment. People with epilepsy often experience warnings before both kinds of attacks. These warnings are called auras and last just seconds. They may include strange memories, hallucinations, ringing in the ears, and unpleasant odors and tastes. They signal the beginning of a seizure.

Medications have been used successfully to reduce attacks or prevent them altogether. Surgery can be an effective cure for epilepsy. Attacks have to be limited to just part of the brain for surgery to be effective, however. Special diets have also proven helpful. They help control the number of attacks people with epilepsy experience.

SENTENCES

Manuscript Form

When writing a paper for school, it is important to follow a manuscript style in order to present information in a neat and organized way. Here is one common manuscript style.

Margins

Leave a one-inch margin on the top, sides, and bottom of each page.

Pagination

One half inch from the top of each page, include a header in the upper right-hand corner. The header should include your last name followed by the page number.

Indention

Paragraphs should be indented half an inch; set-off quotations should be indented an inch from the left margin (five spaces and ten spaces, respectively, on standard typewriters).

Heading

On the title page of your paper, include a heading one inch from the top of the page. The heading should include your full name, your teacher's name, the course name, and the date (day, month, year). Double-space between each line of your heading.

Title

On the title page of your paper, include the title of your paper. Double-space between the heading and the title. Center the title and capitalize the appropriate letters. Double-space between the title and body of your paper.

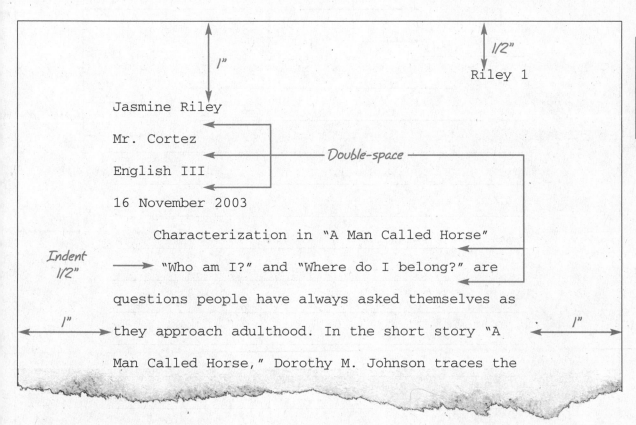

SENTENCES

Manuscript Form (continued)

EXERCISE   The following passage is excerpted from a research paper written on February 3, 2003, by Brian Coley, a student in Mrs. Ferdinand's English III class. Fill in the blanks with the appropriate information to complete the title page according to the guidelines on the previous page.

Title: Animal Images in *The Tragedy of Macbeth*

First Paragraph: William Shakespeare's *Macbeth* is the story of a great man's fall from grace. At the beginning of the play, Macbeth is a loyal supporter of Scotland's King Duncan, but greed for power causes him to kill the king and take the crown for himself. Once he is king, Macbeth is paranoid about losing power, so he kills many more people. When the Scottish nobles see his cruelty, they rally to overthrow Macbeth. The animal images in *Macbeth* symbolize Macbeth's transition from brave soldier to cornered tyrant by emphasizing how his overreaching ambition leads to his destruction.

SENTENCES